WAR, WOMEN AND CHILDREN IN ANCIENT ROME

WAR, WOMEN AND CHILDREN IN ANCIENT ROME

John K. Evans

London and New York

First published 1991
by Routledge
11 New Fetter Lane, London EC4P 4EE

Simultaneously published in the USA and Canada
by Routledge
a division of Routledge, Chapman and Hall, Inc.
29 West 35th Street, New York, NY 10001

Typeset in 10/12 pt Garamond by
Selectmove
Printed and Bound in Great Britain by
Biddles Ltd, Guildford and Kings Lynn

British Library Cataloguing in Publication Data
Evans, John K.
War, Women and children in ancient Rome.
1. Roman Empire. Society. Role of Women
I. Title
305.420937

Library of Congress Cataloguing in Publication Data
Evans, John K.
War, Women, and children in ancient Rome / John K. Evans.
p. cm.
Includes bibliographical references and index.
ISBN 0-415-05723-X
1. Women—Rome—History. 2. Women's rights—Rome—History.
3. Women—Legal status, laws, etc. (Roman Law). 4. Women and
war—Rome—History. 5. Children—Rome—History. I. Title.
HQ1136.E93 1991
305.4'0937—dc20   90-45259

ISBN 0-415-05723-X

MATRI CONIUGI CARISSIMIS

CONTENTS

PREFACE AND ACKNOWLEDGEMENTS

Influenced in large part by the feminist movement, over the last two decades several new fields of study have emerged within the discipline of History. Foremost among these are the history of women, and the history of the family; each has spawned a voluminous and still-growing literature, which embraces not only books and monographs but also an array of periodicals devoted specifically to these areas of interest. Happily, despite the skepticism with which historians of the classical world normally welcome innovative methodologies, students of Greece and Rome have not insulated themselves from these developments. Since the path-breaking publication some fifteen years ago of Sarah B. Pomeroy's *Goddesses, Whores, Wives, and Slaves. Women in Classical Antiquity* (New York, 1975), the literature devoted specifically to Greek and Roman women has swelled to the point that it is now difficult for the interested reader to stay abreast of it all. This literature is noteworthy above all for its impressive diversity of perspective, which ranges from analysis of the erotic treatment of women in Greek and Roman art to textual criticism designed to illuminate the role of women in the early Church. It is, however, almost equally noteworthy for its sophisticated application of methods of analysis first elaborated in other disciplines to the often intractable sources for classical antiquity. In this vein, the structuralist studies of Greek myth and tragedy come instantly to mind. Finally, it should be noted that studies of the family, while not yet able to rival the literature devoted to women *per se* in terms of sheer quantity or methodological sophistication, are also beginning to appear in increasing numbers. It is, for example, only during the course of the last decade that children have become a significant research interest for historians of Greece and Rome.

Undergraduate courses that concentrate exclusively on the history of women in the ancient world have also proliferated, most noticeably in the American universities. Ironically, there is one feature of the literature in this field that makes it relatively easy to organize such courses for students otherwise unfamiliar with classical antiquity, yet at the same time constitutes a serious impediment to the future development of the field at the research level. This is the tendency to treat the history of women in antiquity as a discrete topic, or to put it another way, the failure to integrate women's history into the broader fabric of Ancient History at large. This deficiency is especially evident in Roman history: the last decade has seen the publication of a large number of books devoted to Roman women, but whatever else one may say about them, all of these works share one thing in common – they are divorced from the issues of perennial concern to the broader community of political and social historians of Rome. It is this deficiency that the present exercise will attempt to redress. Its thesis may be briefly stated: so rigidly patriarchal a society as Rome of the Twelve Tables could not send hundreds of thousands of men abroad to prosecute wars of conquest that went on virtually without interruption for the last two hundred years of the Republic's existence without inviting severe erosion of the institutions that kept women and children in thrall. It thus attempts to link the study of Roman women and children to one of the most venerable topics in Roman history, whether the perspective be that of the political or social historian: the domestic consequences of Roman 'imperialism' in the period that begins with the Hannibalic war and concludes with the introduction of the Principate under Augustus. It embraces working-class women as well as the elite, and attempts to elucidate developments in the countryside as well as the cities. Throughout, but most obviously in the two chapters devoted to working women and children, it also attempts to define the limits that a capricious and lacunose source tradition must impose on an investigation of this type. In these two chapters, our conclusions cannot hope to rise above the problematic, but since this work was written with the hope of broadening the current debate about Roman women and children, this is perhaps as it should be.

This study owes a great deal to the painstaking and constructive criticism of two colleagues past and present, D. Brendan Nagle of the University of Southern California, and Thomas Kelly here at the University of Minnesota. Both have been involved in this project from its inception, and have generously taken the time to read and comment upon each chapter in its various incarnations. Because these two men combine breadth of historical vision with a healthy skepticism about the reliability of our literary sources, they have been able to suggest different approaches that might be profitably explored, as well as save me from several potentially embarrassing lapses in judgement. They are, of course, not to be held responsible for any mistakes of fact or interpretation as remain; in the area of Roman law, these would have been far more numerous were it not for the painstaking care with which Jane Gardner of the University of Reading corrected the penultimate draft of the manuscript. It is a pleasure both to acknowledge her contributions to this work, and to the study of Roman women at large.

At this point I should also like to thank several individuals for their help in assembling the plates for this work. I am indebted above all to Natalie Kampen of Barnard College, who generously and promptly supplied Plates 1, 2 and 9 from her own *Image and Status: Roman Working Women in Ostia* (Berlin, 1981). Thomas Wiedemann of the University of Bristol similarly allowed me to reproduce Plate 10 from his book *Adults and Children in the Roman Empire* (London and New Haven, 1989). Martin Kilmer of the University of Ottawa furnished the photographs for Plates 4 and 5, which are published here with the kind permission of Anna Gallina Zevi of the Soprintendenza Archeologica di Ostia. Finally, thanks are due to Karen Einaudi of the Fototeca Unione of the American Academy in Rome, who supplied Plate 3, and to Arnoldo Mondadori Editore S.p.A. of Milan for the use of Plates 6 and 7.

I would also like to take this opportunity to express my appreciation to the Bush Foundation. The Foundation's generous financial support enabled me to take a sabbatical leave in 1988, during the course of which more than half of the research and writing for this project was completed. I am no less grateful to the University of Minnesota itself for a brace of Single Quarter Leave grants that furnished the initial momentum for the project earlier in the decade.

John K. Evans
Minneapolis

PLATES
(between pages 100–101)

ABBREVIATIONS

AAN	*Atti dell'Accademia di Scienze morali e politiche*
AC	*L'Antiquité Classique*
AE	*L'Année Epigraphique*
AG	*Archivio Giuridico*
AHR	*American Historical Review*
AJAH	*American Journal of Ancient History*
AJPh	*American Journal of Philology*
AncSoc	*Ancient Society*
Ann(ESC)	*Annales, ESC*
ANRW	*Aufstieg und Niedergang der römischen Welt*, ed. H. Temporini and W. Haase (Berlin, 1972–)
AULLA	*Australasian Universities Language and Literature Association*
BCH	*Bulletin de Correspondance Hellénique*
BGU	*Aegyptische Urkunden aus den Staatlichen Museen zu Berlin, Griechische Urkunden*
BICS	*Bulletin of the Institute of Classical Studies of the University of London*
BIDR	*Bollettino dell'Istituto di Diritto romano*
CIL	*Corpus Inscriptionum Latinarum*
CJ	*Classical Journal*
CLE	*Carmina Latina Epigraphica*, ed. F. Bücheler, suppl. E. Lommatzsch (Leipzig, 1895–1926)

CP	*Classical Philology*
CQ	*Classical Quarterly*
CR	*Classical Review*
CRAI	*Comptes rendus de l'Académie des Inscriptions et Belles-lettres*
CSSH	*Comparative Studies in Society and History*
CV	*Classical Views*
CW	*Classical World*
DArch	*Dialoghi di Archeologia*
EHR	*English Historical Review*
G&R	*Greece and Rome*
HSPh	*Harvard Studies in Classical Philology*
IG	*Inscriptiones Graecae*
IJ	*Irish Jurist*
ILLRP	*Inscriptiones Latinae Liberae Rei Publicae*, ed. A. Degrassi (Florence, 1957–)
ILS	*Inscriptiones Latinae Selectae*, ed. H. Dessau (Berlin, 1892–1916)
IvOlympia	*Die Inschriften von Olympia*, ed. H. Dittenberger and K. Purgold (Berlin, 1896)
JbAC	*Jahrbuch für Antike und Christentum*
JEA	*Journal of Egyptian Archaeology*
JFamHist	*Journal of Family History*
JHS	*Journal of Hellenic Studies*
JRS	*Journal of Roman Studies*
MDAI(A)	*Mitteilungen des deutschen Archäologischen Instituts, Athenische Abteilung*
MDAI(R)	*Mitteilungen des deutschen Archäologischen Instituts, Römische Abteilung*
MEFR	*Mélanges d'Archeologie et d'Histoire de l'Ecole Française de Rome*
NJA	*Neue Jahrbücher für das klassische Altertum*
NS	*Notizie degli scavi di antichità*
PAPhS	*Proceedings of the American Philosophical Society*

PBSR	*Papers of the British School at Rome*
PCPhS	*Proceedings of the Cambridge Philological Society*
P.Bour.	*Les Papyrus Bouriant*, ed. P. Collart (Paris, 1926)
P. Cornell	*Greek Papyri in the Library of Cornell University*, ed. W.L. Westermann and C.J. Kraemer, Jr. (New York, 1926)
P. Flor.	*Papiri Fiorentini*, ed. G. Vitelli and D. Comparetti (Milan, 1906–1915)
P. Gen.	*Les Papyrus de Genève*, ed. J. Nicole (Geneva, 1896–1900)
P. Grenf.	*New Classical Fragments and Other Greek and Latin Papyri*, ed. B.P. Grenfell and A.S. Hunt (Oxford, 1897)
P. Hibeh	*The Hibeh Papyri*, ed. B.P. Grenfell and A.S. Hunt (London, 1906)
P. Lond.	*Greek Papyri in the British Museum*, ed. F.G. Kenyon and H.I. Bell (London, 1893–1917)
P. Meyer	*Griechische Texte aus Aegypten*, ed. P.M. Meyer (Berlin, 1916)
P. Oxy.	*Oxyrhynchus Papyri*, ed. B.P. Grenfell, A.S. Hunt, et al.* (London, 1898–)
P. Ross.–Georg.	*Papyri russicher und georgischer Sammlungen*, ed. G. Zereteli, O. Krüger and P. Iernstedt (Tiflis, 1925–1935)
P. Ryl.	*Catalogue of the Greek Papyri in the John Rylands Library at Manchester*, ed. A.S. Hunt, J. de M. Johnson, V. Martin and C.H. Roberts (Manchester, 1911–1952)
PSI	*Papiri della Società Italiana*, ed. G. Vitelli, M. Norsa, et al.* (Florence, 1912–)
P. Teb.	*Tebtunis Papyri*, ed. B.P. Grenfell, A.S. Hunt, et al.* (London, 1902–1938)

RD	*Revue Historique de Droit français et étranger*
RE	*Real-Encyclopädie der classischen Altertumswissenschaft*, ed. A. Pauly, G. Wissowa, and W. Kroll (Stuttgart, 1893–1967)
REA	*Revue des Etudes Anciennes*
RFIC	*Rivista di Filologia e di Istruzione Classica*
RIDA	*Revue Internationale des Droits de l'Antiquité*
SB	*Sammelbuch griechischer Urkunden aus Aegypten*, ed. F. Preisigke, *et al.* (Berlin, Strassburg, *etc.*, 1913–)
SDHI	*Studia et Documenta Historiae et Iuris*
TAPA	*Transactions and Proceedings of the American Philological Association*
TRG	*Tijdschrift voor Rechtsgeschiedenis*
ZPE	*Zeitschrift für Papyrologie und Epigraphik*
ZRG	*Zeitschrift der Savigny-Stiftung für Rechtsgeschichte*

I

INTRODUCTION

On the morning of 21 June, 217 BC, the Roman consul C. Flaminius led his unsuspecting army into a well-conceived Carthaginian ambush along the shores of Lake Trasimene in central Italy.[1] A number of sources describe the ensuing disaster in some detail. The most conservative of these sources estimates that 15,000 citizens and Italian allies perished in the engagement, while another 10,000 managed to escape the carnage.[2] News of this defeat understandably created panic in the streets of Rome,[3] but there were other emotions on display as well. The most circumstantial account, that of Livy, is clearly embellished; nevertheless, it convincingly captures the anguish that those who waited for news of the survivors must have experienced:

> Over the next few days a crowd consisting mostly of women lingered at the city gates, waiting for members of their families or for word concerning them. They crowded around everyone who came along, questioning them; nor could they be torn away, especially from acquaintances, before they had inquired into everything in turn. Then, as they walked away, the looks on their faces revealed whether the news that each person had received was good or bad, and friends gathered around those returning home to congratulate or console. The joy and grief of the women was particularly striking. It is said that one woman, suddenly confronted at the gate by a son who was uninjured, died in his embrace; another, to whom the death of her son had been falsely reported, was sitting sadly in her home when he walked in the door. At the very first sight of him, she died from her overwhelming happiness.[4]

A few days later, 4,000 *equites* under the command of the

propraetor C. Centenius were also killed or captured,[5] and the following year witnessed the still-greater disaster at Cannae. The precise magnitude of this catastrophe will forever remain unknown, as perhaps it was unknown at the time. Polybius places the Roman losses at 70,000 killed and 10,000 captured; this figure roughly coincides with that given by Dionysius of Halicarnassus, who calculates that some 75,630 out of a total force of 86,000 men failed to escape the carnage. Livy reduces the casualties to 48,200, but swells the number of prisoners to 18,700; finally, both Appian and Plutarch round off the fatalities to an even 50,000.[6] Whatever the true figure,[7] in Rome itself the reaction was much the same as it had been after the defeat at Trasimene, only more so. Never, Livy says, had the city known such terror and confusion; 'the sound of wailing women was to be heard everywhere, and since nothing had as yet been clearly ascertained, in virtually every home the living and the dead were being indiscriminately mourned.'[8] In order to restore a semblance of calm, the Senate published an edict that directed women to remain in their homes, put restraints on mourning, and imposed silence throughout the city.[9] In the end, however, there were very few families that did not have occasion to lament the loss of a father, husband, brother, or son. A festival for the goddess Ceres, whose worship was restricted to women, had to be cancelled in the immediate aftermath of the defeat: women in mourning were excluded from the rites, and 'at that moment', so Livy claims, 'there was not a matron to be found who was not grieving.'[10] This might be dismissed as mere hyperbole were it not for the fact that in 215 the government was forced to borrow heavily in order to fund the war effort. The revenues generated by the *tributum*, or general property tax, had proven inadequate, and this was specifically attributed to the enormous losses sustained at Trasimene and Cannae.[11] Every soldier, it should be kept in mind, was at this time both a property-owner and a tax-payer as well.[12]

The early years of the Hannibalic war were among the grimmest that Rome would ever experience. Still, it would be fair to say that during the Republic women in mourning were always to be encountered in large numbers, for in this period of Roman history war was the normal state of affairs and peace the exception. When Octavian closed the gates of the temple of Janus in 29 BC, an act that signified that Rome was completely at peace, only two precedents could be found, the most recent in 241 BC![13] This was, we now believe, an exaggeration, but it was by no means an outrageous one.

It appears, for example, that in the period 218–129 BC Rome was at war every year in at least one theater,[14] and widows and orphans were sufficiently numerous to warrant special consideration from the censors.[15]

This last point forcefully reminds us that war not only exacted an emotional toll from Roman women and their children but affected them in other ways as well. In fact, like Roman society at large, during the nearly five centuries of the Republic the political, social, economic and legal standing of Roman women was subject to profound change. Given the elite bias of the historical and literary sources at our disposal, it is hardly surprising that it is the political aspect of this process that has attracted the greatest attention to date. Much of this scholarship, however, is purely descriptive – a narrative of isolated episodes that is virtually indistinguishable from biography.[16] Even with regard to the role of women in politics, therefore, the forces responsible for the changes so often remarked still require explanation. Rome's seemingly unending warfare, for example – the subject of repeated analysis in a number of other contexts – seems always to have exercised a great and at times a decisive influence on the evolving role of women in Roman society, as well as on their relationship with their children.[17] Despite its palpable importance, however, this theme has not yet been the subject of a sustained historical study, an omission that the present work hopes to make good. At the outset, it will focus upon the evolving legal status of Roman women, and attempt to determine the forces (warfare among them) that affected their status. It will then examine feminine ownership and use of property (much of it generated by successful warfare), with all that this implies with regard to the social standing of women in the Roman community. Here the extant evidence draws us remorselessly into the circle of the Roman aristocracy; in order to compensate for this elite bias, the ability of economically less fortunate free-born women to enter a rural and urban work-force increasingly dominated by slave labor suggests itself as a third topic for investigation. Although neglected, the question is nevertheless important, for our sources frequently allude to the expropriation of peasant women and their children in the second century BC, but do not tell us what subsequently became of them.[18] In order to fill this gap, a sustained effort will be made to pinpoint the kinds of work that were available to women, as well as to determine whether access to a given position was affected by considerations of status. This means, above all, examining the degree to which a given profession was monopolized by slave- and freedwomen. The study will then conclude by exploring the relationship between parents and their children. In both the normative and jural sense, this tie also seems to have experienced far-reaching changes during the course of the Republic – but here as well, the forces at work have to date eluded analysis. Because the study of children in Roman society is still in the formative stage, it is too early to draw definitive conclusions; nevertheless, it will at least be suggested here that the emergence of the small child as a valued personality during the course of the second and first centuries BC may also, in the end, be numbered among the domestic consequences of what is commonly known as 'Roman imperialism.'

NOTES

1. For the date, see Ovid, *Fasti* 6.767–768, and the discussion in F.W. Walbank, *A Historical Commentary on Polybius* I (Oxford, 1957) 412–413.
2. Livy 22.7.2 cites 15,000 casualties; a further 10,000, 'who in their flight had scattered across the whole of Etruria, found their way back to Rome by various ways.' Polybius 3.84.7–85.4, and Plutarch, *Fabius Maximus* 3, also list 15,000 casualties, but both add that Hannibal captured another 15,000 prisoners. Appian, *Hannibalica* 10, adjusts these figures to 20,000 dead and 10,000 prisoners; Polybius, Plutarch and Appian are all in agreement that Hannibal released the Italian allies who had fallen into his hands, while the Romans were ultimately enslaved (Livy 34.50.5). The number of Roman dead swells to 25,000 in the accounts of Eutropius 3.9 and Orosius 4.15.5. For further discussion, cf. *inter alia* G. de Sanctis, *Storia dei Romani* III.2 (Turin, 1917) 117–118; Walbank, *A Historical Commentary on Polybius*, I.419–420; A.J. Toynbee, *Hannibal's Legacy* II (London, 1965) 66; and P.A. Brunt, *Italian Manpower, 225 BC–AD 14* (Oxford, 1971) 419 notes 1 and 4.
3. Appian remarks that the citizens stocked the walls with stones, armed the *seniores*, and being in need of weapons, brought down from the temples the spoils of their earlier wars (*Hannibalica* 11).
4. Livy 22.7.11–13. This and all succeeding translations are furnished by the author. The final element of this vivid scene is repeated in Aulus Gellius, *Noctes Atticae* 3.15.4, although he situates it after the battle at Cannae rather than Trasimene.
5. Polybius 3.86.3–5; Livy 22.8.1; Appian, *Hannibalica* 11.
6. Polybius 3.117.3–4; Dionysius of Halicarnassus, *Antiquitates Romanae* 2.17.4; Livy 22.49.15 (casualties), 22.49.13, 49.18, 50.11, 52.1–2, 52.4 (prisoners); Appian, *Hannibalica* 25; Plutarch, *Fabius Maximus* 16.
7. Here modern scholars are in as much disagreement as ancient. De Sanctis, *Storia dei Romani*, III.2.133–135, lists the Roman dead at 20,000–25,000. Brunt, *Italian Manpower*, 419 note 4, argues that 'the number of killed, captured, and missing was about 30,000.' Toynbee, *Hannibal's Legacy*, II.66–68, follows Livy and sets the losses in killed and in unransomed prisoners at 54,700. Walbank, *A Historical Commentary on Polybius*, I.440, calculates that the Romans may have suffered 61,500 casualties and a further 10,000 prisoners, but he rightly warns that 'any

estimate of casualties is likely to be unreliable.'

8. Livy 22.54.8–55.3.

9. Livy 22.55.6–7.

10. Livy 22.56.4.

11. Livy 23.48.7–9.

12. Elegibility for military service at Rome was contingent upon satisfaction of a property requirement. We may infer from Polybius 6.19.2 that the minimum census qualification of 11,000 *asses* in force at the beginning of the Second Punic War had been reduced by the mid-second century BC to 4,000 *asses*. E. Gabba, 'Le origini dell'esercito professionale in Roma: i proletari e la riforma di Mario,' *Athenaeum* new series 27 (1949) 181–183, argues that the reduction occurred in the period 214–212 BC. Brunt, *Italian Manpower*, 75, 77 and 403, opts specifically for 214; *contra*, Walbank, *A Historical Commentary on Polybius*, I.698, 701–702. For the reaction of Roman women to the defeats at Trasimene and Cannae, see also C. Herrmann, *Le Rôle judiciaire et politique des femmes sous le République romaine* (Brussels, 1964) 52–54; and S.B. Pomeroy, *Goddesses, Whore, Wives, and Slaves. Women in Classical Antiquity* (New York, 1975) 177.

13. Varro, *De Lingua Latina* 5.165; Livy 1.19.3; Augustus, *Res Gestae* 13; Velleius Paterculus 2.38.3; Plutarch, *Numa* 20.2. T.R.S. Broughton, *The Magistrates of the Roman Republic* I (Cleveland, 1951) 223, argues for 235 BC, but 241 is more plausible; cf. R.M. Ogilvie, *A Commentary on Livy, Books 1–5* (Oxford, 1965) 93–94; and W.V. Harris, *War and Imperialism in Republican Rome, 327–70 BC* (Oxford, 1979) 190–191 and note 1.

14. Harris, *War and Imperialism*, 9–10, makes an attempt to calculate the intervals of peace. In the period 327–241 BC, this amounted to four or five years at most. From 241 to 30 BC, only 240–239, 128–127 and 116 are certain, and 227–226 possibilities.

15. Livy specifically excludes widows and orphans from the censuses of 465 (3.3.9) and 131/130 BC (*Periochae* 59), while Plutarch makes a more general statement to the same effect (*Publicola* 12). This has induced most scholars to conclude that they were exempt from the *tributum*. In its place, according to Cicero, *De Republica* 2.36, Livy 1.43.9, and Plutarch, *Camillus* 2, they were at least theoretically liable to pay a special levy called *aes equestre*. For fuller discussion, see *inter alia* K.J. Beloch, *Die Bevölkerung der griechisch-römischen Welt* (Leipzig, 1886) 308–309, 312–313; Th. Mommsen, *Römisches Staatsrecht³* III (Berlin, 1888) 236, 256 note 4; Gabba, 'Le origini dell'esercito professionale in Roma,' 187–188; F.C. Bourne, 'The Roman Republican Census and Census Statistics,' *CW* 45 (1952) 134; E. Gabba, 'Ancore sulle cifre dei censimenti,' *Athenaeum* new series 30 (1952) 166; Toynbee, *Hannibal's Legacy*, II.463–465; G. Pieri, *Histoire du cens à Rome des ses origines à la fin de la République* (Sirey, 1967) 177–182; and Brunt, *Italian Manpower*, 22 and 114.

16. This anecdotal technique, particularly commonplace in political histories of Rome, characterizes such standard treatments of Roman women as B. Förtsch, *Die politische Rolle der Frau in der römischen Republik* (Stuttgart, 1935); J.P.V.D. Balsdon, *Roman Women: Their History and Habits* (London, 1962); Herrmann, *Le rôle judiciaire et politique des femmes*; and E. Meise, *Untersuchungen zur Geschichte der Julisch-Claudischen Dynastie* (Munich, 1969). Much of the recent social history of Roman women, it might be added, is also heavily dependent on anecdotal evidence. Thus T. Carp, 'Two Matrons of the Late Republic,' *Women's Studies* 8 (1981) 189–200 = H. Foley (ed.), *Reflections of Women in Antiquity* (New York, 1981) 343–354; and S. Dixon, 'Family Finances: Tullia and Terentia,' *Antichthon* 18 (1984) 78–101 = 'Family Finances: Terentia and Tullia,' in B. Rawson (ed.), *The Family in Ancient*

Rome (London, 1985) 93–120, both explicitly assume that the financial acumen displayed in Cicero's correspondence by his wife Terentia is a characteristic of late Republican noblewomen at large – an imprudent generalization at best.

17. The growth of the *imperium Romanum* has traditionally been the preserve of the political and military historian, and the recent appearance of Harris, *War and Imperialism*; E. Gruen, *The Hellenistic World and the Coming of Rome* (Berkeley, 1984); and A.N. Sherwin-White, *Roman Foreign Policy in the East, 168 BC to AD 1* (London, 1984), demonstrate that it has lost none of its interest in this respect. It has, however, increasingly become the focus of social and especially demographic studies, the most notable of which are Toynbee, *Hannibal's Legacy*; and Brunt, *Italian Manpower*. For an overview of the strengths and weaknesses of this literature, see J.K. Evans, '*Plebs Rustica. The Peasantry of Classical Italy I*: the Peasantry in Modern Scholarship,' *AJAH* 5 (1980) 19–47.

18. The critical (and much-abused) passages are Sallust, *Bellum Iugurthinum* 41.7–8; Plutarch, *Tiberius Gracchus* 8–9; Appian, *Bella Civilia* 1.7–10; and Florus 2.1–2.

II

THE LEGAL STATUS OF
ROMAN WOMEN

THE EARLY REPUBLIC

The most reliable evidence for the role assigned Roman women in the early Republic is the famous Law of the Twelve Tables, which is traditionally dated to 451–450 BC. Here it is quite clear that a Roman female remained throughout life in the condition of a daughter, for she was never excused from male tutelage in one form or another.[1] She was initially in the *potestas* of her father, whose authority over his children the jurist Gaius aptly characterizes as without parallel in human society.[2] A father literally possessed the power of life and death over his children (*ius vitae et necis*), although in practice this was normally invoked only to dispose of infants whom he had decided for one reason or another not to rear. According to Dionysius of Halicarnassus, the legendary Romulus ruled that a father must rear all his sons, but was only obligated to raise his first-born daughter;[3] in fact, it seems clear that he could order the exposure of any new-born infant in his *familia* with impunity.[4] Still, as his children matured, this awesome power of life and death continued to remain at his disposal. One legend recounted by Livy in the first book of his history of Rome is particularly instructive in this regard. We are told that a ruinous war between Rome and Alba Longa was avoided when the Roman king, Tullus Hostilius, and his Alban counterpart agreed to settle their dispute through a trial of arms between two sets of triplets, the brothers Horatii and Curiatii respectively. Predictably, the Romans prevailed: two of the Horatii fell first, but the last brother cleverly managed to dispatch all three of his foes. As it happened, however, his sister was betrothed to one of the Curiatii, and when she learned of his death, openly began to mourn him. This so enraged her brother that he put her to the sword. The young man was subsequently tried and convicted for treason, but when he appealed his conviction to the *populus*, it was set aside. Livy remarks that it was the intervention of his father that decided the outcome. The elder Horatius 'adjudged his daughter to have been rightly put to death; if this had not been the case,' he added, 'he would have invoked his paternal authority and executed his son himself.'[5]

The *ius vitae et necis* was but one aspect of the primitive *patria potestas*. It also entitled a father to sell his children into *mancipium* at Rome or slavery *trans Tiberim*, and to surrender their labor to a creditor in compensation for a debt.[6] It permitted him to dissolve their marriages irrespective of their wishes and despite the fact that children may have been born to the union;[7] and for all intents and purposes it empowered him to choose a husband for his daughter. To be sure, at this early date the latter may have already possessed the right to spurn the engagement that we hear of in classical law, but this would have required her to demonstrate that her father's nominee was morally delinquent.[8] Since Roman women in all periods tended to marry early – there are many examples of girls who married at or even before the age of twelve, which in classical law was the earliest moment at which a bride could enter upon a legitimate marriage (*matrimonium iustum*)[9] – the decision was effectively taken out of their hands.[10]

When a father died, the Twelve Tables acknowledged what must in fact have been a long-established custom, namely that his unmarried daughters automatically passed into the guardianship of their nearest agnatic kinsman (their *tutor legitimus*) unless the decedent had specifically designated another guardian in his will (a *tutor extraneus*).[11] It seems fairly certain that a guardian's authority over his wards was not as wide-ranging as the *potestas* of their father,[12] but his prerogatives were nevertheless of considerable consequence. Thus the authors of the Twelve Tables went on to stipulate that even a mature woman could not alienate conveyable property (*res mancipi*), such as land or slaves, without the approval of a guardian.[13] In addition, a woman could not manumit a slave without his permission,[14] nor contract an obligation or make a valid will.[15] The latter prohibition was soon annulled, however, for the first legal privilege that women apparently obtained was the right to execute a will *per aes et libram*.[16] Still, it should be stressed that this was also strictly subject to the consent of the woman's guardian, for before she could act he first had to transfer her from his own authority to that of a *tutor extraneus* through a ritualized form of fictive sale known as *coemptio fiduciae causa*.[17] When her *tutor* was an agnatic kinsman, however, such permission must have been difficult to obtain since it was precisely to her agnatic relations that a woman's property passed if she died intestate. The agnates, that is to say, could not benefit from such a will, and would surely have assumed that the property at issue would be dispensed in the form of legacies if the *tutor legitimus* was foolish enough to permit such a document to be drawn up.[18]

These restrictions on a woman's freedom of action are obviously formidable, but scholars have so far failed to reach a consensus with regard to the set of assumptions that must underlie them. Although the point will undoubtedly prove contentious, later in this chapter it will be argued that they seem to betray a belief on the part of these early Romans that women were incompetent to manage their own affairs, and left to their own devices would diminish rather than augment the property in their possession. Indeed, according to Gaius the *veteres* expressly cited *levitas animi*, which we may somewhat vaguely translate as 'the inconstancy of the female character,' as the rationale for these elaborate arrangements.[19]

The subordinate status of women in early Rome persisted after marriage, for *matronae* were still counted as daughters. Gaius is quite specific on this point, averring that 'a wife acquires a daughter's rights (*filiae iura*) if for any reason whatever she enters her husband's authority.'[20] He also describes in detail the three forms of marriage that transferred the bride from the *potestas* of her father to the authority (*manus*) of her husband. A wife became *in manu*, for example, if she was 'purchased' by her husband – a procedure known as *coemptio matrimonii causa* (to be distinguished from the fiduciary *coemptio* discussed above). Here again Gaius' language is worthy of note: 'a woman who makes a *coemptio* with her husband so that she may assume the status of a daughter in his household (*filiae loco*) is said to have made a *coemptio* for the purpose of matrimony.'[21] *Confarreatio*, a religious ceremony centered on the sacrifice of a spelt cake to Jupiter Farreus by the bride and groom, was a second and still more binding form of *manus* marriage. It is generally thought that such unions were at one time indissoluble;[22] be that as it may, divorce was certainly possible during the Principate.[23] It required, however, the performance of a second ritual (the *diffareatio*) before a college of priests known as the *sacerdotes confarreationum et diffareationum*, and Plutarch characterizes these rites as numerous,

9

horrible, gloomy and strange.[24] Since *coemptio* and *confarreatio* were so complex, it is hardly surprising that the most common form of marriage *cum manu* was the less complicated arrangement that the jurists designate as *usus*. The Twelve Tables simply mandated that a woman who cohabited with her husband for one year without interruption thereby passed automatically into his *manus*; in order to remain *sine manu*, it was stipulated merely that she spend three nights each year away from his home – presumably returning to her natal family or guardian.[25] *Usus* thus did not involve a formal procedure, but it produced the same results: if a wife lapses into the authority of her husband, Gaius remarks, 'she assumes the place of a daughter' (*filiae locum optinebat*) in his household.[26]

Obviously, therefore, marriage *sine manu* constituted a fourth possibility. This left the young bride under the supervision of her father or guardian,[27] an arrangement that for economic reasons seems increasingly to have appealed to both parties to the marriage. Several decades ago, Schulz forcefully reminded us that a wife *in manu* shared her husband's property with his children *in potestate*, while in a marriage *sine manu* the wife had no claim to his estate at all.[28] Conversely, several scholars have stressed that a daughter who remained subject to her father's *potestas* after her marriage thereby retained her claim to a share of the patrimony.[29] Sarah Pomeroy has recently taken these trains of thought still further, posing the attractive if still speculative suggestion that the appeal of a marriage *sine manu* stemmed precisely from the fact that it enabled both families to prevent the dispersal of their property.[30] The merit of this argument becomes apparent, for example, if one keeps in mind that a woman married *sine manu* could not even alienate her dowry without the approval of her father or guardian. Again, in early Rome the latter was typically an agnatic kinsman who might legitimately expect to inherit from her at some future date, and hence had every reason to prevent her dotal property from passing permanently into her husband's possession.[31]

One final point regarding marriage *cum manu* must be broached here. Simply put, while it is readily apparent that in a *manus* relationship the wife stood *in filiae loco* to her husband, the precise legal implications of this status are not wholly clear. The most important, although by no means the only, question at issue is whether or not husbands possessed the *ius vitae et necis* over their wives *in manu*.[32] Two passages in the compendia of Valerius Maximus and Aulus Gellius would seem to suggest that they did indeed have such authority. Valerius informs us that a certain Egnatius Mecenius, ostensibly a contemporary of Romulus, beat his wife to death when he discovered that she had been drinking wine. No *accusator* came forward to indict him; on the contrary, Egnatius was applauded for his assiduous defense of traditional Roman sobriety.[33] This makes it clear that the public was prepared to countenance a wife's execution by her husband, but strictly speaking, we cannot tell from this anecdote whether a husband who behaved in this fashion was exercising his legal authority or committing murder. Fortunately, Aulus Gellius is much more precise, albeit in a wholly different context: he reports that the elder Cato, in one of his orations, upheld the husband's right to kill his wife out of hand if she was caught in adultery, while she could also be put to death if an investigation determined that she was adulterous or had been drinking wine.[34] These statements seem straightforward enough, but Plutarch claims with equal certitude that a husband could legitimately divorce his wife only if she was guilty of adultery, the theft of his keys (which would give access to the wine cellar), or the poisoning of his children. If he repudiated her for any other reason, he adds, then she was entitled to half of his property, and the balance was devoted to Ceres, the protectress of wives.[35] There is not a word here of the *ius vitae et necis*, but one might be inclined to dismiss Plutarch's testimony out of hand since he refers these regulations to the legendary Romulus. Several additional points, however, induce caution.

First, it should be observed that, according to Gellius, the elder Cato did not limit himself to claiming that a husband who caught his wife *in flagrante delictu* could put her to death with impunity; he also went on to say that a wife who trapped her husband in precisely the same circumstances was powerless to take action against him. Gellius' testimony on this latter point is nicely corroborated by a contemporary of Cato, the comic poet Plautus. He says precisely the same thing in the *Mercator* – while making it no less clear that an adulteress could expect a prompt divorce, not a summary execution.[36] Unfortunately, Plautus' testimony is not decisive on this point: the *Mercator* is adapted from a Greek original, the *Emporos* of Philemon, and it is set in Athens, whose laws required husbands to divorce wives guilty of adultery.[37]

Secondly, Valerius Maximus, Aulus Gellius, Dionysius of Halicarnassus and Plutarch all cite the divorce initiated by Sp. Carvilius Ruga as the first such in Roman history, despite the fact that, with the exception of Plutarch, each of these authors also lodges the transaction somewhere in the period 235–231 BC.[38] This is more than two centuries after the traditional date for the publication of the Twelve Tables, which clearly established procedures for divorce,[39] and several decades after the capricious divorce proceeding undertaken by a certain L. Annius, who was expelled from the Senate by the censors in 307 BC as a consequence of his action.[40] Alan Watson has plausibly argued that Carvilius' divorce caused such a sensation, and generated the confusion that we see in the account of Valerius Maximus in particular, because he repudiated his wife on grounds of sterility. However novel, Carvilius' action certainly would have conformed with the Roman belief that the intent of marriage was procreative. Still, sterility could hardly be considered a matrimonial offense in the same vein as adultery or the murder of one's children, hence the Romans were compelled by Carvilius' action to abandon the notion that divorce was a strictly punitive measure. If Watson's reading of the evidence is correct, then Plutarch's presumption that early Roman law directed a husband to divorce a misbehaving wife rather than execute her has to be taken more seriously.[41]

Plutarch, Gellius and the elder Pliny further observe that it was a venerable tradition among the Romans for the male relatives of a married woman to kiss her at every encounter. They did so in order to determine whether or not she had been drinking – a strange custom that finds its putative explanation in another law attributed to Romulus, this time by Dionysius of Halicarnassus.[42] He states that a woman married *cum manu* could indeed be put to death for drinking or adultery, but only if she was found guilty by a tribunal that included her male relations as well as her husband.

Finally, the elder Pliny adds still another detail that serves to undermine our confidence in the reports that a husband could arbitrarily put his wife to death. In the *Annales* of Fabius Pictor, Pliny tells us, it is claimed at one point that 'a matron was starved to death by her kinsmen (*a suis*) because she had broken into the chest in which the keys to the wine cellar were kept.'[43]

When all of the evidence is taken into consideration, therefore, it appears to have been the case that, during the early Republic, a wife *in manu* could not be summarily executed by her husband unless he actually caught her committing adultery. However, she could be divorced and returned to her family for execution, or could be killed by her husband after consultation with her kinsmen, if she was adjudged guilty of adultery or a fondness for wine.[44] From the point of view of the woman unfortunate enough to be caught, tried and condemned, such fine distinctions would truly have seemed of purely academic interest, but for us they serve as vivid reminders that in early Roman society all women, regardless of their age, were in a state of permanent ritual and jural subordination to their husbands, fathers, or guardians.[45]

THE EMANCIPATION OF ROMAN WOMEN

Most of the burdensome restrictions under which women labored were still in place at the beginning of the Principate. Augustus reaffirmed the principle that an adulterous wife could be put to death, but only by her father if she was still *in potestate*, and only if he caught her in the act either in his own home or that of her husband.[46] Within the confines of his own home, the husband could kill his wife's lover with impunity as well, but this same *lex Iulia de adulteriis* expressly forbade him to lay hands upon his wife.[47] The law ordered him instead to repudiate her, and then bring suit. Conviction brought with it the confiscation of half her dowry and one-third of all other property in her possession, as well as perpetual relegation to an island.[48]

In an effort to promote child-rearing, however, Augustus also instituted the so-called *ius liberorum*. This measure granted exemption from guardianship to all free-born women who gave birth to three children, and to freedwomen with four.[49] Shortly thereafter, the emperor Claudius abolished agnatic guardianship,[50] and in the second century AD Hadrian did away with fiduciary *coemptio*, making it possible for free-born women to write wills without the cumbersome preliminaries of fictive sale and manumission.[51] The *senatusconsultum Tertullianum*, also of Hadrianic date, in certain circumstances allowed mothers to inherit from their children if the latter died intestate;[52] and Antoninus Pius finally put an end to one of the cardinal elements of *patria potestas*, the father's right to compel his children to divorce.[53] The last piece of legislation worthy of note in this regard, the *senatusconsultum Orfitianum* of AD 178, granted a woman's children the right of intestate succession in preference to her brothers, sisters and other agnates – further diminishing her traditional obligations to her lineage.[54]

Although some scholars still interpret the *senatusconsultum Velleianum* – a Claudian or Neronian measure designed to prevent a creditor from suing a woman who had given surety for a loan to a third party – as evidence of a continuing mistrust of feminine capacity,[55] it may nevertheless confidently be averred that the first and second centuries AD witnessed profound changes in the legal status of women. The same can hardly be said, however, of the last two centuries of the Republic. The few changes of consequence during this period all concerned guardians (*tutores*). As Cicero caustically puts it at one point, 'our ancestors wished all women to be in the tutelage of guardians because of their instability of judgement, but the lawyers have devised new kinds of guardians whom women keep under their thumbs.'[56] This somewhat cryptic remark may be directed at the contemporary tactic of placing a woman in the *tutela* of one of her own or her deceased husband's freedmen;[57] conversely, it may simply be a reference to *coemptio fiduciae causa*, which was apparently the most common way of removing a *tutor*. As we saw earlier, the procedure involved an imaginary sale, with the purchaser promptly manumitting the woman in question and thereby becoming her guardian.[58] In their wills, some husbands also made provision for their wives *in manu* to nominate their own guardians, a contrivance known as *tutoris optio*.[59] If we may believe Livy, this was already possible as early as 186 BC, for this was one of the privileges that the Senate granted to Hispala Faecenia for her part in uncovering the Bacchanalian conspiracy.[60] A *senatusconsultum* of unknown date also permitted a woman to apply to the praetor for a new *tutor* to replace one who was absent or otherwise incapacitated;[61] in addition, the praetor could dismiss a guardian, or compel him to sanction an action even against his will.[62]

Some scholars have suggested that these developments robbed the institution of *tutela* of all significance, and thus helped to foster the increasing independence of women in the second and first centuries BC.[63] On closer examination, however, this does not appear to be the case. A wife had to be *in manu*, for example, to take advantage of *tutoris optio*, but marriage *sine manu* seems steadily to have displaced all other marital arrangements, and there is a consensus today that by the second century BC it was clearly predominant.[64] Insufficient attention has also been paid to the fact that a woman could not terminate a guardianship through *coemptio fiduciae causa* without the approval of the guardian in question.[65] If he agreed to put an end to the relationship, arguably he did so for his own convenience and not his ward's. In this context, one should always keep in mind that the Augustan *ius liberorum* not only released women from guardianship but men from service as guardians as well.[66] Similarly, the extreme reluctance of praetors to become involved in disputes between Roman women and their *tutores legitimi* – a heading that encompasses both patrons and agnatic relations[67] – has not received the stress that it deserves. Finally, one may simply observe that Augustus and his advisors, who must have been well informed about the character of *tutela* at the end of the Republic, obviously deemed it to be a real hindrance to women and an equally real imposition upon their guardians. This is the most economic, if not the only possible, explanation for their decision to reward mothers and fathers of three children with dispensation from its burdens and responsibilities.[68]

Nevertheless, it was precisely during the last two centuries of the Republic that the social status of Roman women altered most radically. Scholars customarily point to Cornelia, the mother of the Gracchi: she rejected a proposal of marriage from King Ptolemy VIII Euergetes II Physcon of Egypt, and managed a sizeable household at Misenum, all without any visible intervention from a *tutor*.[69] An equally popular example is Terentia, the long-suffering wife of Cicero, who owned a residential property, woodland, and two blocks of rental housing in Rome that yielded an annual income of 80,000 sesterces.[70] We hear much of Philotimus, the freedman who assisted her in financial matters, but there is no reference to a guardian even in the one instance when one would have been required by law. After her divorce from Cicero in 46 BC, Terentia repaid a loan to Cornelius Balbus by transferring to him a debt that she had been unable to collect from Cicero. It was a clever ruse, and Cicero was clearly of the opinion that it was one of Terentia's own devising.[71]

Maesia Sentia and Gaia Afrania are less frequently mentioned, but no less interesting. In the first century BC, these two women pleaded their own cases before the Praetor's court.[72] They have, however, been overshadowed by Hortensia, who in 42 BC led several hundred of Rome's wealthiest ladies into the forum to confront the triumvirs Antony, Lepidus and Octavian. The latter proposed to help themselves to the property of 1400 matrons, mostly wives of their proscribed enemies, but the strongly sympathetic public response to Hortensia's speech persuaded them to delete 1000 names from the list, and to make good the difference by taxing men with property worth 100,000 sesterces or more.[73]

This was not the first occasion on which Roman women had taken to the streets in an effort to influence public deliberations. When the Senate debated whether or not to ransom the prisoners taken at Cannae, the *curia* was surrounded by a vocal crowd, consisting in large part of concerned wives and mothers. They wanted the captives brought home, but made no active attempt to coerce the senators, and were reduced to bitter tears when the Senate rejected Hannibal's offer and thereby sentenced the men to slavery.[74] Twenty years later, in 195 BC, respectable matrons once again ventured into the public arena, but this time they were more forceful and met with greater success. The issue on this occasion was a proposal to repeal the *lex Oppia*, a sumptuary measure adopted in 215 BC, when Rome's fortunes in the Hannibalic war were at their nadir. It forbade women to own more than half an ounce of gold, to wear multi-colored clothing, or to ride in carriages within a mile of Rome itself or the towns in the *ager Romanus*.[75] The law did not, however, apply to Rome's Latin allies; the women of Rome, therefore, had good reason to resent its discriminatory restrictions, all the more so since the measure had been carried during a crisis but remained in force long after the danger had passed.[76] Predictably, then, matrons greeted the proposal to abrogate the law, which was introduced by the tribunes M. Fundanius and L. Valerius, with the greatest enthusiasm. More to the point, their support proved decisive. They aggressively lobbied the consuls, praetors, and other magistrates, and literally besieged two other tribunes, the brothers M. and P. Iunius Brutus, in their homes until they agreed to withdraw the vetoes with which they were paralyzing the plebeian assembly. Once they had been overawed, the law was repealed without difficulty.[77]

The increasing visibility of women in the second century BC manifests itself in one other way that deserves our immediate attention. In 102 BC, the consul Q. Lutatius Catulus started a new (and, one presumes, politically self-serving) trend when he delivered a public funeral oration for his mother Popilia.[78] Iulius Caesar honored his second wife, Cornelia, and his aunt Iulia, the wife of C. Marius, with similar *laudationes*, both in 67 BC.[79] The practice became increasingly commonplace, and equally ceased to be monopolized by the elite. The social status of Murdia, who was eulogized by one of her sons in the Augustan period, is unknown, but one can hardly mistake the libertine status of Allia Potestas, who was similarly honored by her patron in the third century AD.[80]

Thus by the end of the Republic some women at least were demonstrably capable of managing their own affairs, had intruded successfully in politics and law, and were of sufficient political value to their husbands and male relations to warrant public funeral orations. The independent judgement that these women displayed in political, legal and financial matters was, of course, completely at variance with the subordinate condition to which the law condemned them. More to the point, the ability of noblewomen such as Cornelia efficiently to manage their own affairs could not fail to make an impression upon their male counterparts – and it was upon the latter's presumption of innate female incompetence (*levitas animi*) that, in the final analysis, the jural status of women squarely rested. In the end, as we have seen, the law was overhauled, however slowly and incompletely, in recognition of this fact. Gaius says as much at one point in the *Institutiones* (1.190):

> Indeed, there appears to be almost no valid argument for keeping women of mature age in guardianship. For that which is commonly believed, namely that because of their instability of character women are frequently deceived and for this reason are rightly subjected to the authority of guardians, seems more specious than true. For women who are of mature age do personally conduct their own affairs, and in many cases a guardian gives his approval merely for form's sake.

COMPETING EXPLANATIONS

How, then, are we to account for the increasing independence and assertiveness of Roman women during the last two centuries of the Republic? Scholars have ventured a variety of explanations; one still current, which has been tendered repeatedly in this century, emphasizes the freedom permitted by the increasingly popular option of marriage *sine manu*. A comment to this effect in Sarah Pomeroy's *Goddesses, Whores, Wives, and Slaves* may be taken as representative:

> The marriage without *manus* gave a woman more freedom. She was under the authority of a father or guardian who lived in a different household, while her husband, whose daily surveillance was available, had no formal authority over her. (p. 155)[81]

However attractive it might appear at first glance, there are a number of criticisms that can be levelled against this argument. First, as we have already emphasized, a variety of sources draw attention to the fact that it was the custom of Roman men to kiss their married kinswomen whenever they encountered them in public, not as a sign of affection but in order to determine whether they had been drinking.[82] This demonstrates that distance alone did not preclude Roman men from taking a keen interest in the behavior of their kinswomen – a completely natural reaction, given the fact that divorce for cause entitled the injured husband to keep a portion of his wife's dowry (*retentio propter mores*), and might enable him to retain it all.[83] The husband could thus turn a profit from his wife's immorality, but before we leap to the seductive conclusion that many men would for this reason encourage their wives to behave indiscreetly, it should also be recalled that Roman marriage was explicitly procreative in purpose.[84] Typically, that is to say, the Roman husband was also a father: if he received a dowry from his own wife, it was also the case that he would have to supply one for his daughter when she entered upon marriage – property that could be jeopardized by her subsequent behavior. In this tangled web of propertied relationships, it should be immediately apparent that most husbands would have a vested interest in cooperating closely with their marital relations to guarantee their wives' good behavior, and to punish swiftly and sternly such delinquencies as did occur. This is the moral of the aforementioned story that the elder Pliny attributes to Fabius Pictor, in which a *matrona* was starved to death by her own kinsmen because she had broken into the chest containing the keys to her husband's wine cellar.[85]

A second criticism derives from the first: the size or character of the dowry might insure close scrutiny, and even interference, on the part of the wife's blood-relations. As Pomeroy has herself pointed out, in Roman Egypt a bride whose dowry consisted of land was far more likely to remain in close contact with her father or kinsmen than one who brought *res mancipi* to her marriage.[86] The modest plot of $10\frac{3}{4}$ arouras (about $7\frac{1}{2}$ acres) that one husband received in a marriage contract, for example, virtually guaranteed that father and daughter would remain in close proximity to one another.[87] In this setting, a father would obviously be well positioned to exercise his *potestas* – and the papyri suggest that some fathers at least did invoke their authority to put an end to their daughters' marriages, often

18

for the explicit purpose of recovering their dowry. In the second century AD, several fathers who intervened in this manner ended up in court; we know of two cases that were finally tried before the governor of Egypt. In the first, the plaintiff was the injured son-in-law, but the second was a protracted and bitter dispute between a father and daughter who refused his order to divorce her husband. In each case, the judge ruled against the father, subordinating the principle of *patria potestas* to the wishes of the wife in question.[88]

In Egypt, therefore, marriage did not protect a woman against the capricious exercise of *patria potestas* until the second century AD. It would, of course, be imprudent to use this material to define conditions in Italy, but here as well it should be noted that dowries might consist of land,[89] and that fathers might order their daughters to divorce for strictly financial reasons.[90] It thus seems reasonable to assume that similar legal disputes also occurred in Italy, which eventually inspired the edict of Antoninus Pius safeguarding harmonious marriage against parental interference.[91]

We may safely conclude, therefore, that in many instances the freedom scholars have accorded a woman married *sine manu* was largely illusory.[92] It should, however, also be kept in mind that this presumed freedom rests on the tacit assumption that marriages were invariably virilocal, and that all households took the form of nuclear families. It may well be the case that this was the most typical pattern, but it was by no means universal. In his life of Aemilius Paullus, for example, Plutarch tells us that one of Aemilius' daughters married into the household of the Aelii Tuberones. He describes it in the following terms:

> There were sixteen members of the clan, every single one of them an Aelius. They had one very small house, and one small farm sustained them all. They all lived here in one household along with their several wives and children.[93]

This appears to be a horizontally extended household, and it is certainly fair to suggest that pressure to conform – let us recall that the bride might well have been 15 years of age or younger – would be of far greater consequence than the particular form of marriage that she had contracted.

One final example may be invoked here, for it illustrates still more dramatically how artificial these distinctions between marital categories can be. This lurks in Dio Chrysostomus' seventh, or Euboeic, discourse. Shipwrecked somewhere along Euboaea's inhospitable Aegean shore, Dio tells us that he wandered off and eventually found shelter in an unpretentious peasant homestead. Happily, he then fully details what can best be characterized as a three-generational vertically extended household of extreme complexity (Figure 1).

There is much of value here for anyone interested in marriage patterns in classical antiquity, but for the present it is the two sisters in the third generation that require our attention. Since the elder had moved away to marry a wealthy man, and lived at some distance from her parents, she might conceivably have derived some benefit from a marriage *sine manu*. The younger sister, however, married a male relation brought up in the same household, and the young couple continued to reside there after the wedding. Self-evidently, therefore, the notion that marriage *sine manu* would have created a more favorable environment for the younger sister than marriage *cum manu*, at least so long as both her husband and father were alive, is scarcely to be credited.[94]

A second explanation for the freedom of action that women increasingly enjoyed during the middle and late Republic – and one that differs radically from the institutional role assigned to

Figure 1 A peasant household in Dio Chrysostomus

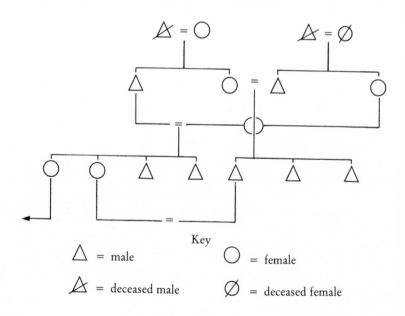

Key

△ = male   ◯ = female

◬ = deceased male   ∅ = deceased female

marriage *sine manu* – has been inspired by the work of the Italian jurisconsult Siro Solazzi. Some sixty years ago he argued, in great detail and with considerable vigor, that the various references to feminine *infirmitas* and *levitas animi* in the corpus of Roman law were without exception Byzantine interpolations.[95] Solazzi's verdict was subsequently endorsed by most students of Roman law,[96] and this in turn generated a widespread loss of confidence in the long-standing belief to which we have already twice made reference, namely that the authors of the Twelve Tables had placed women in perpetual guardianship because of their inconstancy of character. The very notion that women were widely regarded in early Rome as unstable and irresponsible, that is to say, rests squarely on one of these 'contaminated' passages:

> Veteres enim voluerunt feminas, etiamsi perfectae aetatis sint, propter *animi levitatem* in tutela esse . . . exceptis virginibus Vestalibus, quas etiam veteres in honorem sacerdotii liberas esse voluerunt; itaque etiam lege XII tabularum cautum est.[97]

Solazzi's article thus invited renewed discussion of both the origins of female guardianship and the reasons for its increasing irrelevance, although on closer examination the manifest weakness of his argument quickly became apparent. Lanfranchi, for example, drew attention to the fact that inconstancy of character was invoked repeatedly to characterize women in the declamations attributed to Quintilian[98] – a catalogue expanded by Schulz to include passages in Cicero, Valerius Maximus and Seneca.[99] Still, Schulz chose to modify Solazzi's position rather than abandon it altogether. Having duly noted that the first indisputable allusion to feminine incapacity surfaces in Cicero's observation that the *maiores* 'wished all women to be in the tutelage of guardians because of their instability of judgement,'[100] Schulz rightly stressed that such a concept would have been singularly out of place among the elite of the late Republic – and especially so in the case of Terentia's husband! The criticism is, however, largely misdirected, since Cicero explicitly attributes this prejudice to the *maiores*, and not to himself.[101] Nevertheless, this false step is important because it led Schulz to a second and still more critical claim: instead of drawing the conclusion that Cicero was voicing a primitive Roman belief anachronistic in his own day, the similarity between this passage and a well-known dictum in the *Politics* of Aristotle induced him to suggest that it was a Hellenistic import, destined first to enter the mainstream of Roman rhetoric and eventually to be enshrined in the corpus of Roman law.[102] The genesis of *tutela mulierum perpetua*, he then asserted, actually lay in the Roman conviction that women should be excluded from public life: ignorance of the law and business practice, not an innate lack of judgement, sustained the institution.[103] Although Schulz himself did not explicitly draw the requisite conclusion, it follows from this argument that, for Roman women to obtain emancipation, at least some of their number would have to intrude successfully in traditionally male spheres of activity. With this supposition, we have arrived at the heart of this second and still popular explanation for the increasing freedom enjoyed by Roman women.

This hybrid argument of Solazzi and Schulz merits careful scrutiny, above all because it conforms so nicely with the evidence presented above for the growing political, business and even legal acumen of Roman women in the late Republic. Moreover, there is a considerable body of evidence, scattered across several centuries, which testifies to the Roman conviction that there were specifically male and female spheres of activity. Ulpian, for example, informs us that the praetors would not allow women to represent third parties in court, not only because pleading would be unbecoming for a woman but also 'so that women might not perform duties which belong to men.'[104] Again, the authors of the *senatusconsultum Velleianum* reasoned that women who secured loans for third parties should not be sued on this account 'because it is not just that women perform duties appropriate to men and become bound by obligations of this kind in consequence.'[105] A rescript of Severus Alexander also bluntly stated that guardianship was an exclusively male prerogative, while Diocletian and Maximian endorsed anew the principle that women could not represent another party in court.[106] Clearly, then, there were barriers, and we have already seen that women successfully breached them. Were these barriers, however, as Schulz suggests, wholly arbitrary, or were they in fact grounded in a male perception that women were inherently unstable and irresponsible? Here it will be argued that this latter view, which was accepted without reservation until subjected to Solazzi's criticisms, in fact makes better sense of the limited pool of data at our disposal.

At the outset, it should be noted that Schulz's point of departure can no longer be defended, for in the past decade Joëlle Beaucamp has levelled new and still more telling criticisms against Solazzi's original premise.[107] This has not, however, proven fatal to Schulz's

assumptions, which have recently been endorsed with some modification in an important paper by Suzanne Dixon.[108] Like Schulz,
she believes that the notion of feminine incapacity is a Hellenistic
intrusion, but she also adopts an explanation for the origins of
female guardianship that Schulz explicitly rejected, namely the
desire of the agnatic kinsmen to preserve property that would
devolve upon them when their wards died.[109] By the late Republic,
she continues, the original intent of the arrangement had been
obscured, and Romans such as Cicero who took an antiquarian
interest in such institutions falsely concluded from the protective
character of *tutela impuberum* on the one hand, and Hellenistic
apothegms concerning the instability of women on the other, that
their ancestors must have believed women and children equally to
require assistance and protection.

Despite differences of opinion with regard to the original intent
of *tutela mulierum perpetua*, therefore, Schulz and Dixon are in
agreement that the charge of *levitas animi* is first levelled against
Roman women in Cicero, a Hellenistic prejudice utterly alien to
primitive Rome. This is, of course, a classic *argumentum ex silentio*:
where should we expect to see such an idea first surface, if not
precisely in Cicero? More to the point, the concomitant notion
that women in early Rome would have been regarded by their male
contemporaries as stable and responsible personalities contradicts
such evidence as we possess.[110] The frequently attested desire of
Roman men to prevent their wives from drinking, for example,
betrays a fear on their part that wine would unleash their passions,
and lead them on to other and still more serious offenses: it is surely
not coincidence that Aulus Gellius and Dionysius of Halicarnassus
both couple the ban on drinking with that on adultery.[111] This
aversion to excessive display of feminine passion is even embodied
in the Law of the Twelve Tables, for Cicero tells us that it forbade
women to lacerate their cheeks or indulge in excessive lamentation
at funerals.[112] It should be stressed, however, that it is precisely
in its provisions to safeguard agnatic succession that the Law of
the Twelve Tables most clearly betrays this masculine fear that
the emotional instability of women might yield dire economic
consequences. As Dixon appropriately emphasizes, most scholars
are now in agreement that the code's arrangements for the perpetual
tutelage of women reflect the determination of their male kinsmen
to preserve property that would automatically descend to them
through intestate inheritance. This should now be taken as a
given, but it should also be conceded that as an explanation for

tutela mulierum perpetua it is at best only a half-truth. Since institutions do not exist *in vacuo*, but rest upon a set of social assumptions, a further question must be posed: in the archaic period, what was it about women that persuaded Roman men to regard such a procedure as vital to their own interests? Here the Twelve Tables supply one vital clue: the *decemviri* established tutelary arrangements not only for women but also for children (*impuberes*), lunatics (*furiosi*) and spendthrifts (*prodigi*).[113] In each instance, the agnates were summoned to serve as trustees, and in the case of male children, guardianship automatically ceased when they obtained their majority – the moment in time when they were thought to be competent to manage their own affairs. Lunatics and spendthrifts, in contrast, were subject to *tutela perpetua* precisely because they had demonstrated their incompetence, and it is with these two categories that women were conjoined. It is obvious that gender is not the critical element in determining the need for a guardian in the case of *furiosi* and *prodigi*, and this in turn should lead us to suspect that with regard to women as well it was not gender *per se* but some self-evident and lifelong disability that rendered them incompetent to manage their own property, hence in need of *tutela perpetua* as well. As we have already seen, Gaius unequivocally states that the authors of the Twelve Tables (the *veteres*) somewhat vaguely labelled this disability *levitas animi*, and there is one last piece of evidence to be introduced that should clinch the argument in his favor. Children required guardians above all because their powers of reason and judgement were immature, and in the various forms of *manus* marriage that the vast majority of early Roman women contracted, they were relegated to perpetual childhood (*filiae loco*). It cannot be mere coincidence that all children were thought to require guardians, that women were looked upon as children in perpetuity, and that women were also in permanent need of a guardian.

Thus with the collapse of Solazzi's argument against it, there is no longer any reason to doubt the authenticity of Gaius' evidence. What we must now attempt to do is define the content of *levitas animi* more precisely. Here it should first be pointed out that feminine interference in masculine spheres of activity is unlikely to be at issue. Even in the early Republic there was nothing formally to prevent women from crossing gender-defined boundaries and engaging in such 'masculine' activities as drawing up a will *per aes et libram*; rather, Roman law forbade them to do so without male supervision. If, therefore, there was such a thing as an *officium virile* in the archaic community, it does not necessarily follow that the exclusion of women from the activity in question was always rigidly observed. Second and more importantly, we must keep constantly in mind that in whatever period it was introduced, a phrase such as *levitas animi* was devoid of content until Roman men supplied it with meaning by specifying the modes of behavior that they considered 'irresponsible'. Our immediate concern, therefore, is to determine how, if left to their own devices, women could have threatened the inheritance rights of the *agnati*, for it is the latter's right to a woman's property that feminine *levitas animi* jeopardized. Happily, a satisfying answer can be exhumed from Livy's account of the Bacchanalian affair (186 BC). He informs us that the Senate accorded special privileges to Hispala Faecenia, the *liberta* who had brought the cult's more sinister features to public attention. Among these privileges was the right to marry outside of her clan (*enuptio gentis*) – a piece of information that points to the commonplace character of marriage among fellow clansmen and women in early Rome, above all within the propertied classes. Clearly, this device alone would have made it possible for the *agnati* to keep the property that would devolve upon them from an *intestata* within the extended family, hence the more widespread the resort to this modified form of endogamy was, the more puzzling *tutela mulierum perpetua* becomes.[114] In this tightly knit social environment, then, we may now rephrase our earlier question: what could have inspired Roman men to conceive of *tutela perpetua* as a necessary complement to gentile marriage?

In his study of *enuptio gentis*, Watson remarks that a *tutor* could not capriciously withhold his consent when a woman *sui iuris* sought to marry outside of her clan. He makes an exception, however, in the case of women in the first census class. Here women were openly expected to marry inside the *gens*, and if they chose not to do so, 'not only could the *tutor* withhold his consent but it was considered perfectly reasonable and proper for him to do so, he could not be compelled to give his consent and the marriage would not be valid without it.'[115] On this basis, therefore, we may reasonably conclude that the driving force behind *tutela mulierum perpetua* was a fear on the part of the *agnati* that women, by nature creatures of immature judgement whose passions could be inflamed by, *inter alia*, an excess of wine, would seek to contract *manus* marriages that were also exogamous. As we shall see below, as women matured they appear to have had a greater voice in the selection of their husbands, but we should also keep in mind that their mothers might also come into conflict with the *tutores* over the selection of their daughters' husbands – the moral of Livy's tale of the 'Maid of Ardea'. Hence there was ample room for the desires of women to collide with the economic interests of the *agnati*, and it would only be natural for the latter to regard these desires as frivolous and irresponsible. Whether the *agnati* used a catch-phrase such as *levitas animi* to define the source of their fears is hardly relevant; the seminal point is that, in all probability, *tutela mulierum perpetua* is rooted in a masculine conviction that women may allow considerations of property to be superseded by other priorities. It was women's perceived immaturity of judgement on this point, which may be defined from the masculine point of view as the substitution of passion for reason, that induced Roman men to circumscribe both their testamentary rights and ability to marry a man of their own choice.[116]

The perpetual tutelage of Roman women, it must therefore be concluded, was inspired from the very beginning by masculine prejudice – an ironically unreasoning conviction that women are by nature as emotionally unstable as *furiosi* or *prodigi*.[117] Once this point is recognized, however, it should be equally clear that anything which undermined this attitude would serve to weaken the institution as well. In this context, the suggestion that women obtained greater freedom as a direct result of demonstrating their ability to discharge traditional male prerogatives becomes still more compelling. At first glance this comment seems to do little more than take us back to the issue with which this whole discussion began, but in fact it may also now be rephrased: under what circumstances would Roman men, who had so little faith in feminine judgement with regard to matters of property, be forced to allow women to represent their own interests? There is, for example, no source that asserts that marriage *sine manu* compelled Roman women to fend for themselves – indeed, there is no source that actually alludes to the liberating influence of marriage *sine manu* – but there are several that talk of war and its attendant administrative duties in precisely these terms. In the speech urging repeal of the *lex Oppia* that he scripts for L. Valerius, for example, Livy inserts the following remark:

Of course, if you annul the Oppian law, and later wish to prohibit any of the things that the law now forbids, it will no longer be in your power to do so. Some will find daughters, wives, sisters even, less under their control – but never, so long as their men are alive, is feminine servitude shaken off. However, they themselves abhor the freedom that comes with the loss of husbands and fathers.[118]

Writing more than a century later, Tacitus attributes similar thoughts to a certain Valerius Messalinus. During the first five years of Tiberius' reign, Agrippina and Plancina, the wives of Germanicus and Cn. Calpurnius Piso respectively, had shocked Roman society by their conduct in the provinces to which their husbands had been assigned. Repeated interference in their husbands' military duties was not the least of the charges levelled against them,[119] and in AD 21 this touched off a debate on the floor of the Senate. There would be less corruption, some senators reasoned, if magistrates' wives were compelled to remain at home while their husbands served abroad. Most of the *patres*, however, tended to the opposite point of view. Valerius, to whom Tacitus allots a speech on this occasion, bemoaned the fact that all husbands would be penalized because of the inability of one or two to keep their wives in check, while at the same time 'a sex frail by nature would be left unguarded, exposed to its own innate licentiousness as well as the passions of others.'[120] This last thought will have occurred to others in the chamber as well.

A few scholars have seen the significance of these passages,[121] but to date the larger body of evidence suggesting a causal relationship between Rome's ceaseless warfare and the increasing social and economic freedom of Roman women has remained largely unexplored. As one would expect, for example, the Romans themselves were most alert to the moral consequences of warfare that freed women from the *auctoritas* of their husbands, fathers or guardians for extended periods of time. Evidence of this concern first begins to surface during the Second Punic War. In 215 BC, the Senate devised an elaborate ceremonial to introduce the cult of Venus Verticordia, 'the Turner of Hearts'. This cult, we are told, had but one purpose, and that was to discourage adultery.[122] The Senate had good reason to be concerned: during the first four years of the war, at least 108,000 men had been called up to serve with the legions.[123] As it turned out, however, the gesture proved futile. Two years later, in

213 BC, the plebeian aediles M. Fundanius Fundulus and L. Villius Tappulus charged an undetermined number of women with immoral conduct; some at least were found guilty, and ushered into exile.[124] As Pomeroy has noted, this was a highly irregular procedure.[125] Women fell within the jurisdiction of their husbands or kinsmen, not the *res publica*. Normally, then, these charges would have been preferred before domestic tribunals – but the middle years of the Hannibalic war could hardly be considered normal. In this setting the most likely explanation is also the simplest: the men with authority over these adulteresses were either dead or absent from Rome on military service.

Livy's narrative of the punishment meted out to the Bacchanalian conspirators in 186 BC reinforces this conclusion. Adultery, murder, false witness, forged seals, substitution of wills – large numbers of men and women alike, Livy says, were adjudged guilty of these and other capital crimes. 'Convicted women were handed over to their kinsmen, or to husbands with authority over them, so that they might be executed in private. If there was no one qualified to exact punishment, however, it was carried out in public.'[126] The text is unambiguous, and warrants only one conclusion: although it contravened the most fundamental principles of Roman law, in 186 BC there were women in Rome who were no longer subject to *potestas*, *manus*, or *tutela*. This is all the more striking because legislation had already been enacted to redress this situation, conceivably during the course of the Second Punic War itself. The *lex Atilia*, that is to say, stipulated that a woman who became *in nullius manu* should apply to the praetor to appoint a *tutor* for her, a procedure (*tutela a magistratu dativa*) that also required the participation of a majority of the college of plebeian tribunes.[127]

The mere enactment of such legislation, of course, indicates that at the outset of the second century many women found themselves without *tutores*. This makes it easier to comprehend the events of 186 BC, and it becomes easier still if one recalls that there were ten legions in the field during this year – a total of 123,000 men.[128] In the period 200–168 BC, the number of legions fluctuated between a maximum of thirteen (182,400 men) in 190, and a minimum of six in 199 and 197 (101,000 and 102,800 men respectively), but there were more than 100,000 men under arms in twenty-seven of these thirty-three years.[129] Rome had, to be sure, fielded large armies in the past, but warfare in the early Republic was a seasonal affair, and did not impose an intolerable strain upon her institutions. In the second century, in contrast, many recruits could look forward to at least six years of continuous service. This was especially true of those unfortunate enough to be sent out to Spain. The veterans who returned from the Iberian peninsula in 180 BC had been posted there since at least 186; similarly, those who went out in 146 were not brought home until 140.[130] The absence of 100,000 men or more, when prolonged over a number of years and in thousands of cases rendered permanent either by death in the field, desertion, or capture and subsequent enslavement, could not fail to be socially disruptive.[131] Indeed, the *lex Atilia* is quite specific on this point, for it instructed women whose guardians had been taken captive to apply for new *tutores*, while stipulating that the mandate of these appointees would automatically cease if the *captivi* were fortunate enough eventually to return home.[132] Hence there can be no doubt that prolonged transmarine warfare freed women from traditional constraints, and as the Bacchanalian affair indicates, some took advantage of their freedom to indulge themselves in ways that the government was not prepared to countenance.

While the Latin authors are predictably obsessed with the precipitous decline of public morals, the seemingly endless campaigns of the Hannibalic war and the second century BC, which absorbed manpower in such vast quantities, also left Roman women to cope on their own with a number of quite mundane problems. We have already remarked, for example, that the Law of the Twelve Tables – a product of the fifth century BC, when seasonal conflict was the norm – absolutely forbade women to enter into a contract at their own discretion.[133] In the second century, this and other measures originally intended to preserve property for the *agnati* by curbing feminine *levitas animi* remained fully in force; but again, in the interim the dramatic expansion of their domain had forced the Romans to abandon the traditional concept of seasonal military service. In these radically different circumstances, therefore, one might well ask how, *exempli gratia*, a wife left in day-to-day charge of the family farm could hire additional workers for the harvest and other periods of extraordinary labor demand – a routine event in the second century, even when the husband was not away on campaign[134] – or replace a slave or work animal that had died.[135] One might equally ask how betrothals and dowries were arranged for girls of marriageable age, when their fathers were off in a distant military theater. Here it is instructive to note that at some point before his death in 211 BC, the proconsul Cn. Cornelius Scipio

Calvus (cos. 222 BC) wrote to the Senate from Spain to request a successor, so that he might return to Rome and settle his daughter's dowry. Rather than lose so capable an officer, the senators took the matter into their own hands: 'after the dowry had been fixed in consultation with Scipio's wife and kinsmen, the *patres* put up the money from the public treasury, and themselves gave the girl in marriage.'[136]

One would like to know more about the role of Scipio's wife in this affair, but even as it stands, this obscure episode may be profitably contrasted with three well-known stories, the first situated in the fifth and the others in the second century BC. The potential for conflict between the mother and *tutores* over the selection of a husband for a girl whose father was deceased or a prisoner is nicely captured in the legend of the 'Maid of Ardea.' Livy relates that, in this particular instance, the disagreement became so bitter that the mother eventually petitioned the Ardean magistrates to intervene on her behalf – an action that prompted a civil war.[137] It does not particularly matter that the episode is set in Ardea rather than Rome, nor that we are dealing with legend rather than fact: the episode is entirely credible, and surely illustrates the kind of quarrel that must lie behind the remarkable decision to allow praetors to overrule the objections of *tutores* and permit women to pursue a course of action to which they were opposed.[138]

The second story, which was meant to draw attention to the conspicuous *virtus* that Tiberius Gracchus exhibited even in adolescence, in fact reveals how differently marital negotiations might proceed when the girl's father was at home. According to Plutarch, at a banquet of the college of augurs Appius Claudius Pulcher, who was destined not only to hold the consulship (143 BC) but to be *censor* (136) and *princeps senatus* as well, invited young Gracchus to become his son-in-law:

> When Tiberius gladly agreed and the engagement had thus come to pass, Appius returned home. But he had scarcely set foot in the door when he called out to his wife and shouted in a loud voice: 'Antistia, I have betrothed our Claudia.' Completely stunned, she replied: 'Why so suddenly, or why such haste – unless you have obtained Tiberius Gracchus as a husband for her.'[139]

Here matters are arranged between two social equals, but as the third anecdote makes clear, when the two individuals involved were patron and client events would still follow the same arbitrary course. Plutarch tells us that, after the death of his wife, the elder Cato was in the habit of sharing his bed with a young slave-girl, to his son's disgust. This promptly induced Cato to seek out a new bride:

> While going down to the forum with his clients in the usual manner, he called out in a loud voice to a certain Salonius, who had been one of his under-secretaries and was now escorting him, to inquire if he had found a suitable son-in-law for his daughter, who was now of marriageable age. The man said that he had not, nor would he even think of doing so without first consulting Cato. 'Well,' Cato replied, 'I have found you a suitable son-in-law, unless of course you find his age displeasing: he is blameless in all other respects, but he is a very old man.' Salonius instantly urged him to take the matter in hand and betroth his daughter to the man of his choice, since she was also his client and in need of his services. Without further ado, Cato said that he wished to marry the girl himself. At first, as one would expect, the proposal stunned Salonius, who considered Cato to be well beyond marriageable age and himself far from worthy of alliance with a house of consular rank and triumphal standing. He gladly accepted, however, when he saw that Cato was in earnest, and as soon as they reached the forum the betrothal was formally announced.[140]

At last, we can understand how Terentia and Tullia could negotiate the latter's marriage to the notorious P. Cornelius Dolabella in 50 BC without consulting Tullia's father, the orator Cicero. The latter was governor of Cilicia at the time, and politically embarrassed by the match: Cicero wanted to avoid prorogation of his command at all costs, and counted heavily upon the support of his politically influential predecessor, another Appius Claudius Pulcher (cos. 54 BC), to insure his return to Rome. Unfortunately, at the very moment of the marriage, Dolabella was prosecuting Pulcher for *maiestas* and *ambitus*![141] In a desperate attempt to salvage their relationship, Cicero wrote to Pulcher and stressed that the marriage had taken him completely by surprise. He did not expect Pulcher to be skeptical:

there is one thing of which I am not afraid, namely that you will fail clearly to understand that what was done was done by others, to whom I had stipulated that, since I was going to be so far away, they should not seek my advice but do what they thought best.[142]

At this point, we can also grasp more clearly why legislation was required to permit women to petition the praetor to appoint a new guardian to take the place of one who was deceased, absent, or a captive. Naturally, citizens of lesser standing did not receive the solicitous treatment that the Senate was prepared to accord a Cornelius Scipio. Hence a mechanism had to be devised that would allow ordinary women to act in conformity with the law in the absence of husbands or guardians. This, in turn, helps to explain the meaning behind Gaius' comment that a guardian's endorsement was often 'merely for form's sake.'[143] New *tutores* would typically be more distant kinsmen, with predictably less interest in the affairs of their wards. It is thus no wonder that *tutela mulierum perpetua* came to be regarded as an onerous obligation, nor that Augustus would use exemption from it as an inducement to stimulate the birth-rate among the elite in his *lex Iulia de maritandis ordinibus*.[144]

Systemic warfare thus created a situation in which many women were compelled to exercise their own judgement and rely upon their own talents, and thereby fostered feminine independence, but we should not forget that this process could be painful as well as exciting. It is not the case, as Livy correctly reminds us, that every Roman woman wished to be independent.[145] He might have added that mishandled opportunities could yield results that were extremely unpleasant – a point that Tiberius Gracchus, at least, seems readily to have comprehended.

Until the very end of the first century BC, the Roman army relied almost exclusively upon the Italian peasantry to satisfy the bulk of its manpower requirements. The peasant economy of classical Italy, however, typically mixed vegetable and cereals culture with food-gathering, hunting and fishing, and made intensive use of family labor.[146] In a nuclear family, therefore, one would logically expect that the loss of labor attendant upon conscription of the *agrestis* would leave his wife and children in a difficult if not impossible situation. As we shall see later, not all wives and children caught up in these circumstances were equally at risk, but it cannot be denied that some were imperilled. In fact, the danger had already begun to manifest itself as early as the First Punic War, if not earlier. In 256 BC, the consul M. Atilius Regulus landed in Africa, and quickly won what appeared to be a decisive victory.[147] With the end of this protracted and difficult struggle apparently in sight, the Senate decided to prorogue Regulus' command for a second year. This was a singular honor, hence it must have come as a considerable shock to the *patres* when Regulus wrote back and asked to be replaced. He informed the Senate that

> the manager of his farm, a property of seven *iugera* [4.35 acres] in the Pupinian district, had died, and a hired hand had taken advantage of the opportunity to run off with the whole of his equipment and livestock. He therefore beseeched the senators to send out a new general, lest his wife and children be left to starve on this derelict property.[148]

In the event, we are told, the Senate arranged for Regulus' farm to be leased, provisioned his wife and children, and made good his losses at public expense. This particular story, then, had a happy ending; once again, however, it must be emphasized that the families of ordinary soldiers caught up in this same situation would not have been so fortunate. Whether apocryphal or not, this episode permits us to glimpse the ugly reality that lurks behind the speeches in which Tiberius Gracchus decried the expropriation of the peasantry, which he attributed in large part to the burden of military service.[149] To be sure, one must always keep in mind that Tiberius overstated the deracination of the Italian peasantry in order to win support for his legislative proposals, but there still can be no doubt that in certain areas of the peninsula, and notably the environs of Rome itself, many peasant families did suffer wholesale expropriation.[150]

While, therefore, Rome's sustained pattern of aggression abroad had a profound impact on the legal status of all Roman women, irrespective of their position in Roman society, it is equally clear that the ability of the individual woman to cope with the domestic consequences of prolonged warfare was largely determined by status considerations. It is for this reason that we shall next examine the economic impact of war on women in the Roman elite, focussing in particular upon the institutions of dowry and inheritance, and then turn our attention to the lower classes.

NOTES

1   Gaius, *Institutiones* 1.144. The perpetual jural subordination of women has been the subject of frequent comment. Cf. recently, for example, T. Carp, 'Two Matrons of the Late Republic,' *Women's Studies* 8 (1981) 191 = H. Foley (ed.), *Reflections of Women in Antiquity* (New York, 1981) 345; J.P. Hallett, *Fathers and Daughters in Roman Society* (Princeton, 1984) 67; J.A. Crook, 'Women in Roman Succession,' in B. Rawson (ed.), *The Family in Ancient Rome* (London, 1985) 62; and J.F. Gardner, *Women in Roman Law and Society* (Bloomington and Indianapolis, 1986) 5–22.

2   *Institutiones* 1.55.

3   *Antiquitates Romanae* 2.15.2.

4   For further discussion of this point, cf. C. Herrmann, *Le Rôle judiciaire et politique des femmes sous le République romaine* (Brussels, 1964) 14; and J.A. Crook, *Law and Life of Rome* (London, 1967) 108.

5   Livy 1.24–26; cf. Dionysius of Halicarnassus, *Antiquitates Romanae* 4.64.4–67.2. This tale must have already been widely known early in the second century BC, for surviving fragments suggest that Ennius recounted it in some detail in his *Annales*; see J. Vahlen, *Ennianae Poesis Reliquiae*[3] (Leipzig, 1928) nos. 129–136. For the legal issues involved here, see R.M. Ogilvie, *A Commentary on Livy, Books 1–5* (Oxford, 1965) 114–117; for this and other instances of the exercise of *patria potestas* against daughters, cf. S.B. Pomeroy, *Goddesses, Whores, Wives, and Slaves. Women in Classical Antiquity* (New York, 1975) 152–153; and Hallett, *Fathers and Daughters*, 113–115. It remains unclear, however, whether a father could exercise his *ius vitae et necis* capriciously. Thus R. Yaron, 'Vitae Necisque Potestas,' *TRG* 30 (1962) 249; W. Kunkel, 'Das Konsilium im Hausgericht,' *ZRG* 83 (1966) 241–246; and A. Watson, *Rome of the XII Tables* (Princeton, 1975) 42–44, all argue that a son could only be put to death *ex iusta causa*; *contra*, A. Guarino, *Labeo* 13 (1967) 124, whose criticisms are directed against Kunkel's argument; J.-P. Neraudau, *La Jeunesse dans la littérature et les institutions de la Rome républicaine* (Paris, 1979) 170; and more cautiously, W.V. Harris, 'The Roman Father's Power of Life and Death,' in R.S. Bagnall and W.V. Harris (eds), *Studies in Roman Law in Memory of A. Arthur Schiller* (Leiden, 1986) 81–95.

6   Sale *in mancipio*: Gaius, *Institutiones* 1.117; sale into slavery *trans Tiberim*: Cicero, *Pro Caecina* 98; *De Oratore* 1.181; surrender to satisfy a debt: Watson, *Rome of the XII Tables*, 117–121, thus convincingly interprets Livy 2.24.6 and especially Gaius, *Institutiones* 1.132 (cf. 4.79) – purportedly a direct quote from the Law of the Twelve Tables (the fourth tablet, according to Dionysius of Halicarnassus, *Antiquitates Romanae* 2.27.1–3).

7   In 48 BC Cicero contemplated dissolving the marriage of his daughter Tullia to P. Cornelius Dolabella. He discussed the matter at length with his confidant Atticus, but it is quite clear that he did not consult Tullia herself: Cicero, *Epistulae ad Atticum* 11.3; cf. *Epistulae ad Familiares* 14.13 (47 BC). This paternal privilege also surfaces in Plautus, *Stichus* 53, on which see now M. McDonnell, 'Divorce Initiated by Women in Rome,' *AJAH* 8 (1983) 56. A. Watson, *Roman Private Law around 200 BC* (Edinburgh, 1971) 23 n. 8, further adduces *Rhetorica ad Herennium* 2.38, a fragment of a play entitled *Cresphontes* that most scholars have attributed to Euripides. Both Watson and H.D. Jocelyn, *The Tragedies of Ennius* (Cambridge, 1967) 96–97 (fragment 53) and 270–277, believe first that this passage should be attributed to the *Cresphontes* of Ennius, and second that it mirrors Roman rather than Athenian

legal practice. Although Jocelyn's arguments are not compelling and one must therefore suspend judgement on this matter, it is nevertheless certain that this element of *patria potestas* was not abolished before the reign of Antoninus Pius (Paulus, *Sententiae* 5.6.15).

8   *Digesta* 23.1.11–12.

9   Cf. A.G. Harkness, 'Age at Marriage and Age at Death in the Roman Empire,' *TAPA* 27 (1896) 35–51; M. Bang, 'Das gewöhnliche Alter der Mädchen bei der Verlobung und Verheiratung,' in L. Friedländer, *Darstellungen aus der Sittengeschichte Roms*[10] IV (Leipzig, 1922) 133–141; M. Durry, 'Le mariage des filles impubères à Rome,' *CRAI* (1955) 84–91 = *Mélanges Marcel Durry* (Paris, 1970) 17–24; 'Le mariage des filles impubères chez les anciens Romains,' *Anthropos* 50 (1955) 430–432; 'Le mariage des filles impubères dans la Rome antique,' *RIDA* 2 (1955) 263–273; 'Sur le mariage romain,' *RIDA* 3 (1956) 227–243 = 'Autocritique et mise au point,' *Mélanges Marcel Durry*, 27–41; J. Reinach, 'Puberté féminine et mariage romain,' *RD* 34 (1956) 268–273; M. Garcia Garrido, 'Minor Annis XII Nupta,' *Labeo* 3 (1957) 76–88; Watson, *Roman Private Law around 200 BC*, 20–21; A. Ruggiero, 'Il matrimonio della impubere in Roma antica,' *AAN* 92 (1981) 63–71; G. Clark, 'Roman Women,' *G&R* second series 28 (1981) 201–202; and especially M.K. Hopkins, 'The Age of Roman Girls at Marriage,' *Population Studies* 18 (1965) 309–327; B.D. Shaw, 'The Age of Roman Girls at Marriage: Some Reconsiderations,' *JRS* 77 (1987) 30–46; and D.W. Amundsen and C.J. Diers, 'The Age of Menarche in Classical Greece and Rome,' *Human Biology* 41 (1969) 125–132. For a recent review of the entire controversial question of the age at marriage of Roman females, and of the debate over the consummation of pre-pubertal unions, see Gardner, *Women in Roman Law and Society*, 38–41.

10 As she matured, however, she might well have some say in the choice of future husbands. Thus Tullia chose her third husband, Dolabella, in consultation with her mother Terentia, and without regard for her father's political interests. Cf. P. E. Corbett, *The Roman Law of Marriage* (Oxford, 1930) 2–5; J.E. Phillips, 'Roman Mothers and the Lives of Their Adult Daughters,' *Helios* 6 (1978) 69–80; Carp, 'Two Matrons of the Late Republic,' 189–200 = Foley (ed.), *Reflections of Women in Antiquity*, 343–354; and S. Treggiari, 'Consent to Roman Marriage: Some Aspects of Law and Reality,' *CV* 26 (1982) 34–44; and 'Digna Condicio: Betrothals in the Roman Upper Class,' *CV* 28 (1984) 419–451, especially 441–451. For fuller discussion of *patria potestas*, see especially B. Förtsch, *Die politische Rolle der Frau in der römischen Republik* (Stuttgart, 1935) 23–25; W.W. Buckland, *A Textbook of Roman Law from Augustus to Justinian*[3] (rev. by P. Stein, Cambridge, 1963) 102–104; J.A. Crook, 'Patria Potestas,' *CQ* new series 17 (1967) 113–122; A. Watson, *The Law of Persons in the Later Roman Republic* (Oxford, 1967) 98–100; *Roman Private Law around 200 BC*, 28–33; *Rome of the XII Tables*, 40–46; Neraudau, *La Jeunesse*, 169–170; Gardner, *Women in Roman Law and Society*, 6–11; and the especially vivid treatment of A.S. Gratwick, 'Free or Not So Free? Wives and Daughters in the Late Roman Republic,' in E.M. Craik (ed.), *Marriage and Property* (Aberdeen, 1984) 42–45.

11 Gaius, *Institutiones* 1.155; for fuller discussion of this point, see now S. Dixon, 'Infirmitas Sexus: Womanly Weakness in Roman Law,' *TRG* 52 (1984) 345. Gardner, *Women in Roman Law and Society*, 14–22, is not only the most recent but also the most comprehensive, reliable and readable survey of the complex regulations governing *tutela mulieris*.

12 Cf. Watson, *Law of Persons*, 110; and Pomeroy, *Goddesses, Whores, Wives, and Slaves*, 153.

13 Gaius, *Institutiones* 2.47. Cicero, *Epistulae ad Atticum* 1.5.6 appears to be an

oblique reference to this regulation.

14 Cicero, *Pro Caelio* 68.

15 Cicero, *Pro Caecina* 72 is the *locus classicus* for the restriction on assuming obligations. With regard to testation, E. Volterra, 'Sulla capacità delle donne a far testamento,' *BIDR* new series 7 (1941) 74–87; and C. Herrmann, *Le Rôle judiciaire et politique des femmes*, 20–21, argue on the basis of such mythical figures as Acca Larentia (Aulus Gellius, *Noctes Atticae* 7.7.5) that the women of primitive Rome possessed testamentary capacity. As Watson, *Law of Persons*, 152–154; and more recently Crook, 'Women in Roman Succession,' 63, have pointed out, however, this is unlikely in the extreme because it is certain that a woman could not make a will *calatis comitiis* or *in procinctu*, hence could only have obtained such capacity with the introduction of the will *per aes et libram*. McDonnell, 'Divorce Initiated by Women in Rome,' 59, argues that a guardian's consent was also required before his female ward could marry or divorce during the early and middle Republic. Livy's much-discussed tale of the 'Maid of Ardea' (4.9.4–6), however, led R.M. Ogilvie, 'The Maid of Ardea,' *Latomus* 21 (1962) 477–483, to conclude that a *tutor* could veto a marriage *cum manu* but not one contracted *sine manu*. In this episode, which Livy situated in 443 BC, a mother successfully petitioned the Ardean magistrates to endorse her own choice of a husband for her daughter in preference to the nominee of the girl's *tutores*. Even if one assumes that the matter was indeed one of Roman law (which is incautious at best), it should be kept in mind that Livy nowhere explicitly states that the marriage proposed by the mother would be *sine manu*. *Contra* Ogilvie, therefore, it would seem more prudent to conclude from this story that the consent of a guardian was a precondition for marriage during the early Republic, and secondly that we glimpse here the sort of dispute that eventually would result in legislation permitting women to petition the praetor to compel *tutores* to sanction transactions against their will. Ogilvie's reasoning, cautiously endorsed by Watson, *Roman Private Law around 200 BC*, 21 and 40, and *Rome of the XII Tables*, 25–28, has also been sharply criticized by E. Volterra, 'Sul diritto familiare di Ardea nel V secolo a.C.,' *Studi in onore di Antonio Segni* IV (Milan, 1967) 657–677 (thus 668–669 n. 20: 'comunque tutte queste questioni appaiono oziose, dato che il testo di Livio si occupa del diritto di una città diversa da Roma e che la *conventio in manum* è istituto proprio dei Romani e sconosciuto ad altre popolazioni'); and D. Daube, *Roman Law. Linguistic, Social and Philosophical Aspects* (Edinburgh, 1969) 112–116. For further commentary on the role played by agnatic tutors in arranging marriages for their female wards, see the discussion of *enuptio gentis* on pages 25–26.

16 On this, see *inter alia* Watson, *Roman Private Law around 200 BC*, 100–116, and especially 103; and *Rome of the XII Tables*, 60–64.

17 M. Kaser, *Roman Private Law*[3], trans. R. Dannenbring (Pretoria, 1980) 292; and R. Villers, 'Manus et mariage,' *IJ* 4 (1969) 175–176, both argue that *coemptio fiduciae causa* is in fact a late Republican innovation, but this is essentially an argument from silence: the procedure first surfaces in Cicero, *Topica* 18 – and it is precisely in Cicero that we should expect to catch our first glimpse of such an institution. While we do not know precisely when women first obtained the capacity to make a will *per aes et libram*, it cannot have been later than the end of the third century BC. The historicity of the will executed by Hispala Faecenia, the libertine heroine in Livy's account of the Bacchanalian conspiracy of 186 BC (39.9.7), may remain subject to debate, but it is clear from Polybius' detailed account of the testamentary arrangements within the natal and adoptive households of Scipio Aemilianus (31.26–28.9) that Roman women could make wills early in the second century. The property that Scipio

inherited from his biological mother, Papiria, places this point beyond doubt. Quite apart from the fact that Scipio had been adopted out of his natal family (the Aemilii Paulli), which was sufficient in and of itself to sever the agnatic link between them, it was also the case that Papiria had been divorced by his father many years earlier. For fuller discussion, see above all G. Boyer, 'Le droit successoral romain dans les oeuvres de Polybe,' *RIDA* 4 (1950) 169–187; and F.W. Walbank, *A Historical Commentary on Polybius* III (Oxford, 1979) 503–511. For *coemptio fiduciae causa* in general, see Dixon, 'Infirmitas Sexus,' 346; and Crook, 'Women in Roman Succession,' 63–64, and 70.

18 For agnatic succession, see above all *Digesta* 26.4.1.*pr.* The self-interested opposition of *tutores legitimi* to female testation has been stressed by many different authors. See, for example, Villers, '*Manus* et mariage,' 176; S.B. Pomeroy, 'The Relationship of the Married Woman to Her Blood Relatives in Rome,' *AncSoc* 7 (1976) 224; and S. Dixon, 'Family Finances: Tullia and Terentia,' *Antichthon* 18 (1984) 84 = 'Family Finances: Terentia and Tullia,' in B. Rawson (ed.), *The Family in Ancient Rome* (London, 1985) 99; 'Infirmitas Sexus,' 345; and *The Roman Mother* (Norman, Okla., 1988) 46. J.A. Crook stresses the same point in two different papers published in Rawson's collection; see 'Women in Roman Succession,' 60–63; and 'Feminine Inadequacy and the Senatusconsultum Velleianum,' 84. It is regarded as a given in Gardner, *Women in Roman Law and Society*, 13–16, 18–20, *et passim*.

19 Gaius, *Institutiones* 1.144; cf. Ulpian 11.1. It has been argued that such expressions as *levitas animi* are post-classical interpolations, and therefore cannot be taken as representative of Roman thinking in the fifth century BC. On this point, to which we shall return below, see especially the highly influential work of S. Solazzi, 'Infirmitas aetatis e infirmitas sexus,' *AG* fourth series 20 (1930) 3–31; but cf. J. Beaucamp, 'Le vocabulaire de la faiblesse féminine dans les textes juridiques romains du IIIe au VIe siècle,' *RD* 54 (1976) 485–508; as well as Dixon, 'Infirmitas Sexus,' 343–371. Here the essential vagueness of the phrase should also be stressed; in the ensuing discussion, we shall attempt to penetrate its meaning as well.

20 *Institutiones* 1.115b.

21 *Institutiones* 1.113–114. On *coemptio*, see especially Corbett, *Roman Law of Marriage*, 78–85; and Watson, *Rome of the XII Tables*, 14–16. Whether *coemptio* dimly reflects the literal practice of marriage by purchase in archaic Roman society has been hotly disputed; for a review of the literature and an attempt to lodge the discussion in modern anthropological research, see G. MacCormack, '*Coemptio* and Marriage by Purchase,' *BIDR* third series 20 (1978) 179–199.

22 Dionysius of Halicarnassus, *Antiquitates Romanae* 2.25, makes Romulus the author of a law to this effect. In addition, Plutarch, *Quaestiones Romanae* 50, is frequently interpreted in this way, but this passage in fact applies only to the *flamen Dialis* and his wife. On this point, see R. Leonhard, 'Diffareatio,' *RE* 5 (1903) 481; and Corbett, *Roman Law of Marriage*, 220–223.

23 Festus, *Glossaria Latina* v. *diffareatio*. On *confarreatio*, see especially Gaius, *Institutiones* 1.112; Corbett, *Roman Law of Marriage*, 220–223; and Watson, *Rome of the XII Tables*, 11–14.

24 For Plutarch's characterization, see again *Quaestiones Romanae* 50. A fragmentary inscription discovered at Antium and dated to the reign of Commodus mentions this priesthood as part of an equestrian *cursus honorum*; see *CIL* X.6662 = *ILS* 1455. A formal rite, *remancipatio*, was also required to put an end to a marriage where *manus* had been instituted by *coemptio* or *usus*, but this was a far less complicated procedure (Gaius, *Institutiones* 1.137a).

25 The latter has been plausibly suggested by R. Villers, 'Le statut de la femme à

Rome jusqu'à la fin de la République,' *Recueils de la Société Jean Bodin XI: la Femme* (1959) 184; cf. Pomeroy, 'Relationship of the Married Woman to her Blood Relatives,' 216–217. The definitive study of the *trinoctium* remains that of H.J. Wolff, 'Trinoctium,' *TRG* 16 (1938) 145–183. On *usus*, see again Corbett, *Roman Law of Marriage*, 85–90; and Watson, *Rome of the XII Tables*, 16–18; and 'The Origins of *usus*,' *RIDA* third series 23 (1976) 269–270.

26 Gaius, *Institutiones* 1.111. For a full and very careful discussion of the nuances of *manus* in general and the phrase *loco filiae* in particular, see J. Gaudemet, 'Observations sur la *manus*,' *RIDA* 2 (1953) 330–336. Above all, one must carefully distinguish between marriage and *conventio in manum*, a point stressed repeatedly by E. Volterra. See, for example, 'Ancora sulla manus e sul matrimonio,' *Studi in onore di Siro Solazzi* (Naples, 1948) 675–678.

27 Gaius, *Institutiones* 1.136. On marriage *sine manu*, see again Corbett, *Roman Law of Marriage*, 90–94.

28 F. Schulz, *Classical Roman Law* (Oxford, 1951) 119.

29 Thus Wolff, 'Trinoctium,' 177–178; Villers, 'Le statut de la femme à Rome,' 183–184; Herrmann, *Le Rôle judiciaire et politique des femmes*, 33; and Hallett, *Fathers and Daughters*, 90–91.

30 Pomeroy, *Goddesses, Whores, Wives, and Slaves*, 155; 'Relationship of the Married Woman to Her Blood Relatives,' 222. Gratwick, 'Free or Not So Free?,' 46–49, independently arrives at the same conclusion. Villers, '*Manus* et mariage,' 169, shrewdly suggests that the original purpose of the *trinoctium* itself was to assure that the married woman would inherit from her father rather than her husband. The impact of this system on the testamentary rights of legitimate children has been appropriately stressed by Dixon, *Roman Mother*, 45.

31 See Cicero, *Pro Caecina* 73; *Pro Flacco* 86. The rules governing the various forms of marriage may be conveniently consulted in any of the standard manuals on Roman law; cf., for example, Buckland, *Textbook of Roman Law*[3], 118–121; Watson, *Law of Persons*, 19–31; or Gardner, *Women in Roman Law and Society*, 11–14. Among the privileges that the Senate granted to the freedwoman Hispala Faecenia in 186 BC for her part in uncovering the Bacchanalian cult was that of marriage outside of her *gens* (*enuptio gentis*). As Y. Thomas, 'Mariages endogamiques à Rome. Patrimoine, pouvoir et parenté depuis l'époque archaïque,' *TRG* 58 (1980) 370–382, rightly points out, this plainly suggests that marriage in primitive Rome typically joined members of the same clan – the circle immediately beyond the *proximi agnati*, relations with whom constituted incest. This point will be resumed below.

32 The evidence for the husband's putative power of life and death over his wife *in manu* is here set out in full, but one should also note how the masculine belief that the consumption of wine leads women inexorably on to adultery surfaces repeatedly in this material. It will be argued below that this notion, in tandem with other evidence for the presumed emotional instability of early Roman women, underwrites both their perpetual legal relegation to childhood (*in filiae loco*) and the ambiguous concept of feminine *levitas animi*.

33 Valerius Maximus 6.3.9. The tradition that Egnatius was a contemporary of Romulus, however, stems from Pliny, *Naturalis Historia* 14.89. According to Pliny, Egnatius (whom he calls Egnatius Maetennus) was in fact indicted for murder, but the accusation was set aside by Romulus.

34 Aulus Gellius, *Noctes Atticae* 10.23.

35 Plutarch, *Romulus* 22.3. P. Noailles, 'Les tabous du mariage dans le droit primitif des Romains,' *Annales Sociologiques* series C fascicule 2 (Paris, 1937) 10–11, reasonably suggests that the charge of killing her children may be an

elliptical reference to abortion without the husband's consent; cf. Herrmann, *Le Rôle judiciaire et politique des femmes*, 12–14.

36   *Mercator* 819–822.

37   See above all Demosthenes 59.86–87.

38   Valerius Maximus 2.1.4; Aulus Gellius, *Noctes Atticae* 4.3.2, 17.21.44; Dionysius of Halicarnassus, *Antiquitates Romanae* 2.25.7; Plutarch, *Comparison of Theseus and Romulus* 6.6; *Comparison of Lycurgus and Numa* 3.11.

39   The *locus classicus* is Cicero, *Orationes Philippicae* 2.69.

40   Valerius Maximus 2.9.2. For the date, see Livy 9.43.25; and on the episode see especially Corbett, *Roman Law of Marriage*, 218.

41   A. Watson, 'The Divorce of Carvilius Ruga,' *TRG* 33 (1965) 38–50. The argument is repeated in briefer compass in *Rome of the XII Tables*, 31–32.

42   Plutarch, *Quaestiones Romanae* 6; Aulus Gellius, *Noctes Atticae* 10.23; Pliny, *Naturalis Historia* 14.90; Dionysius of Halicarnassus, *Antiquitates Romanae* 2.25.6. The testimony of Gellius and Dionysius has been examined at length by Kunkel, 'Das Konsilium im Hausgericht,' 233–241. It is important to note that, *contra* Watson, *Roman Private Law around 200 BC*, 23, Kunkel believes that *si vinum bibit* in Gellius is governed by the verb *condemnatur*, and not by *multitatur*. This not only makes better sense of the Latin, but also brings Gellius into conformity with Dionysius.

43   Pliny, *Naturalis Historia* 14.89.

44   For a similar review of the evidence, leading to slightly different conclusions, cf. Watson, *Rome of the XII Tables*, 34–38; G. MacCormack, 'Wine Drinking and the Romulan Law of Divorce,' *IJ*10 (1975) 170–174; as well as Pomeroy, *Goddesses, Whores, Wives, and Slaves*, 153–154; and 'Relationship of the Married Woman to Her Blood Relatives,' 217–219. See also Noailles, 'Les tabous du mariage,' 11–14; and especially G. Williams, 'Some Aspects of Roman Marriage Ceremonies and Ideals,' *JRS* 48 (1958) 16–29, who develops a persuasive argument for the view that the ideal wife in the early Republic was one who was dutiful to her husband in all things. Cf. as well T.E.V. Pearce, 'The Role of the Wife as *Custos* in Ancient Rome,' *Eranos* 72 (1974) 16–33, whose persuasive argument that the Roman wife was responsible both for securing her husband's property and looking after the welfare of all who inhabited his home furnishes the necessary context for comprehending the savage punishment meted out to a wife who stole his keys or indulged in excessive drinking. Corbett, *Roman Law of Marriage*, 127–129; and Kunkel, 'Das Konsilium im Hausgericht,' 237–238, both tend to the belief that a husband possessed the *ius vitae et necis* even in a marriage *sine manu* – an important point, since this form of marriage had virtually displaced the various *manus* arrangements by the beginning of the second century BC. Here it should be noted, however, that after Publilia and Licinia were convicted in a praetorian investigation of murdering their husbands, L. Postumius Albinus (cos. 154) and Claudius Asellus respectively, they were surrendered not to the families of their husbands but to their kinsmen, who put them to death in private (Livy, *Periochae* 48; Valerius Maximus 6.3.8).

45   There is only one conspicuous exception to this generalization, and that is the Vestal Virgins, on whom in this vein see especially M. Beard, 'The Sexual Status of Vestal Virgins,' *JRS* 70 (1980) 12–27; in briefer compass, Gardner, *Women in Roman Law and Society*, 22–26.

46   *Digesta* 48.5.22.4; 48.5.23.2–4.

47   *Digesta* 48.5.24.*pr.*; Paulus, *Sententiae* 2.26.4–5.

48   *Digesta* 48.5.24.1; Paulus, *Sententiae* 2.26.14.

49   Gaius, *Institutiones* 1.145, 194.

50   Gaius, *Institutiones* 1.157, 171.

51 Gaius, *Institutiones* 1.115a.

52 *Digesta* 38.17.2; *Institutiones Iustiniani* 3.3.

53 Paulus, *Sententiae* 5.6.15; cf. 2.19.2; *Codex Iustinianus* 5.17.5; *Digesta* 24.1.32.19, and 43.30.1.5. For further discussion, see above all G. Matringe, 'La puissance paternelle et le mariage des fils et filles de famille en droit romain (sous l'Empire et en Occident),' *Studi in onore di Eduardo Volterra* V (Milan, 1971) 224–236.

54 On this last point, see especially Pomeroy, 'Relationship of the Married Woman to Her Blood Relatives,' 226; Dixon, 'Infirmitas Sexus,' 354–355; Crook, 'Women in Roman Succession,' 67–68; and above all Gardner, *Women in Roman Law and Society*, 190–200. On the Augustan legislation concerning marriage and adultery, see now L.F. Raditsa, 'Augustus' Legislation Concerning Marriage, Procreation, Love Affairs and Adultery,' *ANRW* II.13.278–339; K. Galinsky, 'Augustus' Legislation on Morals and Marriage,' *Philologus* 125 (1981) 126–144; and A. Richlin, 'Approaches to the Sources on Adultery at Rome,' *Women's Studies* 8 (1981) 225–250 = Foley (ed.), *Reflections of Women in Antiquity*, 379–404.

55 The *locus classicus* is *Digesta* 16.1.2.1. Crook, 'Feminine Inadequacy and the Senatusconsultum Velleianum,' 83–92; and Gardner, *Women in Roman Law and Society*, 75–76 and 234–235, both argue that this piece of legislation was a direct reaction to Claudius' abolition of agnatic guardianship for women. It was thus designed, they conclude, to protect them from the consequences of their own actions – and particularly from pressure put upon them by their husbands – clear proof that the archetypal male notion of feminine *levitas animi* was still strongly entrenched in Roman society even at this relatively late date. This seems a far more likely explanation of the legislation's purpose that that of H. Vogt, *Studien zum Senatus Consultum Velleianum* (Bonn, 1952) 6–9. Vogt argued that the genesis of the measure lay in the Senate's conviction that *intercessio* was part of the *virile officium*; this may be true, but it can hardly be the whole story since it leaves the emotional basis for this gender-based division of responsibilities still unexplored – a point already made by H. Kreller in his review of Vogt's book, *ZRG* 72 (1955) 402. In fact, it may be readily admitted that many conservative Roman men (including, perhaps, a majority of the Roman Senate) continued to distrust feminine capacity in the first and second centuries AD, but this does not invalidate the argument presented here that this period witnessed the systematic emancipation of women from the cumbersome legal restrictions that had governed their lives since the inception of the Republic. Even with regard to the *senatusconsultum Velleianum*, it should be noted that, according to Ulpian (*Digesta* 16.1.2.3), both Antoninus Pius and Septimius Severus disallowed this immunity (*exceptio*) when it was clearly the woman's intent to deceive the creditor, while Severus Alexander further ruled (*Codex Iustinianus* 4.29.5) that a woman could also be sued for a debt contracted by her husband if she knew that he had pledged her property. Whatever the original intent of the *senatusconsultum Velleianum*, therefore, it was subsequently interpreted in a manner compatible with the emancipation of women effected by the measures referred to above. As we shall see below, Dixon, 'Infirmitas Sexus,' 363–369, has recently pursued a line of reasoning similar to Vogt's, but her argument has not improved upon the flaws in his position.

56 Cicero, *Pro Murena* 27.

57 Thus Dixon, 'Infirmitas Sexus,' 347.

58 Gaius, *Institutiones* 1.114–115a.

59 Gaius, *Institutiones* 1.150–153.

60 Livy 39.19.5.

61 Gaius, *Institutiones* 1.173; cf. Livy 39.9.7. See also Dixon, 'Infirmitas Sexus,' 349; and Crook, 'Women in Roman Succession,' 70.

62 Dismissal of a guardian: *Digesta* 26.10.1, 3–4, 10; his compelled agreement: Gaius, *Institutiones* 1.190. Livy's legendary tale of the 'Maid of Ardea' (4.9.4–6) may be broached here *exempli gratia*. Admittedly the drama, in which the choice of a husband for the young girl became a matter of such bitter dispute between her *tutores* and her mother that the latter appealed to the magistrates to overrule the guardians, is set in Ardea and thus strictly speaking cannot be used as evidence for conditions in Rome. Still, the issue here is sufficiently banal that one may confidently see in it the sort of dispute that would eventually make the need for this praetorian sanction apparent.

63 Cf., *inter alia*, Förtsch, *Die politische Rolle der Frau*, 28–29; E. Sachers, 'Tutela,' *RE* 7A (1948) 1588–1599; J.P.V.D. Balsdon, *Roman Women: Their History and Habits* (London, 1962) 276; M. Arthur, ' "Liberated" Women: the Classical Era,' in R. Bridenthal and C. Koonz, *Becoming Visible: Women in European History* (Boston, 1977) 80–81; R. Vigneron, 'L'antifeministe loi Voconia et les "Schleichwege des Lebens",' *Labeo* 29 (1983) 146–148; and Hallett, *Fathers and Daughters*, 67–68. Pomeroy was also once of this opinion (*Goddesses, Whores, Wives, and Slaves*, 151), but she has subsequently become more skeptical ('Relationship of the Married Woman to Her Blood Relatives,' 224–225).

64 Cf. Corbett, *Roman Law of Marriage*, 90–91; Förtsch, *Die politische Rolle der Frau*, 26–27; Herrmann, *Le Rôle judiciaire et politique des femmes*, 33; Watson, *Law of Persons*, 25; Pomeroy, 'Relationship of the Married Woman to Her Blood Relatives,' 222; Thomas, 'Mariages endogamiques,' 350–351; and Crook, 'Women in Roman Succession,' 59. Whether this consensus is well founded is another question; on this point, see especially Gratwick, 'Free or Not So Free?,' 46. Certainly, the various forms of *manus* marriage subsisted well beyond the second century BC. There is a clear reference to *usus* in Cicero, *Pro Flacco* 84; and Tacitus, *Annales* 13.46 seems to imply a similar arrangement for Poppaea Sabina and the future emperor Otho in AD 57, as has been noted both by H. Furneaux (ed.), *The Annals of Tacitus* II[2] (revised by H.F. Pelham and C.D. Fisher, Oxford, 1907) 215; and R. Villers, 'A propos de la disparition de l'*usus*,' *RD* 28 (1950) 538–547. Gaudemet, 'Observations sur la *manus*,' 325–330, argues for the continuance of *coemptio* into the fourth century AD.

65 Gaius, *Institutiones* 1.115.

66 *Institutiones Iustiniani* 1.25; *Vaticana Fragmenta* 191, 247.

67 Praetorian reluctance: Gaius, *Institutiones* 1.192; on *tutela legitima*, see especially F. de Zulueta, *The Institutes of Gaius* II (Oxford, 1953) 45–46.

68 Cf. Pomeroy, 'Relationship of the Married Woman to Her Blood Relatives,' 225; and especially Dixon, 'Family Finances: Tullia and Terentia,' 84–85 = 'Family Finances: Terentia and Tullia,' 99–100; and 'Infirmitas Sexus,' 354–355, 368.

69 Plutarch, *Tiberius Gracchus* 1.4; *Gaius Gracchus* 19; cf. *inter alia* Förtsch, *Die politische Rolle der Frau*, 56–72; Herrmann, *Le Rôle judiciaire et politique des femmes*, 87–89; and Pomeroy, *Goddesses, Whores, Wives, and Slaves*, 151.

70 Cicero, *Epistulae ad Familiares* 14.1.5 (residential property); *Epistulae ad Atticum* 2.4.5 (woodland); 12.32.2, 15.17.1, 15.20.4, 16.1.5 (rental housing that she brought to Cicero as dotal property, and managed during his exile; cf. *ad Familiares* 14.2.2–3).

71 Cicero, *Epistulae ad Atticum* 12.12.1. On Terentia, see now Carp, 'Two Matrons of the Late Republic,' 189–200 = Foley (ed.), *Reflections of Women in Antiquity*, 343–354; and Dixon, 'Family Finances: Tullia and Terentia,' 78–101 = 'Family Finances: Terentia and Tullia,' 93–120.

72 Valerius Maximus 8.3; cf. Herrmann, *Le Rôle judiciaire et politique des femmes*, 100–101, 107–108; as well as A.J. Marshall, 'Ladies at Law: the Role of Women in the Roman Civil Courts,' in C. Deroux (ed.), *Studies in Latin Literature and Roman History* V (Brussels, 1989) 35–54, for further details.

73 Appian, *Bella Civilia* 4.32–34; Valerius Maximus 8.3; cf. Herrmann, *Le Rôle judiciaire et politique des femmes*, 111–115; and Hallett, *Fathers and Daughters*, 58–59.

74 Livy 22.60–61.10, 34.3.7.

75 Livy 34.1.3; Valerius Maximus 9.1.3.

76 Livy 34.7.5–6.

77 Livy 34.1.7–34.8. This episode has attracted widespread attention; cf., for example, Balsdon, *Roman Women*, 33–36; Herrmann, *Le Rôle judiciaire et politique des femmes*, 52–64; Pomeroy, *Goddesses, Whores, Wives, and Slaves*, 178–181; A.E. Astin, *Cato the Censor* (Oxford, 1978) 25–27; P.A. Johnston, 'Poenulus I, 2 and Roman Women,' *TAPA* 110 (1980) 145–147; J. Briscoe, *A Commentary on Livy, Books XXXIV–XXXVII* (Oxford, 1981) 39–63; and Hallett, *Fathers and Daughters*, 229–230.

78 Cicero, *De Oratore* 2.44.

79 Suetonius, *Divus Iulius* 6.1; Plutarch, *Caesar* 5.2.

80 *CIL* VI.10230 = *ILS* 8394 (Murdia); *CIL* VI.37965 (Allia Potestas). On this topic, see especially F. Vollmer, *Laudationum Funebrium Romanorum Historia et Reliquiarum Editio* (Leipzig, 1891), particularly 453–454 (Popilia) and 484–491 (Murdia); and W. Kierdorf, *Laudatio Funebris. Interpretationen und Untersuchungen zur Entwicklung der römischen Leichenrede* (Meisenheim am Glan, 1980) 111–116. One may also usefully consult the briefer remarks of Hallett, *Fathers and Daughters*, 41–43.

81 Cf. Förtsch, *Die politische Rolle der Frau*, 27; and Herrmann, *Le Rôle judiciaire et politique des femmes*, 33: 'l'autorité paternelle était plus lointaine et moins pesante que n'aurait été celle du mari. Et il faut supposer qu'après la mort du père la tutelle des agnats se faisait plus légère encore. . . . Donc nous pouvons considérer qu'une disposition de la loi des XII Tables contenait déjà le germe d'une émancipation féminine qui rendrait bientôt le mariage *cum manu* exceptionnel.'

82 See again Plutarch, *Quaestiones Romanae* 6; Aulus Gellius, *Noctes Atticae* 10.23; and Pliny, *Naturalis Historia* 14.90.

83 The most notorious case in Republican history was decided by Marius in 100 BC (Valerius Maximus 8.2.3; Plutarch *Marius* 38); a similar episode related by the elder Pliny (*Naturalis Historia* 14.90) has been situated early in the second century BC by Watson, *Law of Persons*, 70. For the penalties in classical law, see Ulpian 6.9.12; for fuller discussion, see Corbett, *Roman Law of Marriage*, 130–133; Watson, *Law of Persons*, 68–72.

84 The *leno-maritus* is first attested in Cicero but surfaces repeatedly thereafter in Latin literature; see V.R. Tracy, 'The *leno-maritus*,' *CJ* 72 (1976) 62–64. The procreative intent of *matrimonium iustum* emerges most clearly in the oath that Sp. Carvilius Ruga swore before the censors on the occasion of his divorce, *uxorem se liberum quaerundum gratia habiturum* (Aulus Gellius, *Noctes Atticae* 4.3.2; cf. 17.21.44); see in addition Dionysius of Halicarnassus, *Antiquitates Romanae* 2.25.7. The phrasing is clearly formulaic: cf. Plautus, *Captivi* 889; and Suetonius, *Divus Iulius* 52.3.

85 See again *Naturalis Historia* 14.89.

86 S.B. Pomeroy, 'Women in Roman Egypt,' in H.P. Foley (ed.), *Reflections of Women in Antiquity* (New York, 1981) 308.

87 *P.Ryl.* 154 (AD 66) = A.S. Hunt and C.C. Edgar (eds), *Select Papyri* I (Cambridge, Mass., 1932) 4. Egyptian marriage contracts often specify that

a wife who spends a day or night away from home without her husband's permission may be summarily divorced, with her dowry completely forfeit; cf., for example, *P.Teb.* 104 = *Select Papyri* 2 (92 BC), and *BGU* 1052 = *Select Papyri* 3 (13 BC). When the dowry took the form of land, this would provide a father with ample incentive to monitor his daughter's behavior! Egyptian marriage contracts may be conveniently consulted in O. Montevecchi, 'Ricerche di sociologia nei documenti dell'Egitto greco-romano, II: i contratti di matrimonio e gli atti di divorzio,' *Aegyptus* 16 (1936) 4–6; in briefer compass, cf. *La papirologia* (Turin, 1973) 203–207. For further discussion, see now S.B. Pomeroy, *Women in Hellenistic Egypt from Alexander to Cleopatra* (New York, 1984) 83–98. Although the above-mentioned contracts cannot be used to document conditions in Roman Italy, it should nevertheless be noted that Plautus, *Mercator* 821–822, also cites a wife's absence from home without her husband's permission as grounds for divorce. R. Yaron, 'Minutiae on Roman Divorce,' *TRG* 28 (1960) 8–12, accepts this at face value; it is quite unclear, however, whether Plautus found this passage in his model, the *Emporos* of Philemon, or wrote it himself for a Roman audience.

88   See again Pomeroy, 'Women in Roman Egypt,' 308–309; and especially N. Lewis, 'On Paternal Authority in Roman Egypt,' *RIDA* third series 17 (1970) 251–258.

89   Thus *Digesta* 23.3.6.1, 23.3.10.1, 23.3.32, 23.3.47, 23.3.50.*pr.*, 23.3.52. For the second century BC, see Plautus, *Miles Gloriosus* 1166, 1277–1278, *Trinummus* 508–509; and above all Appian, *Bella Civilia* 1.10. I. Shatzman, *Senatorial Wealth and Roman Politics* (Brussels, 1975) 53, 277 and 283, suggests that Cn. Pompeius Strabo's property at Tarentum was the dowry of his mother, a niece of the poet Lucilius.

90   See again Cicero, *Epistulae ad Atticum* 11.3, *Epistulae ad Familiares* 14.13; cf. *Rhetorica ad Herennium* 2.38.

91   Paulus, *Sententiae* 5.6.15.

92   Gratwick, 'Free or Not So Free?,' 44, is to my knowledge the only other student of the subject to reach this conclusion.

93   Plutarch, *Aemilius Paullus* 5.4–5; cf. Valerius Maximus 4.4.8–9.

94   This family reconstruction is based upon data scattered in *Orationes* 7.10–11, 20, 47, 65, 67–68, and 76. In predominantly virilocal peasant societies of more recent vintage, such as the present-day Taiwanese, uxorilocal marriage is routinely employed by parents without male offspring to perpetuate their descent line. A.P. Wolf and Chieh-shan Huang, *Marriage and Adoption in China, 1845–1945* (Stanford, 1980) 13–15, 124–126, 218, and 337 point out, for example, that in this century it accounts for some 10–15 percent of all marriages in Taiwan, 15–20 percent in the Yangtze delta, and 40 percent or more in the Yunnan community of West Town. One might logically expect Roman couples to have embraced this strategy as well, for in Roman society casualties on the battlefield aggravated an already high infant and child mortality rate. On this subject see above all M.K. Hopkins, 'On the Probable Age Structure of the Roman Population,' *Population Studies* 20 (1966) 245–264; but cf. I. Kajanto, 'On the Problem of the Average Duration of Life in the Roman Empire,' *Soumalainen Tiedeakatemia* 153 (1968) 1–30; and B.W. Frier, 'Roman Life Expectancy: Ulpian's Evidence,' *HSPh* 86 (1982) 212–251. In fact, (among the elite, at least) adoption was the first resort of those who failed to produce sons, as of those whose sons predeceased them – the *locus classicus* is Cicero, *De Domo Sua* 34–36. Still, it must frequently have been the case that adoptive sons married a natural daughter because the jurists carefully regulated this arrangement (Gaius, *Institutiones* 1.61; *Digesta* 23.2.17.*pr.*, 1; *Institutiones Iustiniani* 1.10.2). One may also reasonably speculate that some (though by

43

no means all) of these marriages were uxorilocal. The evidence for uxorilocal marriage in primitive Rome is assembled in Thomas, 'Mariages endogamiques,' 375–378. R.P. Saller and B.D. Shaw, 'Tombstones and Family Relations in the Principate: Civilians, Soldiers and Slaves,' *JRS* 74 (1984) 124–156, argue on the basis of patterns of commemoration in sepulchral inscriptions that, in the civilian population, 'nuclear family commemorators regularly constitute about 75–90 per cent of the total. This proportion does not vary much, regardless of chronological, geographical, or social differences.' (134) They thus conclude that the nuclear family was the central social institution of imperial life, and that affection, heirship and kinship obligation were more important social dynamics than the *patria potestas*. It should be noted, however, that they consciously exclude the *plebs rustica* from their study (127), which fatally weakens their argument. Given the fact that few of the *plebs urbana* would have owned landed property, we should hardly be surprised to learn that patriarchal authority was of marginal consequence to members of this group. As the authors themselves concede, such 'humble families . . . were primarily working units (rather than property-transmitting units), in which the wife often participated and from which the children drifted away as they grew up.' (138) In the countryside, land-ownership would have given a Roman father more effective leverage over his male offspring, and where it was dispersed in dotal settlements as well as by testament, would have always harbored the potential for the continuing conflict between father and daughter described above. Dowry and testament would also have combined to create a complex social environment in which a given nuclear family would find itself surrounded by other such family farms in the possession of individuals in the extended kinship networks of the husband and wife. It is here that the authors' conclusions about the centrality of the nuclear family are at their most vulnerable: it is not enough to know the relationship between the commemorator and the deceased; we must also ask whether the funeral was attended only by members of the immediate family, so to speak, or by the membership of an extended kinship network surrounding them.

95 Solazzi, 'Infirmitas aetatis e infirmitas sexus,' 3–31, especially 18–31.

96 Cf., *inter alia*, F. de Martino, 'L' "ignorantia iuris" nel diritto penale romano,' *SDHI* 3 (1937) 387–418, especially 409; A. Guarino, 'Appunti sulla "ignorantia iuris" nel diritto penale romano,' *Annali della R. Università di Macerata* 15 (1941) 190, 203; B. Biondi, *Il diritto romano cristiano* II (Milan, 1952) 216–223; Vogt, *Studien zum Senatus Consultum Velleianum* (Bonn, 1952) 8; and U. Zilletti, *La dottrina dell'errore nella storia del diritto romano* (Milan, 1961) 269.

97 *Institutiones* 1.144–145. Solazzi's brief discussion (and rejection) of the phrase *levitas animi* in this passage is lodged in a footnote: 'Infirmitas aetatis e infirmitas sexus,' 30 note 2. Cf. 'Glosse a Gaio,' *Studi in onore di Salvatore Riccobono* I (Palermo, 1936) 170, where he again dismissed the phrase as an interpolation, but unfortunately without further elaboration.

98 F. Lanfranchi, *Il diritto nei retori romani* (Milan, 1938) 615, 621–622; cf. C. Ritter (ed.), *M. Fabii Quintiliani Declamationes Quae Supersunt CXLV* (Leipzig, 1884) 117 (*Decl. 272: infirmitas sexus*), 285 (*Decl. 327: infirmior sexus*), and 403 (*Decl. 368: imbecillior sexus*).

99 Schulz, *Classical Roman Law*, 181–182; cf. Cicero, *Pro Murena* 27 (*infirmitas consilii*); Valerius Maximus 9.1.3 (*imbecillitas mentis*); and Seneca, *ad Marciam* 1.1 (*infirmitas muliebris animi*).

100 *Pro Murena* 27: 'mulieres omnes propter *infirmitatem consilii* maiores in tutorum potestate esse voluerunt.'

101 Schulz concedes the point (*Classical Roman Law*, 181: 'This dictum was wrong

with respect to Roman women in Cicero's own time, as Cicero himself knew very well; his own wife administered her property quite independently'), but he fails to see how it affects his argument. Cf. Dixon, 'Infirmitas Sexus,' 352: 'in this case Cicero was surely presenting what he imagined (or pretended) to be a traditional belief about the nature of women. The gist of his remark is that lawyers thwarted the ancestral intention, which was posited on archaic reasoning.'

102 *Politica* 1260a: 'for the slave is completely without the capacity for judgement; the female has it, but in an unstable form; the child also has it, although its state is immature.' The parallel between the two texts may be admitted at once, but Schulz's conclusion does not follow. It never seems to have occurred to him, for example, that Cicero might have borrowed (consciously or unconsciously) a Greek idiom to express a Roman idea. Schulz's line of reasoning will be more fully criticized below.

103 *Classical Roman Law*, 182–184. It should be carefully noted that this is merely an assertion; Schulz does not introduce any evidence in support.

104 *Digesta* 3.1.1.5: *ne virilibus officiis fungantur mulieres.* Since women such as Maesia Sentia and Gaia Afrania did represent themselves in court, this would seem a more pertinent objection than the argument that pleading was unbecoming for a woman.

105 *Digesta* 16.1.2.1: *cum eas virilibus officiis fungi et eius generis obligationibus obstringi non sit aequum.*

106 *Codex Iustinianus* 5.35.1 (AD 224): *tutelam administrare virile munus est*; 2.13.18 (AD 294): *alienam suscipere defensionem virile officium est et ultra sexam muliebrem esse constat.*

107 Beaucamp, 'Le vocabulaire de la faiblesse féminine,' 485–508. She criticizes Solazzi's assumption that classical jurists would have avoided tautological constructions as well as his failure even to suggest why these purported interpolations were introduced. The decisive objection that she raises, however, is that a Byzantine interpolator would have used the term *fragilitas* instead of *infirmitas*, which disappeared in the fourth century.

108 'Infirmitas sexus,' 343–371.

109 'Infirmitas sexus,' 343: 'Legal historians are generally agreed that the origin of *tutela mulierum* is to be explained in terms of the early Roman system of inheritance and was designed to safeguard male rights rather than to protect women.' *Contra* Schulz, *Classical Roman Law*, 182: 'regard for family interests was not the prevailing motive . . .'

110 Dixon makes this claim in 'Infirmitas sexus,' 344: 'Traditional statements about the nature of women stress their excessive cunning and greed rather than innate ineptitude at commerce.' Women such as Tullia, the daughter of Servius Tullius, who according to Roman legend (Livy 1.46.6–48.7) engineered the murder of her father and the accession to the throne of Tarquinius Superbus, come immediately to mind. It is always dangerous to generalize from such anecdotal evidence, however, especially when it conflicts with reliable but more broadly based traditions, and with contemporary evidence, in this case the Law of the Twelve Tables (*infra*).

111 Thus Pomeroy, 'Relationship of the Married Woman to Her Blood Relatives,' 217.

112 *De Legibus* 2.59.'

113 Children: Gaius, *Institutiones* 1.155; lunatics: *Rhetorica ad Herennium* 1.23; Cicero, *De Inventione Rhetorica* 2.148; cf. *Tusculanae Disputationes* 3.11; Gaius, *Institutiones* 2.64; *Digesta* 26.1.3.*pr.*, 27.10.13; spendthrifts: *Digesta* 27.10.1.

114 A. Watson, '*Enuptio Gentis*,' in A. Watson (ed.), *Daube Noster* (Edinburgh,

1974) 331–341, especially 335–336, argues for the banal character of this form of endogamy among the propertied classes, who would have also been the driving force behind the institution of *tutela mulierum perpetua*.

115   '*Enuptio Gentis*,' 335.

116   For Hispala Faecenia, see Livy 39.19.5, and *infra*. Thomas, 'Mariages endogamiques,' 370–382, nicely develops the interplay between marriage inside the clan and a succession strategy designed to avoid dispersion of agnatic property, and rightly characterizes this strategy as 'endogamie relative.'

117   A conclusion also reached by Gratwick, 'Free or Not So Free?,' 39–40, although he does not argue for his conclusion.

118   Livy 34.7.11–12.

119   *Annales* 1.69, 2.55.5.

120   *Annales* 3.34.

121   In particular Pomeroy, *Goddesses, Whores, Wives, and Slaves*, 179–181; and Carp, 'Two Matrons of the Late Republic,' 192 = Foley (ed.), *Reflections of Women in Antiquity*, 346.

122   Valerius Maximus 8.15.12.

123   P.A. Brunt, *Italian Manpower, 225 BC–AD 14* (Oxford, 1971) 419 – and this is a conservative estimate!

124   Livy 25.2.9–10.

125   *Goddesses, Whores, Wives, and Slaves*, 179; cf. 'Relationship of the Married Woman to Her Blood Relatives,' 219. In both works, she mistakenly calls Fundanius and Villius tribunes instead of aediles.

126   Livy 39.18.4–6. The best analysis of Livy's account of this episode remains that of J.A. North, 'Religious Toleration in Republican Rome,' *PCPhS* new series 25 (1979) 85–103. The execution of the convicted murderesses Publilia and Licinia at the hands of their respective kinsmen in 154 BC again instances the procedure normally followed.

127   Gaius, *Institutiones* 1.185. The freedwoman Hispala Faecenia, the heroine of the Bacchanalian conspiracy, proceeded in precisely this fashion so that she might make a will and institute her lover as her sole heir (Livy 39.9.7), which demonstrates that this measure was in effect in 186 BC. For a date during the Second Punic War, and specifically in 210 BC, see Watson, *Roman Private Law around 200 BC*, 36, together with the references in note 4, to which one should add T.R.S. Broughton, *The Magistrates of the Roman Republic* I (Cleveland, 1951) 279. Crook, 'Women in Roman Succession,' 70, is the most recent scholar correctly to stress the importance of this episode for our understanding of legal procedure during the middle Republic, but it must be added that Livy's account of the Bacchanalian conspiracy makes it clear that many women simply ignored the law.

128   This figure is derived from the calculations of A. Afzelius, *Die römische Kriegsmacht während der Auseinandersetzung mit den hellenistischen Grossmächten* (Copenhagen, 1944), 34–79. His tabulations may now also be conveniently consulted in Brunt, *Italian Manpower*, 422–426.

129   Cf. Afzelius, *Die römische Kriegsmacht*, 47; or A.J. Toynbee, *Hannibal's Legacy* II (London, 1965) 647–652 (legions); and Brunt, *Italian Manpower*, 424 (manpower). As a preamble to the discussion that follows, it needs to be pointed out that Rome's Italian allies will have generated at least half of the men under arms throughout this period. Since citizen and allied soldiers alike were principally recruited from the class of smallholders, however, the wives and children of soldiers in both categories will have been seriously discomfited by their prolonged absence for service overseas. We need not, therefore, discriminate between them. We can also safely presume that the municipal senates of the allied communities had to deal with the same range

of legal problems that confronted the Roman Senate as a practical consequence of this style of warfare. Unfortunately, it does not necessarily follow that they will have invariably arrived at the same solutions, or blindly followed Roman precedent. Here, then, as in so many other settings, our near-total ignorance of developments in Italy at large must temper the line of argument and the general conclusions which follow, particularly with regard to legal developments in the late third and second centuries BC.

130 Livy 40.36.10 (service from 186 to 180); Appian, *Iberica* 78 (146 to 140). Scholars have frequently focussed their attention on the length of service in the second century BC, and on its domestic implications. Cf., for example, R.E. Smith, *Service in the Post-Marian Roman Army* (Manchester, 1958) 1–10; Toynbee, *Hannibal's Legacy*, II.72–100; K. Hopkins, *Conquerors and Slaves* (Cambridge, 1978) 25–37; and J.K. Evans, 'Resistance at Home: the Evasion of Military Service in Italy during the Second Century BC,' in T. Yuge and M. Doi (eds), *Forms of Control and Subordination in Antiquity* (Tokyo and Leiden, 1988) 121–140.

131 Known casualty figures for the period 218–133 BC have been compiled and fully discussed by Toynbee, *Hannibal's Legacy*, II.65–72. One should make particular note of his brief comments at the end of this section on the additional but incalculable loss of life to be attributed to outbreaks of disease in the Roman army. Brunt, *Italian Manpower*, 134, 339, and 688–690, also takes up this point: he estimates that some 40% of the soldiers in the Augustan field armies died in service, with fully half of these casualties attributable to disease.

132 Gaius, *Institutiones* 1.187.

133 See again Cicero, *Pro Caecina* 72.

134 Cato, *De Agricultura* 2.6, 4, 5.4, 144.3–4, 145.1, and 146.3.

135 According to Valerius Maximus (4.4.6), the wife of the consul M. Atilius Regulus was caught up in such a situation during the First Punic War. While her husband was on campaign in Africa, a hired hand ran off with all of the equipment and livestock on their farm. For more on this episode, see below. The balance of the Latin evidence is infuriatingly casual – for example, Plautus, *Stichus* 525–526, in which a husband praises his wife for her management of their household during the three years of his absence. D. Hobsan, 'The Role of Women in the Economic Life of Roman Egypt: a Case Study from First Century Tebtunis,' *CV* 28 (1984) 373–390, employs three registries to explore the economic activity of women in this particular community. Although data from Egypt do not necessarily mirror conditions in the Roman world at large, and in this particular case there is a hiatus of more than two centuries as well, this archive may nevertheless generate some useful insights. One should first note that female guardianship was still an effective institution in Egypt in the first century AD. Secondly, two of the registries stem from a sixteen month period of economic crisis in AD 45–46; and third, the problems which confront us are parochial in the extreme. Hobsan's conclusion will hardly occasion surprise: 'a woman's active economic role is not very extensive, and relates quite directly to her household. As a wage-earner she can wet-nurse to raise cash and she can trade on the real estate which comes to her from inheritance or the money which is in her dowry. We do not find women involved in giving loans or buying and selling animals or renting farm land to any great extent' (388–389). This finding is further confirmed in her study of the economic activity of women in the Fayum village of Socnopaiou Nesos; see 'Women as Property Owners in Roman Egypt, *TAPA* 113 (1983) 311–321. *Tutela mulierum perpetua* obviously circumscribed the economic options of Roman women at the outset of the second century BC in a quite similar way,

and the absence of a guardian (or, for that matter, a father with *potestas* or a husband with *manus*) will have merely exacerbated the situation. While Roman law permitted a woman to petition the *praetor urbanus* for assistance, we tend to overlook the obvious fact that a woman could not avail herself of this opportunity unless she was resident in Rome or could travel to the city. It is highly unlikely that many farm women would have been free to do so.

136   Valerius Maximus 4.4.10. Cf., on this episode, Hallett, *Fathers and Daughters*, 99; for further instances, see Treggiari, 'Digna Condicio,' 421. The classical jurists take up the question of how marriages should be arranged for the children of *captivi* (cf., *infra*, note 139), but it is not at all clear how this dilemma was resolved in the middle Republic. This places the Senate's refusal to ransom the citizens captured by Hannibal at Cannae, and the deep anxiety of the women who occupied the Forum during the debate (Livy 22.60–61.10, 34.3.7) in an entirely new light.

137   Livy 4.9.4–6.

138   Once again, see Gaius, *Institutiones* 1.190.

139   *Tiberius Gracchus* 4.2, and cf. M.I. Finley, 'The Silent Women of Rome,' *Horizon* 7 (1965) 61 = *Aspects of Antiquity* (London, 1968) 133. On this aspect of the *patria potestas*, see especially Matringe, 'La puissance paternelle et le mariage des fils et filles,' 196–223; as well as Treggiari, 'Digna Condicio,' 439. Phillips, 'Roman Mothers and the Lives of Their Adult Daughters,' 69–80, assembles all of the evidence for the participation of Roman mothers in the selection of husbands for their daughters, but this discussion is vitiated by a failure to grasp that the role of the mother and father would change as their daughter matured. Their role typically would be decisive in a first marriage, for example, but less so in second or third marriages. It is this above all that accounts for the active participation of Tullia, the daughter of Cicero, in the choice of her third husband, P. Cornelius Dolabella (*infra*).

140   *Cato Maior* 24.2–4. It should be carefully noted that Salonius agreed to allow Cato to choose a husband for his daughter before he realized that Cato wished the girl for himself. For still another second century example of marriage negotiations proceeding without the knowledge of the girl in question, see Plautus, *Trinummus* 442–581, especially 497–500 and 577–580. Terence, *Andria* 99–102, 238–239, and *Hecyra* 545–546, supply further illustrations; indeed, in the latter instance we are introduced to a wife whom the husband accuses of trying to subvert the arrangements that he has negotiated. Although it may well be the case that Terence is simply reproducing his original here, a work of Menander, his Roman audience would certainly not have found anything in these passages surprising.

141   Cicero, *Epistulae ad Familiares* 3.10.1–5, 3.11.1–3, 3.12.1.

142   *Epistulae ad Familiares* 3.12.2. On this episode, see especially J.H. Collins, 'Tullia's Engagement and Marriage to Dolabella,' *CJ* 47 (1952) 164–168, 186, who stresses that Cicero preferred the candidacy of Tiberius Nero (*Epistulae ad Atticum* 6.6.1; *ad Familiares* 13.64); cf. as well Treggiari, 'Digna condicio,' 441–451; and Gratwick, 'Free or Not So Free?,' 32–37.

143   *Institutiones* 1.190. In the imperial period, the juristconsults repeatedly addressed such issues as the marriage of a son or daughter *in potestate*, and the provision of a dowry for the latter, when the father was absent or had been taken captive. Cf., for example, *Digesta* 23.2.9.1 (a son can marry whomever he chooses if his father has been in captivity for three years); 23.2.10 (a son or daughter may marry if their father has been absent for three years); 23.2.11 (if a son or daughter marries in the absence of the father before three years have elapsed, the marriage is to be considered valid if the partner is not of a character offensive to the father); 23.3.5.4 (a praetor or governor of a province

may arrange a dowry for the daughter of a *captivus* from the latter's estate); and 49.15.12.3 (the son of a *captivus* may marry without his father's consent 'because the circumstances and needs of the moment as well as the public good demanded a marriage'). The attention which imperial lawyers paid to these problems casts into bold relief the difficulties that confronted the wife of a *captivus* during the Republic, or a soldier serving in Spain for six years or more, for whom no such legal guidelines were available.

144   The point is appropriately stressed by Dixon, 'Infirmitas sexus,' 353–354.
145   Livy 34.7.11–12.
146   On the peasant economy, see especially J.K. Evans, '*Plebs Rustica*. The Peasantry of Classical Italy II: the Peasant Economy,' *AJAH* 5 (1980) 134–173.
147   Polybius 1.30.
148   Valerius Maximus 4.4.6.
149   Appian, *Bella Civilia* 1.7, 9; Plutarch, *Tiberius Gracchus* 9.5. It has long been assumed that the second century BC witnessed the virtual extermination of the Italian peasantry and its wholesale replacement by slave labor, principally war captives. Cf., *inter alia*, J. Kromayer, 'Die wirtschaftliche Entwicklung Italiens im II. und I. Jahrhundert vor Chr.,' *NJA* 33 (1914) 152–154; C.A. Yeo, 'The Development of the Roman Plantation and Marketing of Farm Products,' *Finanzarchiv* new series 13 (1951) 323; G. Steiner, 'The Fortunate Farmer: Life on the Small Farm in Ancient Italy,' *CJ* 51 (1955) 58; D.C. Earl, *Tiberius Gracchus: a Study in Politics* (Brussels, 1963) 33–34; Toynbee, *Hannibal's Legacy*, II.165 *et passim*; the review of Toynbee by E. Gabba, *RFIC* 96 (1968) 71 = *Esercito e società nella tarda repubblica romana* (Florence, 1973) 558–559; A.E. Astin, *Scipio Aemilianus* (Oxford, 1967) 162–165; Brunt, *Italian Manpower*, 398, 642–643 *et passim*; and Hopkins, *Conquerors and Slaves*, 4–31. A few scholars, however, have stressed the local and regional variations that invalidate this generalization: cf. M.W. Frederiksen, 'The Contribution of Archaeology to the Agrarian Problem in the Gracchan Period,' *DArch* 4–5 (1970–71) 330–367; D.B. Nagle, 'Towards a Sociology of Southeastern Etruria,' *Athenaeum* new series 57 (1979) 411–441; and J.K. Evans, '*Plebs Rustica*. The Peasantry of Classical Italy I: the Peasantry in Modern Scholarship,' *AJAH* 5 (1980) 19–47. Happily, this research has begun to undermine the traditional *communis opinio*; cf., for example, E. Badian, 'Tiberius Gracchus and the Beginning of the Roman Revolution,' *ANRW* I.1.668–731; P.W. de Neeve, *Peasants in Peril: Location and Economy in Italy in the Second Century* BC (Amsterdam, 1984); and K. Bringmann, *Die Agrarreform des Tiberius Gracchus* (Stuttgart, 1985).
150   The *ager Eretanus* furnishes convincing archaeological evidence; see R.M. Ogilvie, 'Eretum,' *PBSR* new series 20 (1965) 70–112. Here it might be useful to remember that it would be the difficulties encountered by citizens within a day or two of Rome itself that would most likely come to the attention of a plebeian tribune, for access to Rome allowed them an opportunity both to voice their grievances and to influence the outcome of elections in the plebeian assembly.

III

WAR AND THE WOMEN OF PROPERTY

LEGEND AND REALITY

In 509 BC, so Livy writes, the Roman army was camped beneath the walls of Ardea, and a group of young officers retired to the tent of Sextus Tarquinius for a drinking party. During the course of the festivities, the conversation turned to the subject of wives, and a heated argument ensued as each of the revellers praised his own spouse in the most extravagant terms. Finally, Lucius Tarquinius Collatinus suggested that they ride off at once, and catching their wives by surprise, discover their true characters. The horsemen left immediately for Rome, and reaching the city at dusk found the Etruscan princesses enjoying themselves at an elaborate dinner party; then they continued on to Collatia, so that they might put Lucretia, the wife of Collatinus, to the test. 'Despite the lateness of the hour, they found her sitting in her room; surrounded by handmaidens working by lamplight, she was busy with her wool. In this contest among the wives, therefore, it was Lucretia who prevailed.'[1]

In studied contrast to her dissolute Etruscan peers, then, Lucretia is presented to us as the archetypical Roman matron, who 'kept to her house and worked her wool.'[2] As it turns out, in this respect at least the lifestyle of early Roman women does appear to have differed materially from that of their Etruscan counterparts. Tomb paintings make it clear, for example, that well-to-do Etruscan women not only attended dinner parties but shared the banquet couches with men. They were also to be seen with men at sporting events and religious festivals, again without any attempt to separate the two sexes physically.[3] This risqué behavior profoundly shocked Greek literati such as the fourth-century historian Theopompus,[4]

50

and it is certainly safe to assume that Livy was not the first Roman to censure Etruscan women for their freedom and love of luxury.[5]

Lucretia's anonymity was further reinforced, it might be added, by the Roman practice of identifying women not as individuals but as the daughters of their fathers: for example, her name simply means 'the daughter of Lucretius.'[6] Here again, however, Etruscan women were more visible, for each seems to have possessed a *praenomen* in addition to the *gentilicium*.[7]

These differences seem to suggest that, during its Etruscan phase, Roman society exhibited two fundamentally different but co-existing sets of values, in one of which noblewomen were accorded high status and considerable freedom of action, while the other relegated them to a cloistered existence akin to that of their more famous Athenian contemporaries.[8] This parallel can be misleading, however, for in one crucial respect the situation of women such as Lucretia differed substantially from the Athenian norm. Although, as we have seen, it is probable that a modified form of endogamy was widely practiced among the propertied element of early Roman society, still there was no institution in primitive Rome analogous to the Athenian epiklerate.[9] This insured that the property of an Athenian citizen who died without male issue would nevertheless remain within his lineage, for it required his daughter to marry her nearest male kinsman and transmit the estate to the sons born of this union.[10] The Athenian *epikleros* could, therefore, only loosely be described as her father's heir; it would in fact be more accurate to regard her as a conduit by means of which he could pass his property on to his grandsons.[11] The Law of the Twelve Tables, in contrast, makes it clear that Roman women were able to own real as well as movable property in their own right by the middle of the fifth century BC at the latest. The fifth table in particular informs us that, in the event of intestacy, sons and daughters inherited their father's estate in equal shares, with the brothers and sisters of the deceased serving as contingent heirs.[12] As we have already seen, women could not dispose of conveyable property (*res mancipi*) without the consent of their guardians, but it must also be remarked that their enjoyment of such property was otherwise unrestricted.[13] Indeed, since the Twelve Tables does not distinguish between men and women in this regard, it appears that a female co-heir to a family estate (a form of *consortium* known as *ercto non cito*) could institute an action for the compulsory division of the inheritance – the *actio familiae erciscundae* – so that she might exercise exclusive rights over her share of the *patrimonium*.[14]

These property rights, which may well antedate the Law of the Twelve Tables and even the Republic itself, supply the necessary backdrop for two tales that Livy worked up in the fifth book of his *History of Rome* to illustrate the selfless patriotism of women in the Republic's formative years. In the first, set in 395 BC, the *matronae* are said voluntarily to have deposited sufficient gold in the state treasury to redeem Camillus' vow of a tenth part of the Veientine spoils to Apollo. A grateful Senate replied by decreeing that henceforth the women might drive to festivals and games in four-wheeled carriages, and appear on holy and working days in two-wheeled vehicles.[15] Plutarch adds that the women volunteered 8 talents of gold – a considerable sum indeed – but he differs from Livy in claiming that the Senate honored these women of property by granting them the right to be eulogized in funeral orations.[16] Livy reserves this honor for the dénouement of his second tale, which is situated a mere five years later: in 390 BC, he writes, when the Senate proved unable to raise the thousand pounds of gold that it had promised to the Gauls besieging the Capitol, the women of Rome once again made good the difference from their own resources.[17]

Although scholars have traditionally regarded these particular stories as mere annalistic fiction, there were in fact numerous occasions on which the *res publica* requisitioned women's property, above all during the Second Punic War.[18] In 217 BC, the Senate ordered the *matronae* to contribute money to Juno Regina, and the freedwomen to Feronia.[19] Two years later, the Senate enacted the *lex Oppia* in response to the catastrophe at Cannae; this measure, it will be recalled, stipulated that Roman women should not own more than half an ounce of gold, appear in public in a multi-colored garment, or ride in a carriage within a mile of Rome itself or any town in the *ager Romanus*.[20] In 214, the orphans, widows and unmarried women 'contributed' their funds to the treasury; and in 210, we are told, senators, *equites* and plebs alike hastened to replenish the treasury, with each man 'reserving a ring for himself, his wife and children, a gold locket for his son, and one ounce of gold by weight for his wife and each daughter.'[21] Finally, in 207 the curule aediles called upon the *matronae* yet again, this time to dip into their dowries and supply sufficient gold to fashion a basin to be dedicated in the temple of Juno Regina.[22]

It is, therefore, obvious that a considerable amount of property had come into the possession of Roman women by the end of the third century BC, principally through dowry and inheritance. In a purely partible society that was perpetually at war, and steadily enriched by its military endeavors, this is of course precisely what we should expect to see. In the next half-century, however, Rome's conquests generated vast wealth for the Republic, a significant proportion of which ended up in the hands of the elite.[23] Given the staunchly conservative character of Roman society, it was predictable from the outset that *luxus*, or the flagrant display of such wealth, would be sharply condemned by the more traditionally minded, of whom the most visible was the elder Cato.[24] The latter in fact found himself at the center of a profound conflict between old and new outlooks during these five decades – a volatile environment in which women who flaunted their gains could not possibly fail to elicit an emotionally charged and strongly negative reaction. The repeal of the *lex Oppia* brought several such episodes in its train, hence it should hardly occasion surprise to learn that in this period, both the dotal system and the right of women to inherit came under attack.

DOWRY: A VEHICLE FOR CONSPICUOUS CONSUMPTION

The elaborate set of rules that governed dowry in classical Roman law has been preserved for us in minute detail, but the origins and devolution of the system remain shrouded in mystery. The Law of the Twelve Tables is completely silent on the subject, which means that the earliest contemporary sources are, as with so many other topics in Roman history, the second-century authors Plautus and Polybius.[25] Nevertheless, the Romans themselves seem to have been firmly convinced that the institution was as old as the city itself: Dionysius of Halicarnassus specifically cites dowry as one of the many innovations to be attributed to Romulus.[26] The earliest regulations were, therefore, lodged among the so-called *leges regiae*, whose historicity has long been a matter of intense scholarly debate. Watson, among others, has vigorously argued that the annalistic tradition does faithfully preserve the substance of Roman law during the regal period, especially in the case of dowry; Wieacker, in contrast, laments that 'vom vordezemviralen Recht wissen wir so gut wie gar nichts.'[27] In a very real sense, however, the ultimate outcome of this debate is of little consequence because Dionysius merely alludes to the existence of dowry during the monarchy without furnishing any useful details. Indeed, it must be emphasized that there is no circumstantial evidence of any value until late in the third century BC, when the infamous divorce proceedings associated with the name of Sp. Carvilius Ruga compelled the Romans to grant an action for recovery of the dowry in the event of the death of the husband or the dissolution of the marriage (*actio rei uxoriae*).[28] It is safe to infer, on the basis of this reform, that heretofore the husband had enjoyed full ownership of the *dos* and retained it upon the death or divorce of his wife *ex iusta causa*, but it would be most imprudent to venture even an approximate date for the introduction of these rules.

One cannot, therefore, repose much confidence in evidence of a far later date that actually specifies the cash value of dowries in the fifth century BC. This applies especially to Valerius Maximus, who tells us that Tuccia, the granddaughter of the legendary dictator Cincinnatus, brought her husband a dowry of 10,000 *asses*, while an otherwise unknown Megullia was surnamed *Dotata* because her dowry amounted to 50,000.[29] Nothing more can be said about Megullia, but the evidence for Tuccia's dowry is particularly suspicious because it conforms so neatly with the modest means that later tradition accorded Cincinnatus.[30] Hence the first reasonably trustworthy information is once again forthcoming only as we approach the end of the third century. As we have already remarked in another context, during the course of the Second Punic War the proconsul Cn. Cornelius Scipio Calvus, who was then serving in Spain, asked the Senate to relieve him of his command so that he might return to Rome and arrange for his daughter's marriage. The *patres* were understandably reluctant, however, to recall an officer who had so far enjoyed considerable success in the field. Accordingly, they decided to conduct the requisite negotiations themselves, and at public expense eventually gave the girl in marriage with a dowry of 40,000 *asses* (16,000 sesterces, hereafter HS).[31]

The *aerarium* was admittedly in a parlous condition throughout this conflict, but this alone can hardly account for the quantum leap in the scale of dowries that we observe within this very family during the next generation. Polybius, who was certainly well informed about the matter, tells us that Scipio Calvus' nephew, the famous Scipio Africanus, was able to equip his two daughters with dowries of 60 talents (HS 1,440,000) apiece![32] Polybius' narrative does not suggest that Scipio was unduly generous, nor would such a characterization have been warranted: Scipio was, after all, the most successful general of his age, and equally able to finance games on three separate occasions; pay for the construction of an arch on the Capitoline hill complete with seven bronze statues, two equestrian figures, and two marble basins; and send a golden crown to the island of Delos.[33]

Livy casually remarks that the games put on in 205 were funded out of the booty that Scipio had brought back from Spain, but it is eminently probable that most if not all of the lavish public expenditure recounted above was paid for in this fashion. This serves to remind us that neither custom nor law required a Roman general to deposit all of the booty from a successful campaign in the state treasury.[34] The point is of paramount importance, for it has been reasonably estimated that Roman warfare generated at least HS 438,000,000 in the form of booty during the period 200–157 BC.[35] Typically, the victorious commander would distribute some of the booty to his troops proportionate to rank, set aside some for himself and deposit the balance in the *aerarium*. Scipio's use of the funds that he reserved for himself was equally commonplace: much of the money that these senatorial officers kept for themselves was in fact devoted to games and public building projects, both meant to enhance the political standing of their families. In addition to such public munificence, however, triumphant senators were also expected – again in the manner of Scipio – to employ their share of the booty to finance their own political careers or those of their sons, and to dower their daughters.

Unfortunately, the information that we possess with regard to the dotal arrangements of the Cornelii Scipiones is the most detailed at our disposal: the sources for the second century BC have little to say about either the size or composition of dotal property in other elite families. Moreover, all but one of the other specific cash amounts that do appear in the sources for this period derive from Roman comedy. Since these figures had to fit the meter that the poet was using, and may in any event have been copied from the original Greek New Comedy productions, they are obviously suspect. In order, therefore, to set these data and the far larger body of circumstantial evidence about dotal property in the second century BC in a useful context, it will first be necessary to examine the overall pattern of consumptive expenditure within the nobility. This, as it turns out, swelled dramatically in the post-Hannibalic period, and here it will be argued that the size of dowries did in fact increase commensurate with other outlays.

We may suitably begin by stressing that consumptive expenditure in the second century BC followed a well-established pattern, the various elements of which were all designed to strengthen the prestige and *auctoritas* of the individual and family in question. There was, for example, nothing random about the allocation of booty among the infantry, centurions and cavalry in this period. This usually followed the crude but predictable ratio of 1:2:3, hence reflected the broad economic and political divisions to be found within Roman society at large, and particularly in the elective assembly, the *Comitia Centuriata*.[36] This ratio, it should be noted, was rigidly applied in both the least profitable campaigns of the period, and the most lucrative. Thus in 197 BC, for example, the consuls C. Cornelius Cethegus and Q. Minucius Rufus both triumphed from the Cisalpina, Cethegus over the Insubres and Cenomani, and Rufus against the Boii and Ligurians. In both instances, the *pedites* received 7 *denarii* apiece, the centurions 14, and the *equites* 21. Thirty years later, L. Aemilius Paullus gave each soldier 100 *denarii*, and the centurions and cavalry 200 and 300 respectively, on the occasion of his triumph over Perseus of Macedon.[37]

The use of booty to finance public building projects is another prosaic feature of this period, but precisely because it was so useful politically. In 200 BC, for example, the praetor L. Furius Purpurio engaged a Gallic force near Cremona; at the height of the battle, he vowed a temple to Veiovis, which was duly dedicated some six years later.[38] Such vows, conveniently sworn when battle was imminent or actually underway, seem to have been the driving force behind most temple construction in Rome during the second century.[39] Before engaging the Insubres in 197, the above-mentioned Cornelius Cethegus vowed a temple to Juno Sospita, which he personally dedicated three years later.[40] In 181, M'. Acilius Glabrio dedicated a temple to Pietas that his father had pledged a decade earlier, when he fought Antiochus the Great at Thermopylae.[41] During the decisive naval battle off Myonnesus in 189, the propraetor L. Aemilius Regillus insured his victory over Antiochus' fleet by vowing a temple to the Lares Permarini; this was dedicated in 179 by his kinsman, M. Aemilius Lepidus. The latter also erected temples for Juno Regina and Diana, which he had promised in the course of separate encounters with the Ligurians in

187.[42] This same year also witnessed the capture of Ambracia by M. Fulvius Nobilior, who used some of the spoils to build and furnish a temple for Hercules and the Muses.[43] One of his relations, Q. Fulvius Flaccus, inaugurated a temple for Fortuna Equestris in 173, fulfilling a vow sworn six years earlier, during a campaign against the Celtiberians.[44] Warfare in Spain would subsequently inspire the construction of at least two more temples. The booty that L. Licinius Lucullus treacherously obtained from the Caucaei in 151 funded his dedication to Felicitas, while D. Iunius Brutus erected a temple for Mars from the proceeds of his campaigns against the Lusitanians and Callaeci in 138–136.[45] Even so minor a province as Corsica could be made to play a part: in 173, the praetor C. Cicereius vowed a temple to Juno Moneta in the thick of a successful battle, which he dedicated five years later on the Alban Mount.[46]

In this context, the Third and Fourth Macedonian Wars were particularly fruitful for their senatorial participants. In 171, the praetor C. Lucretius Gallus sacked the Boeotian city of Haliartus. Livy draws the reader's attention to the statues and paintings removed from the site; the latter subsequently adorned the temple of Aesculapius at Antium, while Gallus also supplied the town with an aqueduct at a cost of 13,000 *denarii*.[47] Cn. Octavius, who commanded the Roman fleet in 168–167, used his share of the booty to add a double portico to the Circus Flaminius, and to construct a magnificent residence on the Palatine which, according to Cicero, 'was thought to have obtained support for its owner, a new man, in his bid for the consulship.'[48] Finally, after his triumph over the Macedonian pretender Andriscus in 146, Q. Caecilius Metellus Macedonicus also erected a portico, which enclosed the temples of Juno Regina and Jupiter Stator; it was adorned with 34 bronze equestrian statues that Metellus had brought back from Macedon, works of Lysippus that Alexander the Great had commissioned in honor of those who had fallen at the Granicus.[49]

Games and other forms of public entertainment could also be legitimately funded from the spoils of war, and the political intent of such exhibits is again obvious. The first example is also the clearest. In 193 the propraetor P. Cornelius Scipio Nasica vowed games to Jupiter in the midst of a battle with the Lusitanians. Two years later, he asked the Senate to allocate the necessary funds, a request that seemed both novel and unfair. The senators decided, therefore, that whatever games he had vowed on the spur of the moment and without the advice of the Senate should be paid for either from the spoils, if he had set any aside for this purpose, or at his own expense.[50]

In the event, Scipio staged games for a period of ten days; in 189, similar tactics almost secured a censorship for M'. Acilius Glabrio. During the course of his triumph over Antiochus and the Aetolians in 190, he displayed

> 3,000 pounds of silver bullion, 113,000 Attic four-drachma pieces, 249,000 *cistophori*, engraved silver vessels in large numbers and of great weight, royal furniture made out of silver, costly clothing, 45 gold crowns (gifts of the allied communities), and spoils of all kinds.[51]

As a *novus homo*, Acilius would not normally have been an attractive candidate, especially in an intensely competitive field that included two other well-known plebeian candidates, M. Claudius Marcellus (cos. 196) and the elder Cato (cos. 195), as well as three equally illustrious patricians, T. Quinctius Flamininus (cos. 198), L. Valerius Flaccus (cos. 195), and this same Scipio Nasica (cos. 191). Nevertheless, 'the support of the populace inclined towards this man above all, because he had handed out many gifts (*congiaria*), by means of which a majority of the voters had incurred an obligation.' This so angered the *nobiles* that two of the plebeian tribunes, P. Sempronius Gracchus and C. Sempronius Rutilus, formally accused him of illegally sequestering some of the money and booty captured in Antiochus' camp. Nothing came of the accusation, although it did induce Glabrio to abandon his candidacy.[52]

Glabrio's unhappy experience did not discourage other triumphant senators, who must have been impressed by the popular acclaim that his largesse had inspired. In 186, M. Fulvius Nobilior celebrated lavish games in honor of Jupiter Optimus Maximus, thereby discharging a vow sworn on the capture of Ambracia the previous year. He had collected 100 pounds of gold from the allied communities for this purpose, and he requested the Senate to set aside this amount from the money that he planned to deposit in the *aerarium*. The *patres*, in turn, decided to permit the games, but to cap the outlay, apparently at HS 80,000.[53] In 179, the Senate imposed this same ceiling on Q. Fulvius Flaccus, who had made opportune use of his campaign against the Celtiberians by not only vowing the above-mentioned temple for Fortuna Equestris but also games for Jupiter! During the course of this same year, M. Aemilius Lepidus put on games for seven days when he dedicated the temples for Juno Regina and Diana that we also referred to earlier; Flaccus took similar advantage of the opening of his temple for Fortuna in 173, offering theatrical performances over a period of five days.[54] Finally, L. Anicius Gallus climaxed his triumph over king Genthius and the Illyrians in 167 with a vaudevillian offering in the circus that Polybius savagely pillories.[55]

As Polybius' striking analysis of the aristocracy's elaborate funerary ceremonies makes clear, despite their ostensibly domestic character these spectacles offered members of the elite yet another opportunity to accrue political capital – and it can hardly be a coincidence that the cost and scale of these displays mushroomed as booty became more plentiful.[56] Funerary games featuring gladiatorial combat were offered for the first time in 264 BC, when three pairs fought at the funeral of D. Iunius Brutus Pera.[57] Almost five decades later, the death of M. Aemilius Lepidus in 216 BC occasioned three days of games and 22 pairs of gladiators.[58] In 200 BC, four days of games and 25 pairs of combatants commemorated the passing of M. Valerius Laevinus.[59] Sixty pairs fought at the funeral of P. Licinius Crassus in 183, but his death was marked not only by three days of games but also by distributions of meat and a public banquet.[60] These innovations were perpetuated at the funeral of T. Quinctius Flamininus in 174, the cost of which may well have been the highest to date since it also featured theatrical performances.[61] In fact, two anecdotes suggest that such funerary games now routinely cost a half-million sesterces or more. On his deathbed, the well-to-do M. Aemilius Lepidus admonished his sons not to spend more than 1,000,000 *asses* (HS 400,000) on his funeral: Livy's language makes it clear that, by 150 BC, this would have been regarded as a modest sum.[62] This impression is reinforced by Polybius' account of the funeral games that P. Cornelius Scipio Aemilianus and Q. Fabius Maximus Aemilianus celebrated for their father, L. Aemilius Paullus, in 160. The total expense came to 30 talents (HS 720,000), and Polybius indicates that any show, 'if it is done on a grand scale,' would cost at least this much.[63]

The sudden and dramatic increase in funerary expenses that we observe among the nobility at the beginning of the second century recalls, of course, the equally extraordinary surge in the size of the dowries that Scipio Africanus supplied for his two daughters in this same period. This was another form of conspicuous consumption that the adroit politician could put to effective use. The experience of L. Mummius is particularly worthy of note in this regard because it demonstrates that, by the middle of the second century at the very latest, every successful general was expected to dower his daughters out of his share of the booty – indeed, failure to do so was certain to excite public comment. After the destruction of Corinth and Thespiae in 146, Mummius set aside their finest works of art for himself, but not a single item was destined to grace his own home. Rather, this unusually scrupulous man (Livy praises him as an *abstinentissimus vir*) chose in quite traditional fashion to decorate temples and public buildings not only in Rome but also throughout the Italian peninsula and even in Greece and Spain. He removed, for example, the so-called 'Ladies of Thespiae', which were transferred to the temple of Felicitas in Rome, but it is a measure of his self-restraint that he left a Cupid of Praxiteles behind simply because the statue had been consecrated. In equally traditional fashion, Mummius also used some of the booty to build a temple for Hercules Victor in Rome, and to give a banquet for its populace. This was the end of it, however, and both Frontinus and the elder Pliny stress that at his death his strict honesty, and particularly his refusal legitimately to enrich himself with the spoils of war, left his daughter in such poverty that the Senate had to supply her dowry at the public expense.[64]

The dowries that Scipio Africanus arranged for his daughters are the largest that we hear of in the second century, but if we keep in mind how few *abstinentissimi viri* were to be found within the elite at this time, then the few additional figures that have survived may be thought to represent the prevailing scale of expenditure with reasonable accuracy. These suggest that the female offspring of praetorian and consular families could now legitimately expect to receive dotal property worth HS 100,000 or more. The anonymous second wife of L. Aemilius Paullus, for example, is reliably reported to have brought her husband a dowry of 25 talents (HS 600,000). At the very least, this lends greater credibility to the otherwise suspect sum of 20 talents (HS 480,000) that surfaces in Plautus' *Cistellaria*.[65] The *Mercator* offers us a dowry of 10 talents (HS 240,000), *Truculentus* a sum in excess of 6 (HS 144,000), and *Trinummus* a paltry HS 80,000 – the same amount, it might be recalled, that the Senate imposed for the games celebrated by M. Fulvius Nobilior and Q. Fulvius Flaccus, and about double the cost of the aqueduct that C. Lucretius Gallus built for Antium.[66] The largest dowry in the corpus of Terence's comedies is again 10 talents, the smallest a mere 2 (HS 48,000).[67] Apart from these bald and mostly unreliable figures, however, sharply increasing dowries have left their mark on this period in a variety of other ways as well. First, as Polybius makes clear in his panegyric for Scipio Aemilianus, at the beginning of the second century it was already customary for dowries to be paid in three annual installments rather than in a lump sum.[68] Secondly, in this period some aristocrats met with great difficulty when called upon to return the dotal property or its cash equivalent when divorce, or the death of the husband, supervened. Thus the brothers Scipio and Fabius Aemilianus, the heirs of L. Aemilius Paullus, were only able to repay their stepmother's above-mentioned dowry by selling off household goods, slaves and real property. In similar fashion, the heirs of Q. Aelius Tubero had to sell a plot of land in order to restore her dowry to his widow Aemilia, one of Paullus' daughters.[69] As Boyer has justly concluded, these two points strongly suggest that, in the second century, Roman nobles often arranged dowries that exceeded their liquid assets. Here again, this at least suggests that the specific figures which appear in Roman comedy, while anecdotal, do have a wider historical application.[70]

Finally, the rapidly swelling scale of dotal expenditure is indirectly but no less indelibly reflected in the large body of evidence that colorfully delineates the negative impact of this trend on the day-to-day relationships of aristocratic husbands and wives. Lamentably, the most striking of such data again stem from Roman comedy – a genre that, as historical evidence, must always be used with caution. It has been frequently remarked, for example, that Terence reproduces his Greek originals quite closely, so that he is a more reliable source for Athenian institutions than Roman. Plautus, in contrast, often revised his Greek materials, either to make them more intelligible to his Roman audience or to pillory some aspect of the contemporary Roman scene.[71] In this context, it is undoubtedly significant that Terence never pauses to editorialize when marriage negotiations turn to the subject of dowry, while Plautus does so at nearly every opportunity. For Roman women, he concludes, freedom of action and a swollen dowry go hand in hand.[72]

The greater the dowry, that is to say, the less control a husband has over his wife. In the *Aulularia*, one of the players observes that 'a wife without a dowry, she's under her husband's thumb, but the dowered ones harry their husbands with their mischief-making and big-spending' (534–535). He invites his fellow citizens to emulate his own example:

> if the rest of the well-to-do would follow my course and take the dowerless daughters of our indigent citizens as their wives, there would be a great deal more unity in our city, we would experience less envy than is now the case, our wives would be far more reluctant to make trouble for us, and our expenses would be considerably reduced. (478–484) . . . And if someone should ask, 'who are the rich girls with their dowries going to marry if this law of yours should be established for the poor ones?' – why, let them marry whomever they please, so long as there's no dowry in attendance. Do this and they'll submit to their husbands, for instead of bringing them a dowry they'll bring them a better character than is presently the case. Then I'll make those mules of theirs, which now set you back more than a horse, cheaper than Gallic geldings! (489–495)

As Fraenkel has observed, this last reference to *Gallici cantherii* is certainly a Plautine interpolation – the beginning, in fact, of a long and detailed indictment of the behavior of well-to-do *matronae*, which Plautus had ample opportunity to observe at first hand. Deprive them of their dowries, he has Megadorus assert, and

> you'll never again hear them say: 'good sir, I brought you a dowry far in excess of the money you had before. It's only right, therefore, that purple and gold come my way – and maids, mules, coachmen, footmen, pages and litters borne aloft.' (498–502).

After a brief aside by his friend Euclio, Megadorus continues in a still more strident and personal tone:

> At present, no matter where you go, you'll find more wagons parked in front of townhouses than you will on a country-estate. That's a marvellous sight, however, compared with the day when everyone comes round looking for his money. The fuller, the embroiderer, the goldsmith, the woolen worker, the tradesmen who deal in flounces, underclothes, bridal-veils, violet dyes, yellow dyes – they're all standing around. The sleevemakers, they're there too, along with the shoemakers who specialize in balsam scents, the linen dealers and your

ordinary shoemakers. Squatting cobblers, slipper specialists, sandal makers – they're all at the ready, in tandem with the mallow dyers, the brassière makers and the girdle manufacturers. And just when you think you've paid off the lot, 300 more show up, all seeking their share. Your atrium is overrun with weavers, fringe-makers, and men who specialize in jewelry boxes. You bring them in and settle accounts. Now you're sure that everyone's paid off – and then in walk the saffron-dyers: there's always some pest or other hanging about, looking to hit you up for this or that. (505–522)

'These,' Megadorus balefully concludes, 'are just some of the many nuisances and intolerable expenses that huge dowries bring in their wake.' (532–533) In the absence of a secure date for the play, it might be speculated that Plautus contrived this dreary catalog to poke fun at the immediate aftermath of one of the most sensational events to occur in Rome during his lifetime, the stormy debate sparked in 195 BC by the tribunician proposal to repeal the *lex Oppia*. We know from a fragment of Ennius' *Annales* that the elder Cato spoke in favor of retaining the law;[73] the force of his rhetoric, if not his exact words, is certainly captured in the long speech that Livy scripted for the occasion.[74] Here Cato asks his fellow-citizens why respectable *matronae* have taken to the streets, and even stormed the Forum, in their anxiety to have the measure repealed. He answers his own question as follows:

'In order that we may glitter with gold and purple', says one; or 'in order that we may be driven through the city in carriages on festal and working-days, as if in triumph over the conquered and broken law and over your votes, that we have captured and taken away'; finally, 'that there be no limit to our spending, no limit to our luxury.'[75]

Conspicuous feminine consumption, Livy's Cato goes on to say in a thoroughly Plautine vein, will drive Roman husbands to complete distraction:

Do you wish, citizens, to start a competition among your wives, so that the well-to-do shall strive to own what the rest cannot, and the poor, lest they be scorned because of their poverty, spend beyond their means? Let these women once begin to feel ashamed when it is not called for, and they will no longer feel ashamed when they should. The woman

63

who can buy from her own funds will do so; the woman who cannot will pester her husband. And the latter will be reduced to misery, whether prevailed upon or not, since what he fails to give himself he will see given by another man.[76]

In the event, as we have already seen, the opponents of the *lex Oppia* prevailed; the measure was repealed, with not one tribe voting in support of the law. Aemilia, the sister of L. Aemilius Paullus and wife of Scipio Africanus, was one noblewoman who took full and immediate advantage of the altered situation – as we learn once again from Polybius' encomium for her nephew, Scipio Aemilianus. Polybius tells us that, when she took part in the women's religious processions,

> apart from the opulence of her own dress and carriage, the baskets, cups and other instruments of sacrifice carried in her train on these notable occasions were all of silver or gold, while the number of household slaves escorting her, both male and female, was correspondingly large.[77]

All of this property passed to Aemilianus at her death, and he promptly transferred it to his mother Papiria,

> whose means fell short of her high rank. For this reason she had previously shied away from the great religious processions; but now, when an important public sacrifice happened to occur, she drove forth in all Aemilia's splendor and circumstance, including among other things the same mule-drivers, mule team and carriage. As a result, all the women who witnessed the event were amazed by Scipio's kindness and generosity, and raising their hands, prayed that everything good befall him.[78]

We lose sight of Aemilia's estate after the death of Papiria, when Scipio divided it between his two sisters, the wives of Q. Aelius Tubero and M. Porcius Cato (the son of the orator).[79]

This is peer pressure with a vengeance, and one imagines Plautus watching Aemilia or some other noblewoman parading through the streets in this fashion, and muttering to himself about *Gallici cantherii*, going home to pen the *Aulularia*. Polybius supplies, in short, a backdrop against which it becomes easier and easier to understand why Plautus' old gentleman

> cares not at all for those ladies of high rank, those shrews with

bloated dowries shouting this and ordering that; the women who, with their carriages trimmed in ivory, their *haute couture* and their purple, reduce their husbands to servitude by their prodigality. (167–169)[80]

The link between shrewish behavior and a rich dowry recurs in the *Miles Gloriosus*, where the aged Periplectomenus at one point wryly observes that, as a wealthy man, 'I had the option of marrying a woman of the highest birth with a dowry to match – but I had no desire to admit a female that barks into my home.' (679–681) It is, however, precisely to the theme of *dos* as an instrument for the enslavement of the husband that Plautus most often returns. This analogy surfaces, for example, not only in the *Aulularia* but also in the *Asinaria*, where one of the characters grumbles that he 'sold his authority (*imperium*) in return for a dowry.' (87) In the *Menaechmi*, a father summoned by his daughter accurately assumes that 'she's got into an argument with her husband. That's the way it goes with women who feel entitled to treat their husbands like slaves: they're arrogant, and it's all because of their dowries.' (765–767)[81] In the *Mostellaria* as well, the spectators are reminded that they, too, 'have old bags at home, wives who bought you with their dowries.' (281)

The imperious daughter who, in the *Menaechmi*, summons her father to threaten her husband and thereby protect his financial investment reappears in the *Mercator*.[82] Worse still, even the slaves that such *uxores dotatae* brought with them into the marriage (the *servi recepticii*) might harass these unfortunate husbands with impunity. Thus we find Libanus, the servile hero of the *Asinaria*, taunting his master Demaenetus with the fact that Saurea, his wife's inherited slave, 'has more authority (*manus*) in the household than you.' (85–86) A surviving fragment of Cato's speech in support of the *lex Voconia* vividly corroborates this seemingly implausible claim:

In the beginning the woman brought you a great dowry; thereafter, she receives a large sum of money, which she does not entrust to her husband's authority (*potestas*) but gives him as a loan; later, when she is mad at him, she orders her inherited slave (*servus recepticius*) to hound him and demand the sum.[83]

The precarious position of the husband whose wife had brought him a large dowry surfaces periodically in subsequent literature, ranging into the second century AD.[84] It is hardly surprising, therefore, that the censors on occasion had to exhort their fellow-citizens to marry at all. Thus in 131 BC, Q. Caecilius Metellus Macedonicus delivered a speech entitled *De Prole Augenda*; a generation later, his kinsman Metellus Numidicus returned to the theme in his *De Ducendis Uxoribus*. A fragment of this latter speech survives, and it makes for interesting reading indeed.

> If, Romans, we could get along without a wife, we would all abstain from this annoyance; but, since nature has arranged things so that we can neither live with them very comfortably nor without them at all, we must look to our lasting well-being rather than the pleasures of the moment.[85]

This is not, it should now be clear, simply a misogynistic comment, but rather an accurate reflection of a troubled social environment.[86] Once the *actio rei uxoriae* had been introduced late in the third century, it must have become axiomatic that the more welcome the dowry, the greater the leverage that it gave the wife over her husband. This is due to the fact that, while the latter might use the dotal property as he saw fit for the duration of the marriage, in the event of divorce he had to prove that his wife had been morally delinquent or had herself initiated the divorce without cause; if he failed to do so, he was legally obligated to return the entire sum to the woman's father or guardian. It seems reasonable to assume that repayment of a dowry sufficiently large to require three annual installments, and which might well have been used by the husband to pay off existing debts or invested in land or business, could prove awkward in the extreme. We have referred above to the difficulties encountered by the heirs of L. Aemilius Paullus and Q. Aelius Tubero in this regard, but the most celebrated case is that of Cicero. In 48 and 47, he was torn between paying the second and third installments of his daughter Tullia's dowry, or sending her husband Dolabella a notice of divorce. In the event, he opted to pay, although financial difficulties delayed the second installment. In 46, Cicero finally decided to initiate the divorce, while also dissolving his own union with Terentia. Thereafter, she harassed him at every turn to restore the dowry of HS 400,000 that she had brought to the marriage some thirty years earlier. A settlement was reached in 45 only after considerable maneuvering and negotiation; it may have been facilitated in part by Dolabella's prompt repayment of the first two installments of Tullia's dowry (in 44, he would renege on the third) – but only in part. Late in 46, a desperate Cicero found it necessary to remarry; his bride was many years his junior, but sufficiently wealthy to enable Cicero to ease his financial difficulties.[87] Considering all of the misery that Terentia caused him after their divorce, the learned Cicero might well have had occasion to ponder a brief exchange in Plautus' *Epidicus*. 'Heavens, man,' Apoecides remarked, 'a huge dowry is a gorgeous sight;' to which Periphanes laconically replied, 'good god, yes – so long as there's no wife attached!' (179–180)

To be sure, flagrant and unseemly displays of wealth such as those recounted above did not pass without a challenge. If they inspired Plautus, they enraged the elder Cato, and he finally had an opportunity to do something about it when elected to the censorship in 184 BC. He directed the assessors to catalog women's clothing, jewelry, plate, furniture and carriages at ten times their actual value, and he then proceeded to tax them at three times the prevailing rate – altogether, a thirtyfold penalty.[88] Still, Cato could only be censor for a year: in order to have a lasting impact, such a Draconian solution would have to be passed into law. Although the last two centuries of the Republic would witness a great deal of sumptuary legislation, in fact such a measure was never forthcoming.

Roman legislators focussed instead on men's dining habits, and it is instructive briefly to peruse these measures in order to get a sense of what the Senate might have done in the case of dotal property. The *lex Orchia* (*circa* 182), which restricted the number of guests that could be invited to banquets, was followed by two far more comprehensive measures in 161. The first was a senatorial decree aimed specifically at the *principes civitatis* who hosted banquets during the *ludi Megalenses*. They were required to swear an oath before the consuls that they would not spend more than 120 *asses* at each dinner, would serve only domestic wines, and would not set out more than one hundred pounds of silverware. The second measure, the *lex Fannia*, limited the number of dinner-guests to three (except on market days, when five were permitted), and regulated both the cost and the foods consumed at such meals in extraordinary detail. During the *ludi Romani*, *ludi Plebei*, the *Saturnalia*, and on certain other specified occasions, citizens were allowed to spend a maximum of 100 *asses* a day; they could also spend 30 *asses* on ten additional days each month, but for the rest were limited to 10. They were not permitted, however, to serve fowl except for one unfattened hen! The *lex Licinia*, a measure of uncertain date, raised the base figure to 30 *asses*, and also permitted an outlay of 200 *asses* at weddings – this in addition to fixing weights for the amount of dried meat and salted foods that could be consumed. In 81, the dictator Sulla introduced legislation 'which provided that on the Kalends, Ides and Nones, on days of games, and on certain religious holidays, it should be right and lawful to spend 300 sesterces on a dinner, but on all other days not more than 30.' This was quickly followed by the *lex Aemilia* of 78 BC, which again regulated the foods served at banquets; the still more obscure *lex Antia* severely limited the ability of magistrates or magistrates-elect to dine out. Finally, the emperor Augustus raised the ceiling for dinner-parties on ordinary days to 200 sesterces, with 300 permitted on the Kalends, Ides and Nones, and 1,000 at nuptial banquets.[89]

The mere repetition of such legislation testifies to the ineffectiveness of these measures, but here the point to be kept firmly in mind is that, despite their lack of success, conservative senators never ceased their assaults upon this particular manifestation of *luxuria*. In this setting, therefore, the failure of the Senate to follow up Cato's assault on feminine prodigality with legislative action comes as a considerable surprise, and demands explanation.

Prima facie, one might expect Roman nobles to resist any attempt to limit the size of the dowries that they supplied for their daughters. Although there was never a legal requirement that the *dos* correspond to a woman's testamentary portion (indeed, a marriage could even be contracted without a dowry),[90] the same sentiment that required equal division of the estate of an *intestatus* among his *sui heredes* must have urged many fathers to regard dowry in precisely this fashion.[91] Thus it might be argued that, in an era of rapidly increasing wealth in general, fathers who wished to equip their daughters with richer dowries were behaving in a natural and completely predictable manner. Moreover, it might be added, the safeguards established by the *actio rei uxoriae* would have eliminated one brake on larger dowries, while the transfer of property in three annual installments enabled senators to invest their daughters with significantly larger sums than would have been possible if the entire amount had to be paid at once. As plausible as it might appear, however, this explanation simply will not do. Cicero's awkward dealings with Dolabella forcefully remind us that the *actio rei uxoriae* was a lawsuit in which an aggrieved husband might well prevail, retaining a portion of the dowry as child-support (*retentio propter liberos*) or in compensation for his wife's immoral behavior (*retentio propter mores*). More to the point, as we shall see below, in the mid-second century the Senate enacted legislation that severely circumscribed the long-standing and seemingly natural inheritance rights of elite women. Clearly, therefore, one cannot explain the privileged position of dotal property simply by appealing to natural sentiment and recent innovations in the law.

Sarah Pomeroy has proposed a second and quite different solution to this mystery. *Mulierculae*, she rightly reminds us, were with very few exceptions rigidly excluded from the public arena; the *mundus muliebris* consisted of elegant clothing and costly jewels, but little more.[92] Feminine display was, therefore, quite conventional, and this leads her to the following conclusion:

> The explanation for the lack of further sumptuary legislation against women may be found in women's increasing independence from male relatives. Wealthy upper-class women were considered less as appendages of men, and their displays of wealth brought them status in the eyes of women. But whatever women did independent of men was futile and, though potentially irritating to men, ultimately of minor importance to the state.[93]

One might instantly object that men's dining habits were also 'of minor importance to the state' – but that did not deter the Senate from repeated attempts to regulate them. More importantly, however, while it may be conceded that the public display of wealth enhanced the reputation of women among their peers, and while it might even be admitted that the increasing emancipation of women from male tutelage created new opportunities for such exhibitionism, there is absolutely no evidence to suggest that the growing independence of women somehow precluded sumptuary attacks on dotal property. To the contrary, it would have been quite easy for the Senate strictly to regulate the use to which women put their property while leaving the scale of dowries completely unchecked.

Nevertheless, in stressing the influence that manifest wealth exerted on an individual's public standing, Pomeroy has at the very least pointed us in the right direction: if the Senate chose not to pass sumptuary legislation to govern *luxuria* on the part of women, this was due in large part if not exclusively to the political capital that individual senators might accrue from such display. Polybius makes it eminently clear, that is to say, that a woman who publicly flaunted costly possessions not only enhanced her own prestige but that of her male benefactor as well. We have already made reference to the stunning impact of Papiria's first public appearance in Aemilia's finery, and to the high esteem in which the women who witnessed it subsequently held Scipio Aemilianus. Polybius goes on shrewdly to remark that 'this proved to be the original source of his reputation for nobility of character, which quickly spread since it is in the nature of women to gossip incessantly once they have got started on a subject.' As Walbank has observed, Scipio's magnanimity in this instance was undoubtedly calculated to obtain precisely the effect that Polybius describes.[94]

Polybius goes on to relate that Scipio took similar political advantage of two other episodes involving Aemilia's property. As we noted earlier, Scipio Africanus wished to furnish each of his daughters with a dowry of 50 talents, but at the same time he also wanted to leave his wife Aemilia in comfortable financial circumstances. Accordingly, he arranged for each girl to receive 25 talents at the moment of her marriage, with the balance to be paid to his sons-in-law, P. Cornelius Scipio Nasica Corculum and Tiberius Sempronius Gracchus, out of Aemilia's estate when she eventually died. This occurred in 162, and as Aemilia's heir it was incumbent upon Scipio Aemilianus to execute this agreement. When the two young men presented themselves to Scipio's banker, they fully expected to receive only a partial payment – the first of the three installments that Scipio was legally required to surrender – only to be informed that he wished to pay off the entire balance. Presuming that the banker had somehow been misinformed, they immediately sought out Scipio, and reminded him that he was under no legal obligation to hand over this enormous sum all at once. Scipio, however, replied that while he would take full advantage of the law when dealing with strangers, he preferred to behave in a more generous manner with his *amici* and kinsmen. This exchange, so Polybius avers, left Gracchus and Scipio Nasica 'amazed by Scipio's magnanimity and mortified at their own meanness, although they were second to none in Rome.'[95]

Finally, with the death of Papiria a few years thereafter, Scipio had still another opportunity to dispose of Aemilia's personal property, and he again used it to advantage. Despite the fact that they had no legal claim to it, he divided her estate, as well as that of Papiria, between his sisters (the wives of Q. Aelius Tubero and M. Porcius

Cato, the son of the censor) – a gesture that 'gave new life to Scipio's reputation for magnanimity and familial affection.'[96]

Cicero's awkward marriage to the adolescent Publilia, however, conversely demonstrates that a senator might be willing to risk public humiliation as well as domestic tension for the sake of a rich dowry. Antony countered Cicero's Philippics with ribald comments about this union, but marriage nonetheless offered Cicero and other cash poor aristocrats a convenient means of obtaining the capital required to discharge their debts without the embarrassment of mortgaging or selling their landed property. If our sources were more abundant, doubtless we would encounter many schemes to rival that of a certain M. Fulcinius of Tarquinii. He was one of the many thousands of Romans to suffer severe financial setbacks during the turbulent decade of the eighties BC, but he at least was able to improve his situation by giving an estate in the *ager Tarquiniensis* to his wife in exchange for her dowry, which consisted of an unspecified but clearly imposing sum of money. When Fulcinius died, he left their son as his sole heir, but with the stipulation that his wife enjoy the use of his property for the balance of her life (*ususfructus*). Since, therefore, the particular piece of land that he transferred to her would in the end have devolved upon her in any event, this tactic gave Fulcinius access to a great deal of money, and yet cost him nothing. Here again, therefore, we see that it was very much to the advantage of the elite to avoid sumptuary assaults on the dotal system – in marked contrast to the severe restrictions that, in 169 BC, the Senate imposed on the inheritance rights of Roman noblewomen.[97]

INHERITANCE

One of the more remarkable features of the Roman experience is the tenacity with which they adhered to a purely partible system of succession that was formally articulated for the first time in the Law of the Twelve Tables, but almost certainly antedates the Republic itself. Despite the profound social and economic changes that necessarily accompanied the expansion of Rome's *imperium*, and above all the tendency increasingly to view landholding as at once the only secure and honorable form of investment, this system remained unchallenged until 169 BC, when Rome's primacy in the Mediterranean basin was already secure. For at least four centuries, therefore, the sentiment had prevailed that sons and daughters who were still *in potestate* should share equally in their father's estate, along with his wife *in manu*, since she was considered to be *in filiae loco*.[98] In keeping with this sentiment, the first legislative restrictions on testamentary privilege were implemented precisely to safeguard the claims of the *sui heredes* to *patrimonia* that were being severely depleted by legacies to outside parties. Tiberius Coruncanius, who was *pontifex maximus* in the middle of the third century BC, ruled that legatees who received as much of a given estate as the natural heirs also acquired in the process an obligation to care for the deceased – that is, to celebrate his or her mortuary rites (*sacra*) in perpetuity.[99] This clearly indicates that the dispersal of estates through the multiplication of legacies had already become a serious problem at this relatively early date – a problem that the *lex Furia*, a tribunician measure that appears to have been promulgated during the last stages of the Hannibalic War, attempted to redress. This plebiscite limited legacies and *donationes mortis causa* to the already minuscule sum of 1,000 *asses*, while granting an action to the heir against individuals who violated this ceiling for four times the excess amount. The statute specifically exempted, however, all persons within the sixth degree, and one person within the seventh (a *sobrinus*, or cousin on the mother's side); moreover, it seems probable that, like the *lex Cincia de donis et muneribus* of 204 BC, the list of *exceptae personae* went on to embrace the affianced, a husband and wife, and their marital relations. At this moment, then, the Roman elite clearly wished to preserve the long-standing system of purely partible inheritance, even at the cost of delimiting testamentary freedom.[100]

For this reason, it is all the more surprising that, a few decades later, the Senate chose summarily to abandon this principle – or at least no longer to apply it to the aristocracy. With the staunch support of the notoriously conservative elder Cato, in 169 BC still another plebeian tribune, one Q. Voconius Saxa, introduced a bill that was meant either to supplant or to complement the *lex Furia* (it is not clear which). At the heart of this measure there lay two provisions, the first of which forbade anyone to take from an estate a legacy or gift that exceeded the amount left to the *sui heredes*. This clause penalized *cognati* and *adfines* in particular, and thus might be construed as simply a more restrictive version of the *lex Furia*, but it was also considerably more relaxed in the sense that it removed the ceiling of 1,000 *asses* on legacies and gifts to individuals unrelated to the deceased. The second clause, however, was positively Draconian in character. It flatly forbade anyone registered in the first census class to nominate a woman – even an only daughter – as his or her heir, and thus put an abrupt end to the concept of pure partibility.[101] This meant that, for all intents and purposes, a girl who was fortunate enough to have one or more brothers would in future be able to receive her intestate portion in the form of a legacy, while an only daughter was condemned to suffer a heavy financial loss.[102] Hence it is no wonder that, in the next century, Cicero at one point characterized the *lex Voconia* as vile and inhumane (*improbum et inhumanum*), and at another as a measure 'passed for the benefit of men but utterly unjust to women.'[103]

Cicero never elaborates upon these remarks in any detail; indeed, he refers to the objectives of this portion of the bill on only one occasion – a vague and elliptical allusion to the need to impose limits on the amount of property that a woman might own (something which, as Cicero himself recognized, the law did not accomplish).[104] At a still later date, Aulus Gellius makes a passing reference to the measure in a discussion of sumptuary legislation; finally, Augustine condemns it in still more general terms as a blatant instance of man's unjust treatment (*iniquus*) of women.[105] All of this suggests that later Romans themselves were uncertain about the original intent of this clause; it is, therefore, hardly surprising that scholars today are also sharply divided on this issue, discussion of which continues to dominate the literature devoted to the *lex Voconia*.

For the most part, this literature makes for unrewarding reading, above all because so many scholars have favored mono-causal explanations for what was undoubtedly a complex event. This criticism is especially relevant in the case of the anti-feminist, or misogynist, argument that has become so popular in recent years. The proponents of this viewpoint appropriately draw our attention to the only contemporaneous piece of evidence that is at all informative, a fragment of Cato's speech in support of the bill in which he harshly condemns the insolence of independently wealthy *uxores dotatae* (see p. 65 above).[106] This passage, it is claimed, demonstrates that Voconius and his supporters hoped to check the insufferable *superbia* of Roman noblewomen by depriving them of their property[107] – a tactic that at the same time would achieve the closely correlate objective of bridling feminine *luxuria*.[108]

However attractive this supposition may appear at first glance, it is in fact seriously flawed, and cannot be defended without substantial modification. At the outset, it should be stressed that the few surviving lines of Cato's speech harbor a methodological trap that has been consistently ignored. Simply put, although it may be conceded that Cato looked upon Voconius' proposal as a precious opportunity to resume a struggle that must have seemed forever lost with the repeal of the *lex Oppia*, this tells us nothing about Voconius' own motives, much less those of others in the Senate who supported him. Cato, it should be recalled, at the very end of his career concluded every speech before the Senate with the laconic expression *Carthago delenda est*;[109] he was not famous for sticking to the point, and the fact that he chose to attack *uxores dotatae* in a discussion of testamentary legislation is a clear warning that this fragment should be approached with caution.

It should also be kept firmly in mind that this diatribe, despite its notoriety, constitutes an insignificant fraction of Cato's original speech, and that Aulus Gellius chose to excerpt it for reasons of his own. It was, let us recall, Cato's use of the term *servus recepticius* that interested this author, and not the issue that Cato was addressing. We have no way of determining, therefore, whether Cato single-mindedly pursued the evils of feminine arrogance and prodigality on this occasion, or merely voiced this concern in the course of a comprehensive analysis of a larger social issue. What is eminently clear, however, is that we cannot embrace the more misogynistic of these two alternatives simply because it fits our own preconceived assumptions about Cato, or the purported anti-feminism of the Roman Senate in the second century BC.

There is, moreover, a third and still more cogent objection that requires consideration. If the goal of the *lex Voconia* was to deprive aristocratic women of their property with the express intent of eliminating their penchant for *luxuria* and *superbia*, then the measure was extraordinarily misconceived. We have already remarked that everyone registered in the top census class was still free to leave half of his property to his wife or daughter in the form of a legacy. Women might, therefore, still dispose of staggering sums of money – a point certainly not lost on Cicero, who makes it clear that there was nothing to prevent the daughter of one P. Crassus from inheriting HS 100,000,000 in this manner.[110] There were also, as we shall see below, a number of stratagems (some of them obvious) that could be invoked to defeat this section of the law, but the Senate never took action to close these loopholes.

These are insuperable objections, but they by no means exhaust the litany of criticisms to be directed against this anti-feminist hypothesis. One more remains, and this the most telling of all. Although Cato clearly reminded his fellow senators that overlarge dowries were directly responsible for much of the insolent and prodigal behavior of their female counterparts, this body nevertheless refused to sanction any restrictions against dowered property. Since Plautus and even the sober Polybius paint an equally unflattering picture of the dotal system during this period, it seems unlikely that the Senate disagreed with Cato; rather, the *patres* simply chose not to follow his lead. We are, therefore, compelled to draw the conclusion that feminine *luxuria* was not an issue of pressing importance for the majority of the Senate, despite the fact that these same senators did not hesitate to impose detailed sumptuary restrictions upon themselves.

The failure of the Senate to regulate dowry as an instrument for the conveyance of property, or to cap the amount that a woman might take in the form of a legacy, also vitiates another popular explanation for this chapter of the *lex Voconia*. This is the suggestion that the ongoing concentration of wealth in the hands of elite women was in the best interests neither of the *res publica* nor of its leading families. The defenders of this thesis, which has taken a variety of forms, accordingly regard the measure as preservative in intent rather than punitive: the object of Voconius and his friends was not to strip these women of their resources but to secure the traditional property rights of Roman men by restraining a natural sentiment that was remorselessly weakening their position. In its most venerable guise, this theory stipulates that the dispersal of senatorial property undermined the existing social and political order – a general remark frequently conjoined with the more specific observation that a married daughter's share of the *patrimonium* could be permanently lost to her natal family, thus diminishing its resources and, by extension, its political influence.[111] More recently, it has been suggested that the Senate had to take action because heavy manpower losses in the Hannibalic war and the many conflicts that followed during the next four decades had caused a great deal of property to pass into the hands of widows and orphans, who were exempt from the *tributum*. This trend, it is argued, threatened both the fiscal and military infrastructure of the Republic, and thus forced the Senate's hand.[112]

Once again, however, it must be said in response that the *lex Voconia* would have been a remarkably inefficacious device to fulfill either of these two objectives. As Gardner has recently reminded us, the Voconian law did not alter the rules of intestate succession; the estate of an *intestatus* continued to be divided equally among his *sui heredes*, including daughters married *sine manu*. Intestacy, therefore, offered a ready means of circumventing this provision of the statute, and *prima facie* this tactic should have appealed most strongly to the father of an only daughter – the one person whom the law quite severely penalized.[113] A parent blessed with both a son and daughter, in contrast, could leave fully half of his property to the latter in the form of a *legatum partitionis*, an act that would again be in conformity with intestate law as well as natural sentiment.[114] Finally, Pomeroy has cleverly suggested that one could evade the law and bequeath any amount of property to a daughter simply by calling it a posthumous contribution towards her dowry. The 50 talents that Scipio Aemilianus transferred to the two Corneliae is not, as she contends, the earliest instance of this dodge (Scipio Africanus made these arrangements more than a decade before the introduction of the *lex Voconia*), but Pomeroy's point is nevertheless well taken.[115]

There have been a number of other theories tendered in explanation of this mysterious provision, but today none of these commands much of a following.[116] More importantly, we have only begun to enumerate the evasive tactics that the Senate chose to ignore. As we have already seen, a testator could bequeath the entirety of his estate to a male heir, but at the same time grant to his wife (or, presumably, a sister or daughter) usufruct over some or all of his property.[117] Alternatively, he might leave his estate to a male relation or friend, but only on the explicit understanding that the latter would pass it on – typically to the testator's daughter.[118] Such trusts (*fideicommissa*) first became legally binding during the reign of Augustus,[119] but Cicero's sharply condemnatory description of a man who reneged on such an arrangement suggests that, within the upper class at least, these *fideicommissa* were normally considered to be solemn obligations well before this date. While he was still an *adulescens*, Cicero writes, he attended a *consilium* summoned by a senator named P. Sextilius Rufus, the sole heir of a certain Q. Fadius Gallus. In his will, Fadius stated that he had asked Sextilius to pass the whole of his property on to Fadia, his daughter. Although it was obvious that Fadius would never have designated Sextilius as his heir unless he had agreed to this arrangement, the latter nonetheless now denied that he had been party to this scheme, which contravened the oath that he had sworn to uphold the *lex Voconia*. Still, Cicero relates, Sextilius announced that he was prepared to violate his oath and surrender the inheritance, but only if his friends encouraged him to pursue this course. Everyone present knew that Sextilius was lying; still, they unanimously advised him not to give Fadia more than she was legally entitled to inherit – presumably the half-share that she might have received in the form of a *legatum partitionis*. As a result, 'Sextilius kept an exceptionally large estate, although he would not have touched a penny of it if he had followed the advice of men who placed honor and virtue before profit and personal advantage.'[120]

Fideicommissa seem to have become increasingly popular with the passage of time, but Cicero makes it clear that many wealthy citizens nevertheless seized upon a radically different and risk-free tactic to achieve the same result. In the second of his Verrine orations, Cicero notes that in 75 BC a wealthy Sicilian named P. Annius Asellus bequeathed the whole of his estate to his *unica filia*. Although this property was worth far in excess of HS 100,000, Annius' action was still in strict conformity with the *lex Voconia* simply because 'he had not registered' (*neque census esset*). Many scholars, taking this remark literally, have concluded that a citizen could now evade the census with impunity.[121] As Nicolet has emphasized, however, it would be more prudent to assume that Annius was not registered in the first census class, having managed either to conceal a large part of his wealth, or having been enumerated in one of the lesser classes at the last *lustrum*.[122]

During the course of the following year (74 BC), Verres reached an agreement with the reversionary heir, one L. Annius; in return for a suitable bribe, Verres inserted a paragraph in his edict that retrospectively applied the Voconian law to everyone whose fortune made them eligible for the first census class, regardless of their actual registration. Verres used this as an excuse to set aside Annius' will – a legal impropriety that Cicero subsequently used against him with dramatic effect. Above all, Cicero stresses that not one of the governor's praetorian successors incorporated this dubious legal precedent into his own edict, an omission which encouraged many individuals once again to take advantage of this loophole. Cicero refers in passing to a *pecuniosa mulier* named Annaea. 'Since she was not registered [in the first class],' (*censa non erat*) 'on the advice of many of her kinsmen she instituted her daughter as her heir.'[123]

The Voconian law appears, therefore, to have been a dead letter literally from the moment of its inception. Indeed, it is tempting to go further, and dismiss a measure that could be so easily circumvented as a mere legal curiosity. One additional piece of evidence, however, compels us to take this legislation seriously. As we have already frequently remarked, the Law of the Twelve Tables regulated the line of intestate succession, with the *sui heredes* of the deceased (including a wife married *cum manu*) taking equal shares of his estate irrespective of their sex. In the absence of natural heirs, the brothers and sisters of the deceased (his *consanguinei*) were invited to share the *patrimonium*, and if these were also lacking, his nearest agnatic kinsmen (*proximi agnati*) were summoned in their place – again without discrimination between the two sexes.[124] At some point, however, the decision was taken to exclude women from the ranks of the *proximi agnati*; this sharply circumscribed their intestate rights, which now extended no further than their fathers, sisters and brothers. Only one source, the jurist Paul, offers any kind of explanation for this restriction. He tells us that this statute was passed *Voconiana ratione* – an elusive phrase that might be translated as 'in the spirit of the Voconian law', and which seems to suggest a date after 169 BC.[125] Be that as it may, the point to be kept firmly in mind is that the *lex Voconia* was only one of two discrete pieces of legislation introduced to curb the succession rights of Roman women. For all of its seeming incongruities, therefore, the bill that Voconius Saxa laid before the Senate in 169 BC must be regarded as a thoughtful response to a serious social and economic problem; above all, it must not simply be dismissed as the surface manifestation of a misogynistic attitude that, in the minds of a growing number of scholars, characterized the Roman elite in the middle of the second century.

It is likely, then, that Cato and those senators who followed his lead looked upon this bill as an opportune means of checking feminine intemperance at its source, while still others in the Senate regarded it as an instrument that would keep most of Rome's burgeoning wealth in masculine hands. The majority, however, must have had a quite different objective in mind – one that demanded a fundamental departure from the deeply entrenched philosophy of purely partible inheritance yet at the same time did not require even minor changes in the dotal system. More confusing still, while a majority of the Senate clearly agreed on the need for legislative reform of the inheritance system, the general policy that they were trying to implement must have admitted of so many individual exceptions that they deliberately opted to frame the law in language that could be easily circumvented. Unless, that is to say, we wish to believe that the Senate not only failed in 169 BC to anticipate the many loopholes that could be used to defeat the *lex Voconia* but also continued in the decades that followed to remain blind to these tactics, we are compelled to conclude that the supporters of this measure understood that it could not be justly applied in all cases, and made allowance for this fact from the very outset. As a matter of methodological principle, then, any explanation of the *lex Voconia* that fails adequately to account for the ease with which the measure could be evaded, and equally for the failure of the Senate to reform a dotal system that had become the subject of strident complaint, must be found wanting.

Once the issue is posed in these terms, one possible explanation for the Senate's puzzling behavior does suggest itself. This is centered on the profound changes that occurred during the course of the Republic in the institution of marriage. In the beginning, as we have seen, a marriage contract typically presupposed the entry of the wife into the *manus* of her husband – an arrangement that, by the late Republic, had been virtually eclipsed by marriage *sine manu*.

During the early Republic, it is worth briefly repeating, the Roman bride normally not only entered her husband's household but his lineage as well. This was the most important consequence of any marriage *cum manu*, whether it resulted from *usus* or the more formal rituals of *coemptio* or *confarreatio*. Once released from the *potestas* of her father, the bride became *in filiae loco* to her husband, subsequently to share in his *patrimonium* as one of his *sui heredes*. She no longer had a claim to property within her natal descent line; the dowry with which her father equipped her was the last economic transaction between them. If, as many scholars believe, the dotal property that she conveyed to her husband frequently approximated her intestate portion, this would have served only to guarantee her equal treatment with her brothers and sisters who remained *in potestate*.

The value of dowries, however, increased dramatically after the Hannibalic war. This, as we have also seen, was made possible by Rome's highly lucrative warfare abroad, but it resulted no less from a calculation that political advantage was to be obtained from the ostentatious display of wealth. Hence there is every reason to believe that, within the ranks of the nobility, fathers typically made every effort to provide their daughters with the richest dowries that they could afford. This set the stage for the recurrent criticism of feminine *luxuria* and *superbia* that we see in Plautus, and for which Polybius supplies such striking justification; it also inspired the stern measures that Cato levelled against well-to-do women during his censorship, but this might well have been the end of it if marriage *cum manu* had remained the norm in this period. By 169 BC, however, marriage *sine manu* was certainly commonplace, and it may have already superseded the various *manus* arrangements in importance. This had a number of important consequences, but here the relevant point is that for testamentary purposes a married daughter still remained among her father's *sui heredes*. Unless he disinherited her, she would first receive a dowry that was recoverable in the event of divorce or the death of her husband, and later would take an additional share of the estate – either her intestate portion, or a testamentary bequest. Self-evidently, this gave her a distinct advantage over her brothers, and it is suggested here that the fundamental purpose of the *lex Voconia* may well have been to eliminate this advantage. Voconius would have reasoned, that is to say, that having received her share of the *patrimonium* in the form of a dowry, a daughter should surrender her claim to the balance of the estate. By compelling fathers to disinherit their daughters while at the same time leaving the dotal system free of constraints, this was precisely the outcome of his bill.

If this supposition is correct, then the otherwise curious failure of the Senate to close the many loopholes that allowed the law to be so easily circumvented also admits of explanation. While, for example, equity demanded that the testate and dotal shares of brothers and sisters should roughly correspond, it would hardly be just to apply the law blindly against the *unica filia*. The Senate thus chose to compromise, framing the law in general terms but leaving the testator sufficient freedom of action to cope with his individual circumstances. In the case of an only daughter, the testator might leave half of his property to her in the form of a *legatum partitionis*, with the balance reserved for a male kinsman; alternatively, he could name a male heir but request that he hand on the whole of his estate to his daughter (the *fideicommissum*), or achieve the same result by deliberately remaining intestate.

Such flexibility could also be important in a number of other circumstances. A father might, for example, come into substantial wealth after his daughter's marriage, and accordingly seek to increase her share of the *patrimonium*; once again, a *legatum partitionis* would allow him to accomplish this without difficulty.[126]

Polybius' account of the rather complicated arrangements that Scipio Africanus employed to dower his two daughters reminds us of another problem that often had to be overcome – the death of a father with unmarried daughters. Sarah Pomeroy has suggested that the *lex Voconia* permitted posthumous dotal payments, and that under this guise enormous fortunes could be transferred to women; this remains unclear, but the same result could certainly be achieved through legacies or *fideicommissa*.[127]

There were, of course, other legislative strategies that could have been used to secure the inheritance rights of sons *in potestate* against their emancipated brothers and married sisters. It is, perhaps, a further argument in favor of the interpretation of the *lex Voconia* submitted here that the praetors incorporated a definitive solution to this problem into the edict, apparently before the end of the Republic, that may be construed simply as a logical extension of our supposition. Gaius tells us that the praetors came increasingly to recognize that the system of intestate succession defined by the Law of the Twelve Tables was unfair, above all because it rigidly excluded sons and daughters who had been emancipated in favor of more distant agnatic relations. Their dissatisfaction with this arrangement eventually culminated in a decision to invite all of the children of an *intestatus* to share equally in his estate – a procedure known as *bonorum possessio unde liberi*.[128] This, of course, necessitated a concomitant change in the rules of testate succession, hence the praetors quickly ruled that the children of a testator, whether *emancipati* or *sui heredes*, could challenge a will in which they were not disinherited (*bonorum possessio contra tabulas*). Males now had to be excluded by name, females either *nominatim* or in a generic clause.[129]

It soon became obvious, however, that these innovations placed the *sui heredes* in a markedly inferior economic position. Unlike their emancipated brothers and sisters, the latter had no opportunity to accumulate property of their own so long as they remained *in potestate*: anything that they did acquire was considered part of their father's estate. *Exempli gratia*, this meant that if two brothers – one emancipated but not disinherited, and the other still *in potestate* – each received a legacy of HS 10,000 while their father was still alive, the *emancipatus* would in the end receive half of his brother's share because it was technically part of their *patrimonium*. In order to remedy this obvious injustice, therefore, the praetors quickly ruled that, whenever a *suus* suffered a loss because of the

81

intervention of an *emancipatus*, the latter's claim would not be acknowledged unless he agreed to contribute to the settlement a portion of his own property, and thus compensate the *suus* for his loss (*collatio bonorum*). If the *emancipatus* calculated that he in turn would be placed at a disadvantage by this arrangement, then the praetor permitted him to abstain from *bonorum possessio* altogether (*beneficium abstinendi*).[130]

With the passage of the *lex Falcidia* in 40 BC – a measure that superseded both the *lex Furia* and the *lex Voconia* with regard to legacies – the ability of women to receive property in this fashion increased significantly. A passage in Valerius Maximus similarly suggests that the Voconian law's restrictions on women in the first census class had become a dead letter by the end of the Augustan period at the latest.[131] The unfair economic advantage that the wealthy *uxor dotata* enjoyed over her brothers and unmarried sisters *in potestate* thus surfaced anew, but in a still more exaggerated form because of the willingness of the praetors to grant *bonorum possessio*. It should, however, be readily obvious that *collatio* could be adapted to negate this advantage, and this in fact is what the praetors proceeded to do. In the case of a woman married *sine manu* but *sui iuris*, the praetors simply applied the existing procedure of *collatio bonorum* against property that she had accumulated during the course of the marriage. In order to bring her dowry into account, however, a new albeit cognate procedure had to be devised. Since the *dos* was at law the property of the husband, the wife who sought *bonorum possessio* could hardly be required to bring a portion of it into the settlement. On the other hand, she might very well recover the whole of her dotal property upon the termination of the marriage, and thereby upset the equitable balance among the various heirs that the praetor wished to impose. It was for the purpose of resolving this dilemma that the jurists introduced *collatio dotis*. Simply put, the praetor refused to grant *bonorum possessio* to the *emancipata* unless she promised in advance that, upon recovery of her dowry, she would compensate the *sui heredes* by surrendering an appropriate portion of the *dos* to them.

So long as their fathers were alive, of course, most women married *sine manu* remained *in potestate* themselves, and here the historical development of *collatio dotis* proceeded somewhat differently. It should first be remarked that, in the fashion of their unemancipated brothers, they too could not own property, hence were never subject to *collatio bonorum*. A passage in the *Digesta* suggests that the praetor initially invoked *collatio dotis* only against the woman *in potestate* who applied for *bonorum possessio* in order to annul her father's will and claim an intestate portion of his estate. Unfortunately, this innovation cannot be dated, although it must have occurred before the middle of the second century AD since a rescript of Antoninus Pius extended it to women who 'meddled with the estate' (*bonis se immiscere*) of an intestate father.[132] The seminal point, however, is that by this date the jurists had devised in the various forms of *collatio* an effective method for compensating the *sui heredes in potestate* for the significant and unfair economic advantage that dotal and testamentary privilege gave to their married sisters.

WOMEN OF WEALTH IN THE LATE REPUBLIC

It can thus be argued that the *lex Voconia* represents a first attempt to restore the economic balance between married sisters and their brothers *in potestate* that would later give rise to *collatio dotis*. Be that as it may, there can be no doubt that dowry and inheritance were the two institutions principally responsible for the great wealth that many aristocratic women enjoyed in the latter stages of the Republic. Some of these women, it may be observed, continued to flaunt their wealth, or to dispose of it, in ways that had earlier aroused the ire of such disparate personalities as Plautus and the elder Cato. Pliny, for example, has preserved for us the bizarre tale of Gegania, a woman who was as independent as she was rich. She purchased a Corinthian lamp-stand for HS 50,000, and with it a hunchback named Clesippus whom the auctioneer included in the lot. At a dinner-party that she subsequently hosted, she reasoned that it would amuse her guests to see this deformed creature in the nude, and ordered him to be brought into the chamber. Thereupon, Pliny continues, she became so infatuated with him that Clesippus became first her lover and ultimately the sole heir to her estate! The grateful freedman thereafter venerated the lamp-stand, and he perpetuated Gegania's memory with a splendid tomb. As Herrmann has rightly emphasized, it goes without saying that Gegania did not have a *tutor legitimus*; no agnate would ever have given his approval for an action that was at once scandalous and at odds with his own economic interests.[133]

Gegania's eccentric behavior, however, pales in comparison with the still more notorious figures that Sallust puts on display in his account of the Catilinarian conspiracy. At one point, he describes *luxuria* in general terms as a form of madness that induced some women first to dissipate enormous fortunes, then to support themselves by prostitution, and finally, overwhelmed by debt, to venture upon civil war. In order to flesh out this portrait, he then focusses upon Sempronia, a putative descendant of Caius Gracchus, the wife of D. Iunius Brutus (cos. 77), and mother or stepmother of the Caesarian assassin D. Iunius Brutus Albinus. She was, Sallust stresses, a gifted woman and a well-educated one, but the pursuit of *luxuria* had transformed her into a feminine version of Catiline himself:

> There was nothing that she valued less than modesty and chastity; and one could hardly determine which she squandered the more readily, her money or her reputation. As for her sexual needs, they were so strong that she sought out men far more often than she was sought by them. She had on many previous occasions broken her word, reneged on a debt, and been an accessory to murder – poverty and extravagance (*luxuria*) having urged her on from bad to worse.[134]

At the opposite end of the spectrum we meet with women who combined wealth with unquestioned sobriety. The most famous is undoubtedly Cornelia, the mother of Tiberius and Caius Gracchus. In 139 BC, as we have already seen, she spurned a marriage alliance with King Ptolemy VIII Euergetes II Physcon of Egypt, choosing instead to devote herself to the education of her children. After the death of her two illustrious sons, she continued to maintain a large household at Misenum, entertaining Greek and Roman literati while exchanging gifts with kings throughout the Roman world. A famous anecdote, however, makes it clear that wealth never held her in thrall. On one occasion, a Campanian matron whom she was visiting showed her a collection of jewels that, according to Valerius Maximus, were *pulcherrima illius saeculi*. Cornelia refrained from comment, he goes on to say, until her sons returned from school; at that moment, she turned to her hostess and said: 'here are my jewels.'[135]

Terentia is another figure that instantly comes to mind in this context. Cicero may have found her shrewish, miserly and in the end even dishonest, but he never questioned her conjugal loyalty or her business sense. In addition to the HS 400,000 and other dotal property that she brought with her to the marriage, Terentia had sufficient capital of her own to become deeply involved in financial affairs. She owned and managed both urban and rural properties, was able to hold her own in a spirited dispute with a group of *publicani*, and administered Cicero's household (including the rental housing that she had brought him as *praedia dotalia*) during his exile – all without any visible assistance from a *tutor*.[136]

Cicero's orations are also peopled with several memorable and financially independent female characters, who exhibited the same political capacity as their male counterparts. Perhaps the most notorious is Sassia, the villainess of the *Pro Cluentio*. A noblewoman from Larinum, she was the mother of Cicero's client, Aulus Cluentius Habitus, and of a daughter (Cluentia) for whom she arranged a marriage with a family relation named Aurius Melinus. This did not, however (if we accept Cicero's account at face value), deter Sassia from seducing her son-in-law, whom she promptly married after her disgraced daughter's predictable divorce. Young Cluentius, Cicero goes on to say, then earned his mother's undying hatred by coming to his sister's defense, and thereafter Sassia was determined to effect his destruction. In the years that followed, Sassia gave birth to another daughter (Auria), and then witnessed her husband's murder at the hands of a fellow townsman and Sullan partisan, Statius Albius Oppianicus. The latter promptly proposed to the widow, whose fortune he coveted, and Sassia just as promptly consented to the marriage – but only after Oppianicus agreed to murder two of his three sons (how Sassia expected to profit from this remains unclear)! Oppianicus subsequently attempted to murder Cluentius, who for some reason had not disinherited his mother, but his agents were caught in the act, and after long and tortured proceedings Oppianicus himself was eventually charged and convicted, to die in exile. Hoping to implicate Cluentius in Oppianicus' death, Sassia quickly convened a *consilium* of her own and her late husband's *amici*. In the presence of these *homines honesti* (Cicero does not bother to explain how such sinister characters as Oppianicus and Sassia could have such friends), she subjected several slaves to a judicial inquiry on two separate occasions, but failed to extract the necessary confessions despite resorting to the cruelest forms of torture imaginable. Sassia was thus frustrated, but only for the moment. Three years later, she compelled a reluctant Oppianicus the younger (her late husband's sole surviving son) to marry her daughter Auria, and then forced him to take part in still another inquiry into his father's death.

Once again the slaves were put to the torture, but this time with more satisfactory results: one of them confessed to having poisoned Oppianicus, while also implicating Cluentius in the crime. The latter was promptly charged with the murder of Oppianicus, and with corrupting the jury that had convicted and driven him into exile. It was the younger Oppianicus who sat behind the prosecutor's bench, but Cicero makes it eminently clear that it was Sassia who orchestrated the entire proceeding.

It is, admittedly, an unsavory story, and made all the more so by Cicero's colorful obloquy. He concludes his account of Sassia's marriage to her own son-in-law, for example, with the following choice passage:

> Oh! The villainy of the woman, unbelievable, and apart from this one instance unheard of in the whole of human experience! How to describe her animal passions, unbridled and untamed – or her impudence, in a class by itself! Did she quake before the vengeful might of the gods, or the scandal among mankind? Did she dread the nuptial eve itself, with its wedding torches? The bridal chamber's threshold? Her daughter's marriage bed? The very walls that had witnessed the earlier act of consummation? Rather in her lust and frenzy she broke through and overran every barrier: raw passion triumphed over modesty, impudence over prudence, madness over reason.[137]

None of this, of course, should be taken very seriously: Cicero was trying to win his case, and he even boasted after the fact that he had 'thrown dust in the eyes of the judges' in order to do so.[138] A more sympathetic observer might have applauded Sassia for her resolute independence, energy and competence. She had, after all, arranged marriages for her two daughters, and also satisfactorily negotiated a marriage for herself with a notorious Sullan partisan who had overawed most of their fellow townsmen. More to the point, Cicero stresses that it was Sassia who summoned the third and final *consilium*, questioned the slaves under torture, drew up the writ against Cluentius, dispatched the younger Oppianicus to undertake the prosecution, and assembled the witnesses who were to testify against the defendant. It was, in short, simply Sassia's misfortune that Cicero chose to appear for the defense; if they had been on the same side, he would undoubtedly have characterized her in much the same terms that he reserved for Caecilia, the heroine of the *Pro Roscio Amerino*.

Sextus Roscius, a well-to-do member of the gentry in the Umbrian community of Ameria, enjoyed formal ties of *hospitium* with three of the most powerful aristocratic houses in Rome, the Metelli, Servilii and Cornelii Scipiones. Nevertheless, he was murdered while visiting the capital in 80 BC, and his name was retroactively added to the list of the proscribed so that his lands might be confiscated and put up for public auction. The principal beneficiary of this dubious proceeding was Sulla's powerful freedman, L. Cornelius Chrysogonus, who purchased thirteen estates worth HS 6,000,000 for the miniscule sum of HS 2,000. Chrysogonus kept ten of these properties for himself while surrendering the rest to Titus Roscius Capito. The latter was one of Roscius' fellow townsmen and bitterest enemies, who seems to have engineered his assassination. In the weeks that followed, however, Ameria's town-council openly espoused the cause of Roscius' like-named son and heir, who had been reduced to abject and undeserved poverty, and the increasingly nervous conspirators ultimately decided that their title to his property would never be secure so long as the young man remained alive. Accordingly, they began to plot his downfall as well, but Roscius anticipated their designs and prudently fled to Rome, where he took refuge in the house of Caecilia, the daughter of Metellus Balearicus (cos. 123) and sister of Q. Caecilius Metellus Nepos (cos. 98). When Chrysogonus and his agents responded by accusing Roscius of parricide, Caecilia actively intervened on his behalf, persuading first a young *nobilis* named Messalla (presumably M. Valerius Messalla Niger, cos. 61, or M. Valerius Messalla Rufus, cos. 53) to undertake the defense, and ultimately Cicero himself. He, of course, praises Caecilia for her *virtus*, *fides* and *diligentia* – qualities that he assuredly would have discovered in Sassia as well if he had appeared on her behalf.[139]

Despite striking differences in personality and temperament, therefore, these six late Republican noblewomen enjoyed a degree of independence that, even two centuries earlier, would simply have been inconceivable. For these women and others of their class, the swift expansion of the *imperium Romanum* in the post-Hannibalic period had brought great wealth, and the freedom to enjoy it. Still, for all of the attention that we lavish upon them, it must always be remembered that these fortunate women constituted an insignificant fraction of the total Roman population. If we focus our attention instead upon the largely anonymous women of the lower classes, it seems clear that Rome's ceaseless warfare produced far less felicitous results.

NOTES

1 Livy 1.57.3–11; cf. Ovid, *Fasti* 2.741–743; and Dionysius of Halicarnassus, *Antiquitates Romanae* 4.64.2–4. Dionysius, it should be noted, offers a markedly different version of the events leading up to the rape of Lucretia. By Livy's day, of course, the woman who worked at her wool deep into the night was a well-established symbol of chastity; cf. Tibullus 1.3.83–88; and Propertius 1.3.41.

2 The phrase *domum servavit, lanam fecit* appears on a second century sepulchral inscription dedicated to a *matrona* named Claudia (*CIL* I².1211 = VI · 15346= *ILS* 8403); for other early epigraphic references to the *uxor* as *lanifica*, see *CIL* I².1930 and 2161. Lucretia was also the epitome of conjugal chastity, which is emphasized in such early inscriptions as *CIL* I².1221 = *ILS* 7472, and *CIL* VI.26192 = *ILS* 8398.

3 Here one might note, by way of contrast, that at the end of the second century BC a group of six freedmen built a block of seats specifically for women at a theater in Capua (*CIL* I².2506).

4 See Athenaeus, *Deipnosophistae* 12.517d-518b.

5 The material evidence for the social and economic freedom enjoyed by women within the Etruscan elite has been carefully explored. See J. Heurgon, 'Valeurs féminines et masculines dans la civilisation étrusque,' *MEFR* 73 (1961) 139–160; and above all L. Bonfante, 'Etruscan Women: a Question of Interpretation,' *Archaeology* 26 (1973) 242–249; 'The Women of Etruria,' *Arethusa* 6 (1973) 91–101 = J. Peradotto and J.P. Sullivan (eds), *Women in the Ancient World: the Arethusa Papers* (Albany, 1984) 229–239; and 'Etruscan Couples and Their Aristocratic Society,' *Women's Studies* 8 (1981) 157–187 = H.P. Foley (ed.), *Reflections of Women in Antiquity* (New York, 1981) 323–342.

6 For the nomenclature of Roman women, see especially I. Kajanto, 'On the Peculiarities of Women's Nomenclature,' *L'Onomastique latine* (Paris, 1977) 147–158; as well as 'Women's Praenomina Reconsidered,' *Arctos* 7 (1972) 13–30; and 'On the First Appearance of Women's Cognomina,' *Akten des VI. Internationalen Kongresses für griechische und lateinische Epigraphik, München 1972* (Munich, 1973) 402–404.

7 Inscriptions suggest that *Cauia* and *Poplia* were especially popular *praenomina*; see again Kajanto, 'Women's Praenomina Reconsidered,' 17.

8 In the late nineteenth and early twentieth centuries, scholars typically regarded Athenian women as little better than slaves, destined at marriage to enter an environment indistinguishable from the harem. F.A. Wright, *Feminism in Greek Literature: from Homer to Aristotle* (London, 1923, repr. Port Washington, NY, 1969) 1–2, 57–62 and 183–186, is representative of this viewpoint, which still has its advocates today: cf. E.C. Keuls, *The Reign of the Phallus: Sexual Politics in Ancient Athens* (New York, 1985) 6–11 *et passim*; and E. Cantarella, *Pandora's Daughters* (Baltimore, 1987) 46–47. A counterreaction set in with A.W. Gomme, 'The Position of Women in Athens in the Fifth and Fourth Centuries,' *CP* 20 (1925) 1–25 = *Essays in Greek History and Literature* (Oxford, 1937) 89–115; cf. M. Hadas, 'Observations on Athenian Women,' *CW* 29 (1936) 97–100; L.A. Post, 'Woman's Place in Menander's Athens,' *TAPA* 71 (1940) 426–440; H.D.F. Kitto, *The Greeks* (Harmondsworth, 1951) 219–236; C. Seltman, 'The Status of Women in Athens,' *G&R* second series 2 (1955) 119–124; and D.C. Richter, 'The Position of Women in Classical Athens,' *CJ*

67 (1971) 1–8, which includes a brief history of the controversy. V. Ehrenberg, *The People of Aristophanes*[2] (Oxford, 1951, repr. New York, 1962) 192–207; W.K. Lacey, *The Family in Classical Greece* (London, 1968) 151–176; R. Just, 'Conceptions of Women in Classical Athens,' *Journal of the Anthropological Society of Oxford* 6 (1975) 153–170; S.B. Pomeroy, *Goddesses, Whores, Wives, and Slaves. Women in Classical Antiquity* (New York, 1975) 58–60, 79–84; and J.P. Gould, 'Law, Custom and Myth: Aspects of the Social Position of Women in Classical Athens,' *JHS* 100 (1980) 46–51, have adopted positions between these two extremes, while nevertheless stressing that Athenian women were expected to spend most of their time indoors. It is also worth remarking that the Attic orators offer a curious Athenian parallel to the anonymity of Roman women. As Just, 'Conceptions of Women,' 161; and D.M. Schaps, 'The Woman Least Mentioned: Etiquette and Women's Names,' *CQ* new series 27 (1977) 323–330, have pointed out, in the law courts respectable Athenian matrons remain unnamed, unless they are deceased or related to the speaker's opponent.

9   For the peculiar form of endogamy to be encountered in primitive Rome, see again A. Watson, '*Enuptio Gentis*,' in A. Watson (ed.), *Daube Noster* (Edinburgh, 1974) 331–341; and Y. Thomas, 'Mariages endogamiques à Rome. Patrimoine, pouvoir et parenté depuis l'époque archaïque,' *TRG*, 58 (1980) 345–382.

10   It is, however, not at all clear that an heiress who was already married could be compelled to divorce and marry her nearest agnatic kinsman, especially if she had already given birth to a son. For this and other details relevant to the epiklerate, see especially A.R.W. Harrison, *The Law of Athens: the Family and Property* (Oxford, 1968) 9–12, 132–138, and 309–311; as well as D.M. Schaps, *Economic Rights of Women in Ancient Greece* (Edinburgh, 1979) 25–42.

11   For the Athenian woman as transmitter of property, see Gould, 'Law, Custom and Myth,' 43–45. The concept is, however, a venerable one, as D.M. Schaps, 'Women in Greek Inheritance Law,' *CQ* new series 25 (1975) 53–54, makes clear. The property rights of Athenian women remain a difficult topic. For an introduction to this subject, see *inter alia* Harrison, *Law of Athens*, 112–114; or G.E.M. de Ste. Croix, 'Some Observations on the Property Rights of Athenian Women,' *CR* new series 20 (1970) 273–278. The fullest discussion may be found in Schaps, *Economic Rights of Women*, 4–24.

12   *Institutiones Iustiniani* 2.13.5, 3.1.1; Ulpian 26.1; Gaius, *Institutiones* 3.1–13; and Paulus, *Sententiae* 4.8.20.

13   Gaius, *Institutiones* 2.47; cf. Cicero, *Epistulae ad Atticum* 1.5.6.

14   The *locus classicus* is *Digesta* 10.2.1; but cf. Aulus Gellius, *Noctes Atticae* 1.9.12; and Servius, *Ad Aeneidem* 8.642.

15   Livy 5.23.8–11, 25.4–10.

16   *Camillus* 8.

17   Livy 5.50.7. These *matronae* must have been modest as well as selfless, however, since Cicero tells us that the first such eulogy was only delivered in 102 BC (*De Oratore* 2.44)! Diodorus Siculus 14.116 further confuses an already muddled tradition by asserting, *contra* Livy, that the Senate permitted the *matronae* to use carriages in Rome as a reward for their services against the Gauls. Still another explanation for this privilege appears, however, in Ovid, *Fasti* 1.617–628; and Plutarch, *Quaestiones Romanae* 56, both of whom claim that the women refused to bear children until the Senate revoked a decree that prohibited their use of horse-drawn chariots. Scholars have, for obvious reasons, long regarded these explanations as aetiological in nature. Cf., for example, F. Vollmer, *Laudationum Funebrium Romanorum Historia et*

Reliquiarum Editio (Leipzig, 1891) 453–454; and R.M. Ogilvie, *A Commentary on Livy, Books 1–5* (Oxford, 1965) 741.

18 Ogilvie, *Commentary on Livy*, 741, in fact suggests that these tales were propaganda devised during the course of the Punic Wars to stimulate donations from the *matronae*.

19 Livy 22.1.17–18.

20 Livy 34.1.3; Valerius Maximus 9.1.3.

21 Livy 24.18.13–14 (214 BC); 26.36.5, 12 (210).

22 Livy 27.37.9–10.

23 Much of the evidence for the economic consequences of Roman imperialism in the period 200–150 BC may still be most conveniently consulted in T. Frank, *An Economic Survey of Ancient Rome* I (Baltimore, 1933) 109–214. The enrichment of the elite in this period has been examined in detail by I. Shatzman, *Senatorial Wealth and Roman Politics* (Brussels, 1975) 12–18, 241–261, *et passim*.

24 Cato's ceaseless attacks on *luxus* have been frequently explored, and have often served as a point of departure for a still broader discussion of the conflicting habits of thought and behavior that characterized the Roman elite in this period. Cf., for example, H.H. Scullard, *Roman Politics 220–150 BC*² (Oxford, 1973) 153–159; and A.E. Astin, *Cato the Censor* (Oxford, 1978) 91–103.

25 For an introduction to the subject, cf., *inter alia*, F. Schulz, *Classical Roman Law* (Oxford, 1951) 122–130; B. Nicholas, *An Introduction to Roman Law* (Oxford, 1962) 88–90; W.W. Buckland, *A Textbook of Roman Law from Augustus to Justinian*³ (rev. P. Stein, Cambridge, 1963) 107–111; M. Kaser, *Roman Private Law*³, trans. R. Dannenbring (Pretoria, 1980) 298–303. P.E. Corbett, *The Roman Law of Marriage* (Oxford, 1930) 147–210; A. Watson, *The Law of Persons in the Later Roman Republic* (Oxford, 1967) 57–76; and J.F. Gardner, *Women in Roman Law and Society* (Bloomington and Indianapolis, 1986) 97–116, examine the institution in exhaustive detail. It is, however, an instructive commentary on how little is known about dowry in early Rome that it warrants only one paragraph in A. Watson, *Rome of the XII Tables* (Princeton, 1975) 38–39; it receives less than four pages in his *Roman Private Law around 200 BC* (Edinburgh, 1971) 24–27.

26 *Antiquitates Romanae* 2.10.2.

27 A. Watson, 'Roman Private Law and the *Leges Regiae*,' *JRS* 62 (1972) 100–105; *Rome of the XII Tables*, 39 note 35; F. Wieacker, 'Die XII Tafeln in ihrem Jahrhundert,' *Les Origines de la république romaine* (Geneva, 1967) 300. Corbett, *Roman Law of Marriage*, 147–148, also defends the antiquity of dowry, but is appropriately vague with regard to the moment of its introduction ('some form of dowry had been in use at Rome long before the time of Cato and Plautus'). C. Herrmann, *Le Rôle judiciaire et politique des femmes sous le République romaine* (Brussels, 1964) 10–11, is of the opinion that the *leges regiae* 'rapportent une tradition archaïque certes, mais postérieure à la chute de Tarquin.'

28 Aulus Gellius, *Noctes Atticae* 4.3.1–2, who excerpted the information from the *De Dotibus* of Cicero's *amicus*, Servius Sulpicius.

29 Valerius Maximus 4.4.10; cf. F. Münzer, 'Tuccia,' *RE* 7A (1939) 768; 'Megullia,' *RE* 15 (1931) 333.

30 This has left its mark upon a wide variety of Roman sources. Cf. Livy 3.13.8–10, 26.8–11; Dionysius of Halicarnassus, *Antiquitates Romanae* 10.8.4, 17.3–6; Valerius Maximus 4.4.7; Columella, *De Re Rustica* 1.*pr.*13; and Pliny, *Naturalis Historia* 18.20.

31 Valerius Maximus 4.4.10. The Roman government carried out a major reform of its currency *circa* 211 BC. During the first half of the second century (the period of greatest concern in this chapter), 1 talent = 6,000 *denarii* = HS

24,000 = 60,000 *asses*. For the details of this currency adjustment, see in particular M.H. Crawford, 'War and Finance,' *JRS* 54 (1964) 29–32.

32 Polybius 31.27.2.

33 Scipio put on games during his aedileship in 213 (Livy 25.2.6–8); upon his return from Spain in 205 (Livy 28.38.14); and in 201 or 200 to celebrate his triumph in Africa (Polybius 16.23.7). He built the Capitoline arch in 190 (Livy 37.3.7), but the date of the dedication on Delos (*SIG*² 588; *SIG*³ 617) remains uncertain.

34 For fuller discussion of the reasoning that underlies this assumption, see especially I. Shatzman, 'The Roman General's Authority over Booty,' *Historia* 21 (1972) 177–205; cf; M. Pape, *Griechische Kunstwerke aus Kriegsbeute und ihre öffentliche Aufstellung in Rom* (Diss. Hamburg, 1975) 27–33.

35 The evidence has been conveniently assembled by Frank, *Economic Survey*, I.127–138.

36 The spoils awarded to military tribunes, quaestors and legates, who were often *amici* or kinsmen of the commander, were of course more generous still; see Shatzman, 'Roman General's Authority,' 203.

37 Livy 33.23.7 (Cethegus); 33.23.9 (Rufus); 45.40.5 (Paullus). A complete list of the cash distributions to soldiers in the period 201–167 BC may be found in P.A. Brunt, *Italian Manpower, 225 BC–AD 14* (Oxford, 1971) 394. The booty that Paullus brought back to Rome from Macedon has been inventoried by Pape, *Griechische Kunstwerke*, 14.

38 Livy 31.21, 34.53.7, 35.41.8. These passages, which contradict one another with regard to the date and place of the dedication, have elicited considerable discussion. See J. Briscoe, *A Commentary on Livy, Books XXXI-XXXIII* (Oxford, 1973) 112–114.

39 On the construction of temples and porticoes from the proceeds of booty, see again Pape, *Griechische Kunstwerke*, 38–47.

40 Livy 32.30.10, 34.53.3. There is an element of confusion in these passages as well, on which see again Briscoe, *Commentary on Livy*, 227.

41 Livy 40.34.4–6; Valerius Maximus 2.5.1. At least some of the booty from Scarpea, which was stormed shortly after the battle at Thermopylae (cf. Livy 36.19.6), was finally put on display in the Etrurian city of Luna (*ILLRP* I.321a); for further discussion, see Pape, *Griechische Kunstwerke*, 10–11.

42 Livy 40.52.4–7; Macrobius, *Saturnalia* 1.10.10 (Regillus); Livy 39.2.7–11, 40.52.1–3 (Lepidus).

43 *CIL* VI.1307 = *ILS* 16; Cicero, *Pro Archia* 27; Pliny, *Naturalis Historia* 35.66; Servius, *Ad Aeneidem* 1.8. Some of the booty from Ambracia ended up on display in Tusculum (*CIL* I².616), the home of the *gens Fulvia* (Cicero, *Pro Plancio* 20); cf. Pape, *Griechische Kunstwerke*, 12–14.

44 Livy 42.3, 10.5.

45 Appian, *Iberica* 50–55; Cicero, *In Verrem* 2.4.4; Strabo 8.6.23; Dio Cassius 22.76.2; Augustine, *De Civitate Dei* 4.23 (Lucullus); Cicero, *Pro Archia* 27, and on this passage, *Scholia in Ciceronis Orationes Bobiensia*; Appian, *Iberica* 71–73; Valerius Maximus 6.4.1, 8.14.2; Pliny, *Naturalis Historia* 36.26; and Priscian 8.17 (Callaecus).

46 Livy 42.7.1, 45.15.10.

47 Livy 42.63.3–12, 43.4.6–7; cf. Pape, *Griechische Kunstwerke*, 201–202.

48 Cicero, *De Officiis* 1.138; *Res Gestae Divi Augusti* 19; Velleius Paterculus 2.1.2; Pliny, *Naturalis Historia* 34.13; Festus, *Glossaria Latina* v. *Octaviae porticus*; Pape, *Griechische Kunstwerke*, 15.

49 Cicero, *In Verrem* 2.4.126; Vitruvius, *De Architectura* 3.2.5; Velleius Paterculus 1.11.3–4; Pliny, *Naturalis Historia* 34.31, 64. For further discussion of the *porticus Metelli*, see especially F. Coarelli, *Guida archeologica di Roma*²

(Rome, 1975) 246–247; and Pape, *Griechische Kunstwerke*, 15–16.

50 Livy 35.1.4–12, 36.36.1–2.

51 Livy 37.4.8–5.3, 46.2–4.

52 Livy 37.57.9–15; on the charges against Glabrio, see once again Shatzman, 'Roman General's Authority,' 191–192.

53 Livy 39.5.7–10, 22.1–2. It is not clear from Livy's account whether Nobilior was allowed to spend 80,000 sesterces or *denarii*. Since the former would amount to 20 pounds of gold and the latter 80, most scholars have favored the lower figure. Whatever the sum, Livy tells us that actors travelled from Greece to Rome to honor the proconsul, that the ten-day long celebration included lion and panther hunts, and that he was the first to include athletic contests in the festivities.

54 Livy 40.44.8–12, 42.10.5 (Flaccus); 40–52.1–3 (Lepidus).

55 Polybius 30.22; cf. Livy 45.43.1–8.

56 Polybius 6.53.1–54.2. The political content of the funerary games described below was long ago seized upon by M. Gelzer, *The Roman Nobility*, transl. R. Seager (Oxford, 1969) 110–112.

57 Livy, *Periochae* 16; Valerius Maximus 2.4.7; Servius, *Ad Aeneidem* 3.67.

58 Livy 23.30.15.

59 Livy 31.50.4.

60 Livy 39.46.2.

61 Livy 41.28.11.

62 *Periochae* 48.

63 Polybius 31.28.5–6. Terence introduced his *Adelphoe* as part of this funerary celebration, in addition to reproducing his *Hecyra*. The latter did not fare well, however, for the performers were virtually driven from the stage by an unruly audience expecting a gladiatorial show (*Hecyra* 39–42).

64 Pausanias 7.16.8; Dio Cassius 21.72 (Mummius sets aside votive offerings, statues and paintings for himself). Cicero, *De Officiis* 2.76; *In Verrem* 2.1.55; Livy, *Periochae* 52; *Periochae Oxyrhyncheae* 53; Strabo 8.6.23 (he embellishes towns throughout Italy as well as Rome); cf. *CIL* I².627 = IX.4882 = *ILS* 21a (Trebula Mutuesca); I².628 = IX.4540 = *ILS* 21b (Nursia); I².629 = XI.1051 = *ILS* 21c (Parma); I².631 = IX.4966 = *ILS* 21d (Cures Sabini); E. Bizarri, 'Titolo Mummiano a Fabrateria Nova,' *Epigraphica* 35 (1973) 140–142 (Fabrateria Nova). Polybius 39.6 (Mummius adorns temples at Delphi and Olympia); cf. *IG* IV.183 = IV².3060; W. Peek, *Neue Inschriften aus Epidauros* (Leipzig, 1972) 30–31, no. 47 (Epidaurus); *IG* V. 2.77 (Tegea); VII.433 (Oropus); 1808 (Thespiae); 2478–2478a (Thebes); *BCH* 83 (1959) 683 (Tanagra); *IvOlympia* 278–281, 319 = *SIG*².310 = *SIG*³.676 = *ILS* 8768 (Olympia); *CIL* I².630 = II.1119 = *ILS* 21d (Italica). Cicero, *In Verrem* 2.4.4 ('Ladies of Thespiae'). *CIL* I².626 = VI.331 = *ILS* 20 (temple for Hercules Victor); I², p. 505 (public banquet). Frontinus, *Strategemata* 4.3.15; Pliny, *Naturalis Historia* 34.36 (Mummius' daughter in poverty). For a recent overview of Mummius' career, see Pape, *Griechische Kunstwerke*, 16–19; or H. Philipp and W. Koenigs, 'Zu den Basen des L. Mummius in Olympia,' *MDAI(A)* 94 (1979) 193–216, especially 193–204.

65 Polybius 18.35.6; Plautus, *Cistellaria* 559–563.

66 Plautus, *Mercator* 703–704; *Truculentus* 845; *Trinummus* 1158.

67 Terence, *Andria* 950–951; *Heautontimorumenos* 838, 940. G. Boyer, 'Le droit successoral romain dans les oeuvres de Polybe,' *RIDA* 4 (1950) 183 note 40, justly characterizes the dowry of two talents in the latter play as that 'd'une jeune fille de famille aisée, mais qui n'appartient certainement pas à l'aristocratie.'

68 Polybius 31.27.5.

69   Polybius 18.35.6; Valerius Maximus 4.4.9. We also encounter the compulsory
      return of the dowry, presumably through an *actio rei uxoriae*, on several
      occasions in Plautus; cf. *Amphitruo* 928; *Miles Gloriosus* 1166–1167, 1277–
      1278; *Stichus* 204.

70   Boyer, 'Le droit successoral,' 183–184; cf. S. Dixon, 'The Marriage Alliance in
      the Roman Elite,' *JFamHist* 10 (1985) 364–365. It should be kept in mind as
      well that, throughout this period, mothers also contributed to their daughters'
      dowries from their own property – a point that places the financial difficulties
      experienced by elite families in a still more telling light. On this point, see
      S. Dixon, *The Roman Mother* (Norman, Okla., 1988) 216.

71   On this point cf., *inter alia*, E. Segal, *Roman Laughter*[2] (Cambridge, Mass.,
      1987) 92–93.

72   This observation, it must be admitted, would not be universally accepted
      today. One may note, for example, that P. Grimal, 'A propos du *Truculentus*.
      L'antiféminisme de Plaute,' *Mélanges Marcel Durry* (Paris, 1970) 86–89,
      considers Plautus' various diatribes against *uxores dotatae* to have been blindly
      reproduced from his Greek originals. Certainly, Plautus was not the first
      author to lament the unhappy lot of the man who married a richly dowered
      wife: one finds comments to this effect in Greek prose as well as comedy.
      Plato, *Leges* 774c is a conspicuous example; still others have been assembled
      by Post, 'Woman's Place in Menander's Athens,' 428 (to which one should
      add Alexis, fr. 146 Kock). Nevertheless, most scholars still appear to endorse
      the position of E. Fraenkel, *Plautinisches im Plautus* (Berlin, 1922) 137–141,
      who argued that the recurrent assaults on the dowry system in general,
      and Megadorus' long tirade against dowered wives in *Aulularia* 475–537
      in particular, constitute some of the most obvious Plautine revisions in the
      entire corpus of his plays. Cf., for example, Herrmann, *Le Rôle judiciaire
      et politique des femmes*, 64–65. In claiming that Plautus 'stets die römische
      Gesellschaft seiner Schaffensperiode vor Augen hat' when fashioning his
      female characters, however, E. Schuhmann, 'Zur sozialen Stellung der Frau
      in den Komödien des Plautus,' *Altertum* 24 (1978) 97, goes too far. She
      is forced to take this position because she wishes to use Plautus as a tool
      of Marxist social analysis, specifically to demonstrate that every aspect of
      class cleavage that surfaces in his plays reflects the rapid influx of wealth
      into Roman society in the post-Hannibalic period. Although Schuhmann's
      position is too extreme, as we shall see below, there is sufficient corroborative
      evidence from other sources to make it clear that, whether substantially edited
      or not, Plautus' unsympathetic treatment of *uxores dotatae* would have struck
      a responsive chord in his Roman audience.

73   See J. Vahlen, *Ennianae Poesis Reliquiae*[3] (Leipzig, 1928) no. 352.

74   Livy 34.2–4. There has been a prolonged debate over the authenticity of
      this speech; for a convenient summary of the literature, see P.A. Johnston,
      '*Poenulus* I, 2 and Roman Women,' *TAPA* 110 (1980) 147 note 9; and Briscoe,
      Commentary on Livy, 39–43.

75   Livy 34.3.9. As Johnston, '*Poenulus* I,2 and Roman Women,' 150–152,
      shrewdly remarks, Livy's *ne ullus modus sumptibus, ne luxuriae sit* consciously
      recalls Adelphasium's lament, at the end of her long harangue against endless
      bathing, that *modus muliebris nullus est* (230). Shortly thereafter, she is also
      made to remark that *modus omnibus rebus, soror, optimus est habitu* (237).
      Livy's Cato also repeatedly refers to feminine *pudor* (34.2.8, 2.10, 4.12,
      4.13, 4.16) – perhaps deliberately recalling Adelphasium's famous *bon mot*,
      *meretricem pudorem gerere magis decet quam purpuram, magisque meretricem
      pudorem quam aurum gerere condecet* (304–305). As is tentatively suggested
      here with regard to the *Aulularia*, Johnston persuasively argues that the

debate over the *lex Oppia* inspired the *Poenulus*, with Adelphasium arguing the position of Cato and her sister Anterastilis that of his tribunician rival Valerius Tappo.

76 Livy 34.4.16–17.

77 Polybius 31.26.3–5.

78 Polybius 31.26.6–8.

79 Polybius 31.28.8–9. These transactions have been frequently reviewed, especially in the last decade. Boyer, 'Le droit successoral,' 169–187, remains fundamental; but cf. Shatzman, *Senatorial Wealth*, 247–249; J.P. Hallett, *Fathers and Daughters in Roman Society* (Princeton, 1984) 44–45; S. Dixon, 'Polybius on Roman Women and Property,' *AJPh* 106 (1985) 151 *et passim*; and J.A. Crook, 'Women in Roman Succession,' in B. Rawson (ed.), *The Family in Ancient Rome* (London, 1985) 70–71.

80 It is clear from a few surviving fragments that Lucilius also took up this theme of feminine prodigality; see 682–685M.

81 Cf. *Menaechmi* 795–796 ('do you expect your husband to be your slave?').

82 *Menaechmi* 734–738; *Mercator* 787–788.

83 Aulus Gellius, *Noctes Atticae* 17.6. Gellius here discusses the meaning of *servus recepticius* at length; it is normally translated today as 'dowered slave,' but H. Kornhardt, 'Recipere und servus recepticius,' *ZRG* 58 (1938) 162–164; and S. Solazzi, 'Servus recepticius et dos recepticia,' *SDHI* 5 (1939) 222–225, argue persuasively that he was part of the *magna pecunia* – that is, part of an inheritance – rather than dotal property. Cf. R. Vigneron, 'L'antiféministe loi Voconia et les "Schleichwege des Lebens",' *Labeo* 29 (1983) 145–146, who also rightly notes that Gellius' *tum magnam pecuniam recipit* refers to a legacy or inheritance. Segal, *Roman Laughter*[2], 22–26, duly notes that the typical Plautine wife is *irata* rather than *morigera*, and suggests that the Plautine theme of marital discord was a deliberate parody of the Roman norm of feminine *obsequentia*. Cato's fragmentary remarks, however, in tandem with the still more celebrated oration on marriage by Metellus Numidicus (see below), suggest to the contrary that Plautus was in fact satirizing increasingly flagrant displays of feminine independence within the Roman elite. As we have already seen, Johnston, '*Poenulus* I,2 and Roman Women,' 143–159, also reached this conclusion. Similarly, D. Konstan, 'Plot and Theme in Plautus' *Asinaria*,' *CJ* 73 (1978) 221, argues that the 'despotic posturing' of Libanus when he pretends to be Saurea amounts to a commentary on the power that *servi recepticii* and their mistresses had come to exercise in contemporary Roman households.

84 Cf., for example, Horace, *Carmina* 3. 24; Seneca, *De Matrimonio* fr. 87; Martial 8.12; and Juvenal 6.136.

85 Livy, *Periochae* 59; Suetonius, *Divus Augustus* 89; cf. Lucilius 678–679, 686M (Macedonicus); Aulus Gellius, *Noctes Atticae* 1.6.1–2 (Numidicus). Most scholars have presumed that there was in fact only one oration – Macedonicus' – but following the lead of J.C. Rolfe, M. McDonnell, 'The Speech of Numidicus at Gellius, *N.A.* 1.6,' *AJPh* 108 (1987) 81–94, persuasively argues for two.

86 It is, however, still labelled as misogyny in such recent works as J.-P. Neraudau, *Etre enfant à Rome* (Paris, 1984) 183–184.

87 Cicero, *Epistulae ad Atticum* 11.2.2, 3.1, 4a, 23.3, 25.3 (Tullia's dowry); Plutarch, *Cicero* 8.2 (Terentia's dowry); Cicero, *Epistulae ad Atticum* 12.12.1, 19.4, 21.3, 22.1, 23.2 (negotiations with Terentia); *Epistulae ad Familiares* 6.18.5; *Epistulae ad Atticum* 12.8, 13.29, 16.15.2 (negotiations with Dolabella); Plutarch, *Cicero* 41 (Cicero's remarriage). For further discussion, see now T. Carp, 'Two Matrons of the Late Republic,' *Women's Studies* 8 (1981) 189–200 = H. Foley (ed.), *Reflections of Women in Antiquity* (New York,

1981) 343–354; and S. Dixon, 'Family Finances: Tullia and Terentia,' *Antichthon* 18 (1984) 78–101 = 'Family Finances: Terentia and Tullia,' in B. Rawson (ed.), *The Family in Ancient Rome* (London, 1985) 93–120.

88   Livy 39.44.2–3; Plutarch, *Cato Maior* 18.

89   The two most important sources for this fascinating aspect of Roman culture are Aulus Gellius, *Noctes Atticae* 2. 24 (he surveys each of the various measures, with the sole exception of the *lex Orchia*); and Macrobius, *Saturnalia* 3.17. For the Orchian law, cf. Festus, *Glossaria Latina* v. *obsonitavere; percunctatem patris familiae nomen; Scholia in Ciceronis Orationes Bobiensia* (on Cicero, *Pro Sestio* 138). On the *lex Fannia*, cf. as well Lucilius 1172M; Pliny, *Naturalis Historia* 10.139; Athenaeus, *Deipnosophistae* 6.274c; and Macrobius, *Saturnalia* 3.13.13, 16.4. For the *lex Licinia*, cf. Lucilius 1200M, 1353M; on the Augustan measure, Suetonius, *Divus Augustus* 34.1. For ritual feasting at the various games, see most recently J.H. D'Arms, 'Control, Companionship, and *Clientela*: Some Social Functions of the Roman Communal Meal,' *CV* 28 (1984) 334–338.

90   Lucullus married the infamous Clodia, the sister of the impoverished aristocrat Appius Claudius Pulcher, despite the fact that she was *indotata* (Varro, *De Re Rustica* 3.16.2). Horace admonished Scaeva not to seek a dowry for his *soror indotata* from his patron (*Epistulae* 1.17.46).

91   A point emphasized by Hallett, *Fathers and Daughters*, 91–92; cf. A.S. Gratwick, 'Free or Not So Free? Wives and Daughters in the Late Roman Republic,' in E.M. Craik (ed.), *Marriage and Property* (Aberdeen, 1984) 46–47.

92   The *locus classicus* is Livy 34.7.7–10.

93   *Goddesses, Whores, Wives, and Slaves*, 181–182.

94   Polybius 31.26.10; cf. F.W. Walbank, *A Historical Commentary on Polybius* III (Oxford, 1979) 505.

95   Polybius 31.27.16.

96   Polybius 31.28.9. Polybius stresses that the two Aemiliae had no testamentary claim on Papiria's property, but *contra* Boyer, 'Le droit successoral,' 180–181, it is highly unlikely that this was solely because the *lex Voconia* of 169 BC forbade women within the first census class to be named as heirs. B. Kübler, 'Das Intestaterbrecht der Frauen im alten Rom,' *ZRG* 41 (1920) 36–37, persuasively argues that the Law of the Twelve Tables is the relevant statute, since it defined the two girls as the natural heirs of their father, Aemilius Paullus, and not their mother, whom he had divorced. It must also be stressed here that a father who did not provide his daughter with a sufficient dowry was apparently subject to public ridicule; see, for example, Cicero, *Pro Quinctio* 98; Martial 7.10.14; and the comments on this passage of D. Daube, *Roman Law. Linguistic, Social and Philosophical Aspects* (Edinburgh, 1969) 103.

97   Plutarch, *Cicero* 41; Cicero, *Pro Caecina* 10–11, on which see further B. Rantz, 'Les droits de la femme romain tels qu'on peut les apercevoir dans le *pro Caecina* de Ciceron,' *RIDA* 29 (1982) 265–280; and B.W. Frier, *The Rise of the Roman Jurists: Studies in Cicero's* Pro Caecina (Princeton, 1985) 4–27. Gelzer, *Roman Nobility*, 23–25, presents a masterfully succinct analysis of the financial difficulties that attended a class whose capital was heavily invested in land. Dowries were such an important source of ready cash that, as Gratwick, 'Free or Not So Free?,' 47 cleverly remarks, 'the rich male divorcee would find that he could not afford *not* to be married, as a person today with a mortgage cannot afford to be without a job.'

98   For the intestate rights of the *sui heredes* and of the *agnati proximi*, both male and female, stipulated in the Twelve Tables, see again *Institutiones Iustiniani* 2.13.5, 3.1.1; Ulpian 26.1; Gaius, *Institutiones* 3.1–13; and Paulus, *Sententiae*

4.8.20. For the inheritance rights of the wife *in manu*, the critical passage is Gaius, *Institutiones* 3.3. For further discussion of this issue, and of the testamentary capacity of women under the *testamentum per aes et libram* (to which reference is made in Lucilius 519–520, 1350M), see now Watson, *Roman Private Law around 200* BC, 98–105; cf. *The Law of Succession in the Later Roman Republic* (Oxford, 1971) 176–178; and *Rome of the XII Tables*, 66–67.

99   Cicero, *De Legibus* 2.52; for the date of his priesthood, see Livy, *Periochae* 18. The shift in responsibility for the mortuary cult from the *sui heredes* to unrelated legatees had a profound long-term impact on the very concept of ancestor worship among the Romans; this topic has been recently and fully explored by J.K. Evans, 'The Cult of the Dead in Ancient Rome and Modern China: a Comparative Analysis,' *Journal of the Hong Kong Branch of the Royal Asiatic Society*, 25 (1985) 119–151.

100   For the various provisions of the *lex Furia*, see Gaius, *Institutiones* 2.224–225, 4.23; *Epitome Ulpiani pr.* 2; *Institutiones Iustiniani* 2.22.pr.; *Vaticana Fragmenta* 301–302; and the discussions of A. Steinwenter, 'Lex Furia testamentaria,' *RE* 12 (1925) 2356–2360; Watson, *Law of Succession*, 163–167; or *Roman Private Law around 200* BC, 114–116.

101   These clauses are both taken up by Gaius, *Institutiones* 2.226 and 274, in the latter of which he sets the floor for the first census class at 100,000 *asses*. Dio Cassius 56.10. 2, in contrast, puts the figure at 25,000 drachmas, or HS 100,000. The measure is also discussed, or in some cases referred to in passing, by Cicero, *In Verrem* 2.1.104–114; *De Finibus* 2.55; *De Republica* 3.17; *Pro Balbo* 21; Livy, *Periochae* 41; C. Ritter (ed.), *M. Fabii Quintiliani Declamationes Quae Supersunt CXLV* (Leipzig, 1884) 78–81 (*Decl.* 264); Pliny, *Panegyricus* 42.1; Aulus Gellius, *Noctes Atticae* 20.1. 23; Festus, *Glossaria Latina* v. *recepticium servum*; Servius, *Ad Aeneidem* 1.573; Augustine, *De Civitate Dei* 3.21. *In Verrem* 2.1.110 suggests, *contra* Gaius, *Institutiones* 2.226, that both of these clauses may have applied only to those registered in the first class; predictably, their disagreement on this point has spawned an extended modern controversy as well. Kübler, 'Intestaterbrecht,' 22–23; Steinwenter, 'Lex Furia testamentaria,' 2359; 'Lex Voconia,' *RE* 12 (1925) 2423; B. Biondi, *Successione testamentaria donazioni* (Milan, 1943) 380; A. Berger, *Encyclopedic Dictionary of Roman Law* (Philadelphia, 1953) 561; P. Simonius, *Die Donatio Mortis Causa im klassischen römischen Recht* (Basel, 1958) 32; U. Wesel, 'Ueber den Zusammenhang der *lex Furia, Voconia* und *Falcidia*,' *ZRG* 81 (1964) 312; Astin, *Cato the Censor*, 113 note 33; and Kaser, *Roman Private Law*³, 381, are among those who would restrict it to the first class. This has been explicitly rejected by, *inter alia*, O. Karlowa, *Römische Rechtsgeschichte* II (Leipzig, 1901) 940–941; while P.F. Girard, *Manuel élémentaire de droit romain*⁸ (rev. F. Stenn, Paris, 1929) 975 remarks that it applied 'peut-être à eux, peut-être à tout le monde.' For further details, see the discussion of Watson, *Law of Succession*, 167–170. The point is important, however, precisely because the *lex Voconia* was far less favorable to blood and marital relations than the *lex Furia*, yet more generous to unrelated legatees. If the Voconian legislation applied only to the first census class, that is to say, then the *populus Romanus* at large will not have been freed from the ceiling of 1,000 *asses* imposed on legacies and gifts by the *lex Furia* until the enactment of the *lex Falcidia* in 40 BC, a restriction that will have grown progressively more inconvenient with the passage of time. As Rantz, 'Les droits de la femme romain,' 277 has correctly pointed out, however, since it is highly unlikely that the legacy that Aebutius received from Caesennia came to less than 1,000 *asses* (Cicero, *Pro Caecina* 17), on balance it does appear that this clause of the *lex Voconia* did indeed apply to all classes, and not just to the first.

102 A point underscored by Steinwenter, 'Lex Voconia,' 2420–2421; and more recently by Vigneron, 'L'antiféministe loi Voconia,' 141–142; and Crook, 'Women in Roman Succession,' 65–66.

103 *In Verrem* 2.1.105; *De Republica* 3.17.

104 *De Republica* 3.17 (*cur autem, si pecuniae modus statuendus fuit feminis, P. Crassi filia posset habere, si unica patri esset, aeris milliens salva lege, mea triciens non posset . . .*).

105 Aulus Gellius, *Noctes Atticae* 20.1.23; Augustine, *De Civitate Dei* 3.21.

106 Aulus Gellius, *Noctes Atticae* 17.6.

107 Thus Steinwenter, 'Lex Voconia,' 2426–2427; Watson, *Law of Succession*, 29; Astin, *Cato the Censor*, 113–118 (one of the few to stress that no single explanation will suffice); Vigneron, 'L'antiféministe loi Voconia,' 145–146; S. Dixon, 'Infirmitas Sexus: Womanly Weakness in Roman Law,' *TRG* 52 (1984) 361; Hallet, *Fathers and Daughters*, 92–93, 227–228.

108 Steinwenter, 'Lex Voconia,' 2426–2427; Boyer, 'Le droit successoral,' 176; Berger, *Encyclopedic Dictionary of Roman Law*, 561; Simonius, *Die Donatio Mortis Causa*, 32–33; Pomeroy, *Goddesses, Whores, Wives, and Slaves*, 162–163; Villers, *Rome et le droit privé* (Paris, 1977) 60; Astin, *Cato the Censor*, 116; B. Rawson, 'The Roman Family,' in B. Rawson (ed.), *The Family in Ancient Rome* (London, 1985) 18–19; Crook, 'Women in Roman Succession,' 66.

109 Appian, *Libyca* 69; Diodorus Siculus 34/5.33.3; Velleius Paterculus 1.13.1; Pliny, *Naturalis Historia* 15.74; Florus 1.31.4; Plutarch, *Cato Maior* 27.2.

110 *De Republica* 3.17.

111 Thus Wesel, 'Zusammenhang,' 314; Astin, *Cato the Censor*, 116–117; Kaser, *Roman Private Law*[3], 352, 381; Vigneron, 'L'antiféministe loi Voconia,' 148, 153; and Rawson, 'The Roman Family,' 18–19.

112 Cf. S. Pomeroy, 'The Relationship of the Married Woman to Her Blood Relatives in Rome,' *AncSoc* 7 (1976) 222; Carp, 'Two Matrons of the Late Republic,' 192 = Foley (ed.), *Reflections of Women in Antiquity*, 346; Hallett, *Fathers and Daughters*, 92–93; and S. Dixon, 'Breaking the Law to Do the Right Thing: the Gradual Erosion of the Voconian Law in Ancient Rome,' *Adelaide Law Review* 9 (1985) 520.

113 Gardner, *Women in Roman Law and Society*, 174 – merely the latest in a long series of works to underscore this point. Cf., *inter alia*, Steinwenter, 'Lex Voconia,' 2420; R. Villers, 'Le statut de la femme à Rome jusqu'à la fin de la République,' *Recueils de la Société Jean Bodin XI: la femme* (1959) 186; Pomeroy, 'Relationship of the Married Woman to Her Blood Relatives,' 223–224; Vigneron, 'L'antiféministe loi Voconia,' 148; Crook, 'Women in Roman Succession,' 65–66; and Dixon, 'Breaking the Law,' 523. The incidence of intestacy within the Roman elite is, however, a matter of considerable controversy; cf., above all, D. Daube, 'The Preponderance of Intestacy at Rome,' *Tulane law Review* 39 (1964/65) 253–262; and *contra*, J.A. Crook, 'Intestacy in Roman Society,' *PCPhS* new series 19 (1973) 38–44.

114 Cf. Kübler, 'Intestaterbrecht,' 27; Steinwenter, 'Lex Voconia,' 2420–2421; Watson, *Law of Succession*, 128–129; *Roman Private Law around 200 BC*, 111–112; Villers, *Rome et le droit privé*, 518; Vigneron, 'L'antiféministe loi Voconia,' 149; Crook, 'Women in Roman Succession,' 65–66; Dixon, 'Breaking the Law,' 522–523; and Gardner, *Women in Roman Law and Society*, 170.

115 'Relationship of the Married Woman to Her Blood Relatives,' 223–224, with reference to Polybius 31.27; cf. Herrmann, *Le Rôle judiciaire et politique des femmes*, 84; Dixon, 'Breaking the Law,' 522; and Gardner, *Women in Roman Law and Society*, 177.

116   The most ingenious of these alternative explanations was introduced more than a century ago by P. Gide, *Etude sur la condition privée de la femme*[2] (Paris, 1885) 148, who argued that the law was designed to strengthen agnatic tutelage. He rightly observed that the easiest way for an individual to leave the entirety of his estate to a daughter was to remain intestate, but this would also have the effect of subordinating her to a *tutor legitimus*. Buckland, *Textbook of Roman Law*[3], 290–291, still endorses this position, but as Vigneron, 'L'antiféministe loi Voconia,' 143–144, has correctly objected, this tactic would benefit only a daughter or wife *in manu*, while the *lex Voconia* applied to all women in the first census class, including those who were *sui iuris*. For further discussion, see Gardner, *Women in Roman Law and Society*, 174.

117   Cicero, *Pro Caecina* 11; cf. *Topica* 17. It is probable that Scipio Africanus' otherwise curious postponement of the final payment on the dowries of his two daughters (Polybius 31.27) is an early example of usufruct, although it must be emphasized again that it cannot have had anything to do with the *lex Voconia*. For further discussion, see Vigneron, 'L'antiféministe loi Voconia,' 151–152.

118   Kübler, 'Intestaterbrecht,' 27; Steinwenter, 'Lex Voconia,' 2420; Herrmann, *Le Rôle judiciaire et politique des femmes*, 84; J.A. Crook, *Law and Life of Rome* (Ithaca, 1967) 125; Daube, *Roman Law*, 96–97; Watson, *Law of Succession*, 35–37; Pomeroy, 'Relationship of the Married Woman to Her Blood Relatives,' 223–224; Vigneron, 'L'antiféministe loi Voconia,' 150–151; Dixon, 'Breaking the Law,' 523–524; and Gardner, *Women in Roman Law and Society*, 177–178.

119   *Institutiones Iustiniani* 2.23.1, 25.*pr.*

120   *De Finibus* 2.55.

121   Thus Herrmann, *Le Rôle judiciaire et politique des femmes*, 84; Pomeroy, 'Relationship of the Married Woman to Her Blood Relatives,' 223; Vigneron, 'L'antiféministe loi Voconia,' 149–150; Hallett, *Fathers and Daughters*, 96; and Gardner, *Women in Roman Law and Society*, 177.

122   C. Nicolet, *The World of the Citizen in Republican Rome*, trans. P.S. Falla (London, 1980) 72; cf. Villers, 'Statut de la femme à Rome,' 186; and Dixon, 'Breaking the Law,' 525. Vigneron, 'L'antiféministe loi Voconia,' 149–150; and Gardner, *Women in Roman Law and Society*, 170, consider these possibilities in addition to outright evasion. In Cicero's day, deliberate evasion of the census was still a criminal offense, for which an individual could be sold into slavery (*Pro Caecina* 99; cf. Dionysius of Halicarnassus, *Antiquitates Romanae* 4.15.6); he stresses, however, that Annius was protected both by *edicta praetorum* and *consuetudo iuris* (*In Verrem* 2.1.104).

123   *In Verrem* 2.1.104–114.

124   See again *Institutiones Iustiniani* 2.13.5, 3.1.1; Ulpian 26.1; Gaius, *Institutiones* 3.1–13; and Paulus, *Sententiae* 4.8.20.

125   *Sententiae* 4.8.20; cf. Gaius, *Institutiones* 3.14. Paul categorically insists that the Twelve Tables did not distinguish between male and female *agnati* (*ceterum lex XII tabularum nulla discretione sexus agnatos admittit*). He also describes this reform as part of the *ius civile*, hence the presumption that it involved statutory legislation. Proposed dates for the measure vary widely. Schulz, *Classical Roman Law*, 223, suggests that it was a part of the *lex Voconia* itself. Crook, 'Women in Roman Succession,' 60, argues for a date shortly thereafter ('perhaps it arose by juristic interpretation of intestacies resulting from the operation of the *lex Voconia*'). Watson, *Law of Succession*, 70, is vaguer still ('perhaps in the Republic, perhaps later'). The best discussion remains that of Kübler, 'Intestaterbrecht,' 24.

126   We catch a glimpse of this sentiment in, for example, *Digesta* 35.2.14.*pr.* A father has named his son and recently divorced daughter as co-heirs to his

estate. In a *fideicommissum*, however, he requests that his daughter pass her share on to her brother, setting aside only one-sixth of it to supplement her dowry. Clearly, this request was meant to place the brother and sister on equal terms. For further discussion of this passage, see H. Ankum, 'La femme mariée et la loi Falcidia,' *Labeo* 30 (1984) 44–46.

127 Polybius 31.27; Pomeroy, 'Relationship of the Married Woman to Her Blood Relatives,' 223–224. For further discussion of the legal procedures involved here, see especially Boyer, 'Le droit successoral,' 174–175; and Walbank, *A Historical Commentary on Polybius*, III.506.

128 Gaius, *Institutiones* 3.18–19, 25–26; Ulpian, 28.8. Both F. De Zulueta, *The Institutes of Gaius* II (Oxford, 1953) 125–126; and Watson, *Law of Succession*, 183–184, stress that Cicero apparently had no knowledge of this praetorian innovation, and date it to the very end of the Republic or the early Empire. Kaser, *Roman Private Law*³, 333; and Crook, 'Women in Roman Succession,' 61, place this reform with equal vagueness in the later Republic. Crook believes that henceforth a woman married *cum manu* could inherit in both lineages; *contra*, Schulz, *Classical Roman Law*, 228, who argues that an *emancipatus* could not be in another's *potestas*.

129 Gaius, *Institutiones* 2.125, 135; Ulpian 22.23. For the date, see again Schulz, *Classical Roman Law*, 270–273; and Zulueta, *Institutes of Gaius*, II.98–99.

130 The critical passages are *Digesta* 37.6.1.5; and *Codex Iustinianus* 6.20.9. Brief but satisfactory accounts of *collatio bonorum* and *beneficium abstinendi* may be found in Schulz, *Classical Roman Law*, 229–231, 270–273; Nicholas, *Introduction to Roman Law*, 248–249; Buckland, *Textbook of Roman Law*³, 324–325, 370; and Kaser, *Roman Private Law*³, 333, 369.

131 Cf. Gaius, *Institutiones* 2.227, 254; Paulus, *Sententiae* 3.8, 4.5.5; Ulpian 24.32, 25.14; and *Digesta* 35.2.1 (*lex Falcidia*); Valerius Maximus 7.8.2.

132 The *locus classicus* is *Digesta* 37.7.1.*pr.*; cf. *Codex Iustinianus* 6.20.5. For further discussion one should now consult J.F. Gardner, 'The Recovery of Dowry in Roman Law,' *CQ* new series 35 (1985) 451–452; or *Women in Roman Law and Society*, 109–111; cf., in briefer compass, Schulz, *Classical Roman Law*, 231–232; Buckland, *Textbook of Roman Law*³, 325–326; Kaser, *Roman Private Law*³, 370; and Crook, 'Women in Roman Succession,' 61. While most scholars believe that, like *collatio bonorum*, *collatio dotis* was a praetorian innovation of the late Republic or early Empire, A. Guarino, *Le collazione ereditarie, corso di diritto romano* (Naples, 1945) 135–147; and 'Collatio Dotis,' *BIDR* new series 8–9 (1947) 259–276, has vigorously argued that it was a creation of imperial lawyers in the second century AD. His argument, however, rests upon the questionable assumption that the reference to the praetor's edict in the opening sentence of *Digesta* 37.7.1.*pr.* has been interpolated, which he adduces from the equally faulty premise that the awkward Latin that we read there must *ipso facto* be a product of the Late Empire.

133 *Naturalis Historia* 34.6; Herrmann, *Le Rôle judiciaire et politique des femmes*, 109–110. Fortuitously, Clesippus' own funerary inscription has survived; see *CIL* I².1004 = X.6488 = *ILS* 1924.

134 Sallust, *Coniuratio Catilinae* 24.3–25. Although F. Münzer, *Römische Adelsparteien und Adelsfamilien* (Stuttgart, 1920) 272–273, argued that Sempronia was in fact the daughter of Caius Gracchus, her pedigree is very much in doubt; see especially R. Syme, 'Bastards in the Roman Aristocracy,' *PAPhS* 104 (1960) 327 = *Roman Papers* II (Oxford, 1979) 516–517; *Sallust* (Berkeley, 1964) 133–135; and cf. J.P.V.D. Balsdon, *Roman Women: Their History and Habits* (London, 1962) 47–49; and E. Gruen, *The Last Generation of the Roman Republic* (Berkeley, 1974) 422 and note 67.

135 Proposed marriage alliance: Plutarch, *Tiberius Gracchus* 1.4–5. Her sons were tutored by Diophanes of Mytilene (Cicero, *Brutus* 104, 211), and possibly by Blossius of Cumae (*Tiberius Gracchus* 8.4–5). Cornelia's management of her estate at Misenum: Plutarch, *Caius Gracchus* 19.2–3; the anecdote: Valerius Maximus 4.4.*pr.* For further discussion of Cornelia, see above all B. Förtsch, *Die politische Rolle der Frau in der römischen Republik* (Stuttgart, 1935) 56–72; more briefly, E.E. Best, Jr., 'Cicero, Livy and Educated Roman Women,' *CJ* 65 (1970) 201; A.H. Bernstein, *Tiberius Sempronius Gracchus, Tradition and Apostasy* (Ithaca, NY, 1978) 42–50; or D. Stockton, *The Gracchi* (Oxford, 1979) 22–26.

136 See Cicero, *Epistulae ad Familiares* 14.1.5 (urban property); *Epistulae ad Atticum* 2.4.5 (woodland); 2.15.4 (dispute with tax collectors); 12.32.2, 15.17.1, 15.20.4, 16.1.5 (*praedia dotalia*); *ad Familiares* 14.2.2–3 (management of Cicero's household, in part at her own expense). For further discussion, see especially Carp, 'Two Matrons of the Late Republic,' 189–200 = Foley (ed.), *Reflections of Women in Antiquity*, 343–354; and Dixon, 'Family Finances: Tullia and Terentia,' 78–101 = 'Family Finances: Terentia and Tullia,' 93–120. Best, 'Cicero, Livy and Educated Roman Women,' 200, suggests that Cicero inherited his own political and business acumen from his mother Helvia, but this is hardly implied by Plutarch, *Cicero* 1.

137 *Pro Cluentio* 15; cf., for further and equally compelling instances of Cicero's assassination of Sassia's character, 188, 192–194, and 199.

138 Quintilian, *Institutio Oratoria* 2.17.21. This did not, however, deter Herrmann, *Le Rôle judiciaire et politique des femmes*, 100, from incautiously characterizing Sassia as 'une femme, dont le génie était mauvais, pouvait ainsi mener une famille à sa ruine.'

139 For Caecilia's role in these events, and Cicero's fulsome praise of her sterling qualities, see especially *Pro Roscio Amerino* 27, 147, and 149.

Plate 1 Pompeii, Via dell' Abbondanza, shop of M. Vecilius Verecundus. At left of shop entrance, a badly faded wall painting showing, *top*, Mercury emerging from a temple; *below*, a saleswoman sitting behind a counter displaying her wares to a man seated to the right (cf. p. 119).

Plate 2 Pompeii, Via dell' Abbondanza, shop of M. Vecilius Verecundus. At right of shop entrance, a wall painting showing Venus Pompeiana in a chariot drawn by four elephants with, *below*, this highly detailed description of a cloth factory. In the center, four standing workers are kneading material for fulling in two wooden troughs supported by tables to left and right of a wood-burning oven. Three seated workers are preparing strips of cloth, while a figure standing on the far right (Verecundus?) exhibits the finished product (cf. p. 119).

Plate 3 Via della Foce, Museo Ostiense, inv. no. 134. Marble relief depicting a saleswoman standing behind a make-shift counter of chicken and rabbit cages. She appears to be handing a piece of fruit to a male customer. Two other men are engaged in conversation to the left, while a pair of monkeys and a large basket frame the scene on the right. In the background, a snail, a second figure standing behind the saleswoman, and a pair of fowl hanging from a gibbet (cf. pp. 121, 154 n. 76).

Plate 4 Isola Sacra tomb no. 100, Museo Ostiense, inv. no. 5204. Terracotta relief of a mid-wife (Scribonia Attice, or her mother) attending a birth (cf. p. 124–125).

Plate 5 Isola Sacra tomb no. 100, Museo Ostiense, inv. no. 5203. Terracotta relief of a physician, M. Ulpius Merimnus, treating a patient's leg. He is the husband or father of the preceding *opstetrix* (cf. p. 125).

Plate 6 Pompeii, *lupanar* of Africanus and Victor. Entrance to one of the *cellae meretriciae*, with erotic wall paintings situated above the entrance and adjacent walls (cf. pp. 137, 162, n. 138).

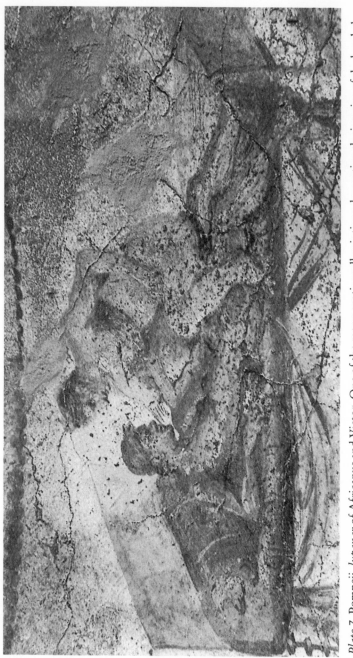

Plate 7 Pompeii, *lupanar* of Africanus and Victor. One of the many erotic wall paintings decorating the interior of the brothel, depicting in this instance a prostitute and her customer in the popular *Venus conversa* position (cf. p. 137).

Plate 8 The Louvre, inv. no. 659. Childhood sarcophagus of M. Cornelius M. f. Statius depicting, *left to right*, a nursing scene; the infant in the arms of a male figure (the father?); the child driving a sheep-drawn chariot; the child engaged in recitation before his father or *paedagogus* (cf. p. 168).

Plate 9 The Vatican, Museo Chiaramonti, inv. no. 1632. A fragmentary childhood sarcophagus of unknown provenance depicting, *left to right*, an infant being breast-fed and bathed; the child driving a sheep-drawn chariot (cf. p. 168).

Plate 10 Herculaneum, a reconstructed wall-painting depicting a *magister* beating one of his pupils, who has been hoisted onto the shoulders of a fellow-student (cf. pp. 170, 201 n. 22).

IV

WAR AND WORKING WOMEN

THE PLEBS RUSTICA

For the relatively few women who were members of the Roman elite, the last two centuries of the Republic brought significant and, for the most part, welcome change. Despite efforts to curb their inheritance rights, Roman noblewomen came into possession of sizeable fortunes, and increasingly were able to administer them with minimal interference from their husbands or guardians. These changes, it should now be clear, were both an unexpected and – in some masculine quarters, at least – unwelcome result of Rome's prolonged and highly profitable transmarine warfare. Still, it should always be remembered that these campaigns also routinely required the conscription or voluntary recruitment of scores of thousands of Italian peasants. Rome's far-flung wars of conquest, therefore, could not help but affect the lives of hundreds of thousands of free-born but less privileged and thus completely anonymous Italian women. Many of these, it is safe to assume, also experienced unprecedented independence in this period – but in economically more vulnerable circumstances. It is these women, so many of whom must have lived at or near the economic margins of Italian society, who are the subject of this chapter.

The anonymity of these peasant women is, however, something that cannot be too strongly emphasized since it poses severe difficulties for anyone trying to investigate them. For the last two centuries of the Republic in particular, we are almost wholly dependent upon literary evidence that is at once finite in quantity, often capriciously anecdotal or tantalizingly vague, and uniformly contaminated by an urban elite bias. So formidable an array of obstacles should discourage any attempt to calculate with precision

101

the number of women whose lives were directly influenced by Rome's overseas expansion. Obviously, the still more select category of women who lost their homes due to the prolonged absence or death of a husband or father under arms, and who were forced to take refuge in the peninsula's cities and towns as a result, will prove even more elusive. One must, therefore, be content with a broad and incomplete sketch rather than a detailed description of this particular facet of Rome's post-Hannibalic expansion. Nevertheless, especial attention will be paid to pinpointing the skills that country women routinely developed, and to assessing their opportunities for employment in a marketplace that came increasingly to be dominated by slave and freed labor.[1]

The anecdotal character of much of the evidence, and the limited value of such sources, may be succinctly illustrated by reviewing the career of one Spurius Ligustinus, certainly the best-known of all Roman smallholders. In 171 BC, Livy tells us, a host of volunteers who anticipated an easy and lucrative campaign presented themselves for the newly declared war with Macedon. As a result, no fewer than 23 former chief centurions (*primi pili*), Ligustinus among them, found it impossible to re-enlist at their old rank. Rather than accept a lesser posting, they appealed to the plebeian tribunes to intercede on their behalf. An assembly was duly summoned, but after both sides had presented their case Ligustinus had a change of heart and came forward to announce that he was willing to serve at whatever rank the recruiting officers deemed appropriate. This brought the entire episode to a felicitous and suitably patriotic conclusion, but for our purposes it is the speech that Livy scripted for the occasion that merits the most careful scrutiny, for here he has Ligustinus recount the details of his background and long military career. A Sabine peasant, Ligustinus had inherited less than an acre of land (one *iugerum*) from his father, and there is nothing to indicate that he ever attempted to expand this modest holding. Instead, he seems to have looked upon military service as the primary source of his family's income. He joined the army as a common soldier at the outset of the Second Macedonian War (200 BC), but in the third year of the campaign was promoted to the rank of centurion by Titus Quinctius Flamininus. Upon discharge, he immediately volunteered for service in Spain, where he once again earned promotion to the rank of centurion, this time from the elder Cato. He volunteered yet again for the war against Antiochus and the Aetolians, in which he also served as a centurion, and in the years that followed he fought twice more in Spain as well as in two unidentified campaigns. In all, he completed 22 *stipendiae* in a space of thirty years, four of them as a *primus pilus*. His share of the booty from these various military exercises amounted to at least 304 *denarii*, and it must have been this money that allowed him to support a wife and eight children on his tiny plot of land.[2]

There is a wealth of useful information in this passage, but it must also be conceded that it raises a number of important questions, none of which can be satisfactorily answered at the present time. Livy mentions in passing, for example, that Ligustinus' wife was his agnatic first cousin. This is the earliest such union that we hear of in Roman history; indeed, a fragment of Livy published in the last century indicates that the customary ban on marriage among agnates within the sixth degree remained inviolate until shortly before the outbreak of the Hannibalic war.[3] This household thus recalls the similar but still more complex arrangements described by Dio Chrysostomus in his Euboeic discourse. This is a pattern that, at the very least, suggests the possibility of widespread endogamy among the peasantry, who might have regarded it as an efficient device to prevent the dispersal of their property.[4]

Livy also remarks that Ligustinus' bride was *indotata*: she brought nothing more to the marriage than her 'free birth and chastity' (*libertatem pudicitiamque*). In Roman society, dowry was never regarded as a necessary preliminary to *matrimonium iustum*, so there is nothing in this statement that requires us to reject it out of hand. At the same time, however, it must also be admitted that the pertinent literary and legal evidence alike imply that a dowerless union would have been highly unusual. The literary sources in particular lead us to believe that fathers who were unable to equip their daughters with a suitable dowry expected to be treated with contempt, and accordingly would resort to desperate measures to avoid such humiliation. Plautus, a contemporary of Ligustinus, nicely captures the feelings of such a parent in his *Trinummus*, although here the unfortunate Lesbonicus is the prospective bride's brother rather than her father. Lesbonicus is a typical Plautine spendthrift; the play opens with his father Charmides travelling abroad, while at home Lesbonicus has already squandered the family fortune. All that remains, apart from 3,000 gold Philippics that Charmides secretly entrusted to his friend Callicles, is a small farm outside the city; Lesbonicus has even been forced to sell the family's Athenian townhouse. At this point Lysiteles, who is in love with Lesbonicus' anonymous sister, induces his father (Philto) to approach the young man and negotiate a dowerless marriage. This leads to an awkward and embarrassing exchange. 'My son sent me here,' Philto announces, 'to unite our two families in marriage and friendship. He wishes to marry your sister; my sentiments are the same, and I wish it, too.' Lesbonicus takes this as a deliberate insult: 'Sir,' he says, 'I no longer know you; although your own affairs have prospered, you are mocking my misfortunes.' Pressed harder, Lesbonicus then attempts to draw the conversation to a close with a remark that he clearly expects Philto to comprehend and appreciate. 'It is only right that I recognize my station in life; my family's position is inferior to yours, so you must look elsewhere for a marital alliance.' Philto, however, remains undaunted, and Lesbonicus finally agrees to the union – but only on the condition that Philto accept the afore-mentioned farm, the family's last resource, as his sister's dowry. He is acutely aware that, without a dowry, the public at large may draw the conclusion that his sister has entered concubinage rather than marriage. Lesbonicus is determined to avoid this ghastly prospect, even if it means that he must sink still deeper into poverty, but it is his own *dignitas* that is at issue, not his sister's reputation. 'Who would be deemed more vile than me?' he asks Lysiteles. 'And in any event, if you took her without a dowry all the talk around town would embellish your reputation and slander mine. You'd get the honor and glory and I'd get – whatever they tossed at me.'5

The play has, of course, a happy ending. Callicles comes up with a clever scheme to furnish Lesbonicus with a thousand gold Philippics for his sister's marriage, and Charmides arrives home just in time to give the couple his blessing. The reader should always remember, however, that this is a significant sum of money, and that this comedy is in fact peopled with characters and values drawn from the urban elite. It thus shares a bias common to Roman literature at large, and this in turn compels us to wonder whether the Plautine obsession with dotal property betrays a peculiarly aristocratic concern not shared by Roman society as a whole. Horace also introduces us to an *agrestis* of modest means who was unable to supply a dowry for his sister, and the nexus between poverty and dowerless marriage is made still clearer by Varro. One of the figures in his *De Re Rustica*, the once-impoverished *nobilis* Appius Claudius Pulcher, admits that circumstances forced him to betroth one of his sisters (the notorious Clodia) to Lucullus without a dowry. He then goes on to say that 'it was only after he [Lucullus] had relinquished a legacy to me that I began, for the very first time, to drink honey-wine in my own home' – an event that clearly marked his escape from poverty.[6] There is nothing here to suggest, however, that ignominy attached itself to an *indotata* who combined poverty with an unblemished reputation. Once again, therefore, we may legitimately ask whether the dowerless union between Ligustinus and his cousin was an anomaly, or an event that permits us to glimpse one of the many hidden realities of rustic Italian life.

Livy also celebrates the fact that Ligustinus and his wife produced eight children; this is by no means the largest family that we hear of in the second century,[7] but it again calls into question the conventional wisdom that large families were the exception rather than the rule among the Italian peasantry. This claim rests in very large part upon a single fact – the reduction of the property qualification for military service from 11,000 to 4,000 *asses*.[8] Although the date of this reform remains unclear,[9] and thus the circumstances that occasioned it are equally uncertain, today historians nevertheless take it for granted that it must have been a calculated response to the ongoing deracination of the Italian peasantry, and the difficulties that this would entail for military recruitment.[10] One could hardly deny that decades of uninterrupted warfare, often on two or more fronts simultaneously, exacted a ruinous toll among the *rustici* summoned to arms; still, it should also be recognized that a high birth-rate among the peasantry, and the concomitant testamentary dispersal of landed property, would also sharply diminish the pool of eligible recruits. The fact that he repeatedly volunteered for service, for example, implies that Ligustinus was enrolled among the *proletarii*, but it says nothing about his father's standing. In fact, he could easily have been an *assiduus*: it must have been fairly common to find a father registered in the fifth and lowest class of the *assidui*, only to have his children reduced to the ranks of the *proletarii* as a result of the division of landed property that accompanied his death. Ligustinus could, therefore, have inherited his proletarian status, but it is equally possible that it resulted from sharing the *patrimonium* with one or more siblings. Livy does not, unfortunately, impart the information that we require to choose among these possibilities, but the large family with which Ligustinus and his wife were blessed will in any event serve to illustrate the point of this discussion. A lifetime of military service, with a centurion's share of the booty in each campaign, should have served to emancipate Ligustinus from the poverty that he knew as a young man; since he had six sons to succeed him, however, it is distinctly possible that the division of his estate nevertheless perpetuated the family's proletarian classification.[11] In sum, given the lacunose condition of the evidence and the complex character of the issues involved, it would be foolhardy to claim that large families were commonplace among the peasantry, and equally delusive to go on claiming that they were not.

Since Ligustinus was abroad for more than two decades, the betrothal and marriage of his two daughters posed at least a potential problem, and we would very much like to know how it was resolved. Did Ligustinus arrange suitable matches for the girls during the intervals when he was at home, or was the matter attended to in his absence by a family council, with his wife (or possibly a male relation) taking the lead? Was there a manifest tendency in these circumstances for the extended family to prefer an endogamous marriage? Would the dotal property tend to be reduced or even eliminated in marriages that were negotiated in the absence of the father? Here as well, we have just enough evidence at our disposal to frame the questions, but no hope of arriving at satisfactory answers.

Finally, it should be noted that the holding of one *iugerum* that Livy assigns to Ligustinus was so small that it was in all probability largely devoted to a vegetable garden, with some space set aside for poultry and a few small animals.[12] In the absence of the *rusticus*, the necessary labor for a farm unit of this size could be supplied by the wife and children: even at a very young age, the latter would be able to perform simple tasks such as shepherding the livestock.[13] In general, however, peasants who were liable to conscription must have had holdings of sufficient size to be able to sow wheat and barley, the traditional subsistence crops in antiquity, and it is here that in many cases the prolonged absence of the principal cultivator would have made itself most severely felt.[14] Hopefully, the smallholder would be able to draw upon his extended family for assistance, but many *agrestes* called off to war must have found it necessary to choose between allowing the land to lie idle, or hiring casual workers (*operarii*) to carry out some or all of the most labor-intensive tasks, in particular ploughing and reaping the harvest.[15] The elder Cato takes it for granted that such *operarii* will be readily available in the countryside,[16] but how could even the most astute peasant cultivator make arrangements in advance that would cover every contingency while he was on campaign in Spain or the

Balkans? The crisis that confronted the wife and children of the consul M. Atilius Regulus in 256 BC nicely illustrates the problem. As we have seen, he had a modest holding of seven *iugera* (4.35 acres), which he placed in the charge of a farm-manager (*vilicus*) while he was on campaign in Africa. During his absence, however, the *vilicus* died, and one of these hired hands absconded with his equipment and livestock, leaving his family to starve. This particular story ends with the Senate intervening to assist the consul's family;[17] the operative point, of course, is that the wife of an anonymous conscript would often have had to fend for herself. Here as well, then, we would like to use anecdotal evidence as a point of departure, and go on to form some idea of the number of peasant women who, trapped in similarly traumatic circumstances, forfeited their homes and even their lives. There is, as it turns out, additional evidence that can be brought to bear, but it is no less frustrating than the material that we have just reviewed. With this caveat, we introduce the second difficulty intrinsic to the subject matter of this chapter – sources that revel in generalizations which defy precise location in space, and often, in time.

This imprecision characterizes each of the four overworked passages that define the expropriation of the Italian peasantry during the second century BC as one of the most important elements underlying the abortive reform legislation of Tiberius Gracchus. Sallust, for example, remarks at one point that

> the populace was burdened with military service and poverty. While the generals carried off the spoils of war and shared them with a few friends, the parents or small children of the soldiers, if they had a powerful neighbor, were being driven from their homes.

Plutarch, who seems to be reading from a speech that Tiberius delivered from the rostrum, is equally vague.

> The wild beasts that wander about Italy have, each and every one of them, a cave or lair that they call home. The men, however, who fight and die for Italy enjoy the common air and light, and nothing else; bereft of house and home, they roam aimlessly about with their wives and children. The generals are, therefore, resorting to outright lies when they exhort the soldiers entering battle to engage the enemy in defence of their tombs and shrines: among these many Romans, there is not

a man to be found who has an hereditary altar or a family tomb.[18]

These sources hint at a countryside in crisis, but here too, it is important to note that they raise more questions than they answer. First, they do not permit even a crude estimate of the number of women and children driven from their homes, much less still finer distinctions between, for example, families that suffered complete expropriation and those fortunate enough to be resettled in new colonial foundations.[19] Second, they do not indicate whether the threat of expropriation confronted the peasantry everywhere in peninsular Italy to the same degree, or constituted a greater menace in some districts than others. Finally, we cannot determine whether the deracination of the peasantry proceeded at a steady pace throughout the century, or responded in cyclical fashion to broader economic trends that influenced capital investment in land. There is, to be sure, an implicit assumption on the part of many historians today that members of the Roman elite typically invested the profits of business and war in rural property. It should be recalled, however, that Cicero obtained a handsome return from the urban rental properties that Terentia brought him as part of her dowry. This demonstrates that, by the end of the Republic, Rome itself afforded many opportunities for landed investment – and in the second century, when the population of the capital swelled dramatically, the construction of new *insulae* must at times have siphoned off a great deal of money that would otherwise have been used to expand rural holdings.[20]

It should, then, be obvious that one cannot accept these vague allusions to an embattled peasantry at face value. At the same time, however, it must also be admitted that any attempt to firm up these generalizations instantly runs foul of the most glaring contradictions. There is, on the one hand, a considerable body of evidence, both epigraphic and archaeological, which suggests that the peasantry flourished in many regions of Italy as late as the second century AD. Other data, however, archaeological as well as literary, point in precisely the opposite direction. Hence it seems appropriate first to delineate these contradictions and then, rather than choose between them, attempt to elaborate a historical context capable of accomodating both sets of data. In this way, it may be possible to pinpoint with somewhat greater accuracy the *rustici* whom Sallust, Plutarch and other sources relegate to such tortured fates.

The notion that the Italian peasantry had been completely displaced by slave labor during the last two centuries of the Republic, and the correlate belief that small farms had wholly given way to large estates, or *latifundia*, was first called into question by Mommsen more than a century ago. He shrewdly recognized that, in the second century AD, the Italian smallholder was still tenaciously clinging to the soil around Ligures Baebiani, an Apenninic community near Beneventum. He drew this conclusion from a single inscription, the long and very detailed register of properties that were mortgaged in support of the town's alimentary project. In all, sixty-six holdings were pledged, with values ranging from HS 501,000 to a minuscule 14,000. Eight of these properties (12 percent of the whole) were valued at HS 25,000 or less, and although even the smallest would have dwarfed the single *iugerum* of a Spurius Ligustinus, it must still be stressed that these are genuinely small holdings: not one of them comes to even 5 percent of the largest declaration. In an earlier age, such men would have formed the backbone of the Roman army – and it is proprietors of this sort that historians have in mind when they talk about the expulsion of the peasantry from the Italian countryside.

Mommsen was considerably less sanguine about the survival of the peasantry in the area around Veleia, another Apenninic hill town located a few hundred miles to the north. Trajan funded an alimentary scheme here as well, and the inscription detailing the forty-six mortgages that underwrote the project does suggest a radically different pattern of landholding. The largest declaration amounts to HS 1,600,000, which is more than triple the value of its counterpart at Ligures Baebiani. More to the point, the smallest estate to be pledged at Veleia (HS 50,000) equals or exceeds in value fully twenty-nine of the sixty-six properties (44 percent) in the Samnite community. What Mommsen failed to keep in mind, however, is that at Veleia the *alimenta* was designed to assist some 300 families, and there is absolutely nothing to suggest that all of these lived within the confines of the town. Indeed, the remains of the site make it clear that Veleia was a very small community, so it is eminently probable that some of those who received assistance were marginal cultivators in the surrounding district.[21] This implies what should always have been obvious in any event, namely that in both Ligures Baebiani and Veleia, there was a body of cultivators whose properties were considerably smaller than those mortgaged by the participants in the program.

It is only, however, when we turn to the archaeological data, and specifically to the surface surveys conducted in south-eastern Etruria, that we begin to catch sight of these elusive *rustici*. According to Plutarch, Tiberius Gracchus had already found this area to be severely underpopulated as early as 137 BC: there were still, to be sure, slave shepherds and cultivators, but the peasantry had simply vanished. A century later, Propertius could even describe Veii, the most celebrated of Rome's Etruscan rivals, as completely abandoned.[22] At first glance, therefore, this would appear to have been one of the regions that our sources have in mind when they talk in such global terms about the deracination of the Italian countryside. If this is in fact the case, however, then what these sources have conveyed to us is at best a half-truth. When he traversed the region in 137, Tiberius will have taken either the via Flaminia, Cassia or Aurelia – paved highways that furnished direct access to Rome's burgeoning markets. Given the high cost of land transport in peninsular Italy,[23] it seems reasonable to assume that the concentration of land immediately adjoining these roads had already advanced sufficiently for it to catch Tiberius' attention, and it was probably proceeding at a similar pace in the valley of the Tiber as well.[24] Still, along the steep ridges that lay between these highways Tiberius would have encountered a wholly different pattern of landholding. It is here that we enter the domain of the subsistence cultivator, and it is important to note that it was not until the second century AD that the population of the district finally reached its apogee. By this date, even the most marginal and inaccessible land had been brought under cultivation, and we come across holdings that are reminiscent of the tiny *fundus* of Spurius Ligustinus. Along the Monte Forco ridge in the *ager Capenas*, for example, G.D.B. Jones directs our attention to a series of five farms, none of which was appreciably larger than the rest:

> The ridge crest is in some places no more than ten metres wide and this makes it difficult to see that any of the farms possessed a cultivable holding larger than 10 *iugera*. Taking into account the very steep slopes on either side, which in places would only have served as a foraging ground for pigs and goats, the amount of workable ground available to most of the farms in question was probably nearer half that figure.[25]

For the anonymous inhabitants of these five sites, life was unquestionably hard, and unfortunately there were no longer lucrative wars of conquest to generate a supplemental income. It is, then, probably not mere coincidence that, like Veleia and Ligures Baebiani, Capena established an alimentary program.[26]

Thus the modest holdings that Mommsen inferred at Ligures Baebiani have also left their trace in southern Etruria – and not simply in the *ager Capenas*.[27] It was this archaeological material that induced Martin Frederiksen to conclude that 'a large belt of territory in the immediate neighbourhood of Rome was in the hands of small farmers, or at least of small holdings.'[28] This finding, it should now be clear, requires modification in only one important respect: these peasant farmsteads were not evenly distributed across the Etrurian landscape, but tended to cluster on marginal soil in zones well removed from the major highways and natural lines of communication and trade.

It is also, then, in the most rugged and remote portion of the *territorium* of Ligures Baebiani that we would logically expect to confront the smallholders to whom Mommsen first drew our attention. This is certainly where we find them across the mountains, in Apulia's Biferno valley. At the end of the Republic, and throughout the first two centuries AD, the lower reaches of the valley witnessed a steady concentration of land into larger units, and it has been suggested that soil previously devoted to intensive polycultural farming was now employed for the grazing of sheep. In the upper valley, however, and especially in the area around Larinum, small farmsteads proved far more tenacious, and their proprietors applied themselves without interruption to an economy that combined stock-raising with the cultivation of vegetables and cereals.[29] Archaeologists have also reported a dense concentration of small farms in a centuriated area to the east of Luceria, another Apulian community. Here the individual units seem to have been about 10 *iugera* in size,[30] and at Samnite Venafrum as well, cultivators on this scale must have been continually in evidence. Cicero describes the whole surrounding district as *plena virorum fortissimorum*, and a century earlier the elder Cato took it for granted that underemployed *rustici* would be ready to hand in this same region whenever circumstances called for the hiring of casual labor.[31]

The evidence for the survival of the Italian peasantry into the second century AD is, therefore, impressively diverse in character, and in the places and times to which it applies. Clearly, then, the received (and still popular) tradition that Roman imperialism resulted in the systemic destruction of the free smallholder, and his replacement with slave labor, requires significant modification.[32] At the same time, however, one must also avoid exaggerating the numbers of these invisible *rustici*. The fact that small farmers were still to be found in the upper Biferno valley during the early Empire, for example, serves only to dramatize the fact that they were systematically displaced by large estates in the lower valley. Further to the south, in Magna Graecia, there is a sharp decline in the number of rural sites in the lower Bradano valley after the third century BC – a pattern that seems to repeat itself throughout the hinterland of Metapontum.[33] A fundamental shift in the pattern of land use, from cultivation to the pasturage of sheep and goats, has been suggested, and this might also account for the similar paucity of Roman material in the countryside around Croton, Heraclea and Tarentum.[34] The literary record also suggests that some of the Etrurian coastal towns, such as Volaterrae, had suffered massive depopulation by the end of the Republic, but it is Latium above all that gives meaning to the celebrated phrase *solitudo Italiae*. With varying degrees of specificity, a number of authors make reference to the desolate state of once-proud cities such as Tusculum and Aricia: perhaps the most telling comment comes from the younger Pliny, who casually describes the area around Laurentum as teeming with flocks of sheep and herds of horses and cattle.[35] In the case of Eretum, the available archaeological data reinforce the literary portrait. Surface surveys indicate that the *ager Eretanus* was steadily absorbed into estates that averaged some 500 *iugera* in size, and at some point in the early Empire, one of these properties actually displaced the town of Eretum itself.[36]

It would appear, then, that smallholders were not uniformly at risk throughout peninsular Italy, nor can it even be claimed that mere proximity to a major city played a decisive role in determining their fate. In the case of Rome, for example, while the *rustici* seem to have disappeared completely from the Latin plain, they not only survived but apparently proliferated on the far more rugged Etrurian landscape to the immediate north of the city. Rather, the evidence currently at our disposal seems to suggest that the most vulnerable peasants were those who lived on land adjacent to highways or navigable rivers that provided efficient access to urban markets, or in zones that were amenable to large-scale pastoral enterprises. Conversely, far less risk attached itself to those who lived in areas that were not conducive to the grazing of large herds of cattle or flocks of sheep – and, surprising as it might seem, to those in districts that came to be dominated by *villae rusticae* specializing in viticulture or other capital-intensive modes of agricultural investment. At Pompeii, it has been remarked, there were many small farmsteads interspersed among the larger estates;[37] it was here that the local magnates undoubtedly found much of the occasional labor that the elder Cato, as we have now seen, looked upon as indispensable during the harvest season. In fact, once the truly symbiotic nature of the relationship between the smallholder and these well-to-do villa owners is placed in its proper perspective, then one may readily posit the continuing existence of large numbers of peasants in much of peninsular Italy during the late Republic and early Empire.[38]

It is thus quite likely that many, and perhaps even a majority, of the *rustici* lived in an essentially timeless environment that was largely unaffected by the dramatic expansion of the *imperium Romanum*. In this setting, many peasant women who lost husbands and fathers – and widows and orphans were sufficiently numerous in Roman society to warrant separate classification in the census[39] – may well have stayed on the land. Remarriage obviously suggests itself as a possibility, with the parcel of land and its *instrumenta* forming an impressive dowry, but there are other alternatives that warrant consideration as well. The still popular belief that a conscript's family was especially vulnerable to violent expropriation during his absence, for example, rests not only on a vague remark in Sallust but also on an implicit assumption that such households were nuclear units with but a single adult male in residence. The multi-generational vertically extended household to which Dio Chrysostomus introduces us in his Euboeic discourse, however, and the still more famous but similarly structured *familia* of the Aelii Tuberones, should serve to remind us that there were other forms of household organization.[40] Moreover, even in nuclear families the death or protracted absence of the *rusticus* would not have inevitably resulted in unendurable economic distress for his wife and children. By the time that he had completed 22 *stipendiae*, Livy tells us, Spurius Ligustinus had four adult sons still living at home – more than enough labor to keep his *fundus* cultivated while he was away on campaign. At an earlier point in the marriage, when these children were still small, his wife would probably have resorted to their underemployed kinsmen for any additional help that she might require: in fact, keeping in mind that Ligustinus and his bride were agnatic first cousins, it is quite conceivable that the two households were physically adjacent to one another.[41]

Nevertheless, it is not only clear that smallholders were systematically displaced from some parts of the peninsula but that an indeterminate number of widows and orphans were thrown back on their own resources in the process. We have already referred to the public execution of several of the female participants in the Bacchanalian scandal, who lacked kinsmen or *tutores* to whom they could be surrendered for punishment in private.[42] We have also seen that this highly unusual event conforms with the institutional evidence, and above all with the provisions of the *lex Atilia* that governed the appointment of a *tutor* for any woman who became *in nullius manu*.[43] Naturally, it is impossible to pinpoint all of the circumstances that might produce this anomalous legal situation; still, on the basis of the evidence that has now passed in review, it does seem safe to conclude that the heaviest concentration of women and children thus affected were those whose husbands and parents were drawn off by Rome's transmarine warfare. One may also reasonably conclude that, within this broad group of women and children who lacked masculine protection, those who were most threatened with expropriation were to be found precisely in Latium. It was their land that was most coveted by generations of the elite, and for which the evidence speaks most clearly of massive depopulation and concentration of property. It was from this district that the rural poor might most easily immigrate to Rome, and attract the attention of the senatorial politician. Thus in 187 BC, responding to a request from the Latins themselves, the Senate expelled 12,000 of their citizens from the capital – a step that was repeated in 177 and 173.[44] It is, of course, not at all likely that the Latin ambassadors were eager to reclaim widows and orphans, but it is highly probable that these are the unwilling and impoverished refugees from the countryside for whom, according to our sources, Tiberius Gracchus later evinced such great sympathy and concern.

Nor would these emotions have been misplaced, for the admittedly sketchy evidence that can be brought to bear strongly suggests that, once removed from the land, peasant women would have found it exceptionally difficult to obtain gainful employment. Quite apart from the stiff competition increasingly offered by imported slave labor, there was also a deeply rooted prejudice to be overcome, namely the universally endorsed assumption that the gods had fashioned woman as a domestic helpmate for man. In the preface to the twelfth book of his *De Re Rustica*, which is largely concerned with the duties of the *vilica*, Columella succinctly expresses this attitude when he writes that

> god has allotted to man the ability to withstand heat and cold, long journeys, and the toils of peace and war – that is to say, agriculture and military service. To woman, however, whom he made unfit for all these matters, he has entrusted the supervision of domestic affairs. Indeed, since he had assigned to this sex the functions of guardianship and care, for this very reason he also made woman more timid than man, recognizing that fear contributes a great deal to scrupulous stewardship.[45]

Columella found this sentiment fully elaborated in a Ciceronian translation of Xenophon's *Oeconomicus*, which reveals something of its impeccable pedigree, but it must be stressed that for once we are in the presence of an outlook that the elite had in common with other strata of Roman society. Natalie Kampen has noted, for example, that the same poses and gestures are attributed to male and female vendors in commercial and funerary iconography; in the case of artisans, however, formal distinctions between the two sexes are painstakingly maintained. Male craftsmen are typically located in a realistic setting, while with but few exceptions female artisans are situated in an allegorical or mythological context. It is hard to resist her conclusion that this artistic distinction gives visual expression to a fundamental conviction: for women, there was only one suitable workplace, and that was their own homes.[46]

It should hardly occasion surprise, therefore, to learn that the skills acquired by these peasant women – indeed, by the overwhelming majority of the female members of Roman society in all periods – were purely domestic. In this regard our sources, both poetic and prose, admit of no exceptions whatsoever. Thus our most detailed source, Columella, emphasizes that the *vilica* (and, by extension, the farm-wife) was responsible for sweeping the house and cleaning out the pens – tasks that, more than two centuries earlier, Plautus and the elder Cato assigned to her as well.[47] Predictably, these and other sources also make her responsible for the preparation of meals, which involved not only cooking but also grinding meal, preserving fruits and vegetables, tending the henhouse, milking the animals, and even apparently chopping firewood.[48] A third major area of responsibility centered on the manufacture of clothing, although it is by no means clear that this ever assumed the dimensions of a cottage industry.[49] Plautus counted spinning and weaving among the domestic skills, and it is well known that the emperor Augustus arranged for his daughter and granddaughters to be taught how to spin and weave; indeed, he even made a point of wearing home-spun garments. In an epitaph from roughly the same period, *lanificium* is one of the virtues attributed to the well-to-do Murdia, along with *modestia, probitas, pudicitia, obsequium, diligentia* and *fides*.[50] Columella sadly remarks that in his day (the middle of the first century AD) wool-working was held in contempt by the typical noblewoman, but this only meant that henceforth it would be the duty of the *vilica* to superintend the production of clothing on the estate, and Columella fully expected that she would be competent to perform the work as well. In the third century AD, wool-working could still be counted among the virtues of a deceased freedwoman – just as, more than four hundred years before, it could be said in praise of a certain Claudia that 'she kept to her house and worked her wool' (*domum servavit, lanam fecit*).[51]

Columella also makes the *vilica* responsible for the health of the slaves attached to an estate, and it is inherently probable that every peasant wife could draw upon a vast store of folk remedies that emphasized herbal cures for both illness and injury.[52] Some practical experience in mid-wifery must have been especially commonplace, although here the folk practices that have come down to us would have been ineffectual at best, and often would have placed the mother's life at risk.[53] Finally, we may take it for granted that these women were also active in the physically taxing but indispensable chore of harvesting plants in the wild; these provided food for the table, and could also be exchanged in the local marketplace for such vital commodities as salt and iron.[54]

The setting in which a displaced *rustica* could put these skills to fullest use would obviously be as a *vilica* on one of the estates in the neighborhood, and we do hear of a few women serving in this capacity who may have been free-born.[55] The agricultural writers, however, take it for granted that the *vilica* will be a slave, and we must accordingly assume that any *ingenua* whom we encounter in this position was the product of unusual circumstances. Casual labor, particularly in the harvest season, would have offered more widespread opportunities to women already inured to such hard work. There is a passing reference in Dio Chrysostomus to women hired to pick grapes, and this converges nicely with a recurrent feature of the excavation reports from Pompeii. Here agricultural tools are continually being discovered, in shops and nondescript houses as well as the residences of the municipal elite. Their owners, as Frederiksen rightly concluded, either had small garden plots outside the city, or took their own tools with them when they found work further out in the countryside.[56]

Still, one could hardly hope to eke out even the barest existence solely from the proceeds of such seasonal labor. More reliable employment would have to be found, and this was the imperative that drove men and women alike to abandon the country for the cities.

THE PLEBS URBANA

Maidservants

Although Dio Chrysostomus casually remarks that a woman who worked as a hired servant did not thereby dishonor herself, it is in fact difficult to see how peasant women could have put their housekeeping experience to fruitful use in an urban setting. In the great aristocratic households of the early Empire – and presumably in the last century of the Republic as well – the ability to read and write defined one category of personal attendant, which was comprised of readers (*lectrices, anagnostriae*), secretaries (*amanuenses, notariae*) and scribes (*librariae*). There is no evidence to indicate widespread literacy among the rural poor (nor, for that matter, among their urban counterparts), hence it is hardly surprising that there are no *ingenuae* to be found among the sixteen women so classified in inscriptions from the city of Rome.[57]

Women who practiced skills that called for formal training make up a second category. Here one encounters masseuses (*unctrices*), beauticians (*tractatrices*), barbers (*tonstrices*) and hairdressers (*ornatrices*). The corpus of inscriptions yields the names of only four masseuses and beauticians in Rome, and all were slaves.[58] The number of barbers and hairdressers on record is much larger – there are forty-four for Rome alone – but of these fully twenty-seven were slaves, and a further thirteen were freedwomen. The status of the remaining four must be listed as uncertain, but at the same time it has to be emphasized that we know of no free-born women who were employed in these jobs.[59] The sole reference to *ornatrices* in Roman law also presumes slave status, while Ovid and Juvenal both suggest that hairdressers were among the *servae* most likely to be physically abused by their wealthy mistresses.[60] Indeed, the vast majority of these professionals seem to have served exclusively in aristocratic households: although Plautus and Martial both refer to *tonstrices* who had their own shops, only three of the forty-six relevant Roman inscriptions are dedicated to women of this sort.[61] All three, it should be added, were freedwomen, but even if they had been indisputably free-born, they would in all likelihood have been of urban and libertine ancestry. There is, in short, nothing in our sources to suggest that these skills were ever a part of the domestic training of a *rustica*.

Finally, it should also be noted that there were a variety of female attendants in these large urban *familiae* who staffed unskilled positions, and it might be thought that an *ingenua* could find employment in one of these capacities. Roman noblewomen needed servants to fold their clothes (*vestiplicae/vestispicae*), to serve food (*ministrae*), and especially to escort them when they went out in public (*pedisequae*). Once again, however, in the city of Rome itself there are five female clothes-folders, five serving-women, one female doorkeeper (*ostiaria*) and nineteen *pedisequae* whose funerary inscriptions have survived; without exception, these appear to have been either slaves or freedwomen. Natalie Kampen comments that 'there seems little chance that anyone other than a slave or client would take on such utterly subordinate work, nor would a wealthy woman be likely to pay wages to a free *pedisequa* with a life separate from her employer's interests.' The latter of these two observations appears intrinsically more likely than the first; there was, however, still another practical consideration that must have often caused these humble tasks to be set aside for female slaves, and particularly new additions to the household. Since the demeanor, and in many instances the talents of these *servae* would have been unknown, their performance in an undemanding position must have often been used to gauge whether or not they were fit for promotion to more challenging duties.[62]

Craftswomen

Despite the fact that the relevant epigraphic data derive for the most part from the late Republic and early Empire, it seems equally clear that peasants of either sex were even less likely to find employment in the workshops of Rome, Pompeii, or the many other towns and cities of post-Hannibalic Italy. This is most obvious in the

118

case of crafts associated with the burgeoning luxury trade, which at all times called for both aptitude and long training. We know of one child, Viccentia, who was already spinning gold thread (*auri netrix*) when she died at the age of 9; since her legal status is uncertain, we cannot tell whether she was being trained by her parents, or had been apprenticed by her owner.[63] A similar background is to be anticipated for such professionals as Sellia Epyre, an *auri vestrix* who maintained a shop on the via Sacra, as well as Thymele Marcella, who dealt in or worked with silk (*siricaria*).[64] For the purposes of this discussion, however, the most interesting of these highly specialized craftswomen are Fulvia Melema and the *liberta* Septicia Rufa. Both were involved in the production of gold leaf (*brattiariae*), and each was conjoined with a freed partner, Gaius Fulcinius Hermeros and Aulus Septicius Apollonius respectively. We may safely presume that Septicius Apollonius was either Rufa's *patronus* or her *collibertus*; in either event, there is a strong possibility that the couple was married. There would have been nothing unusual in this: the tendency for female artisans to be paired with men in the inscriptions, many of whom were clearly their husbands, has often aroused comment.[65] In tandem with the ambivalence of the occupational terminology, however, it does pose one major difficulty that is most clearly illustrated by two paintings at the entrance to the dye shop of the *purpurarius* Verecundus, on Pompeii's Via dell' Abbondanza. The scene on the right doorpost shows seven workers engaged in various stages of the cloth-dying process, with an eighth figure (presumably Verecundus) holding up the finished product for display. On the left doorpost, in contrast, the scene centers on a woman who sits behind a low table exhibiting her wares (plates 1–2). This points to a division of labor between craftsmen and saleswomen, and it compels us to ask whether the various individuals registered above were in fact artisans (this is clear only in the case of the 9-year-old Viccentia), or simply retailed finished products that the men turned out in a workroom at the back of the shop.[66] The question is of critical importance, for if there was such a formal or informal division of labor, then the gravest obstacle blocking the path of a displaced peasant seeking work in the city would not have been the absence of acquired skills but the family orientation of the Italian crafts industry.[67]

In certain professions, it is simply not possible to determine whether women were producers or retailers. Thus in another shop along the via Sacra, four freedmen and one freedwoman

(Babbia Asia) specialized in the delicate job of cutting gem-stones (*gemmarii*). Here again, we are dealing with a tightly knit group of servile origin, and one may well suspect that the *gemmaria* was a saleswoman, but there is no evidence to prove the point. There are some occupations, however, in which it is reasonably safe to assume that women sold the finished product and nothing more. Here we enter, *inter alia*, the prosaic realm of the Dalmatian *plumbaria* Aurelia Vernilla. Although Kampen takes her to be a lead worker, it should be noted that her husband's name also appears on the tombstone in question, which rightly persuaded Le Gall to list her as 'certainement un commercante qui se contentait de vendre du plomb à qui en avait besoin.'[68] Other spousal combinations worthy of note in this context include the free-born *clavarius* P. Aebutius and his wife, the *liberta* Cornelia Venusta; she is identified as a *clavaria*, but all this probably means is that she sold the nails that her husband forged.[69] A similar division of labor may be suspected in the case of the late imperial *aurifex* (goldsmith) Masumilla, who was in business with a certain Severinus, but the most enlightening example of all is supplied by three apparently related libertine couples in the purple cloth trade. The first couple are the late-Republican *purpuraria* Veturia Fedra and her *collibertus*, D. Veturius Nicepor. Their shop was in the area around the monuments of Marius; in the early Empire, Veturia Tryphera and her husband D. Veturius Atticus plied this trade on the vicus Iugarius, while L. Plutius Eros and Plutia Auge, who dedicated an inscription to a Veturia Attica, were in business on the nearby vicus Tuscus. There is no more vivid example of the two features that seem to characterize so much of the Italian *artisanat* – servile roots, and familial organization.[70]

In sum, therefore, the doubts that we have raised about the participation of women in the crafts industry apply to virtually every inscription in which women are given a professional title suggesting a role in production. We may suitably conclude by drawing attention to the four *unguentariae* whose names have come down to us. The husband of one woman lavishly praises her in a verse inscription, but we still cannot tell whether she was involved in the production of perfume, its sale, or both. Two other women of uncertain status, the Ummidiae, are associated with a like-named Ummidius who could easily have been their *patronus* or *collibertus*, hence their roles must be considered similarly unclear.[71] Indeed, there are only three women in the entire corpus of evidence at our disposal of whom it can be said with certainty that they actually worked in a trade – the Ostian shoe-maker (*sutrix*) Septimia [Stra]tonice, and two freedwomen from Rieti, the Fonteiae Fausta and Gnome, who were employed as bakers (*furnariae*).[72]

Saleswomen

When we focus our attention upon tradeswomen, there does not appear to be any appreciable divergence from this pattern of libertine status and shared responsibility, with its household connotations. One freedwoman who dealt in incense, Hilara, is paired with a *libertus* who is probably her husband. Two other freed *thurariae* (the Treboniae, Irena and Ammia) were in business with no less than five freedmen; these seven individuals had all been emancipated by three different but clearly related Trebonii, and one would like to know a great deal more about the intricacies of their relationships with each other as well as with their *patroni*.[73] Among wives who are associated with their husbands, we also find the seed dealer (*seminaria*) Atinia Tyrannis; Aulia Hilaritas, who dealt in preserved foods (*conditaria*); the anonymous *negotiatrix oleariae et vini ex provincia Baetica*; the Narbonensian *negotiatrix* Leo; and Abudia Megiste, the libertine *negotiatrix frumentariae et legumenariae ab scala Mediana*.[74] Another freedwoman, the fishmonger (*piscatrix*) Aurelia Nais, is conjoined with her *patronus* Aurelius Phileros, but we cannot determine whether he is also her husband.[75] Indeed, the inscriptions furnish only three clear cases of tradeswomen who are not linked with one or more men, namely the barley dealer Pollecla, the Spanish cloth-seller (*lintearia*) Fulvia, and the Pompeian money-lender (*faeneratrix*) Faustilla.[76]

The clothing industry

The one conspicuous exception to this otherwise uniform pattern of libertine production and trade lies, as might logically be expected, in the Roman equivalent of the modern garment industry. The manufacture of clothing was, as we have already seen, the only marketable skill that virtually every free-born Roman girl could expect to master and put to extensive use throughout her adult life. Some *ingenuae* clearly produced or repaired clothing in a commercial setting: the jurists take it for granted that an action for damages can be brought against a sewer (*sarcinatrix*) or weaver (*textrix, staminaria*), and it does not matter whether she is free-born or a slave.[77] In the literary sources, there are also recurrent allusions to *ingenuae* engaged in piece-work; the most celebrated passage of Roman vintage is to be found in Pausanias, who remarks that in Patrae there were so many women employed as weavers that they heavily outnumbered the men in the town. The majority of these authors also comment upon the physically demanding character of the tasks involved, and without exception they suggest that poverty alone could compel a woman to undertake such arduous work.[78]

The largest body of garment workers that we know by name are the eleven women employed as *staminariae* in the Pompeian workshop of M. Terentius Eudoxus. Their status is uncertain, but the two female weavers whose epitaphs have survived in Rome were clearly of servile origin.[79] One of these tombstones derives from the monumentum Statilorum; we possess a significant number of inscriptions from this source that suggest a deep involvement on the part of the Statilii in the commercial production of clothing during the Julio-Claudian period. Fully eight of the eleven spinners (*quasillariae*) on record in Rome, for example, were slaves in this household; the other three women also appear to have been *servae*, one of them in the *familia Caesaris*.[80] The funerary inscriptions of three slave-women employed by the Statilii as *sarcinatrices* have come down to us as well, and it is distinctly possible that their services were for hire. In each instance, the name of the *dominus* is omitted from the text – in sharp contrast to the slave and freedwomen serving in this capacity in the various branches of the imperial household, who seem to have restricted their activities to repairing clothes for their fellow servants.[81] Most of the other *sarcinatrices* who appear in the inscriptions must be registered as *incertae*, but it should again be pointed out that there are no securely attested *ingenuae* on this list, and it is quite likely that all of the *incertae* in question enjoyed servile or libertine status.[82]

It is equally worth remarking that, in the few cases outside the monumentum Statilorum where the inscriptions permit us to identify a garment worker in a commercial setting, the libertine pattern that we have previously established immediately asserts itself. This is especially obvious in the case of Cameria Iarine, a freedwoman who either specialized in the production of linen clothing, or who retailed garments worked up by her husband and *collibertus*, Lucius Camerius. The husband and wife are styled *vestiarii tenuiarii*, and maintained a shop on the heavily commercialized vicus Tuscus. Another *liberta*, Avillia Philusa, is similarly conjoined with four freedmen in a consortium of *vestiarii de Cermalo minusculo*.[83] Finally, we even encounter a professional *sarcinatrix* from the Six Altars, the *liberta* Matia Prima; one imagines that she received her training from the anonymous *domina* who emancipated her.[84]

In conclusion, then, since free-born women engaged in the commercial production of clothing continue to surface in literary and legal sources of imperial date, we may certainly presume that in the post-Hannibalic period at least some of the displaced *rusticae* would have been able to support themselves by doing piece-work. Nevertheless, freedwomen and even slave-staffed enterprises of the type associated with the Statilii would have offered increasingly stiff competition during the ensuing generations, above all in Rome itself. Given the dearth of relevant inscriptions for the last century and a half of the Republic's existence, we cannot follow this economic conflict in any detail. It is at least clear, however, that the pattern described above, which was firmly established in the early Empire, took shape during the Republican period.[85] Hence the singular absence of *ingenuae* in the epigraphic data may once again be something more than mere coincidence: there is a strong possibility that they were unable to arrange for commemorative inscriptions because they were the most impoverished segment of the work-force in this industry, and thus unable to afford them.

Mid-wives

Some peasant women may similarly have been able to trade upon their practical experience as mid-wives (*opstetrices*), although in Rome itself this profession also seems to have come increasingly under the domination of women who received their training in the great aristocratic households. One of the chapters of the *lex Aquilia*, a *plebiscitum* that scholars generally date to the third century BC, apparently defined the liability of mid-wives for malpractice; shortly thereafter, Plautus has one of his characters complain about the high prices that *opstetrices* charge for their services.[86] In tandem, these two passages make it clear that professional mid-wives were to be found in post-Hannibalic Rome; indeed, if the *lex Aquilia* is in fact to be dated to the early third century, mid-wifery may rank among the earliest professions undertaken by women in Roman society. Nevertheless, it is most unlikely that many of its practitioners could have met the high standards set by the physician Soranus, particularly in the Italian countryside. He believed that an accomplished *opstetrix* must be literate, free from superstition, keen-witted, blessed with a good memory, in full possession of her various faculties, physically fit, and have soft hands. Here he specifically excludes women who work with wool: this would cause their hands to become calloused, and further add to the discomfort of their patients. With regard to her character, he goes on to say that a mid-wife should remain aloof from gossip, be at all times sober and virtuous, and above all avoid venality, a flaw that might easily induce her covertly to administer an abortifacient for a price. This was, however, precisely the crime for which the *lex Aquilia* sought to define punitive damages, hence one must wonder how many of these *opstetrices* were superstitious and corrupt, to say nothing of the other deficiencies that Soranus catalogs![87]

During the early Empire – once again the period from which most of our epigraphic evidence derives – fully qualified mid-wives may have been more commonplace, especially in the larger towns and cities. The *Corpus Inscriptionum Latinarum* registers the names of twenty-five *opstetrices*, and it is certainly possible that the four slave- and freedwomen who attended members of the imperial family met all of Soranus' exacting requirements.[88] Similarly high standards may well have applied within other wealthy households, where mid-wives were also a part of the permanent staff.[89] Some of these *libertae* eventually established their own private practices, as we see in the case of Grattia Hilara, an *opstetrix a Monte Esquilino*.[90] The eight *incertae* were in all probability independent professionals as well, and some of them may have been of free birth. This has been claimed, for example, in the case of Claudia Trophime, whose tomb was dedicated by her son and grandson, T. Cassius Trophimus and Ti. Cassius Trophimianus respectively.[91] It is conceivable that Valeria Syre and Autronia Fortunata, whose tombstones were erected by children who give evidence of their free birth, were also *ingenuae*.[92] It should not, however, be taken for granted that ingenuous mid-wives were themselves the daughters of free-born citizens, much less that they immigrated to cities such as Rome from the surrounding countryside. It is equally possible that they received their training from libertine mothers in the same profession; three pieces of evidence clearly demonstrate that medicine, like retail trade and the *artisanat*, could be a family enterprise. In the Isola Sacra necropolis, the door of one of the chamber tombs is flanked by a pair of terracotta reliefs that show a mid-wife attending a birth, and a physician treating a patient's leg. The *medicus* is M. Ulpius Merimnus – a name suggestive of libertine status – and the figure of the *opstetrix* represents either Scribonia Attice, her anonymous mother, or both (plates 4–5). The second piece of evidence is a Pergamene inscription dedicated to a doctor named Panthia by Glycon, her husband and fellow physician. A third inscription, this time from North Africa, similarly conjoins a *medicus* (Faustus) and an *opstetrix* (Irene). Panthia was obviously free-born, while Irene was in all probability Faustus' slave, but the jural status of the two Ostian women remains uncertain.[93]

Still, this should not obscure the seminal point: the possibility must always be taken into consideration that women who practiced some aspect of medicine in an urban setting, especially during the imperial period, either received their training inside an aristocratic *familia*, or from one or both parents, who themselves may have been trained in this milieu. If, therefore, some of the *rusticae* expropriated from their smallholdings in Latium during the second century BC were able to support themselves as *opstetrices* in Rome, here again they would have encountered increasing competition from freedwomen, whose credentials must on the whole have been superior to those of their rural counterparts. It would probably be imprudent, however, to place too much emphasis on this last point. If we simply keep in mind that Roman society was at all times and in all places and classes rife with superstition, then it should be obvious that there would always have been a market for country women who practiced the traditional techniques which Soranus obliquely decries, in the cities as well as the countryside. Indeed, we cannot even claim with any certainty that the popularity of these superstitious methods waned over the course of time.[94]

Physicians

These conclusions probably apply with equal force to the small group of female physicians (*medicae/iatromeae*) for whom we have an epigraphic record. In addition to Panthia, we know of at least four other free-born women who practiced medicine during the Principate, all of them resident in the provinces. A short inscription from Cilicia Trachea records a second husband-and-wife team (Obrimos and Ammeis), while the Galatian community of Neoclaudiopolis has supplied us with the name of Domnina; she was commemorated by her husband, who chose to omit his own name from the text. There is nothing to indicate that he was her colleague as well as her spouse, so we must probably look elsewhere for the source of her training. This is equally true in the case of Antiochis, who was honored by the council and people of Lycian Tlos. Since she personally commissioned a statue to mark the occasion, it seems fair to assume that she was not even married. Finally, we are similarly uninformed with regard to the family background and personal history of the African physician Asyllia L.f. Polia.[95]

When we turn to Italy, however, and especially to Rome, the vast majority of the female physicians are once again either slaves or freedwomen. We may take it as a given that those who attended members of the imperial family received their training inside the *familia Caesaris* itself, and the more well-to-do senatorial houses may also have had *medicae* who passed on their knowledge and skills to servile apprentices.[96] What is more surprising is the number of slave or libertine medical practitioners who demonstrably were not associated with elite households. In Rome alone, we meet with five such individuals, and in each instance it is to be presumed that the woman either began her career as a medical apprentice, or gradually and less formally developed her skills by assisting her owner in a medical setting. This latter explanation seems particularly appropriate for the Terentiae, Nice and Prima, who both worked as *medicae* after obtaining their freedom. Two other freed physicians, Minucia Aste and Venuleia Sosis, were emancipated by female owners, and it is certainly possible that their former mistresses were doctors as well.[97] Italy at large adds two more names to this roster: Sentia Aste, whose conjugal partner commemorated her as his *contubernalis*; and Iulia Sabina, whose husband was also her *collibertus*.[98]

Five female physicians remain, all but one of them an *incerta*. Iulia Pye and Valia Calliste are little more than names, but the free birth of Primilla is clearly recorded on her tombstone. Since she died at the age of 44, and at her death had been married to L. Cocceius Apthorus for thirty years, it seems obvious that she completed her medical training during the course of her marriage. Once again, however, there is absolutely nothing on the stone that would permit us to register either Cocceius or Primilla's father, L. Vibius Melito, as doctors in their own right, so her professional background is as mysterious as those of Domnina and Antiochus. Finally, these same doubts also surround the figures of Valeria Berecunda, *iatromea regionis suae prima*, and Scantia Redempta, *antistes disciplinae in medicina.* Although her daughter was certainly free-born, we still cannot determine whether Valeria was herself an *ingenua* or a freedwoman; it is, however, quite likely that Scantia was of free birth. She was commemorated by her parents, who somewhat maliciously remark that, with her death, her husband at once 'lost his wife, his own personal physician, and his principal source of revenue.'[99]

All of these women, it should be kept in mind, practiced medicine during the Principate, and many of them undoubtedly lived up to the demanding standards that prevailed within the imperial household. Even at this relatively late date, however, there were still healers to be found who relied on a far older and more primitive body of medical lore that utilized charms, incantations, exorcisms and the like to prevent or cure injuries and illness.[100] We have already referred to the exotic remedies recommended by the elder Cato, but two centuries later many members of the Roman aristocracy continued to regard superstition as the best form of preventive medicine. The elder Pliny tells us, for example, that C. Licinius Mucianus, who played such an instrumental role in Vespasian's rise to power and who was consul on three different occasions, prevented eye inflammation by placing a fly in a piece of white linen cloth and wrapping it around his neck. A generation earlier, the consul M. Servilius Nonianus (AD 35) similarly warded off eye disease by scratching the letters *rho* and *alpha* on a scrap of papyrus, which he then fastened around his neck with a piece of linen thread. Anecdotal evidence of this sort warrants the assumption that, just as in the field of obstetrics, there would have been ample opportunity at any time after the Second Punic War for peasant women steeped in the complexities of folk medicine to support themselves in Rome. Although professionally trained *medicae*, both freed and free-born, would again have offered considerable competition, and in the abstract would have employed more rational and effective procedures, in a society where so many people believed in the efficacy of magic one may legitimately doubt whether they were typically the healers of first choice.[101]

Wet-nurses

In any event, the impression remains that the number of women who were prepared to enter upon careers in medicine or obstetrics was probably at all times quite modest. In contrast, the sheer mass of data at our disposal makes it clear that many women did find work as wet-nurses (*nutrices*). This is not at all surprising: quite apart from the fact that childbirth often claimed the life of the mother, we must also take into consideration the many exposed infants who were picked up and reared as slaves. As Suzanne Dixon has rightly pointed out, these circumstances recurred with sufficient frequency that a Roman child could claim any woman who assumed responsibility for its upbringing – a mother, foster mother, grandmother or *nutrix* – as its *mamma*.[102]

At the present time, Latin inscriptions allude to or supply us with the names of one hundred and five *nutrices*, while the Egyptian papyri nicely complement this material by furnishing wet-nursing contracts whose detailed provisions are in striking conformity with the teachings of Soranus.[103] The latter describes the archetypical *nutrix* as a woman in her 20s or 30s who has given birth to two or three children of her own. She should, he says, be healthy, and have a large frame and ruddy complexion; more to the point, her breasts should be of medium size, soft and unwrinkled, and yield an overabundance of milk. With regard to her temperament, she should have sufficient self-control to refrain from, *inter alia*, intercourse and alcohol: it was commonly believed that these temptations reduced lactation, and caused the milk to spoil in the process. In addition, she should be even-tempered, tidy, and of a sympathetic nature – qualities that would serve to protect the infant from abuse or neglect. Finally and above all, she should be a Greek, so that the child would be exposed to the highest form of language from the very outset![104]

The anonymous author of the essay *De Liberis Educandis* also endorses this last point, and in Egypt at any rate, wet-nursing contracts routinely contained language requiring the *nutrix* to abstain from sexual relations for the duration of the agreement. Anyone who violated this particular clause, which was explicitly designed to protect the infant against spoilt milk, risked not only the loss of her wages but also severe punitive damages. Thus in 13 BC the ingenuous (but apparently unmarried) Didyma entered into a contract to nurse a foundling for sixteen months, at a monthly salary of 10 silver *drachmae* and 2 *cotylae* (a half-liter) of oil. She agreed to 'take proper care both of herself and the child, and neither to damage her milk, lie with a man, become pregnant, or nurse another child.' In the event that she violated any of these provisions, she was liable to return 150 percent of her wages, and to pay an additional 500 *drachmae* in damages. Married women, it might be added, were not accorded any special sexual privileges. In

9/8 BC a certain Diodora, who was both free-born and married, also agreed to nurse a foundling, this time for a period of two years. She received in compensation 8 silver *drachmae* and some modest gifts of food each month, in return for which she promised not 'to lie with a man, or to take any additional child, as her milk might then fail.'[105]

The extant Egyptian wet-nursing contracts lasted from six months to three years, and involved slaves as well as free-born and married women.[106] Although we would expect Latin contracts to be of similar duration, we do not in fact know the length of time for which any Roman *nutrix* was actually hired. It is, however, eminently clear that the social composition of the wet-nursing profession in Italy was identical to that of Egypt. During the latter stages of the Republic, for example, it already seems to have been taken for granted that the sons and daughters of the great aristocratic houses would be reared by slave nurses, and the contempt that many Roman moralists levelled against mothers who neglected their offspring in this manner did nothing to alter the situation.[107] No fewer than thirty-three of the *nutrices* who survive in Latin inscriptions are associated with aristocratic families (32 percent), and sixty-five of the sixty-eight women whose status can be ascertained were either slaves or freedwomen (95 percent). Two passages in the *Digesta* also allude to slave nurses; indeed, one of them uses the phrase *Stichus nutricis meae nepos liber esto* as a formulaic example of posthumous manumission.[108] Nevertheless, this great legal encyclopedia also refers in several places to hired nurses, and these legal passages merely supplement a still more impressive corpus of literary references that range from early in the second century BC to the late second century AD. One of these sources, the imperial scholar Festus, actually refers to a specific location in the Forum Holitorium as the *columna lactaria* – a place where one could apparently go and arrange to hire a suitable *nutrix*.[109] Clearly, then, Livia Benigna and the still more elusive Turtura C.f. – the only ingenuous wet-nurses whom we encounter in the Latin inscriptions – must represent a much larger body of women who supported themselves in this fashion.[110]

Self-evidently, no one could enter this profession unless she had recently given birth, so the number of expropriated *rusticae* who were prepared to take it up without delay was probably quite small. One cannot exclude the possibility, however, that a far larger number chose deliberately to become pregnant in order to qualify for this work. Alternatively, a woman may have become pregnant as an unintended consequence of working as a prostitute, and subsequently decided to turn to wet-nursing. Certainly, anyone who wanted to pursue wet-nursing as a full-time career had to commit herself to multiple pregnancies, so Soranus' description of the ideal *nutrix* as a woman with two or three children of her own is not at all unrealistic. It is rather the prohibition on sexual activity (if this aspect of the Egyptian contracts in fact had a wider application) that will have proved especially cumbersome. Bradley and others have emphasized the great hardships that the observance of celibacy would have inflicted upon a husband and wife, but it is the economic penalty that concerns us here. If a *nutrix* chose scrupulously to observe this clause in order to avoid the heavy financial loss that she risked by ignoring it, then it follows that a lengthy period of unemployment would ensue upon the termination of each agreement. In theory at least, she might have filled this hiatus by continuing in service as a dry-nurse (*nutrix assa*), or perhaps by giving the child its earliest educational instruction (*paedagoga*). The *literati* clearly expected the latter profession to attract the free-born poor, but it must also be conceded that, at least in the Egyptian wet-nursing contracts, there is no evidence for the transition from *nutrix* to *paedagoga* that the Roman authors open up as a possibility.[111] We must, therefore, suspect that the ban on sexual activity was widely ignored, or that *nutrices* found other means of employment during those periods when they were no longer lactating.

Mourners and gladiators

However exotic it may appear today, wet-nursing was by no means the only profession that allowed women to exploit their bodies for economic gain. Despite the ban that the Law of the Twelve Tables imposed on orchestrated displays of grief at Roman funerals, there seems to have been a considerable market for hired female mourners (*praeficae*) in the second century BC.[112] Female gladiators, it seems, also began to ply their trade at some point in the Republic. Until they were banned from the arena by Septimius Severus, free-born women were attracted to various forms of combat in sufficient numbers to inspire Juvenal to a vicious assault on their collective character. Nero and Domitian actually encouraged women to participate, and it is clear that such activity was by no means limited to Rome. We possess, in particular, a fragmentary Ostian inscription that refers to a gladiatorial exhibit funded by a *duumvir* named

Hostilianus: the program included female sword-fighters. The most important piece of evidence, however, is the recently discovered *senatusconsultum* from Larinum. This decree, which was passed in AD 19, prohibited men and women of senatorial or equestrian rank from appearing on stage or in the arena, and it mentions in passing a still earlier measure (AD 11) that had already applied this ban to all free-born women under the age of twenty. There is, it must be emphasized, nothing in the text to suggest that female gladiators were a recent innovation, nor does the literary tradition imply that a single scandalous episode led to the enactment of the first of these two laws.[113] We may assume, therefore, that prior to AD 11 adolescent *ingenuae* entered the arena, but predictably we can estimate neither their numbers nor the moment in time when they first appeared on the scene, much less their social origins. One could argue, for example, that the hard work to which *rusticae* were continually exposed would have made them peculiarly suitable for such a profession, but in the abstract it is equally if not more probable that the women in question were the daughters of freed gladiators, who had received their training from their fathers.[114]

Entertainers

The extension of this prohibition to the stage further implies that young free-born women found employment as actresses (*scaenicae*), and the evidence for the Republic does indeed suggest that theatrical performers began their careers at an early age. A variety of sources furnish us with the names of seventeen Republican and Augustan female stage entertainers (primarily mimes), and in three instances we are supplied with the woman's age at the moment of her death. The oldest was an *incerta* named Luria Privata, who passed away at the age of 19; the youngest, the *liberta* Eucharis, was saluted by her parents as *docta erodita paene Musarum manu* despite the fact that she died at fourteen. The third figure, Ecloga, was also still in her teens (18) – and despite recent claims to the contrary, she is the only person in this group for whom slave status is actually on record.[115] Indeed, the only other acknowledged freedwoman in the group is the notorious Volumnia Cytheris, whose affair with the triumvir Marcus Antonius exposed the latter to Cicero's caustic wit.[116] At least one Republican actress, the Sicilian Tertia, was certainly free-born, and it is quite likely that Antiodemis, the

Cypriote singer who travelled to Rome in the second century BC, was similarly of free birth.[117]

There is, then, no compelling reason to assume that Luria Privata, or any of the other eleven *incertae* on this list, were slaves or *libertae*. Cicero casually mentions that one of these actresses, Dionysia, earned the impressive sum of HS 200,000 from her work on stage, and a number of contracts from Roman Egypt show that entertainers could earn a respectable income even if they were limited to performing at local festivals. In one case, for example, a castanet dancer named Isidora agreed to perform for six days, together with two other dancers of her own choosing; this trio received 36 *drachmae* a day for their efforts, in addition to food and transport. In still another and more complex document, four flageolet players hired out their services for a period of seven days. They received two *drachmae* to cover the costs of their transportation, a daily wage of eighteen drachmas for each of the first six days of the contract, and six more in the form of a gratuity. These performers thus received a good deal more than was earned by weavers in Egypt – and such entertainers were everywhere and at all times in great demand (in Rome itself, the number of mime-actresses alone was sufficiently large that at some point they decided to organize themselves into a guild).[118] In the abstract, therefore, one would presume that the prospect of a regular income must have attracted free-born women with the requisite talents and physical appearance to the stage with some regularity. The early age at which at least some of these professionals began to undertake their training, however, raises the possibility that the Roman stage, like the Roman crafts industry and the modern circus, was in large part a family enterprise in which one generation passed on its skills and techniques to the next. This would easily account for the consistent reputation enjoyed by the *puellae Gaditanae*, whose erotic dance routines were so seductive that, as Martial puts it, 'they would have caused Hippolytus himself to masturbate.' The apprenticing of young children might also have been employed as a device to recruit new talent, and indeed Egypt once again supplies us with the illuminating example of an agreement in which a pupil's musical instruction is prearranged in the most elaborate detail.[119] Nevertheless, apprenticeships would have constituted little more than a variation on the basic theme of education within the family, in the sense that both would have served to deny mature women the formal training needed to master a particular skill and put it to highly lucrative use.

This is not to say, however, that *rusticae* would have found it impossible to obtain an entrée into one of the many artistic professions already to be encountered not only in Rome but also in towns large and small in the middle and late Republic. The parents of Eucharis went to great lengths to emphasize that their daughter was an entertainer of the highest class, who 'graced the games of the nobles with her dancing, and was the first to appear before the populace in a Greek play.' They wanted to make sure that no one would confuse her with dancers of a quite different sort, such as the pseudo-Virgilian tavern-keeper (*copa*) Syrisca. 'Practiced at the art of swaying her quivering limbs to the rhythm of the castanets, she dances round her smoke-filled tavern with a Greek scarf crowning her head, tipsy and obscene, shaking her noisy reeds against her elbow.' Horace, Juvenal and other authors of the imperial period considered entertainers on this level to be indistinguishable from prostitutes – a point of view repeatedly enunciated in the law codes.[120] At a still earlier date, Plautus and Terence both allude to slave prostitutes being trained in music, and during the Republic mime-actresses who appeared on stage at the *ludi Florales* were already stripping on demand. It is, then, hardly surprising that when one of Cicero's clients was excoriated for participating in the gang-rape of a young actress at Atina, he did not even bother to dispute the charge. The defendant had, he says, simply acted 'in accordance with a well-established tradition at staged events, above all in the country towns.'[121] At this level of society, while formal training in dance or music might have been an asset, it could hardly have been considered an indispensable qualification. Physical beauty and loose morals were more important, and some *rusticae* at least will have qualified on both counts.[122]

Bar-maids and waitresses

Actresses and dancing girls were not, of course, the only women whose activities lent themselves to prostitution. The jurists also ruled that the imperial legislation governing adultery did not necessarily apply to female innkeepers, much less to shopkeepers (*tabernariae*) – a position fully compatible with the Greek and Latin literary portrait of the *tabernaria* as a woman of loose morals.[123] The graffiti on the walls of Pompeii make it clear that this was not simply an upper-class prejudice, but at the same time they also suggest that the *tabernarius* might be an individual of equally dubious character. Here we are introduced, that is to say, to Amaryllis, a female weaver who was nicknamed the *fellatrix*, and at the same time to the fruit vendor Felix, who advertised the services of Mula and Fortunata on the walls of his shop. At 2 *asses*, it might be added, Fortunata charged what appears to have been the going rate for sexual services in this first-century port town.[124]

It was, however, precisely in Italy's cook-shops (*popinae*) and taverns (*cauponae*) that working women doubled most frequently as prostitutes (*meretrices*). Ulpian, we are told, legally defined a *meretrix* as 'any woman who openly sells herself, not only one who does so in a brothel but also if (as is often the case) she works in a shop, tavern or other place of business and does not preserve her modesty.'[125] The presumption that bar-maids and waitresses routinely prostituted themselves also underlies a pair of rulings issued by the emperors Alexander Severus and Constantine – and the epigraphic evidence not only validates this assumption but also reveals the antiquity of the practice. The single most celebrated document stems from Aesernia; here it is recorded that, among other expenses, an overnight guest at an inn consumed 1 *sextarius* of wine, bread and relishes worth 1 and 2 *asses* respectively, and purchased the sexual services of one of the bar-maids for 8 *asses*.[126] Predictably, however, the walls of Pompeii have proven to be far and away the richest source of information on this subject. *Futui copanam*, the anonymous author of one graffito laconically remarks: he was a customer in the *caupona* of Sotericus, on the heavily trafficked Via dell'Abbondanza (I,12,3), where a certain Valeria engaged in fellatio.[127] Further along this same boulevard, a woman named Asellina ran a bar that specialized in the serving of hot drinks (*thermopolium*); we know the names of three of her bar-maids – Aegle, Smyrina and Maria – and a particularly graphic phallic carving on the right doorpost at the entrance to the bar makes it clear that they were also available for sexual purposes (IX,11,2).[128] At a third establishment on this road, the *caupona* of Ermes (II,1,1.13), the customers were served by Palmyra. To some at least, she was more familiarly known as *sitifera* ('the randy animal'); one of her co-workers, whose name has not come down to us, bore the still more sexually explicit epithet of *culibonia* ('hot ass') – an undoubted allusion to her ready availability for anal intercourse.[129]

Would-be customers did not, however, have to restrict themselves to the city's principal avenues. Fortunata and Euplia plied their trade in the *caupona* of Phoebus, which was situated in the Vicolo del

Panettiere (VII,3,26–28). With evident pride, the latter tells us that 'she slept with the most virile of men, and dispatched them one and all' – a boast not at all unworthy of a woman who is described elsewhere as *laxa landicosa* ('the yawning cunt').[130] One visitor to the *caupona* of Euxinus, which was in the vicinity of the amphitheater (I,11,11), has left behind an equally expressive distich. 'Candida', he writes, 'has taught me to hate black women. I shall go on hating them, if I can, and if not, then I shall make love to them in spite of myself.'[131] With its dense concentration of facilities offering sexual gratification, it seems reasonable to conclude that the area around the Insula del Menandro actually constituted something akin to the modern 'red-light district'. The Casa del Menandro itself (I,10,4.15) was flanked by a brothel and a *caupona*; in the former, the *meretrices* Primilla and Ianuaria seem to have commanded a large following of satisfied customers (I,10,5). The floors above a nearby bar jointly managed by Afra Helpis and her husband Demetrius have revealed cubicles that were certainly used for purposes of prostitution, in part perhaps by the women who worked downstairs (I,2,18–19). Cicada, Fortunata, Mandata, Primigenia and Serena entertained their clients at the adjacent *thermopolium* of Innulus and Papilio (I,2,20.21), while a number of men have commemorated their visits to Quinta, who received them in an inn owned by Q. Mestrius Maximus and his wife Irene.[132] It is no wonder, then, that authors with such disparate purposes as Horace, Columella and Tacitus took it for granted that bars and cook-shops were synonymous with brothels, or that a passage in the *Digesta* seems to imply the availability of prostitutes at every country inn.[133]

Nevertheless, it would be extremely imprudent to assume that every woman who served food or wine doubled as a prostitute. The anonymous husband of the Tiburtine *popinaria* Amemone, for example, erected a funerary inscription praising her as a *coniunx sancta*. It is also worth pointing out that, in spite of the suggestive character of her name, there is nothing to indicate that the *seribibi* who frequented the *caupona* adjoining Pompeii's Casa dell'Orso expected Hedone to cater to their sexual desires (VII,2,44). The most salutary warning of all, however, stems once again from the Insula del Menandro. Here, in a *caupona* immediately adjacent to the *domus* itself (I,10,2.3), it is clear that two of the bar-maids, Capella Bacchis and Prima, were also *meretrices*; although the figure is no longer legible, the price that Prima charged for her favors was at one time scratched on the walls. One might, therefore, conclude that a third serving-girl, the *ancilla* Iris, was similarly for hire, but there is no compelling reason to interpret a graffito involving her in this way. A certain Severus, who was obviously a regular patron, aimed the following lines at one of his rivals:

> The weaver Successus loves Iris, a maidservant in this bar, but she does not care for him. Nonetheless, he continues to call on her, and she has taken pity (*commiseretur*) on him. A rival wrote this; farewell.

It is, perhaps, conceivable that the term *commiseretur* masks sexual activity reluctantly undertaken, but this is hardly the most natural interpretation of the verb, and it is only necessary if one assumes that all *popinariae* and *vinariae* were, without exception, *meretrices* as well.[134]

The emphasis that has so far been placed upon *cauponae*, *thermopolia* and *popinae* as centers of prostitution should not, of course, be allowed to obscure the fact that many of these establishments were managed by women. In addition to Asellina, whose *thermopolium* has already been mentioned in passing, the Pompeian inscriptions introduce us to Pherusa, the owner of a *caupona* in the neighborhood of the amphitheater and palaestra (III,6,1). She was active in local politics – a trait that she shared with Fortunata and Pollia, who tended bars on the Via Consolare (VI,3,18–20) and Via di Nola (V,2,17–20) respectively.[135] It was women of this sort that the jurists must have had in mind when they decided that the proprietresses of inns and taverns were not necessarily subject to the laws governing adultery. We may readily believe, therefore, that each of these four tavern keepers was free, and it might even be speculated that the Augustan legislation on adultery was a source of concern for some or all of their number. At the same time, however, it must also be pointed out that the relevant statutes applied to the free-born and the libertine alike. We cannot, then, legitimately presume that these women were *ingenuae*, and the graffiti naturally do not record their jural status. Hence while one may safely conclude that *ingenuae* could obtain employment as bar-maids and waitresses, it is simply not possible to determine whether free-born women managed bars and cook-shops in first-century Pompeii, much less whether displaced *rusticae* might have carved out niches for themselves in this business at a still earlier date. What is clear is that many of these enterprises were jointly managed by a husband and wife, and thus offer still another example of the pattern that we have previously discerned in the retail trade and crafts industries. Hence we cannot discount the possibility that many bars and restaurants were run as essentially household businesses, or that the women whom we see managing on their own were the wives, daughters or freedwomen of male entrepreneurs whose names have not come down to us. In short, the country woman who hoped to make a living in such a facility – be it a bar in the heart of Rome or an obscure country inn – may have been welcomed as a servant or prostitute, but equally may have found lack of capital and family connections serious obstacles to opening her own establishment.[136]

Prostitutes

Popinae, cauponae and the like were not the only places in which prostitutes were to be found in abundance. In Pompeii alone, twenty-two brothels (*lupanaria*) have been unearthed to date. While many were adjacent to or above *cauponae*, several were bordellos pure and simple. The largest of these, the *lupanar* of Africanus and Victor (VII.12.18–20), has yielded more than one hundred graffiti, along with the names of some twenty of the women who received clients in its many chambers.[137] These *cellae meretriciae* were extremely small and poorly ventilated, with masonry beds inadequately covered by a coarse mattress: in several of the cells, the beds still reveal indentations that were gradually deepened by clients who failed to take off their shoes.[138] A wide variety of literary sources, which are in clear agreement with this archaeological material, paint a somewhat fuller picture of cramped, dark and dirty cubicles, with grimy walls and soiled bedding, the air heavy with the smoke given off by lamps scattered among the unventilated chambers. Herein, we are told, everyone was welcome – *ingenui*, freedmen and slaves alike – so long as they could pay the price posted above the door to each cell. The *unguentarius* Phoebus was one of many satisfied customers in the *lupanar* of Africanus and Victor, but some brothels seems to have harbored an element of risk for those who visited the premises: the author of a Beneventine epitaph, at any rate, went to considerable pains to inform passers-by that the libertine madam Vibia Calybene had never resorted to defrauding her clients (*sine fraude aliorum*).[139]

We can identify seven of the women who worked in a *lupanar* on the Vicolo del Labirinto, near the Torre Decima (VI,11,16). A certain Timeles is by far the most interesting, for in one graffito she is styled *fellatrix* and in another *extaliosa* – clearly an allusion to anal intercourse.[140] These are the most circumstantial pieces of evidence that we possess for the range of activities undertaken by Pompeii's prostitutes, and they lead one to suspect that, as often as not, the considerable variations in price registered in the graffiti should be viewed as a comment on the variety of sexual services available rather than on the physical attractiveness or popularity of the individual *meretrix*. Above all, this would explain the different prices charged within a given brothel. We have already drawn attention to Felicla and Drauca; both worked in the *lupanar* of Africanus and Victor, but the former received 2 *asses* from one of her clients while the latter earned a *denarius*. We observe much the same thing in the *lupanar* of Somene – one of two in Pompeii under female management (IX,5,19). Here, we are told, Optata's fee also came to 2 *asses*, but at the same time her co-worker Spes was bringing in 9![141]

The women who worked the streets of Pompeii were no less active, and seem to have charged a similar range of prices. The Greek *meretrix* Eutychis – one of several whores who used the phrase *bellis moribus* to advertise her aptitude for love-making – charged 2 *asses* for her favors, while Attica demanded 16. Was she especially beautiful? Alternatively, did she cater to the needs of a select clientele with unusual preferences?[142] The scribbler who immortalized her did not bother to supply this information, but we are indebted to him nonetheless: without this and literally scores of other epigraphic references to the prostitutes who labored in the streets, brothels and bars of Pompeii, the many satiric passages describing their counterparts in Rome itself could never be accepted at face value. Here too, we are told, the *meretrix* sought out her customers in the streets, alleys and archways; prostitutes were also particularly in evidence around the city walls, and in the Subura. The latter, it should be noted, was the most densely populated district of the capital, and during the late Republic and early Empire came to be regarded as a veritable den of iniquity.[143] Rome's whores also lingered in and around the temples (especially those affiliated with the various eastern deities), marketplaces and public baths – and, if we may take Martial at his word, even plied their trade in the graveyards![144] They circulated as well among the crowds in attendance at the circus or theater, and found more permanent residence in the city's innumerable bars, cook-shops and brothels.[145] Despite their seeming ubiquity, however, in all of these sources there is nothing to suggest that the supply of *meretrices* ever outstripped demand. Rather, our Latin authors seem to imply that Rome's male populace had an insatiable need for their services. One might, of course, dismiss this as yet another example of the satiric penchant for exaggeration, but there is a more sensible explanation for this phenomenon. In Pompeii, the graffiti make it clear that slaves, and freed and free-born industrial workers, found prostitutes to be the most convenient, affordable and socially acceptable sources of sexual gratification. If we presume that they furnished the same sort of outlet for the far larger lower class of Rome, then this would nicely explain why the poets repeatedly refer to the high visibility of prostitutes in the Subura – again, the area of the city in which this segment of the population was most densely concentrated. It is, however, equally important to recognize that young men in the upper classes also looked upon the *meretrix* as a socially acceptable vehicle for satisfying their sexual needs. Cicero takes it for granted that the young gentleman will consort with prostitutes, and even goes so far as to claim that this was fully in accord with the *mos maiorum*. A century earlier, the elder Cato soundly approved of this custom, which he viewed as preferable to the seduction of married women. He had, in fact, only one reservation: the young *nobilis* should indeed frequent brothels, but not too often. The idea, he once exclaimed, was to visit such establishments, not live there.[146]

Naturally, Rome and Pompeii were not the only two places in the Roman world where prostitution flourished. Horace and Dio Chrysostomus casually refer to prostitution in such remote locales as the towns and villages of Lucania and Libya, while the whores of Corinth, in contrast, were renowned throughout the Empire. In the Corinthian temple of Aphrodite alone, we are told, there were no less than a thousand prostitutes (*hierodouloi*) on hand.[147] Anecdotal evidence of this type, which is widespread in both space and time, leads one to conclude that the working poor could find reasonably priced prostitutes even in the most obscure corners of the *imperium Romanum*[148] – and therein lies a problem. It is commonly assumed today that, throughout the Roman period, whores were recruited almost exclusively from the ranks of slaves and freedwomen; at the same time, however, it is also generally conceded that females always constituted a distinct minority of the total slave population.[149] Unless, therefore, one further wishes to presume that the percentage of female slaves engaged in prostitution was very high, or that a significant number of the free and enslaved poor led celibate lives, then these two suppositions would appear to be blatantly contradictory. In fact, while it may be readily conceded that many of the bar-maids and prostitutes whom we meet in the Pompeian graffiti and the pages of Latin literature were slaves or freedwomen, there is ample evidence to suggest that *ingenuae* also pursued this profession.[150] Here we may discount the infamous but relatively small tribe of Roman noblewomen, who took advantage of the periodic relaxation of morals to behave in ways that invited charges of prostitution. Such notorious late Republican figures as Clodia and Sempronia did not, after all, demand a fee for their services, nor is there anything to indicate that the women who tried to dodge the Augustan laws on adultery by registering with the aediles as prostitutes actually intended to sell themselves to any and all comers.[151] The number of *matronae* whom Caligula, Nero, Commodus and Messallina (the consort of Claudius) apparently forced to enter prostitution must have been equally small, but these tales are important nonetheless because they remind us that enslavement was not the only form of compulsion that introduced free-born women to this squalid and degrading existence.[152] A wide variety of sources, scattered across virtually the whole of Roman history, testify to the fact that prostitution was not simply the last but often the only resource available to free women mired in poverty.

The most impersonal evidence may be extracted from the corpus of Roman law. At one point in the *Digesta*, Ulpian quite casually remarks that a woman who turns to prostitution out of economic necessity should not for this reason escape prosecution under the Augustan statutes governing adultery. The Theodosian Code furnishes a still more revealing passage: in AD 428, the emperors Theodosius and Valentinian deprived fathers who prostituted their daughters of their *potestas*, while urging indigent women who had drifted into prostitution to seek help from their bishop, provincial governor or any other interested party.[153] Admittedly, this decree is far too late to be of any immediate relevance to this discussion, but it is important to note that the link which it establishes between *penuria* and voluntary prostitution, or prostitution by a parent, is almost as old as Roman literature itself. Plautus, an author who exhibits a particularly keen understanding of the dynamics of prostitution, repeatedly alludes to the courtesan's commonplace fear that advancing age would translate into lost income and consequent impoverishment. One obvious way to avoid this bleak prospect was to train a daughter to take over the trade – a scenario that Plautus elaborates in the *Cistellaria*. Here the *meretrix* Syra is made to confess that she compelled her daughter Gymnasium to follow in her footsteps 'not because of vanity, but to make sure that I wouldn't go hungry.'[154] Some five centuries later, according to the Greek historian Zosimus, parents were forced to prostitute their daughters in order to pay the *chrysargyron*, a new tax imposed by the emperor Constantine. Neatly bridging the gap between these two authors, the younger Seneca similarly observes that people 'would not only betray a friend in order to prolong their lives but would even personally introduce their children to prostitution.'[155]

Clearly, then, the Plautine *meretrix* was not the only person prepared to prostitute a child in order to escape from poverty. We shall never know, of course, how many Roman parents were economically compelled to take such a desperate step, but against this grim backdrop we may at the very least appreciate why, century after century, free-born women would have fallen into prostitution. Terence and Martial poke fun at the starving whore, and the fourth-century Christian theologian Lactantius unsympathetically excoriates women who must earn this 'utterly abominable bread' merely in order to survive.[156] Nevertheless, these three writers undoubtedly come much closer to the truth than some of the Christian *literati*, who were predisposed to assume that the whore was, by and large, a licentious creature addicted to sexual pleasure.[157] More so than any other author, Terence makes it eminently clear that, for many women, there were only two choices – privation, or prostitution.[158] To be sure, his plays are in all likelihood straightforward translations of Greek New Comedy originals, but in this instance, it still seems safe to conclude that a Roman audience would not have been unduly surprised by the recurrent image of the *ingenua* who, simply to survive, must resort to prostitution.

At what moment in time did women first begin to practice the *artes meretriciae* inside the Roman community? Self-evidently, this is also a question to which there is no possible answer, but it is quite likely that the profession was very old indeed. As David Daube has astutely observed in the course of a brilliant discussion of nominalization as a tool of historical analysis, the noun *meretrix* (literally, 'the earneress') derives from the verb *merere* ('to earn'). Since women were already working in a variety of settings in the early second century BC, one might have expected that the term *meretrix* would still have a generic meaning, but in fact Plautus and Terence always use it in its accepted classical sense of 'prostitute.' It thus seems clear that the noun had already emerged from the verb in the distant past – at a remote moment in time when prostitution was the sole or predominant commercial activity in which Roman women could engage. In this sense, as Daube again points out, its development would have paralleled that of the modern English term 'professional'.

> For a long time this signified a *meretrix*: there was no other profession for females. Nowadays they have more openings and if you hear of a lady that she is a professional, you had better enquire before you make a date or you might find yourself landed with an estate agent or a dentist.[159]

The further back in time that one goes, of course, the less plausible the notion becomes that the *meretrix* was customarily a slave or freedwoman. Indeed, one may legitimately ask whether the early Romans would even have applied a term such as *merere* to their chattel property.

FINDINGS

While we shall never know how many women were actually involved, one may reasonably conclude that most of the expropriated *rusticae* whom Sallust, Plutarch, Appian and Florus describe in such global terms stemmed from the environs of Rome itself, and particularly from the decaying communities of the Latin plain. A sizeable body of evidence, primarily epigraphic in nature, has also been introduced in this chapter to pinpoint the urban occupations in which such women might sustain themselves, but this should not be allowed to obscure the tentative nature of many of its conclusions. As with so many other topics in Roman history, the present exercise has been hindered by a chronic shortage of evidence, but worse still by its uneven spatial and chronological distribution. We possess a respectable amount of information about the women of Rome and Pompeii, but the rest of Italy remains, in the historical sense, virtually a featureless landscape. Above all, our ignorance of developments in the Italian countryside is almost total. With regard to chronology, one must never lose sight of the fact that our data are heavily concentrated in the late Republic and early Empire, with a secondary cluster of information for the early second century BC. While the problem is hardly new, it is nevertheless frustrating to see the climax in the one period of historical trends whose antecedents lay in the other, and yet be unable to follow the progression of events from a distance, much less with any precision. Among the professions surveyed in this chapter, for example, we would like to analyze weaving, medicine, obstetrics and wet-nursing in far greater detail, for in each instance we are dealing with an occupation that clearly attracted free-born women, but with increasing competition from slave and freed labor. One might logically conclude, therefore, that displaced *rusticae* would have found it relatively easy to obtain work in these fields during the years immediately after the Hannibalic war, but that it would have become progressively more difficult to do so in the decades that followed, when more and more skilled slaves entered Italy from Greece, Asia Minor and the Near East. If it is not simply a quirk of the evidence, the increasing incidence of slavery in second-century Rome might also account for the curious paucity of references to professional mourners in the sources for the late Republic and early Principate. Conversely, we know that free female gladiators were already in evidence at the end of the Republic, but we do not know how many women turned to this profession, nor the point in time at which they first began to appear in Italy's arenas. Rome's professional female entertainers are a similarly enigmatic group. By the end of the first century BC, women were undergoing increasingly specialized training in preparation for careers as actresses, dancers and musicians on the legitimate stage, but at the same time these artists were also to be found in innumerable taverns, where their skills and training were employed above all sexually to arouse their male clientele. The degree of specialization that we observe at the end of the Republic obviously implies a period of gradual development over the preceding century, but it cannot be followed in any detail. More to the point, we cannot speak with any assurance about the ethnic and jural background of the first women to appear on the stage or in the coarser environment of the Roman *cauponae*. Anecdotal references to the *puellae Gaditanae* – or to their equally notorious counterparts from Syria and Lydia – permit us to infer that slaves and freedwomen from particular towns or ethnic groups were frequent purveyors of the seamier kinds of entertainment to be found in imperial Rome, but they tell us nothing about their predecessors in the second century

BC.[160] At best, we can only conclude that, once again, women of servile origins would have come increasingly to dominate a profession in which ingenuous women may have originally played some part.

The one profession that was already well established at the end of the Second Punic War, and to which free-born women were driven by poverty across the whole subsequent course of Roman history, was prostitution. The harlot was in all probability the first female 'professional' in the Roman community, and it seems altogether probable that, throughout the history of Rome, prostitution in its various guises was capable of absorbing most if not all surplus female labor, slave, freed and free-born alike.[161] In order properly to appreciate this point, of course, one has to keep two others in mind – the strongly domestic orientation of Roman retail trade and crafts production, and the limited but widely shared range of domestic skills that country women would have brought with them to the city. The former will have served to exclude immigrants, male and female alike, from an extraordinary mix of occupations, while the latter will have resulted in a glut of candidates for the few available jobs in which these skills could be put to profitable use. This combination of circumstances must have made it easy, for example, to find a mid-wife, and it is no longer quite so surprising to learn that the Forum Holitorium functioned as a virtual guild hall for would-be *nutrices*. Thus in the end we are left with the seemingly inescapable conclusion that the production of clothing (in the form of piece-work), and to a much greater extent prostitution, were the only occupations in which large numbers of *ingenuae* forced to fall back upon their own resources would find work ready to hand. The one was physically taxing, and the other must have been degrading in the extreme for women brought up in accordance with the pristine *mores* of Italian society. Both offered little more than a wretched hand-to-mouth existence, and the figure of Amaryllis, the Pompeian weaver who was nicknamed the *fellatrix*, further reminds us that the two professions may not have been mutually exclusive. In striking contrast, then, to the social and economic emancipation that the conquest of an empire brought to so many aristocratic women, for literally thousands of the anonymous wives and daughters of the equally anonymous men serving in the ranks, Rome's unending wars of conquest held out only the promise of a bleak present and still more hopeless future.[162]

NOTES

1   It might be thought that tabulating the number of men under arms in general, and casualty figures in particular, would permit a crude estimate of the number of women threatened with dispossession. As P.A. Brunt, *Italian Manpower, 225 BC–AD 14* (Oxford, 1971) 226–227 and 694–697, has rightly pointed out, however, casualty figures are among the least reliable data to be exhumed from the ancient sources.

2   Livy 42.34–35.2. As a centurion, his share of the booty in the war against Philip of Macedon came to 50 *denarii* (Livy 34.52.12). He would have received another 54 *denarii* on returning from Spain with Cato (Livy 34.46.3), and 50 more on the occasion of M. Fulvius Nobilior's triumph over the Aetolians (Livy 39.5.17). His last two Spanish campaigns will have earned him 100 *denarii* from Q. Fulvius Flaccus and 50 from Tib. Sempronius Gracchus (Livy 40.43.7, 41.7.3), but he will also have been enriched at the end of the campaigns that Livy mentions but does not specify. Since the narrative seems to unfold in strict chronological order, these two campaigns must have occurred in the period 187–182 BC. Both consuls campaigned in Liguria during each of these six years, and it is likely that this is the theater in question; for references, see T.R.S. Broughton, *The Magistrates of the Roman Republic* I (Cleveland, 1951) 367–381. These campaigns may also have been quite lucrative; when L. Aemilius Paullus triumphed over the Ligurian Ingauni in 181, for example, the *pedites* received 30 *denarii* apiece (Livy 40.34.8). For a convenient summary of the monetary distributions to soldiers in the period 201–167 BC, see Brunt, *Italian Manpower*, 394.

3   See P. Krüger, 'Anecdoton Livianum,' *Hermes* 4 (1870) 371–372; for further discussion, cf. A. Watson, *Roman Private Law around 200 BC* (Edinburgh, 1971) 20; *Rome of the XII Tables* (Princeton, 1975) 24; and J.F. Gardner, *Women in Roman Law and Society* (Bloomington and Indianapolis, 1986) 35 and note 18.

4   See again Figure 1, which is based upon Dio Chrysostomus, *Orationes* 7. 10–11, 20, 47, 65, 67–68, and 76, as well as the related discussion of the deficiencies in the argument for the primacy of the nuclear family posed by R.P. Saller and B.D. Shaw, 'Tombstones and Roman Family Relations in the Principate: Civilians, Soldiers and Slaves,' *JRS* 74 (1984) 124–156. Y. Thomas, 'Mariages endogamiques à Rome. Patrimoine, pouvoir et parenté depuis l'époque archaïque,' *TRG* 58 (1980) 348–351, also draws attention to this element of Ligustinus' speech, and rightly connects it with *Digesta* 28.7.23–24 – our firmest evidence for the use of endogamy as a mechanism to avoid undue dispersion of the *patrimonium*. K. Hopkins, 'Brother–Sister Marriage in Roman Egypt,' *CSSH* 22 (1980) 342–343, discounts this explanation for Egypt's notoriously unique variant on endogamy, primarily because of the active market in agricultural real estate revealed in the papyri. There is, however, nothing to indicate that the Italian peasantry widely regarded land as a commodity to be bought and sold like any other.

5   *Trinummus* 442–453, 688–691. It is the ambivalence surrounding the distinction between *concubinatus* and *conubium* that sets this play in a firmly Roman context; for further discussion of concubinage in Roman society, see now S. Treggiari, 'Concubinae,' *PBSR* new series 36 (1981) 59–81.

6   Horace, *Epistulae* 1.17.46; Varro, *De Re Rustica* 3.16.2.

7 Tiberius Gracchus and Cornelia, for example, produced twelve, of whom three reached adulthood (Plutarch, *Tiberius Gracchus* 1.3–5).

8 Livy 1.43.8; Polybius 6.19.2.

9 It has often been lodged in the Hannibalic war, and specifically in the period 214–212 BC. See, for example, E. Gabba, 'Le origini dell'esercito professionale in Roma: i proletari e la riforma di Mario,' *Athenaeum* new series 27 (1949) 181–182; Brunt, *Italian Manpower*, 75, 77, 403. Contra, A.J. Toynbee, *Hannibal's Legacy* II (Oxford, 1965) 88–89 ('at some date before 214 BC'); F.W. Walbank, *A Historical Commentary on Polybius* I (Oxford, 1957) 698 ('Gabba's date for the reduction is not convincing'); R.E. Smith, *Service in the Post-Marian Roman Army* (Manchester, 1958) 4 ('it would seem to have been made during the second century'); and D.C. Earl, *Tiberius Gracchus: a Study in Politics* (Brussels, 1963) 32 ('sometime before 150').

10 Thus Gabba, 'Origini dell'esercito professionale,' 180; and again in his review of Toynbee, *RFIC* 96 (1968) 71 = *Esercito e società nella tarda repubblica romana* (Florence, 1973) 558–559; Smith, *Post-Marian Roman Army*, 4; Earl, *Tiberius Gracchus*, 32; Toynbee, *Hannibal's Legacy* II.36, 88–89, 165 *et passim*; Brunt, *Italian Manpower*, 402–404; K. Hopkins, *Conquerors and Slaves* (Cambridge, 1978) 4–5, 12, 25–37; and C. Nicolet, *The World of the Citizen in Republican Rome*, trans. P.S. Falla (London, 1980) 111.

11 For further discussion of this overlooked point, see above all J.K. Evans, 'Resistance at Home: the Evasion of Military Service in Italy during the Second Century BC,' in T. Yuge and M. Doi (eds), *Forms of Control and Subordination in Antiquity* (Tokyo and Leiden, 1988) 121–140, especially 129–131.

12 For the pattern of land use in the subsistence economy of Roman Italy, see J.K. Evans, '*Plebs Rustica*. The Peasantry of Classical Italy II: the Peasant Economy,' *AJAH* 5 (1980) 135–144.

13 For children engaged in pastoral and agricultural work, cf., *inter alia*, Ovid, *Fasti* 4.511; and Columella, *De Re Rustica* 8.2.7, 11.2.44.

14 It seems appropriate to point out at this juncture that the terms *rusticus*, 'smallholder' and 'peasant' are used interchangeably throughout this chapter. They are applied in particular to the lowest class of the *assidui*, and to the *proletarii*, but it should be kept in mind that, whatever their relations with the elite, in many respects these two groups cannot be treated as identical, much less relegated to an amorphous 'lower class' in the modern sense of the term. It should now be apparent that monoculturalism is not used as a defining characteristic of this element of rural Italian society, nor can it necessarily be assumed that all of the individuals in question actually lived on the land. Partible inheritance, and to a lesser extent dowry, must have often caused smallholdings to be scattered in small allotments, most conveniently reached from a central *vicus*. For further discussion of this point, see P. Garnsey, 'Where Did Italian Peasants Live?,' *PCPhS* 25 (1979) 10–11. The rigid systems of classification sometimes favored by historians – *inter alia*, H. Dohr, *Die italischen Gutshöfe nach den Schriften Catos und Varros* (Cologne, 1965) ii (10–80 *iugera* constitute 'Kleinbetriebe', 80–500 *iugera* 'mittelgrosse Betriebe', and still larger properties are 'Grossgüter') – are also explicitly rejected here. It is instead assumed that the Republican smallholding was characterized by intensive use of family labor, and that the household unit consumed the majority of what it produced.

15 Most women would have found it difficult if not impossible efficiently to use the typical Roman plough, or sole-ard. This was designed in such a way that it had a pronounced tendency to catch in the soil, and it required a constant

and very heavy downward pressure to drive a straight furrow with an even depth. For further discussion, see K.D. White, *Roman Farming* (London, 1970) 174–177; and M.S. Spurr, *Arable Cultivation in Roman Italy* (London, 1986) 27–40.

16 *De Agricultura* 4, 5.4, 13.1, 22.3, 144–146.

17 Valerius Maximus 4.4.6.

18 Sallust, *Bellum Iugurthinum* 41.7–8; Plutarch, *Tiberius Gracchus* 8–9; cf. Appian, *Bella Civilia* 1.7–10; and Florus 2.1–2.

19 A seminal point first developed at length by G. Tibiletti, 'Ricerche di storia agraria romana,' *Athenaeum* new series 28 (1950) 183–208; cf. M.W. Frederiksen, 'The Contribution of Archaeology to the Agrarian Problem in the Gracchan Period,' *DArch* 4–5 (1970–71) 348–349.

20 E. Rawson, 'The Ciceronian Aristocracy and Its Properties,' in M.I. Finley (ed.), *Studies in Roman Property* (Cambridge, 1976) 85–102, is a representative recent example of the traditional focus on senatorial investment in agriculture. For the expansion of Rome in the second century, and the concomitant growth in the city's investment potential, see H.C. Boren, 'The Urban Side of the Gracchan Economic Crisis,' *AHR* 63 (1958) 890–902; P. Garnsey, 'Urban Property Investment,' also in Finley (ed.), *Studies in Roman Property*, 123–136; and B.W. Frier, *Landlords and Tenants in Imperial Rome* (Princeton, 1980) 21–34.

21 *CIL* IX.1455 = *ILS* 6509 (Ligures Baebiani); *CIL* XI.1147 = *ILS* 6675 (Veleia). In addition to Th. Mommsen, 'Die italische Bodentheilung und die Alimentartafeln,' *Hermes* 19 (1884) 393–416 = *Gesammelte Schriften* V (Berlin, 1908) 123–145; see F.G. de Pachtere, *La Table hypothécaire de Veleia* (Paris, 1920); J. Carcopino, 'La table de Veleia et son importance historique,' *REA* 23 (1921) 287–303; M. Besnier, 'A propos de la table hypothécaire de Veleia,' *REA* 24 (1922) 118–122; P. Veyne, 'La table des Ligures Baebiani et l'institution alimentaire de Trajan,' *MEFR* 69 (1957) 81–135; 'Les Alimenta de Trajan,' in *Les Empereurs romains d'Espagne* (Paris, 1965) 163–179; F.C. Bourne, 'The Roman Alimentary Program and Italian Agriculture,' *TAPA* 91 (1960) 47–75; R. Duncan-Jones, 'The Purpose and Organisation of the Alimenta,' *PBSR* new series 19 (1964) 123–146; *The Economy of the Roman Empire*[2] (Cambridge, 1982) 288–319, 333–342, 382–385; P. Garnsey, 'Trajan's Alimenta: Some Problems,' *Historia* 17 (1968) 367–381; E. Champlin, 'Owners and Neighbours at Ligures Baebiani,' *Chiron* 11 (1981) 239–264; and J.K. Evans, '*Plebs Rustica*. The Peasantry of Classical Italy I: the Peasantry in Modern Scholarship,' *AJAH* 5 (1980) 31–33, who also discusses the thorny problems that surround the very meaning of the term *latifundia* (pp. 23–25). On this latter difficulty, see also K.D. White, 'Latifundia,' *BICS* 14 (1967) 62–79.

22 Plutarch, *Tiberius Gracchus* 8.7; Propertius 4.10.29–30; cf. Lucan 7.392.

23 The *locus classicus*, for the second century BC, is Cato, *De Agricultura* 22.3. He tells us that it costs HS 72 to transport an oil mill purchased at Suessa for HS 400 and fifty pounds of oil to Venafrum – a distance of 25 miles. The freight charges for a mill purchased at Pompeii for HS 384 and transported over a distance of 75 miles came to HS 280, or 73 percent of the purchase price! For further discussion, see J. Hörle, *Cato's Hausbücher* (Paderborn, 1929) 193, 197, 255; and C.A. Yeo, 'Land and Sea Transportation in Imperial Italy,' *TAPA* 77 (1946) 221–224; in a more general vein, A.M. Burford, 'Heavy Transport in Classical Antiquity,' *EHR* second series 13 (1960) 1–18. Many Roman authors, but the agricultural writers above all, show a lively awareness of the high economic (and social) costs of land transport; in addition to Cato (1.3, 8.2), cf., *inter alia*, Varro, *De Re Rustica* 1.16.2–6, 1.69.1; Columella, *De Re Rustica* 1.3.3, 3.2.1; Pliny, *Naturalis Historia* 19.30; and Gregory

of Nazianzus, *Orationes* 43.34. In southern Etruria, many owners of large estates went to the considerable expense of constructing paved *diverticula* to link their properties with these highways. Cf. G. Duncan, 'Sutri,' *PBSR* new series 13 (1958) 88–90; G.D.B. Jones, 'Capena and the Ager Capenas,' *PBSR* new series 17 (1962) 166, 169; 18 (1963) 115; A. Kahane, L.M. Threipland and J.B. Ward-Perkins, 'The Ager Veientanus, North and East of Veii,' *PBSR* new series 23 (1968) 80, 89, 113, 117, 139; and P. Hemphill, 'The Cassia–Clodia Survey,' *PBSR* new series 30 (1975) 151.

24 For the Tiber as a commercial avenue to the Roman marketplace, see Strabo 5.2.10; and especially Pliny, *Epistulae* 5.6.12.

25 Jones, 'Capena,' 147. For the *ager Capenas* as a whole, he adds, 'it is the small farms that form the majority of the sites described.'

26 *AE* 1954, 167.

27 Cf. J.B. Ward-Perkins, 'Notes on Southern Etruria and the Ager Veientanus,' *PBSR* new series 10 (1955) 57 (along the via Veientana, 'none of the individual sites is of any great wealth or importance'); Kahane, Threipland and Ward-Perkins, 'Ager Veientanus,' 149 ('here, for every two sites already occupied under the Republic a third came into being during the 150 odd years following the accession of Augustus. Few of these were individually of any great size ...'); Duncan, 'Sutri,' 96–97 ('the majority of the buildings seem to have been farmhouses of varying sizes, but most of them not very large. Judging from the density of sites, each farm would have been a comparatively small unit and the countryside would have been divided up among a series of such individual holdings').

28 'Contribution of Archaeology,' 346; using the same body of evidence, D. Brendan Nagle, 'The Etruscan Journey of Tiberius Gracchus,' *Historia* 25 (1976) 487–489; and 'Towards a Sociology of Southeastern Etruria,' *Athenaeum* new series 57 (1979) 411–441, has independently drawn the same conclusion.

29 See G. Barker, J. Lloyd, and D. Webley, 'A Classical Landscape in Molise,' *PBSR* new series 33 (1978) 48; and Garnsey, 'Where Did Italian Peasants Live?,' 17–18.

30 A date *circa* 120 BC has been suggested for these *fundi*, and it has been speculated that they were part of the Gracchan settlement scheme; cf. Frederiksen, 'Contribution of Archaeology,' 342– 344; and Garnsey, 'Where Did Italian Peasants Live?,' 11.

31 Cicero, *Pro Plancio* 21–22; Cato, *De Agricultura* 4, 5.4, 13.1, 22.3, 144–146. At 144.3, Cato cautions the prospective estate owner to make sure that the casual laborers do not steal firewood from the property. This certainly suggests that these *operarii* lived in the immediate neighborhood, in contrast to the organized gangs of rural laborers that, for example, the grandfather of the future emperor Vespasian brought to the Sabine district each year from Umbria (Suetonius, *Divus Vespasianus* 1.4).

32 *Inter alia*, T.W. Potter, *Roman Italy* (Berkeley, 1987) 98, 152, continues to argue that there were 2–3 million slaves in Italy at the end of the first century BC, out of a total population of 6–7.5 million. Since he further believes that the vast majority of these slaves were employed in agriculture, he is compelled (despite certain misgivings) to endorse the correlate assumption that the peasantry suffered mass expropriation during the last two centuries of the Republic (52, 96, 98–118, 152–153, *et passim*). In fact, any attempt to estimate the number of slaves in Italy at a given moment raises insuperable difficulties, which have too often been ignored in our haste to construct a social history of Roman Italy that emphasizes the horrors of slavery – a point that has been succinctly stressed in a review of this book by J.K. Evans, *AJA*

92 (1988) 451–452.

33 Thus U. Kahrstedt, *Die wirtschaftliche Lage Grossgriechenlands in der Kaiserzeit* (Wiesbaden, 1960) 105–107; the much more recent reports of C. D'Annibale on the field survey of the Chora of Metaponto, and of B. Cabaniss on the faunal material in the kiln deposit at Pizzica-Pantanello, in J.C. Carter (ed.), *The Territory of Metaponto, 1981–82* (Austin, 1983); and J.C. Carter, L. Costantini, C. D'Annibale, J.R. Jones, R.L. Folk and D. Sullivan, 'Population and Agriculture: Magna Grecia in the Fourth Century BC', in C. Malone and S. Stoddart (eds), *Papers in Italian Archaeology IV: the Cambridge Conference* I (Oxford, 1985) 281–312.

34 Kahrstedt, *Grossgriechenlands in der Kaiserzeit*, 80 (Croton), 101–102 (Heraclea), and 118–120 (Tarentum). The care that one must exercise when using this material for historical purposes is, however, brought home by Kahrstedt's report on Croton. At 'S. Severina, 20 km vom Meer, 3–4 südl. des Neto, war immer durch griechische und römische Bauglieder, Gräber, Vasen, Lampen und Münzen bekannt.'(80)

35 Strabo 5.2.6 (Volaterrae); cf. 5.2.3 (Caere). The list of communities that had decayed or even disappeared in and around Latium by the beginning of the Principate is a long one: Alba (Lucan 7.394); Antemnae (Strabo 5.3.2); Aricia (Cicero, *De Lege Agraria* 2.96); Bovillae (Cicero, *Pro Plancio* 23); Collatia (Cicero, *De Lege Agraria* 2.96; Strabo 5.3.2); Cora (Lucan 7.392); Cures (Strabo 5.3.1); Eretum (Strabo 5.3.1); Fidenae (Cicero, *De Lege Agraria* 2.96; Horace, *Epistulae* 1.11.8; Strabo 5.3.2); Fregellae (Strabo 5.3.10); Gabii (Cicero, *Pro Plancio* 23; Dionysius of Halicarnassus, *Antiquitates Romanae* 4.53.1; Horace, *Epistulae* 1.11.7; Lucan 7.392); Labicum (Cicero, *Pro Plancio* 23; Strabo 5.3.2); Lanuvium (Cicero, *De Lege Agraria* 2.96); Laurentum (Lucan 7.394; Pliny, *Epistulae* 2.17.2–3); Trebula (Strabo 5.3.1); and Tusculum (Cicero, *Pro Plancio* 21; *De Lege Agraria* 2.96).

36 R.M. Ogilvie, 'Eretum,' *PBSR* new series 20 (1965) 75–80.

37 E. Lepore, 'Orientamente per la storia sociale di Pompei,' in *Pompeiana. Raccolta di studi per il secondo centenario degli scavi di Pompei* (Naples, 1950) 148–156.

38 This question has been thoroughly explored, and the above conclusion most forcefully stated, by D.W. Rathbone, 'The Development of Agriculture in the "Ager Cosanus" during the Roman Republic: Problems of Evidence and Interpretation,' *JRS* 71 (1981) 10–23. Drawing upon survey and excavation in the *ager Cosanus*, and notably at the Settefinestre villa, he concludes that 'in the rest of Italy we must suppose that the vast majority of the seasonal labour force was recruited from families who had their own small farms which provided them with their basic subsistence. In other words, not only did the villa system in Roman Italy require a large seasonal labour force, but a numerous free (and, probably, poverty-stricken) peasantry was the only possible source to supply this demand.'(15)

39 Livy 3.3.9, *Periochae* 59; Plutarch, *Publicola* 12. Cf. Cicero, *De Republica* 2.36; Livy 1.43.9; and Plutarch, *Camillus* 2.

40 Dio Chrysostomus, *Orationes* 7.10–11, 20, 47, 65, 67–68, 76; Plutarch, *Aemilius Paullus* 5.4–5; Valerius Maximus 4.4.8–9.

41 Livy 42.34.1–12.

42 Livy 39.18.6.

43 Gaius, *Institutiones* 1.185–187.

44 Livy 39.3.4–6 (187); 41.8 (177); 42.10.3 (173).

45 *De Re Rustica* 12.*pr.* 4–5.

46 N.B. Kampen, 'Social Status and Gender in Roman Art: the Case of the Saleswoman,' in N. Broude and M.D. Garrard (eds), *Feminism and Art*

History (New York, 1982) 63–77.

47 Columella, *De Re Rustica* 12.3.8; Cato, *De Agricultura* 143.2; Plautus, *Mercator* 397.

48 Plautus, *Mercator* 396–398, 416; Cato *De Agricultura* 143.2–3; Horace, *Epodi* 2.39–48; Pseudo-Virgil, *Moretum* 37–38, 50–51, 119 (although here both Scybale and Simylus are engaged in food preparation); Columella, *De Re Rustica* 12.3.3, 8–9; Juvenal 14.161–172. In our legal sources, cleaning and cooking are also presumed to be the foremost occupations of women on rural estates; see *Digesta* 33.7.12.5. For further discussion, see J.M. Frayn, *Subsistence Farming in Roman Italy* (London, 1979) 104–114.

49 On this point, see again Frayn, *Subsistence Farming*, 143–144.

50 Plautus, *Mercator* 396, 416, 518–520; Suetonius, *Divus Augustus* 64.2, 73; *CIL* VI.10230 = *ILS* 8394. Cf. *CIL* II.1699, VI.1527, 31670 = *ILS* 8393 (the *laudatio Turiae*), and VI.11602 = *ILS* 8402 (*hic sita est Amymone Marci optima et pulcherrima / lanifica pia pudica frugi casta domiseda*). Here one should make particular note of the last-named virtue, *domiseda*, which means 'she who stays at home'. The maid who stayed indoors to work at her wool by lamplight was an equally praiseworthy person in Latin poetry; cf. Tibullus 1.3.83–88; Propertius 1.3.41; and Juvenal 6.288–291. In the late Empire, *lanificium* continues to be associated with *pudicitia*; cf., *inter alia*, Ausonius, *Parentalia* 2.4, 16.4; and Symmachus, *Epistulae* 6.67.

51 Columella, *De Re Rustica* 12.pr.9, 12.3.6; *CIL* VI.37965 (Allia Potestas); *CIL* I².1211 = VI.15346 = *ILS* 8403 (Claudia).

52 *De Re Rustica* 12.1.6, 3.8. For an insight into folk medicine in second-century Italy, see Cato, *De Agricultura* 115, 122–123, 125–127, and 156–160. *Exempli gratia*, he is particularly enthusiastic about the curative effects of cabbage, recommending at one point (157.10) that the most effective cure for blurred vision is to bathe the eyes in the heated urine of a person who eats cabbage on a regular basis.

53 This subject is explored in graphic detail by V. French, 'Midwives and Maternity Care in the Roman World,' in M. Skinner (ed.), *Rescuing Creusa: New Methodological Approaches to Women in Antiquity*, *Helios* 13.2 (1987) 69–84, especially 70–71.

54 These played a vital role in the peasant economy, since they provided both food for the table and commodities to be sold in the marketplace. Cf. J.M. Frayn, 'Wild and Cultivated Plants: a Note on the Peasant Economy of Ancient Italy,' *JRS* 65 (1975) 32–39 = *Subsistence Farming*, 57–72; and Evans, 'Peasant Economy,' 134–173. For further discussion of the traditional spheres of activity assigned to *matronae*, see now M. Eichenauer, *Untersuchungen zur Arbeitswelt der Frau in der römischen Antike* (Frankfurt, 1988) 33–41.

55 Notably the *vilicae* Cania Urbana (*CIL* III.2118), Cania Ursina (III.5611) and the *actrix* Prastina Maximina (XI.1730). Asia Minor offers a fourth example, a woman named Eirene; see H.W. Pleket, *Epigraphica II: Texts on the Social History of the Greek World* (Leiden, 1969) no. 28 (Pisido-Phrygian borderland). *CIL* V.7348 is too fragmentary to permit of any conclusions, but Dama was not only a slave but a *vilica vicaria* (XI.871 = *ILS* 7369), while Flora was in all likelihood a slave as well (III.5616). For further discussion, see J. Le Gall, 'Métiers de femmes au Corpus Inscriptionum Latinarum,' *Mélanges Marcel Durry* (Paris, 1970), 126; and Eichenauer, *Arbeitswelt der Frau*, 100–102.

56 Dio Chrysostomus 7.114; Frederiksen, 'Contribution of Archaeology,' 352–353; cf. Virgil, *Eclogues* 8.37–38. In fourth-century Athens, we also hear of women who were forced by their impoverished circumstances to hire themselves out as grape pickers (Demosthenes 57.45). One wonders what

happened to the children of women who worked in this fashion. I.T. Sanders, *Rainbow in the Rock, the People of Rural Greece* (Cambridge, Mass., 1962) 87, describes an encounter with a female migratory worker, a widow with four children: 'she had had to leave her four children at home twenty-five days ago and had had no word from them since then, even though her village was only a relatively few kilometers away. Apparently she had gone on working in the harvest fields for winter bread, clinging to the belief that "no news was good news," but her drawn face showed her long concern: "I left them with only a piece of bread to eat. I don't know how they made out."'

57 Cf. *CIL* VI.8786, 33473 = *ILS* 7771, VI.33830, 34270, *AE* 1928, 73 (*lectrices, anagnostriae*); among the *librariae, notariae* and *amanuenses*, there are only three *incertae* (*CIL* VI.3979, 9540 = *ILS* 7397, VI.33892 = *ILS* 7760), with eight securely attested slaves or freedwomen (*CIL* VI.7373, 8882, 9301, 9525 = *ILS* 7400 = *AE* 1982, 46, VI.9541–9542, 37757, 37801). See S. Treggiari, 'Jobs for Women,' *AJAH* 1 (1976) 78; N. Kampen, *Image and Status: Roman Working Women in Ostia* (Berlin, 1981) 118 ('it does seem clear that secretaries tended to be slaves and freed slaves who probably received their educations in the personal service of imperial or wealthy women'); and Eichenauer, *Arbeitswelt der Frau*, 103–104.

58 *CIL* VI.4045, 9096, 9097 = *ILS* 1790, and VI.37823; *CIL* XIV.3035 is too fragmentary to interpret. See Treggiari, 'Jobs,' 80; cf. 'Jobs in the Household of Livia,' *PBSR* new series 30 (1975) 53; and Eichenauer, *Arbeitswelt der Frau*, 111. The *tractatrix* in Martial 3.82 is also clearly of servile status.

59 *CIL* VI.5539, 5876, 6368, 7296, 7297 = *ILS* 7418, VI.7656, 8850, 8879, 8959–8960, 9345, 9690, 9726, 9727 = *ILS* 7419, VI.9731, 9732 = *ILS* 7420a, VI.9733 (conjoined with 9195 by *AE* 1979, 76a), 9735, 33099, 33370a, 33425, 34274, *AE* 1971, 52 (*ser.*); VI.3993–3994, 4717, 8944, 8957–8958, 8977, 9642a4, 9736 = *ILS* 7618, VI.9941, 13402, 37469 = *ILS* 9426, VI.37811–37811a (*lib.*); VI.5865, 9174, 9734 = 33101, 33784 (*inc.*). See Treggiari, 'Jobs,' 78–80; 'Household of Livia,' 52; Kampen, *Image and Status*, 118–119; cf. Gardner, *Women in Roman Law and Society*, 241. It should be observed that the social pattern remains the same when we move beyond Rome and its immediate environs: *CIL* III.2116 (*ser.?*); V.1740 (possible *ingenua*); V.4194 (*lib.*); X.1935 = *ILS* 7841d (*inc.*); X.1941 (*ser.*); X.1942 (*lib.*); XII.4514 (*lib.*); and XIV.5306 (nine *ser.*). With regard to the latter inscription, S. Treggiari, 'Lower Class Women in the Roman Economy,' *Florilegium* 1 (1979) 85 note 47, speculates that they may have been members of a shop or school, which would have offered vocational training analogous to the secretarial and bookkeeping skills taught in the *paedagogium*. This raises the interesting but ultimately unanswerable question of whether vocational education ever emancipated itself from the apprenticeship arrangements that we see among, for example, weavers in Roman Egypt. It is clear from Plutarch, *Cato Maior* 21.7 that slaves were already being apprenticed early in the second century BC, and the practice continued without interruption for the balance of Roman history. Cf., for example, Petronius, *Satryicon* 94 (apprentice barbers); and *Digesta* 32.1.65.3 (hairdressers). For the various methods used to educate slaves, see C.A. Forbes, 'The Education and Training of Slaves in Antiquity,' *TAPA* 86 (1955) 321–360. For the *paedagogium* in particular, one should still begin with S.L. Mohler, 'Slave Education in the Roman Empire,' *TAPA* 71 (1940) 262–280. K.R. Bradley, 'Child Labour in the Roman World,' *Historical Reflections* 12 (1985) 311–330, is at once the most recent and informed study of the apprenticing of children in antiquity.

60 *Digesta* 32.1.65.3; Ovid, *Amores* 1.14.15–16; Juvenal 6.490–495.

61 Plautus, *Truculentus* 405–406; Martial 2.17 (this may, however, be a cryptic

allusion to a prostitute); *CIL* VI.9736 = *ILS* 7618 (a *liberta* with a shop on the vicus Longus), VI.37469 = *ILS* 9426 (a *liberta* who was also in business on the vicus Longus, in conjunction with a *tonsor* who may have been her husband), and VI.37811a = *ILS* 9427 (a *liberta* in the campus Martius). On these inscriptions, see especially the discussion in Treggiari, 'Jobs,' 102 note 31; 'Lower Class Women,' 75; cf. 'Domestic Staff at Rome in the Julio-Claudian Period, 27 BC to AD 68,' *Histoire Sociale* 6 (1973) 244–245, where she briefly discusses the place of the *ornatrix* in the organizational structure of the great urban *familiae* of the early Empire. For the training of and services provided by *ornatrices* and *tonstrices*, as well as an account of the tools that they used in their work, see M. Maxey, *Occupations of the Lower Classes in Roman Society* (Chicago, 1938) 52–53, 94–96.

62   The clothes-folder in *CIL* VI.9901 = *ILS* 7444 was a slave; those mentioned in *CIL* VI.33393, 33395 and 37825 were libertine. The status of the *vestispica* in *CIL* VI.9912 = *ILS* 7431 remains unclear. Servile *pedisequae* are registered in *CIL* VI.4006 = *ILS* 7888, VI.4355, 5200, 5821, 6335–6336, 7410, 9266, 9773–9774, 9775 = *ILS* 7443, VI.9776, 9779–9781, 33477 and *AE* 1945, 110. Those in *CIL* VI.9777–9778 may be *libertae*. Four *ministrae* were slaves (*CIL* VI.9290b, 9637, 9638a, 9639), one a freedwoman (VI.9640). The status of the *ostiaria* (*CIL* VI.6326 = *ILS* 7438) is uncertain. See Maxey, *Occupations of the Lower Classes*, 62–63; Treggiari, 'Jobs,' 80–81; 'Household of Livia,' 53; Kampen, *Image and Status*, 120; Gardner, *Women in Roman Law and Society*, 241; and Eichenauer, *Arbeitswelt der Frau*, 104–105, 109–112. Italy at large furnishes two more *servae* who worked as clothes-folders (*CIL* IX.3318 = *ILS* 7430; *AE* 1985, 173). For the promotion of female slaves from position to position within the urban *familia*, see Juvenal 6.497–498.

63   *CIL* VI.9213 = *ILS* 7691 – an inscription erected by one or both parents, but this does not necessarily mean that she was under their jural control; cf. Treggiari, 'Lower Class Women,' 67; Kampen, *Image and Status*, 126; and H. Gummerus, 'Die römische Industrie I: das Goldschmied und Juwelier-gewerbe,' *Klio* 14 (1915) 166 note 80, who emends the inscription to read VIXIT.AN.XVIIII. M.VIIII. This hardly seems necessary: although not directly relevant to Italy, it is nevertheless of some interest that twenty-eight of the twenty-nine surviving Egyptian apprentice contracts that are cataloged by Bradley, 'Child Labor,' 311–330, involved minors, and each of the five females on his roster was a slave.

64   *CIL* VI.9214a = *ILS* 7692 (*auri vestrix*); VI.9892 = *ILS* 7600 (*siricaria*). The former was either a tailor who worked with gold cloth, or a person who embroidered with gold thread. Another freedwoman, Domitia, seems to have specialized in the setting of pearls (*margaritaria*), while Antistia Delphis was a freed mosaicist (*tesseraria lignaria*) whose position certainly required training and may also have called for considerable artistic ability (*CIL* VI.5972; V.7044 = *ILS* 7288). Artistic talent, for example, is on display in the mosaic floors of two of the three bars outside the Ostian barracks of the *vigiles*, but mosaicists could also be called upon to execute crude repairs on an existing floor, as we note in the case of the tavern of Alexander Helix. See G. Hermansen, *Ostia: Aspects of City Life* (Edmonton, 1981) 143–146, 172–175; and more generally Le Gall, 'Métiers de femmes,' 125; Treggiari, 'Lower Class Women,' 67; and Kampen, *Image and Status*, 126.

65   Thus Treggiari, 'Lower Class Women,' 76; Kampen, *Image and Status*, 126–127; 'Social Status and Gender', 66–67; and Gardner, *Women in Roman Law and Society*, 239. One notes, for example, that the above-mentioned Sellia Epyre was commemorated by her husband, Q. Futius Olympicus.

66   *CIL* VI.6939, 9211 (*brattiariae*). It is symptomatic of the problem that

Le Gall, 'Métiers de femmes,' 125–126; and Eichenauer, *Arbeitswelt der Frau*, 29, 128–129, treat the two *brattiariae* as saleswomen; while Treggiari, 'Lower Class Women,' 66–67, thinks that they were active craftswomen. Kampen, *Image and Status*, 126, is appropriately ambivalent. In her long discussion of the role of women in the crafts industry and retail trade (83–98, 127–131), however, Eichenauer is clearly sensitive to the ambivalent character of the evidence in this respect. In this particular case, we do know that at least one woman – a certain Cuculla – did work in Verecundus' shop; she supported the candidacy of C. Iulius Polybius for the duumvirate (*CIL* IV.7841). For this Pompeian material, see further Kampen, 'Social Status and Gender,' 66–67.

67 Once it is acknowledged that these small craftsmen often worked in tandem with a wife who retailed their products, then the role of women, and especially freedwomen, in the Italian economy assumes a significance hitherto unsuspected. *Exempli gratia*, we know of a freed ivory-worker (*eborarius*), M. Aelius Apollonius, who purchased a tombstone for himself and his wife Lepida (*CIL* VI.33423 = *ILS* 7705), while a freedwoman named Titia Eutychia commemorated her husband, the comb-maker (*pectinarius*) L. Maesius Terentinus, and their two children (*CIL* V.98 = *ILS* 7721). In both instances, one may readily believe that the *uxor* played an active role in the business. The tendency for production to occur within a familial setting is critical to our understanding of the late imperial phenomenon of compulsory admission to guilds for those who married the daughters of professional men – a far less revolutionary change than it appears to be. Cf., for the application of this procedure to the guild of the breadmakers, *Codex Theodosianus* 14.3.2, 14.3.14, and 14.3.21. M.B. Flory, 'Family in *Familia*: Kinship and Community in Slavery,' *AJAH* 3 (1978) 79–81, briefly illustrates how the sharing of work served to create a sense of community within the slave *familia*, which persisted after the manumission of the individuals involved. P. Garnsey, 'Independent Freedmen and the Economy of Roman Italy under the Principate,' *Klio* 63 (1981) 368–370; and M.I. Finley, *The Ancient Economy*[2] (London, 1985) 64, also draw attention to the predominant position of freedmen in Roman industry and commerce. It is very much to be regretted that we do not have epigraphic evidence for the manufacturers of crowns and garlands (*coronariae*) to whom Pliny, *Naturalis Historia* 21.3 refers. At *Thesmophoriazusae* 446–448, Aristophanes introduces a widow with five small children who eked out a marginal existence for her family by making garlands and selling them in the marketplace. The demand for these products must have been constant in the smaller towns of the Empire as well as the large cities, and this kind of artisanal work would have efficiently lent itself to a cottage industry. It is here, more so than in any other craft, that we might logically expect *rusticae* to have found opportunities for work.

68 *CIL* VI.9435 (*gemmarii*): III.2117 (*plumbaria*). Cf. Treggiari, 'Lower Class Women,' 67; Kampen, *Image and Status*, 126; and Le Gall, 'Métiers de femmes,' 125. Many women have left their names on lead pipes, but most can be confidently identified as well-to-do entrepreneurs, such as Annea Iucunda (*CIL* XV.7303 = *ILS* 8683), Hostilia Fortunata (XV.7564), and the *clarissima femina* Cornelia Praetextata (XV.7750). One may also presume that women such as Manilia Flaccilla (*CIL* XIV.1987, XV.7736) and Septimia Callicratia (XIV.1991, XV.7757), who are attested in two or more discrete locations, owned the businesses in question. One cannot, however, claim with certainty that any of the women in this category personally sold the products of their establishments, much less actually worked as *plumbariae*.

69 *CIL* V.7023 = *ILS* 7636; cf. Le Gall, 'Métiers de femmes,' 125; Treggiari, 'Lower Class Women,' 70; and Kampen, *Image and Status*, 113, 126.

70   *CIL* VI.9206 (Masumilla); 37820 = *ILS* 9428; *NS* 1922, 144; and *CIL*
      XIV.2433 = *ILS* 7597 (the *purpurariae*). See Treggiari, 'Lower Class Women,'
      71; Kampen, *Image and Status*, 126; and Gardner, *Women in Roman Law and
      Society*, 238. Was the freedwoman Pompeia Helena, who is styled *aurificis
      Caesaris* (*CIL* VI.4430), a goldsmith, or as seems more likely, a custodian of
      gold ware in the manner of the *ad argentum* [...]cogyris Marcella (VI.4425)?
      Another *purpuraria*, Eurania Mu[...], also appears in conjunction with a male
      partner (*CIL* VI.9848), and one may safely be inferred in the case of Baebia
      Veneria (II.1743). It is only on the highly fragmentary inscription *CIL* VI.9846
      that we find a group of four *libertae*, the Viciriae Creste, Nice, Ta[...], and I(?)
      [...], without a male figure in evidence.

71   *CIL* VI.10006, 33928. There is also ample room for doubt in the case of Licinia
      Primigenia (*CIL* X.1965), the Puteolan *incerta* who died at the age of 71. She
      was commemorated by her son, so it is at least possible that she was associated
      with a husband for some or all of her career. Pompeia Iphigenia was already an
      unguentaria when she died at age 9; presumably, she was either an apprentice,
      or was being brought up in her family's trade (*CIL* XII.1594). Cf. Le Gall,
      'Métiers de femmes,' 124; Treggiari, 'Lower Class Women,' 70; and Kampen,
      Image and Status, 113, 126.

72   *CIL* XIV.4698 (*sutrix*); IX.4721–4722 (*furnariae*). There is a third *furnaria*
      on record, the Carthaginian freedwoman Valeria Euterpe; however, she
      worked with a freedman, so the possibility cannot be dismissed that she
      was a vendor (*CIL* VIII.24678). Three other women, the *resinaria* Iulia
      Agele, the *calcaria* Laturnia Ianuaria, and the much later Christian *lagunaria*
      Leontia, probably dealt in resin, lime and glass products rather than producing
      them (*CIL* VI.9855 = *ILS* 7658 [*resinaria*], *ILS* 7663 [*calcaria*], *CIL* VI.9488
      [*lagunaria*]). For further discussion, see again Maxey, *Occupations of the Lower
      Classes*, 22–23; Le Gall, 'Métiers de femmes,' 124–125; Treggiari, 'Lower Class
      Women,' 70–72; and Kampen, *Image and Status*, 64–69, 113, and 126. The
      Pompeian *alicaria* Glyco (*CIL* IV.4001), whom Le Gall (125) calls a 'pâttisière'
      in fact seems to have been a prostitute; cf. Festus, *Glossaria Latina* v. *alicariae*;
      Plautus, *Poenulus* 266; and the comments of J.N. Adams, *The Latin Sexual
      Vocabulary* (Baltimore, 1982) 153. The *timpanaria* Donata of *AE* 1972, 715, and
      the libertine *tibicina* Philippa (*AE* 1985, 329), are also more likely to have been
      musicians than manufacturers of cymbals or drums on the one hand, and flutes
      on the other. Finally, we do not know whether the *officinatrix* Iunia Crocale
      owned or managed her workshop (*CIL* VI.9715), whatever it may have been.

73   *CIL* VI.9933, 9934; cf. the discussion of Treggiari, 'Lower Class Women,'
      70.

74   *CIL* XIV.2850 = *ILS* 3689 (*seminaria*); VI.9277 (*conditaria*); *AE* 1973, 71 (the
      wine and oil dealer from Spain); *CIL* XII.4496 the Narbonensian *negotiatrix*);
      and VI.9683 = *ILS* 7488 (the *negotiatrix* in cereals and vegetables). Leo,
      Abudia Megiste, the anonymous Spaniard and still another Megiste (*CIL*
      VI.814) are the only vendors on our roster to label themselves as *negotiatrices*,
      but it is clear from *Digesta* 14.4.5.2 and 34. 2.32.4 that the title had a wider
      application; cf. Treggiari, 'Lower Class Women,' 72; Kampen, *Image and
      Status*, 113; and 'Social Status and Gender,' 66.

75   *CIL* VI.9801 = *ILS* 7500 (*piscatrix*). The status of the men who are com-
      memorated with Ursa, Antistia Victorina and Cassia Domestica, who sold
      fruit (*pomaria*), beans (*fabaria*) and linen (*linaria*) respectively, are similarly
      in doubt (*CIL* VI.37819; III.153 = 6672; and V.5923 = *ILS* 7560. Cf. Le
      Gall, 'Métiers de femmes,' 125; Treggiari, 'Lower Class Women,' 72; Kampen,
      Image and Status, 113; and 'Social Status and Gender,' 66.

76   *CIL* VI.9684 (Pollecla); II.4318*a* = *ILS* 7562 (Fulvia); IV.4528, 8203–8204

(Faustilla). The Pompeian *vinaria* with the suggestive name of Suavis is more likely to have been a barmaid than a wine dealer (*CIL* IV.1819); the *negotiatrix* Megiste is a still more elusive figure (VI.814). Cf. Treggiari, 'Lower Class Women,' 72; and Kampen, *Image and Status*, 113. It is also quite likely that the person who dedicated the elaborate funerary inscription in which an anonymous female meat dealer is depicted at the top of a stone frieze, with the moving verses of Virgil, *Aeneid* 1.607–609 at the bottom, was the woman's husband (*CIL* VI.9685). Other friezes and wall paintings, such as the portrait of a female vegetable dealer in Pompeii's Praedia Iulia Felix (Kampen, 'Social Status and Gender,' 66), or the Ostian poultry dealer in plate 3 (*Image and Status*, 52–59), do not permit us to discern the precise circumstances that occasioned the work, hence we cannot even guess at the identity and motives of the person who paid for it. Indeed, even the gender of such vendors may sometimes be in dispute. Thus Kampen (*Image and Status*, 59–64) believes that the vegetable dealer depicted on a relief in the Museo Ostiense is female, while D.C. Bellingham, *JRS* 74 (1984) 228, argues that this figure is 'probably male.' The literary evidence can be equally intractable: Petronius naturally does not bother to supply the legal and marital status of the old woman who sells vegetables in the marketplace and drums up customers for a local brothel on the side (*Satyricon* 1.6–7). For a complete roster of Roman crafts and tradeswomen, see Appendix 1.

77 *Digesta* 15.1.27.*pr.* This accords well with the evidence for the apprenticing of weavers in Roman Egypt that Bradley, 'Child Labour,' 311–330, has accumulated. While the five women introduced to the trade were all slaves, it is of interest that fourteen of the fifteen male apprentices were free-born (there were, in addition, two male slaves who were learning to card wool, and one *ingenuus* who was mastering the art of mat weaving).

78 In addition to Pausanias 7.21.14 and Terence, *Andria* 74–79 – a passage that probably derives from Athenian New Comedy – cf. Cicero, *De Legibus* 2.45; Tibullus 1.6.77–80, 3.16 (a fragment of the poetess Sulpicia); Martial 4.19; Juvenal 8.43; and Apuleius, *Metamorphoses* 9.5. For further discussion, see Maxey, *Occupations of the Lower Classes*, 31–33, 38–39; Treggiari, 'Lower Class Women,' 68–69; G. Clark, 'Roman Women,' *G&R* second series 28 (1981) 198–199; Kampen, *Image and Status*, 121; and Gardner, *Women in Roman Law and Society*, 238. The nexus between poverty and wool-working is at its clearest, however, in Xenophon, *Memorabilia* 2.7.9. Here Socrates tells a certain Aristarchus, whose household contains a host of unmarried female relatives whom he is unable to feed, to buy wool and put them to work in the commercial production of clothing.

79 *CIL* IV.1507, on which see further M. D'Avino, *The Women of Pompeii*, transl. M.H. Jones and L. Nusco (Naples, 1967) 15–16; *CIL* VI.6362 = *ILS* 7432*b* (monumentum Statilorum); and VI.33371. Cf. also Tibullus 1.3.83–88; and the comments of Treggiari, 'Jobs,' 82; and Kampen, *Image and Status*, 122.

80 See *CIL* VI.6339–6341, 6342 = *ILS* 7432*c*, VI.6343–6345, 6346 = *ILS* 7432*d* (*servae Statilorum*); VI.9495, 9849*a* (*servae*), 9850 = *ILS* 7433 (*familia Caesaris?*); and cf. Treggiari, 'Domestic Staff at Rome,' 245–246; 'Jobs,' 82; and Kampen, *Image and Status*, 122.

81 *CIL* VI.6349–6350, 6351 = *ILS* 74352*b* (*servae Statilorum*); household of Livia: *CIL* VI.3988 (*ser.*), 4028 (*lib.*), 4029 (*ser.*), 5357 (*ser.*), 8903*b* (*ser.*), 9038 (*lib.*); households of other imperial women: *CIL* VI.4434 (*ser.*), 4467 = *ILS* 7882*b* (*lib.*), 4468 (*ser.*), 9037 = *ILS* 1788 (*ser.*), 9039*b* (*ser.*).

82 *CIL* V.2542, 2881, XI.5437, *AE* 1981, 502 (*lib.*); *CIL* VI.6726, 9882 (*ser.?*), 9881, 9884 = *ILS* 7567 (*lib.*), VI.9875–9876, 9877*b*, 9879–9880, 9883, 33907

(*inc.*). This qualification also applies to women who weighed wool (*lanipendae*). Six are known to have been slaves (*CIL* VI.9496–9497, 34273, 37721, IX.4350, XIII.447), while three must be considered *incertae* (*CIL* VI.9498, IX.3157, *AE* 1969–70, 49). Cf. Le Gall, 'Métiers de femmes,' 124; Treggiari, 'Jobs,' 82–85; 'Lower Class Women,' 68–69; Kampen, *Image and Status*, 121–122; and Gardner, *Women in Roman Law and Society*, 238.

83 *CIL* VI.37826 (Cameria Iarine), 33920 (Avillia Philusa). Another *vestiaria*, Pompeia Trofhime, may well have been a freedwoman; her husband was a *conditor gregis russatae*, and not a very well-off one, to judge from the poor quality of the Latin on their inscription (*CIL* VI.10072 = *ILS* 5305). The other female tailors of whom we hear are slaves, four of them in the imperial household (*CIL* VI.923, 963*b*, 5206 = *ILS* 1755, imperial *vestificae*; VI.8557, an imperial *vestiaria*; VI.9980 = *ILS* 7428, a servile *vestifica*). *CIL* VI.9744 also refers to a *vestifica*, but is too fragmentary to permit of any conclusions. Cf. Treggiari, 'Jobs,' 84–85; 'Lower Class Women,' 67–68; and Kampen, *Image and Status*, 122. *CIL* VI.9493, which refers to a *tonstrix* named Mecia Flora in a context which suggests that she was a cloth-shearer rather than a barber, has now been classified as a forgery; cf. VI.33809. Still, *tonsores* and *tonstrices* could be cloth-finishers (*Digesta* 33.7.12.6).

84 *CIL* VI.9884 = *ILS* 7567 (Matia Prima).

85 Passages such as Plautus, *Menaechmi* 205; and *Miles Gloriosus* 687–689, suggest that clothing was already being produced for sale in Rome at the beginning of the second century BC. There is corroborative evidence to be found in such sources as Plutarch, *Cato Maior* 4.4 and Livy 39.44.2–3 (Cato's sumptuary tax on, *inter alia*, women's clothing), but there is nothing in these materials to indicate the scale or importance of the garment industry at this relatively early date, much less the degree to which women participated in it.

86 *Digesta* 9.2.9.1 (cf. 50.13.1.2); Plautus, *Miles Gloriosus* 697. For the date of the *lex Aquilia*, see *inter alia* F. Schulz, *Classical Roman Law* (Oxford, 1951) 587 ('most probably of the third century BC'); B. Nicholas, *An Introduction to Roman Law* (Oxford, 1962) 218 ('passed probably in the third century BC'); M. Kaser, *Roman Private Law*[3], transl. R. Dannenbring (Pretoria, 1980) 186, 255 (*circa* 286 BC); F. De Zulueta, *The Institutes of Gaius* II (Oxford, 1953) 209 (287 BC); and Watson, *Roman Private Law around 200 BC*, 151 and note 7 (287 BC). If many mid-wives were as incompetent as Terence's Lesbia (*Andria* 228–233), then such legislation was badly needed. For a late and more serious example, cf. Ammianus Marcellinus 16.10.19.

87 Soranus, *Gynaikeia* 1.1.3–2.4. The superstitious practices to which Soranus briefly alludes were in all probability part of the folk medical tradition drawn upon by the *sagae*, or 'wise women,' on whom see J. Scarborough, *Roman Medicine* (London, 1969) 17–19, and the discussion below.

88 *CIL* VI.8948 (*ser.*), 4458, 8947 = *ILS* 1840, VI.8949 (*lib.*).

89 *CIL* VI.6325, 6647, 6832 (*ser.*), 8192, 8207 (*lib.*).

90 *CIL* VI.9721–9721*a*; cf. 9723 (Poblicia Aphe) and 37810 (Teidia). Grattia and Poblicia were manumitted by women, Teidia by a Sextus Teidius. There is no discernible pattern of female ownership of *opstetrices* in the inscriptions, and in the case of freedwomen who are not associated with one of the great aristocratic houses of Rome, it is not at all obvious how they mastered their skills. Could slave women be apprenticed for training as mid-wives, in the same manner as weavers?

91 *CIL* VI.9720; cf. Le Gall, 'Métiers de femmes,' 128.

92 *CIL* VI.9724 (Valeria Syre), XI.4128 (Autronia Fortunata). *CIL* VI.9725 is too fragmentary to be of use, and III.8820, VI.9722 and XIII.3706 do not furnish enough information to warrant even the most tentative speculation

with regard to the status of the women in question. There are two other provincial *opstetrices* who have recently surfaced, Cleopatra in Narbonese Gaul (*AE* 1979, 396), and Aurelia Macula in Africa (*AE* 1980, 936). They are either *libertae* or *ingenuae*.

93 See G. Calza and G. Becatti, *Ostia*⁹ (Rome, 1974) 71; Kampen, *Image and Status*, 69–72 (Isola Sacra necropolis); Pleket, *Epigraphica II*, no. 20 (Pergamum); and *CIL* VIII. 4896 (Faustus and Irene).

94 For further discussion, see Le Gall, 'Métiers de femmes,' 127–128; Treggiari, 'Jobs,' 86–87; Kampen, *Image and Status*, 69–72, 116; Gardner, *Women in Roman Law and Society*, 240; Eichenauer, *Arbeitswelt der Frau*, 217–245; and above all French, 'Midwives and Maternity Care,' 69–84. For examples of the use of enchantments and other forms of magic and religion in childbirth, see G. Luck, *Arcana Mundi* (Baltimore, 1985) 142–143; and H.D. Betz, *The Greek Magical Papyri in Translation* I (Chicago, 1986) 319.

95 Pleket, *Epigraphica II*, nos 12 (Antiochis), 26 (Domnina), 27 (Obrimos and Ammeis); *CIL* VIII.24679 (Asyllia Polia). Antiochis may be identical with the well-known medical practitioner in Galen 13.341. There are five other provincial *medicae* who were free, and possibly free-born: Iulia Saturnina (*CIL* II.497 = *ILS* 7802), Iulia Quintiana (II.4380), Flavia Hedone (XII.3343), Metilia Donata (XIII.2019), and the anonymous *medica* of XIII.4334. *CIL* II.4314 = *ILS* 5299 is still more fragmentary, and its anonymous *medica* must also be cataloged as an *incerta*. The same holds true for the African *medica* Geminia (*CIL* VIII.806).

96 *Familia Caesaris*: *CIL* VI. 8711 = *ILS* 7803, VI.9084 (*ser.*); VI.8926, *AE* 1972, 83 (*lib.?*); *CIL* VI.8639.*b*.9 (*inc.*). Senatorial household: *CIL* VI.6851.

97 *CIL* VI.9615 = 33812 (Minucia); 9616 (the Terentiae); and 9617 (Venuleia). Cf. *CIL* VI.9510 (a *serva*, Apella). Martial 5.9 supplies a vivid, and predicably caustic, description of the medical apprentice at work; while we are not specifically informed on this point, there is no reason to think that these 'interns' were invariably male.

98 *CIL* V.3461 (Sentia); IX.5861 (Iulia).

99 *CIL* VI.7581 = *ILS* 7804 (Primilla), VI.9477 = *ILS* 7806 (Valeria), VI.9478 (Valia), 9614 (Iulia), X.3980 = *ILS* 7805 (Scantia). For further discussion, see again Le Gall, 'Métiers de femmes,' 128–129; Treggiari, 'Jobs,' 86; Kampen, *Image and Status*, 116; and Gardner, *Women in Roman Law and Society*, 240–241. *Opstetrices* and *medicae* for whom we have epigraphic information are cataloged in Appendix 2 (*infra*).

100 The *locus classicus* is *Digesta* 50.13.1.3.

101 Pliny, *Naturalis Historia* 28.5.23–29; cf. 24.43, where we learn that Servilius' personal physician, Servilius Democrates, used goat's milk to restore the health of the consular's daughter – a salutary reminder that not all of the doctors who served the elite were *ipso facto* above resorting to folk remedies. In fact, it is abundantly clear that many of the *servi medici* had received minimal training from 'physicians' who were themselves little more than charlatans. On this point, see the sobering comments of Forbes, 'Education and Training of Slaves,' 343–353. Servilius, it might be added, was not only a highly educated man but also a historian renowned for his *eloquentia*; see R. Syme, 'The Historian Servilius Nonianus,' *Hermes* 92 (1964) 408–414 = *Ten Studies in Tacitus* (Oxford, 1970) 91–109. Betz, *Greek Magical Papyri* I.242–244 *et passim*, has translated no fewer than 77 different magical cures for a wide variety of diseases, fractures and accidents, ranging from amulets and spells to deal with dog bites or scorpion stings to cures for headaches and gout. With regard to the literary evidence, see, *inter alia*, Pliny, *Naturalis Historia* 28.66, 81–82, 262, 32.135; and Galen, who gives the names of many *medicae* as well

as the specific recipes that they recommended to alleviate or cure illnesses in their various specialties. Cf. 13.58, 85, 143 (Origeneia), 244 (Eugerasia), 250, 341 (Antiochis and Fabulla), 310 (Samithra), 311 (Xanite), 507 (Salome), 707 (Valeria Secunda) and 840 (Maia). For the widespread use of folk remedies in pediatrics, see especially J.-P. Neraudau, *Etre enfant à Rome* (Paris, 1984) 80–82. Eichenauer, *Arbeitswelt der Frau*, catalogs the *medicae* who appear in the literary and Christian sources for the Principate and late Empire (163–191), as well as those for whom epigraphic evidence survives (200–216).

102   S. Dixon, 'Roman Nurses and Foster Mothers: Some Problems of Terminology,' *AULLA* 22 (1984) 9–24.

103   For the Egyptian material, see above all J. Herrmann, 'Die Ammenverträge in den gräko-ägyptischen Papyri,' *ZRG* 76 (1959) 490–499; and K.R. Bradley, 'Sexual Regulations in Wet-Nursing Contracts from Roman Egypt,' *Klio* 62 (1980) 321–325. Bradley and Eichenauer respectively catalog many of the relevant Latin inscriptions in 'Wet-Nursing at Rome: a Study in Social Relations,' in B. Rawson (ed.), *The Family in Ancient Rome* (London, 1985) 201–229, at 204–206; and *Arbeitswelt der Frau*, 274–283; their rosters are updated in Appendix iii below. Bradley also briefly returns to this subject in *Slaves and Masters in the Roman Empire: a Study in Social Control* (Oxford, 1987) 70–73.

104   Soranus, *Gynaikeia* 1.19–20; cf. Galen 6.9; Oribasius 3.120–135; and the discussion in R. Etienne, 'La conscience médicale antique et la vie des enfants,' *Annales de Demographie Historique* 9 (1973) 15–46 = 'Ancient Medical Conscience and the Life of Children,' *Journal of Psychohistory* 4 (1976) 131–161, especially 148–149.

105   Pseudo-Plutarch, *De Liberis Educandis* 3e–f; cf. Quintilian, *Institutio Oratoria* 1.1.12; and Tacitus, *Dialogus de Oratoribus* 29.1. *BGU* 1107 = A.S. Hunt and C.C. Edgar (eds), *Select Papyri* I (Cambridge, Mass., 1932) 16 (Didyma); S.M.E. van Lith, 'Lease of Sheep and Goats / Nursing Contract with Accompanying Receipt,' *ZPE* 14 (1974) 145–162 (Diodora). Since the notion that sexual intercourse ruined a mother's milk does not seem peculiar to Egypt, we may safely presume that similar restrictions governed the professional wet-nurses whom we encounter in the Latin inscriptions.

106   For further details, see Appendix iv.

107   Cf., *inter alia*, Plautus, *Aulularia* 698; *Poenulus* 28–31; *Trinummus* 512–513; Terence, *Adelphoe* 972–977; Lucretius, *De Rerum Natura* 5.222–234; Cicero, *De Amicitia* 74; *Tusculanae Disputationes* 3.1.2; Quintilian, *Institutio Oratoria* 1.1.4–5; Tacitus, *Dialogus de Oratoribus* 28.4; *Germania* 20.1; Plutarch, *Moralia* 608d; Juvenal 6.592–593; and Aulus Gellius, *Noctes Atticae* 12.1. For further discussion, see Neraudau, *Etre enfant*, 77–78; and S. Dixon, *The Roman Mother* (Norman, Okla., 1988) 3, 122–129.

108   *Digesta* 34.1.20; cf. 40.2.13. For the social background of the Latin *nutrices*, see again Appendix iii.

109   *Digesta* 24.1.28.2, 33.2.34.1, 41.7.8, 50.13.14; cf. Plautus, *Aulularia* 815; *Miles Gloriosus* 698; *Truculentus* 903–904; Dio Chrysostomus 7.114; Tacitus, *Dialogus de Oratoribus* 28.4; Pseudo-Plutarch, *De Liberis Educandis* 3c; Soranus, *Gynaikeia* 2.87; Juvenal 6.354; Festus, *Glossaria Latina* v. *lactaria* ('columno in foro dicta, quod ibi infantes lacte alendos deferebant'). The Forum Holitorium antedates the Hannibalic war, and was the site of one of the many omens that occurred in 218 BC (Livy 21.62.2). For a brief introduction to the history of the site, see F. Coarelli, *Guida archeologica di Roma*[2] (Rome, 1975) 278–286.

110   *CIL* VI.32049 (Turtura); *AE* 1960, 249 (Livia). For a third possibility, cf. *CIL* VI.8942 = *ILS* 1839. For further discussion of the *nutrices*, see Maxey,

Occupations of the Lower Classes, 53–55; Treggiari, 'Jobs,' 87–89; Kampen, *Image and Status*, 109; Gardner, *Women in Roman Law and Society*, 241–243; and Eichenauer, *Arbeitswelt der Frau*, 246–291. One Greek passage is also worthy of note in this context. According to Demosthenes 57.45, wet-nursing was a commonplace occupation for fourth-century Athenian citizen women who were living in poverty.

111 Epigraphic references to *paedagogae* are extremely rare; cf. *CIL* V.3519 (*lib.*), VI.6331 = *ILS* 7447*b* (*lib.*), VI.9754 (*civ.*), 9758 (*inc.*); VIII.1506 (*inc.*), IX.6325 (*inc.*); and the comments of Treggiari, 'Jobs,' 90; as well as Eichenauer, *Arbeitswelt der Frau*, 125–126. For the hiring of poor men and women in particular as child-minders, see Tibullus 1.3.83–88; Epictetus 3.26.7; and Plutarch, *Moralia* 830a-b.

112 Cf. Cicero, *De Legibus* 2.59 (the Twelve Tables); Plautus, *Truculentus* 495–496; Lucilius 954–955M; Varro, *De Lingua Latina* 7.70; and Aulus Gellius, *Noctes Atticae* 18.7.3.

113 Tacitus remarks that the genesis of a *senatus consultum* of AD 19 lay in the behavior of a certain Vistilia, a woman of senatorial standing who wished to register with the aediles as a prostitute (*Annales* 2.85). Unfortunately, one cannot determine whether this issue was also taken up in the Larinum decree, or addressed in a separate piece of legislation. On this point, see B. Levick, 'The *Senatus Consultum* from Larinum,' *JRS* 73 (1983) 110–114.

114 Hostilianus: M. Cebeillac-Gervasoni and F. Zevi, 'Révisions et nouveautés pour trois inscriptions d'Ostie,' *MEFR* 88 (1976) 612–620. Larinum decree: *AE* 1978, 145, with German translation in H. Freis, *Historische Inschriften zur römischen Kaiserzeit* (Darmstadt, 1984) no. 31; and text, English translation and commentary in Levick, '*Senatus Consultum* from Larinum,' 97–105. Both texts are discussed in J. Reynolds, M. Beard, R. Duncan-Jones and C. Roueché, 'Roman Inscriptions, 1976–80,' *JRS* 71 (1981) 126 (Larinum), 137 (Ostia). See also Tacitus, *Annales* 15.32 (Nero); Suetonius, *Domitianus* 4.1; Martial, *Spectacula* 6b (Domitian); Juvenal 6.246–267; and Dio Cassius 76.16 (Septimius). There are brief discussions in Gardner, *Women in Roman Law and Society*, 247–248; and Eichenauer, *Arbeitswelt der Frau*, 80–82.

115 Gardner, *Women in Roman Law and Society*, 247, has mistakenly claimed that 'those performers known to us by name were slaves or freedwomen, with names usually of Greek origin.' Eichenauer, *Arbeitswelt der Frau*, 63, similarly writes that 'zusammenfassend lässt sich über die Gruppe der Schauspieler sagen, dass sie durchwegs Sklaven oder Freigelassene waren.' In fact, many of the names that we encounter were clearly chosen for the stage, so they cannot be regarded as a reliable guide to either jural status or ethnic background. On this point see especially C. Garton, 'A Republican Mime-Actress?,' *CR* new series 14 (1964) 238–239 – an article that tentatively adds the otherwise unknown figure of Emphasis, the dedicator of *CIL* I².1359 = VI.33112, to the roster of Republican *mimae*.

116 *CIL* I².1214 = *ILS* 5213 (Eucharis); VI.10110 = *ILS* 5216 (Ecloga); VI.10111 = *ILS* 5215 (Luria); Cicero, *Epistulae ad Atticum* 10.10.5, 10.16.5, 15.22; *Orationes Philippicae* 2.58–62, 69 (Volumnia).

117 Cicero, *In Verrem* 2.3.78 (Tertia); *Anthologia Palatina* 9.567 (Antiodemis). See Appendix v for a complete roster of the known Republican and Augustan actresses, and for fuller discussion of the individual cases, C. Garton, *Personal Aspects of the Roman Theater* (Toronto, 1972), 231–283.

118 Cicero, *Pro Roscio Amerino* 23 (Dionysia); *P. Cornell* 9 = *Select Papyri* I.20 (Isidora). On the latter, see especially W.L. Westermann, 'The Castanet Dancers of Arsinoe,' *JEA* 10 (1924) 134–144; this highly useful article also discusses the contents of seven other similar contracts (*P. Flor.* 74; *P. Gen.*

73; *P. Grenf.* 67; *P. Lond.* 331; and *P. Oxy.* 519, 1025 and 1275). For the four flageolet players, see *P. Lond.* 1917; and the discussion of H.I. Bell, 'A Musician's Contract,' *JEA* 10 (1924) 145–146. On the *sociae mimae*, see *CIL* VI.10109 = *ILS* 5217; if Horace, *Satirae* 1.2.1–4 may be taken at face-value, then the flute-girls in Rome would also have been sufficiently numerous to organize themselves into a guild, the *collegia ambubaiarum*. With regard to the universal appeal of theatrical and stage entertainment, the recent comments of R. MacMullen, *Paganism in the Roman Empire* (New Haven, 1981) 18–25, are very much to the point.

119 Martial 14.203; cf. 1.41.12, 3.63.5, 5.78.26–28, 6.71; Statius, *Silvae* 1.6.71–73; Pliny, *Epistulae* 1.15.3; Juvenal 11.162–176 (*puellae Gaditanae*); and *P. Hibeh* 54 (apprenticeship). Terence, *Phormio* 80–90 introduces us to a *serva* who is learning to play the cithara at school (*citharistria, citharoeda*), but the context may be Athenian. A school in which pupils were trained to become *puellae Gaditanae* is, however, on record (*CIL* VI.9013). Sepulchral inscriptions that record the age-at-death of female musicians and dancers certainly suggest that training began at a young age throughout the Empire, and not simply in Egypt. Cf. *CIL* VI.10143 (9, *saltatrix*), 10127 = *ILS* 5262 (12, *saltatrix*), VIII.12925 = *ILS* 5260 (14, *saltatrix*), VI.7285 (20, *cantrix*), VI.7286 (20, *choraule*), VIII.126 (22, *musica*), VI.10144 (22, *saltatrix*), II.3465 = *ILS* 5256a (25, *sinfoniaca*), VI.9230 (30, *cantrix*) and VI.8693 (35, *cantrix*).

120 *Copa* 1–4; Horace, *Satirae* 1.2.57–59 (' "nil fuerit mi", inquit, "cum uxoribus umquam alienis". Verum est cum mimis, est cum meretricibus, unde fama malum gravius quam res trahit.'); *Epistulae* 1.14.25 (*meretrix tibicina*); Juvenal 2.90 (*tibicina*); 3.62–65; Suetonius, *Nero* 27.2 (*ambubaia*); Plutarch, *Sulla* 36.1 (entertainers in general); *Antonius* 9.8 (*sambucistria*); Augustine, *Sermones* 153.6 (*lyristria*); and *Codex Theodosianus* 4.6.3, 15.7.2, 15.7.8–9, 15.7.12, and 15.13.1.

121 Plautus, *Rudens* 41–46; Terence, *Phormio* 80–86; Valerius Maximus 2.10.8; Lactantius, *Divinae Institutiones* 1.20.10; Cicero, *Pro Plancio* 30. In fact, both Plautus and Terence clearly considered female musicians at large to be little more than prostitutes; cf. Plautus, *Epidicus* 213–221 (*fidicina*); *Mostellaria* 960 (*fidicina* and *tibicina*); Terence, *Adelphoe* 747 (*psaltria*).

122 For an imperial example of a *rustica* learning the art of erotic dancing, see Juvenal 6.63–66 ('Thymele tunc rustica discit'). Livy 39.6.8 tells us that *psaltriae* (female lute-players) and *sambucistriae* (female *sambuca* players) were first introduced to Rome in the triumph that Manlius Vulso celebrated over the Galatians in 187 BC. Plautus, *Stichus* 380 seems to re-inforce Livy's contention, for the *sambucistriae* in this play are Asiatic slaves; cf. Terence, *Adelphoe* 388, 404–405, 451–452, 558–560, 742–747 (servile *psaltriae*), 616–617, 742–743 (servile *sambucistriae*). Indeed, all of the female flute-players (*fidicinae, tibicinae*) and singers (*cantrices, cantatrices*) in Plautus and Terence are servile or libertine in standing; cf. Plautus, *Aulularia* 280–281, 292, 332–333; *Epidicus* 45–52, 130–132, 213–221, 241– 244, 267–269, 274–279, 293–296, 312–319, 352–353, 363–372, 411–413, 463–501, 702–705; *Mostellaria* 934, 960, 971; *Stichus* 380–381, 542; *Trinummus* 252; and Terence, *Eunuchus* 985. However, just as Eichenauer, *Arbeitswelt der Frau*, 60–79 rightly points out that the character of the comic *meretrix* has in every case clearly been shaped to fit the plot, so it must be stressed that the young woman's servile status is equally central to the play's development. In this particular case, therefore, we should not allow ourselves to be seduced by the impressive consistency of the comic evidence, especially since there are so many *incertae* in the epigraphic roster of dancers and musicians. See Appendix vi.

123 Cf. *Codex Theodosianus* 4.6.3, 9.7.1, 15.13.1; *Digesta* 3.2.4.2, 23.2.43.9; *Codex*

Iustinianus 5.5.7 (innkeepers); Paulus, *Sententiae* 2.26.11; *Digesta* 23.2.43.*pr.*; Asclepiades 25; Petronius, *Satyricon* 1.6–7 (*tabernariae*). Tibullus 3.16.3, with its reference to the prostitute armed with a wool-basket, may also be relevant here.

124 See *CIL* IV.1507, 1510 (Amaryllis); 8185 (Mula and Fortunata); and the comments of M. Della Corte, *Case ed abitanti di Pompei*³ (Naples, 1965) 120–121, 323–324; and D'Avino, *Women of Pompeii*, 15–16, 43. For a catalog of the Pompeian inscriptions that furnish the prices charged by prostitutes, see Appendix vii; as S.B. Pomeroy, *Goddesses, Whores, Wives, and Slaves. Women in Classical Antiquity* (New York, 1975) 201; and Duncan-Jones, *Economy of the Roman Empire*², 246, both point out, some of these figures may be malicious rather than real, but it hardly seems likely that all of them would be scurrilous. H. Herter, 'Die Soziologie der antiken Prostitution im Lichte des heidnischen und christlichen Schrifttums,' *JbAC* 3 (1960) 70–111, remains the most important study of this largely neglected topic. For a brief and less discursive overview of prostitution in Roman society, see Treggiari, 'Lower Class Women,' 73–75; or Eichenauer, *Arbeitswelt der Frau*, 112–125.

125 'Palam quaestum facere dicemus non tantum eam, quae in lupanario se prostituit, verum etiam si qua (ut adsolet) in taberna cauponia vel qua alia pudori suo non parcit' (*Digesta* 23.2.43.*pr.*).

126 *Codex Iustinianus* 4.56.3 (Alexander); *Codex Theodosianus* 9.7.1 (Constantine); *CIL* IX.2689 = *ILS* 7478 (Aesernia).

127 See *CIL* IV.8442, and the discussion in Della Corte, *Case ed abitanti*³, 348; and especially in E. La Rocca, and M. and A. de Vos, *Guida archeologica di Pompei*² (Rome, 1981) 230–231. Cf. the equally succint *futuui* [sic] *ospita(m)* of *CIL* XIII.10018, 95 (Bonn). The most comprehensive index of Pompeian buildings and their functions, which is accompanied by a superb set of maps of the site, may be found in H. Eschebach, *Die städtbauliche Entwicklung des antiken Pompeji*, *MDAI (R)* suppl. vol. 17 (Heidelberg, 1970) 165–179.

128 See *CIL* IV.7863, 7873 (Asellina); 7862 (Aegle); 7866 (Maria); 7863–7864 (Zmyrina). Zmyrina may be synonymous with the Ismurna who supported the candidacy of Popidius (IV.7221); cf. Della Corte, *Case ed abitanti*³, 307–308; D'Avino, *Women of Pompeii*, 55; and La Rocca and de Vos, *Pompei*², 208.

129 *CIL* IV.8473 (Culibonia); 8475 (Sitifera); cf. Della Corte, *Case ed abitanti*³, 366; D'Avino, *Women of Pompeii*, 18–19; and Adams, *Latin Sexual Vocabulary*, 110–111. The epithet *sitifera* also seems to be a sexual play on words: one of the most popular coital positions in Roman erotica was styled *more ferarum*. Lucretius describes it, and emphasizes that it was a favorite of prostitutes because they believed it would prevent pregnancy (*De Rerum Natura* 4.1264–1277). A Pompeian bronze survives that nicely illustrates the position; see M. Grant, A. De Simone and M.T. Merella, *Eros in Pompeii: the Secret Rooms of the National Museum of Naples* (New York, 1975) 88–89. For further discussion, see M.C. Marks, 'Heterosexual Coital Positions as a Reflection of Ancient and Modern Cultural Attitudes' (Diss. SUNY Buffalo, 1978) 63–69 *et passim*.

130 *CIL* IV.111 and 2310e (Fortunata); 2310b (Euplia); cf. Della Corte, *Case ed abitanti*³, 149–150, 339–340; D'Avino, *Women of Pompeii*, 45. If she is identical with the Euplia f. of *CIL* IV.5048, then Euplia becomes the first ingenuous *meretrix* that we know by name. For *laxa landicosa*, see again Adams, *Latin Sexual Vocabulary*, 46, 79, 97–98.

131 La Rocca and de Vos, *Pompei*², 226–227.

132 *CIL* IV.8360 (Primilla); 8361 (Ianuaria felas); 2993zg (Afra); 2993db (Cicada); 3916, 8988 (Primigenia); 3922 (Mandata); 3928–3930, 8978 (Serena); 8984 (Fortunata). Cf. Della Corte, *Case ed abitanti*³, 272 (Afra), 273–274 (Cicada,

Mandata, Primigenia, Serena), 299 (Primilla and Ianuaria); and D'Avino, *Women of Pompeii*, 43–44 (Quinta).

133   Horace, *Epistulae* 1.14.21–26; Columella, *De Re Rustica* 1.8.2; Tacitus, *Historiae* 3.83; *Digesta* 5.3.27.

134   CIL XIV.3709 = *ILS* 7477 (Amemone); IV.1679 (Hedone); 8238, 8246 (Capella); 8248 (Prima); 8258–8259 (Iris). As Hedone's inscription makes clear, the basic rate of 2 *asses* that Pompeian prostitutes charged for their services was only half the cost of a serving of Falernian wine: *assibus (singulis) hic bibitur; dupundium si dederis, meliora bibes; qua[rtum] (assem) si dederis, vina Falerna bibes.* Cf. Della Corte, *Case ed abitanti*³, 180 (Hedone), 292–293 (Capella, Prima, Iris); D'Avino, *Women of Pompeii*, 16–18; and La Rocca and de Vos, *Pompei*², 185–186, 306. *AE* 1980, 216, an inscription discovered between Aquinum and Casinum at the site of a sanctuary of Venus, provides a concrete example of how generalizations about the sexual role of *popinariae* and *vinariae* can lead to abuse of the evidence. Four unrelated freedwoman set up a kitchen (*culina*) to serve visitors to the sanctuary. Although there is nothing in the inscription to indicate it, the editor of the text takes it for granted that the four women were doubling as prostitutes. Gardner, *Women in Roman Law and Society*, 249–250, takes this assumption a stage further by speculating that 'they may have met after gaining their freedom; or perhaps their owners had hired them out, to a brothel-keeper or (in view of the catering connection) the proprietor of a *caupona*.' At least one *popa* in Pompeii, the freedwoman Critonia Philema, seems to have been married (*CIL* IV.9824). The only other relevant inscription (*CIL* IV.5424) is too fragmentary to be of any use. T. Kleberg, *Hôtels, restaurants et cabarets dans l'antiquité romaine* (Uppsala, 1957) remains fundamental to any study of the food service industry in the Roman world; for prostitution, see pp. 16, 37, 89–91 *et passim*.

135   *CIL* IV.111 (Fortunata); 368 (Pollia); 7749 (Pherusa); cf. Della Corte, *Case ed abitanti*³, 42, 130, 381–382; and D'Avino, *Women of Pompeii*, 30–32. A certain Sulinea also owned a *thermopolium* in the *insula occidentalis* (VI,Occ. 3.4); see Eschebach, *Städtebauliche Entwicklung*, 135.

136   We have already made reference to Demetrius and Afra Helpis, and to Q. Mestrius Maximus and Irene – two couples in business near Pompeii's Casa del Menandro. Nymphius and Caprasia ran a *caupona* (VI,10,3.4.18) on the Via di Mercurio (*CIL* IV.171, 207). C. Hostilius Conops and Hirtia Psacas managed a *hospitium* and *caupona* (I,2,8) near the Porta Stabiana (IV.3905), while L. Vetutius Placidus and Ascula ran one of Pompeii's larger establishments (I,8,8.9) on the Via dell'Abbondanza (IV.7288, 7291, 7295, 8194*a*); cf. Della Corte, *Case ed abitanti*³, 55–56, 265, 325–326; and D'Avino, *Women of Pompeii*, 30–32. The celebrated Aesernian tavern was also managed by a husband and wife (*CIL* IX.2689 = *ILS* 7478).

137   See *CIL* IV.2172 (Attica); 2258 (Attines); 2198, 2256 (Beronice); 2198, 2206 (Callidrome); 2215 (Cressa); 2193 (Drauca); 2288 (Faustilla); 2173, 2199–2200, 4023, 4066, 8917 (Felicla); 2224, 2259, 2275 (Fortunata); 2189 (Helpis); 2201*a*, 2227*a*, 2233, 2236 (Ianuaria); 2174 (Ias); 2239 (Issa Fabia); 2203–2204 (Mula); 2273, 2292–2293 (Murtis); 2268, 2271 (Myrtale); 2178*a*, 2278 (Nice Cretesiana); 2178*b* (Panta); 2202 (Restituta); 2221, 2225–2228 (Victoria). Only Murtis (2273, 2292) and Myrtale (2268) are said to have engaged in fellatio, but this was probably not the only service that they offered. *Placidus hic futuit quem volvit*, we read in one graffito (2265) – a claim that undoubtedly could have been asserted by any visitor, so long as he was able to pay the price that each *meretrix* charged. This may well have varied. We know that Felicla charged 2 *asses* (4023), but it appears that Drauca commanded a *denarius* (2193).

138   One can form an impression of the interior of this *lupanar* from plates 6 and

7; cf. the discussions in Della Corte, *Case ed abitanti*[3], 203; D'Avino, *Women of Pompei*, 48; and La Rocca, *Pompei*[2], 302–304.

139 Cf. Plautus, *Poenulus* 265–270, 831–838; Horace, *Satirae* 1.2.3; Seneca, *Controversiae* 1.2.1, 1.2.21; Petronius, *Satyricon* 7; Martial 4.4.9, 11.45.1, 12.61.8; Dio Chrysostomus, *Orationes* 7.133; Juvenal 6.121–132; Apuleius, *Metamorphoses* 7.10; *CIL* IV.2184 (Phoebus); IX.2029 = *ILS* 8287 (Vibia). Three Pompeian graffiti suggest that customers were equally aware of a quite different kind of danger – sexually transmitted disease. *CIL* IV.760: *destillatio me tenet* ('I have discharge'). It seems reasonable to assume that this is a reference to some form of drainage associated with a venereal disease. *CIL* IV.1882: *accensum qui pedicat, urit mentulam* ('he who sodomizes an *accensus* will burn his member'). There is a play on words here: an *accensus* is a magisterial attendant, but the verb *accendere* means 'to set on fire.' *CIL* IV.1516: *Hic ego nu(nc) futue formosa(m) fo(r)ma puella(m), laudata(m) a multis, sed lutus intus erat* ('in this place I had sex with a girl who was beautiful on the outside, and praised by many – but on the inside she was filth personified'). The literary evidence for venereal disease in the Roman world is at its clearest in Pliny, *Epistulae* 6.24; cf. Martial 6.66.

140 *CIL* IV.1378, 1387, 1388 (*fellatrix*), 1388a (*extaliosa*). One of the other *meretrices* in residence, Nymphe, is also identified as a *fellatrix* (1389). The services offered by Aphrodite (1382, 1384), Restituta (1374), Secunda (1376, 1389), Spendusa (1403) and Veneria (1391) are left unspecified. Cf. Della Corte, *Case ed abitanti*[3], 60–61; D'Avino, *Women of Pompeii*, 46; and Adams, *Latin Sexual Vocabulary*, 116.

141 *CIL* IV.5105 (Optata); 5127 (Spes); cf. 5120 (Glycera *mordax*); 5118, 5145–5146 (Nebris); 5108 (Partenope); 5125 (Phoebe); 5119 (Suavis); and 5089–5090, 5094, 5104, 5117, 5127, 5130–5131, 5137, 5150, 5153 (Successa). A woman named Venus ran a brothel on the Via dei Soprastanti (VII,6,34–36); the whores in residence included Cloe (IV.1646); Iucunda (1633, 1643); Mystis (1639); Quintilia (1634); Restituta (1631); Rufa (1629a); and Veneria (1642). For further discussion, see again Della Corte, *Case ed abitanti*[3], 162–163, 170–171; and D'Avino, *Women of Pompeii*, 44, 47. The prices charged by prostitutes in Rome seem to have been comparable to those in Pompeii. Cf. Petronius 8.4; Martial 1.103.10; and Juvenal 6.125 (1 *as*); Martial 2.53.7 (2 *asses*); Martial 9.32.3 (1 *denarius*). Horace, *Satirae* 1.2.121–122; Propertius 2.23.15–22; and Dio Chrysostomus, *Orationes* 7.140 all allude to the ready availability and cheap cost of commercial sex, but without offering specific figures.

142 *CIL* IV.4592 (Eutychis); 1751 (Attica). The above-mentioned Restituta (*CIL* IV.2202), and the *verna* Successa (IV.4025–4026), both advertised themselves as *bellis moribus* (IV.4025–4026). The most informative graffito, however, concerns a certain Nicopolis (IV.8171: *Nicopolis, futui te ego et Proculus et Fructus Holconi*); cf. Della Corte, *Case ed abitanti*[3], 332.

143 Catullus 58; Horace, *Carmina* 1.25; Propertius 2.22.3, 2.23.15, 4.7.19; Martial 1.34.6, 2.63.2; Juvenal 11.171–175 (streets, alleys, bridges, archways); Martial 1.34.6, 3.82.2, 12.32.22 (city walls); Horace, *Epodi* 5.58; Propertius 4.7.15; Persius, *Satirae* 5.32; Martial 2.17 (here the reference to a *tonstrix* seems to have an obscene connotation), 6.66.2, 11.61.3–4, 11.78.11 (the Subura). Plautus, *Menaechmi* 338–342 paints a vivid picture of *meretrices* in the port towns who seized upon potential customers as soon as they disembarked from their ships; the play is set in Epidamnus, but the comment would probably apply equally well to Pompeii, Ostia or any other port of consequence in the Roman world.

144 Plautus, *Poenulus* 265–270, 339; Juvenal 6.489, 9.22–26 (temples); Dio Chrysostomus, *Orationes* 7.133 (temples and marketplaces); Martial 2.52; Tacitus, *Historiae* 3.83; *Digesta* 3.2.4.2 (baths); Martial 1.34.8, 3.93.15 (graveyards).

145 Lucilius 1034M; Horace, *Satirae* 1.6.113; Juvenal 3.65 (circus); Propertius 2.23.4 (theater); Horace, *Epistulae* 1.14.21; Tacitus, *Historiae* 3.83 (cook-shops and brothels).

146 See Cicero, *Pro Caelio* 48–50; Horace, *Satirae* 1.2.31–35; and the comments on this passage in the scholia of Porphyrion and pseudo-Acron.

147 Horace, *Epistulae* 1.15.21 (Lucania); Dio Chrysostomus, *Orationes* 5.25 (Libya); Strabo 8.6.20; Aulus Gellius, *Noctes Atticae* 1.8 (Corinth).

148 Cf. S. Treggiari, 'Family Life among the Staff of the Volusii,' *TAPA* 105 (1975) 401 note 37: 'clients of brothels were mostly slaves (who lived in households with an unnatural balance of the sexes) and the free poor.'

149 S. Treggiari, 'Libertine Ladies,' *CW* 64 (1971) 197: 'the common streetwalker was probably most often of slave or freed status. The same seems true of the more accomplished and expensive *meretrix*.' She reiterates this conclusion in 'Lower Class Women,' 73; cf. Pomeroy, *Goddesses, Whores, Wives and Slaves*, 201 ('it is impossible to determine the status of the women who worked in brothels from the information in graffiti, but it seems likely that they were slaves or freedwomen'); and Bradley, *Slaves and Masters*, 117 ('the number of slaves who functioned as prostitutes appears to have been great'). Only Herter, 'Soziologie der antiken Prostitution,' 78–79, explicitly argues for a mix of slave, libertine and free-born women in the profession. For recent discussion on the gender imbalance, see *inter alia* P.R.C. Weaver, *Familia Caesaris* (Cambridge, 1972) 172; Treggiari, 'Domestic Staff at Rome,' 248; 'Family Life among the Staff of the Volusii,' 395; 'Household of Livia,' 58; Pomeroy, *Goddesses, Whores, Wives, and Slaves*, 194; Flory, 'Family in *Familia*,' 87–88; W.V. Harris, *War and Imperialism in Republican Rome, 327–70* BC (Oxford, 1979) 84 note 2; Bradley, *Slaves and Masters*, 73–74, 147; and W.V. Harris, 'On the Roman Slave Supply and Slave Breeding,' in M.I. Finley (ed.), *Classical Slavery* (Cambridge, 1987) 42–64.

150 Servile backgrounds may be assumed above all for women from the eastern provinces, who enjoy such an unsavoury reputation among the Latin poets. See, for example, Lucilius 123–124M; Propertius 2.23.21–22; pseudo-Virgil, *Copa* 1–4; Statius, *Silvae* 1.6.70; and Juvenal 3.62–66, 8.158–163; cf. as well Dio Chrysostomus, *Orationes* 7.134; Athenaeus, *Deipnosophistae* 13.576c, 577a, 595a; and Philostratus, *Epistulae* 47.

151 See Cicero, *Pro Caelio* 57–58 (Clodia); Sallust, *Coniuratio Catilinae* 25 (Sempronia); Tacitus, *Annales* 2.85; Suetonius, *Tiberius* 35.2 (evasion of the adultery laws). The registration of prostitutes with the aediles certainly dates back to the middle of the second century BC, but the procedure may be much older; see Aulus Gellius, *Noctes Atticae* 4.14, and the comments of Broughton, *The Magistrates of the Roman Republic* I.455. It is clear from *Digesta* 23.2.47 that at least some women of senatorial rank did engage in prostitution, but we do not know precisely when or how many may have been involved. This curious phenomenon may have inspired Apuleius' seemingly misogynistic description of the kidnapped maiden who eagerly looked forward to enslavement in a brothel (*Metamorphoses* 7.10).

152 See Suetonius, *Gaius Caligula* 41.1; Dio Cassius 58.28.9 (Caligula); Tacitus, *Annales* 15.37; Dio Cassius 62.15.4–6 (Nero); S.H.A., *Commodus* 2.8; and Juvenal 6.115–132; Dio Cassius 60.31.1 (Valeria Messallina).

153 *Digesta* 23.2.43.5; *Codex Theodosianus* 15.8.2.

154 *Cistellaria* 38–45; cf., *inter alia*, *Mostellaria* 196–202, 216–217; and Terence, *Heautontimorumenos* 389–391. Herter, 'Soziologie der antiken Prostitution,'

89–90, draws attention to the fact that, although beauty was an essential qualification for a successful *hetaera*, it hardly ever appears among the attributes of respectable *matronae*. This reinforces the intrinsically plausible argument of E. Schuhmann, 'Zur sozialen Stellung der Frau in den Komödien des Plautus,' *Das Altertum* 24 (1978) 97–105, who stresses that the strident acquisitiveness of the Plautine *meretrix* resulted from a healthy appreciation of her low social status and precarious economic position.

155   Zosimus 2.38.3; Seneca, *Epistulae* 101.15 (*etiam amicum prodere ut diutius vivant et liberos ad stuprum manu sua tradere*). For further references, see Herter, 'Soziologie der antiken Prostitution,' 77–79.

156   Terence, *Eunuchus* 934–940; Martial 3.82.28; Lactantius, *Divinae Institutiones* 5.8.7 (*nec feminam necessitas cogeret pudorem suum profanare, ut victum sibi obscenissimum quaerat*).

157   Notably Firmicus Maternus, *Mathesis* 6.31.91 (the *meretrix* combines greed with passion); and Johannes Chrysostom, *Homiliae in Epistolam ad Hebraeos* 15.3 (he explicitly rejects hunger and poverty as sufficient excuses to engage in prostitution).

158   Cf. *Heautontimorumenos* 446–447: 'thereafter, although it was against her will, she was compelled to make a living through prostitution' (*ea coacta ingratiis postilla coepit victum volgo quaerere*); *Andria* 797–799: 'it is said that Chrysis lived in this street, the woman who opted dishonorably to earn a fortune here rather than live in her own land in honest poverty' (*in hac habitasse platea dictumst Chrysidem, quae sese inhoneste optavit parere hic ditias potius quam in patria honeste pauper viveret*); 70–79: 'meanwhile, about three years ago a woman migrated here from Andros and settled in the neighborhood – a beautiful woman in her prime, who was forced to move because of poverty and the studied neglect of her relatives. . . . At first she lived a chaste existence, with thrift and hardship, earning a living by distaff and loom; but afterwards, a lover showed up and offered her a fortune, first one and then another. Since everyone's natural inclination is to prefer the delights of the flesh to hard work, she took him up on the offer, and then went to work as a courtesan' (*interea mulier quaedam abhinc triennium ex Andro commigravit huc viciniam, inopia et cognatorum neglegentia coacta, egregia forma atque aetate integra . . . Primo haec pudice vitam parce et duriter agebat, lana ac tela victum quaeritans; sed postquam amans accessit pretium pollicens unus et item alter, ita ut ingeniumst omnium hominum ab labore proclive ad lubidinem, accepit condicionem, dein quaestum occipit*).

159   *Roman Law: Linguistic, Social and Philosophical Aspects* (Edinburgh, 1969) 10.

160   In the course of a long and detailed description of the Saturnalia, Statius refers to female entertainers from these three locations (*Silvae* 1.6.67–74). It is hardly coincidence that they are made to personify the nocturnal licentiousness that was a hallmark of this, the most uninhibited of all Roman celebrations.

161   Although he approaches the subject from a completely different point of view, T.A.J. McGinn, 'The Taxation of Roman Prostitutes,' *Helios* 16 (1989) 79–110, reaches a similar conclusion.

162   Cf. the summary remarks of Treggiari, 'Lower Class Women,' 78–79; and Kampen, *Image and Status*, 30, 133–134; both mention prostitution, but without any particular emphasis.

V

PARENT AND CHILD

THE ENIGMA OF ROMAN CHILDHOOD

At some point, it now appears, early in the third century AD, a Christian apologist named Minucius Felix published his *Octavius*, a religious dialogue among three friends that climaxes in predictable fashion with the conversion of the pagan interlocutor.[1] The debate unfolds as the participants stroll along the beach outside Ostia, but in its early stages Minucius pauses to sketch the following scene:

> Then our party came to a place where several small boats, having been drawn up on the shore, rested above ground on oaken rollers so as to prevent rot. There we saw a group of small boys, who were eagerly vying with one another in a game of ducks and drakes. This is what the game is all about: you choose a well-rounded shell from the shore – one that has been rubbed smooth by the pounding of the waves – and holding it horizontally in your fingers while stooping as low to the ground as you can get, you send it spinning across the water. Once thrown, it should either skim the surface of the sea, gliding smoothly along, or conversely shave the tops of the waves, only to resurface time and time again. Among the boys, the one whose shell has gone the farthest and skipped the most declares himself the winner.[2]

This charming picture of children at play repeats itself in many different forms in the literature of the late Republic and Empire. A century or so earlier, for example, the younger Pliny describes the *pueri* of Hippo Diarrhytus as *quos otium lususque sollicitat*; their time was given over to fishing and swimming, and one of the boys brought his town unwelcome notoriety by striking up a friendship with a dolphin, which allowed him to ride on its back.[3] At still earlier moments in time, both Horace and the younger Seneca allude to yet another seaside activity that has long been the province of the very young – building castles in the sand.[4] One did not, however, have to live near the sea to indulge in a game of tag, or to mimic one's elders by playing at soldiers or pretending to be a bishop or a magistrate presiding over a tribunal.[5] There was in addition a bewildering variety of balls and ball games, for boys and girls alike, as well as Roman versions of the modern leap-frog and blind-man's bluff.[6] Roman children also used coins to play heads or tails (*navia aut capita*), as well as *par impar* – here one player held a certain number of coins in his hand, while the other had to guess, as the name suggests, whether the figure was odd or even. A third and cognate game, *micatio* (the lineal antecedent of the modern Italian *morra*), also involved two players: each rapidly extended some or all of the fingers of his right hand while simultaneously attempting to guess the total number that had been held out.[7] This kind of entertainment could become addictive: Suetonius informs us that Augustus, who was himself a notorious gambler, sometimes gave considerable sums of money to his guests so that they could play at dice (*tali/tesserae*) or *par impar* over dinner. The Roman passion for gambling with dice, which inspired learned treatises on a staggering number of games, in fact seems to have been instilled in childhood as well. Thus the satirist Persius fondly recalled the days of his youth, when nothing counted for more than the next throw of the dice or spin of a top. Dice, coins, nuts – these were the tokens that Roman children placed at risk in games that call to mind such diverse forms of modern amusement as marbles, lagging for coins, and tossing cards into a hat.[8] Just as the dedication of her dolls to Juno or Venus marked an obvious *rite de passage* for the Roman bride, so the scattering of nuts among children flocking around the wedding party was an equally symbolic gesture on the part of the groom.[9]

Although dolls were by no means the only toys with which Roman girls played, we may safely infer both from this ritual act as well as from the frequency with which they surface in tomb furnishings that they were the most important. Dolls sculpted out of clay, wood, bone and ivory have all survived; some of these figures, such as the famous example taken from the tomb of Crepereia Tryphaena, which is now on permanent display in Rome's Antiquarium Comunale (the Palazzo Caffarelli), are actually jointed! Their poses could thus be changed along with their clothing, giving their young owners the opportunity to exercise their imaginations to the fullest. Plutarch's touching account of how his infant daughter used to insist that her *nutrix* offer a breast to her favorite doll permits us at least to glimpse this elusive world of the Roman child's imagination.[10]

The spinning top that so fascinated the youthful Persius seems to have enchanted many another Roman youth as well. Both Tibullus and Virgil specifically refer to it as a toy that especially appealed to boys, and the same is probably true of the riding sticks and mouse-drawn miniature carts to which Horace alludes.[11] In the wealthier households, as scenes on sarcophagi in the Louvre (M. Cornelius Statius) and the Vatican Museum make clear, older boys might even drive small chariots of their own, which were harnessed to a dog, pony, or goat (plates 8–9).[12] There is every reason to believe, then, that in the late Republic and Empire, the world of the small, free-born child was typically replete with toys and games. It is so described by a variety of Roman authors – and, more convincing still – in a pair of simple but deeply moving inscriptions. *Dum vixi, lusi* ('so long as I lived, I played'), we read on the tombstone of Geminia Agathe, who died at the age of 5. In the case of Crocale, who passed away before her fourteenth birthday, this theme recurs in the form of a plea addressed to the *puellae* who came upon her tomb: 'play, you happy little girls, so long as life permits it, for often a malevolent fate carries off even the most winsome among us.'[13]

For the modern reader, and particularly the enlightened parent, these idyllic images are familiar and therefore comforting, but we should hasten to add that this composite portrait of Roman childhood is both incomplete and delusive. Quite apart from the deliberate exposure or murder of unwanted babies – practices that are well-documented, even if they defy the best attempts of modern scholars to quantify them[14] – there is ample evidence for what is now termed child abuse in the Roman world. Predictably, slave children were most vulnerable to sexual and other forms of exploitation. The fictional Trimalchio is perhaps the most celebrated of the *deliciae*, those handsome little boys who catered to the sexual whims of their male or female owners, but it is above all in Martial's epigrams that pederasty is a commonplace occurrence between master and slave.[15] *Domini* could and did resort to a variety of depilatories to keep their *deliciae* free of bodily hair, and even used different regimens in an attempt to delay the onset of puberty.[16] The most radical technique was castration, and sources from Martial to Ammianus Marcellinus attest the continuation of this practice in the face of increasingly severe imperial legislation designed to prevent it.[17] Slave dealers also catered to the Roman fascination with physical abnormality – a market in which dwarfs commanded particularly high prices. The prudent merchant apparently did not, however, rely on nature's whims to keep up his supply of these unfortunates; as Neraudau so graphically puts it, 'certains étaient fabriqués par les ramasseurs d'enfants exposés, qui en enfermaient quelques-uns dans des caisses pour interrompre leur croissance.'[18]

The vast majority of the children sold into slavery in Italy during the last two centuries of the Republic had, of course, been taken captive in the far-flung wars of conquest that were the hallmark of this age. Plutarch's narrative, for example, makes it clear that children made up a significant proportion of the 60,000 Cimbri whom Marius is said to have captured after his decisive victory at Vercellae in 101 BC.[19] Such slave children had absolutely no legal protection against the abuses described above, and unlike at least some of the children born into slavery (*vernae*), whose numbers would increase so sharply during the Principate, these young *captivi* self-evidently could not count upon the sentimentality of their owners to alleviate their situation. It should thus hardly occasion surprise to learn that homosexuality in general and pederasty in particular first became commonplace features of Roman social life during this period. As Verstraete has appropriately emphasized, the acceptance of homosexuality, especially among the Roman elite, must be numbered among the many domestic consequences of the dramatic post-Hannibalic expansion of the *imperium Romanum*: at this time Roman law already had mechanisms in place that were designed to protect free-born minors from sexual exploitation, but it did not exhibit a like concern for slave children of either sex.[20]

Given the extremely brutal treatment of so many slave children, it is all the more important to stress that, Roman law notwithstanding, their free-born counterparts were also physically and sexually abused. The mild-mannered Seneca, for example, bluntly recommends that parents should beat a child who is in need of discipline, and it is quite clear that schoolboys were routinely subjected to a litany of horrors that included both corporal punishment and sodomy. Thus Horace nicknamed one of his teachers, L. Orbilius Pupillus, 'the rod' (*plagosus*). His reputation must have been well earned, for he inspired still another of his students, the poet Domitius Marsus, to immortalize his penchant for wielding the whip and rod in a line of verse.[21] Roman literature, pagan and Christian alike, continues to reveal *magistri* who behaved in this fashion into the late empire and beyond, but the most banal and therefore most persuasive piece of evidence stems from first-century Pompeii. Here, in a school run by a certain C. Iulius Helenus, a surviving grafitto makes it clear that students who neglected their lessons could expect a flogging from the master.[22]

In their graffiti, the students in this school also cast Helenus as a pederast: the terms *fellator* or *cinaedus* appear on the walls in three different places. These particular graffiti might be dismissed as nothing more than malicious slurs, without any basis in reality, but this would not obviate the fact that many teachers did take sexual advantage of their pupils. Juvenal refers in passing to the corrupting influence of one *magister*, while according to Suetonius, the eminent grammarian Q. Remmius Palaemon was as well known for his unnatural vices as for his formidable learning. Once again, however, it is an inscription that furnishes the most telling evidence of all. On his funerary epitaph, a teacher named Furius Philocalus proudly tells us that 'in dealing with his students he exhibited the highest degree of chastity, while he also wrote out wills honestly, neither turning away nor injuring anyone.' It need hardly be added that, if these virtues had been widely observed, there would have been little point in enumerating them.[23]

There were other settings in which *liberi* might also be sexually exploited. Writing late in the second century AD, Artemidorus of Daldis analyzed the meaning of dreams in which fathers and mothers have sexual intercourse with their sons. Some parents, at least, were prepared to indulge such fantasies: Martial, for example, ridicules an openly incestuous relationship in which the mother and son perversely referred to themselves as *soror* and *frater*. We also hear of well-born Roman children who were sodomized or forced to engage in fellatio with men outside their families. The aged emperor Tiberius is the central figure in the most notorious such episode. After his retreat to Capri, we are told, he surrounded himself with a troop of children – one of them the future emperor Aulus Vitellius – whom he abused in this manner. Moral outrage has led many scholars to reject the very existence of these *spintriae*, but the story is too widely documented to be so cavalierly rejected. In any event, there are a great many allusion to pederastic relationships in Roman literature – and we are not entitled to claim that the *pueri* in quesion were invariably slaves.[24]

It is little wonder, then, that Saint Augustine, whose own

instructors were very much in the tradition of Orbilius 'the rod', looked back upon childhood as a period of unmitigated horror. 'Who would not recoil in terror and elect to die,' he inquires at one point, 'if it was submitted to him that he must suffer either death or a return to childhood?'[25] Thus the sense of nostalgia that we have noted, *exempli gratia*, in Persius' satires, is singularly absent in Augustine's essays. Curiously, however, as children the two authors seem to have been equally zealous in their play, and equally resolved to go on playing even at the expense of their studies. It was at this point that their experiences apparently diverged; there is nothing in his poetry to indicate that Persius ever received the stern corporal punishment that was meted out to Augustine – and it is unlikely in the extreme that either man had been sodomized as a child. Hence their dramatically different recollections of a childhood that in both cases seems to have been free of sexual abuse graphically demonstrate how complex the pattern of child development was in ancient Rome. This in and of itself should serve to discourage rosy generalizations about Roman child-rearing, but it must also be emphasized that the surviving evidence hints at complex and fundamental changes in both the affective and jural ties between parent and child over time, and particularly during the last two centuries of the Republic. These developments are especially visible within the elite, but at times the evidence does have a wider application. In this context, one student of the subject has already remarked that, in the whole of the Plautine corpus, there are only two allusions to the child at play, while dolls of Roman style have yet to be discovered from the republican era.[26] When compared with the rich and diverse store of literary and archaeological evidence for the Principate – data that have not by any means been exhaustively surveyed in the preceding pages – this paucity of republican material points to a world in which free-born children either had far less opportunity to play, or one in which their activities were of less consequence to adults. Such seeming contradictions in the evidence for Roman childhood constitute, in fact, only the most obvious manifestations of this pattern of affective and jural change, which is still only dimly perceived yet was clearly of the most profound importance. However difficult the task, therefore, we must nevertheless try to gauge the dimensions of these developments. Above all, since these changes in the parent–child relationship were taking place during the same period in which slave children were first being introduced to and brutalized by Roman society in large numbers, we must ask whether, paradoxically, the increasing affection for small, free-born children that we see so clearly among the elite was also ultimately a product of this era's ceaseless warfare. It is still too early to answer this question firmly in the affirmative, but as we shall discover, the evidence at least suggests that such a causal link did in fact exist.

MODERN INSIGHTS

According to Roman legend, in 488 BC an exiled patrician named Cn. Marcius Coriolanus led the Volsci, one of Rome's most bitter enemies in the tribal warfare that consumed fifth century Latium, on a march against the city. The events that allegedly followed are treated at varying length by Livy, Plutarch and Dionysius of Halicarnassus. These three authors are in agreement that, with the very existence of their homes and families in jeopardy, the *matronae* prevailed upon Coriolanus' wife and mother to lead a delegation of women and children to his camp, in the hope that he could be persuaded to abandon the campaign. At this point, Livy's account radically diverges from that of Dionysius, which is closely followed by Plutarch. In Livy's version, when he recognized that his mother was drawing near,

> Coriolanus, who was nearly beside himself, leapt from his seat and hastened to embrace her. With tears giving way to anger, however, she said: 'Tell me, before I accept your embrace, have I come to an enemy or a son? Am I a captive in your camp, or your mother?'

With considerable hauteur, she then proceeded to lecture him on the meaning of patriotism and filial piety, and overawed by this timely display of *materna auctoritas*, he immediately decided to give up the campaign. Dionysius, in contrast, scripts a very long speech in which Veturia also appeals to her son's sense of patriotism and *pietas*, but his Coriolanus remains completely unresponsive to this tactic. It is only when she falls to the ground at his feet that he is finally moved, and submits to her will.[27] At this point, the two traditions once again converge: it was in the aftermath of this extraordinary triumph, and in order to honor the *matronae* for their heroism, that the Senate decided to dedicate a temple to Fortuna Muliebris.[28]

There is, at first glance, little to distinguish the discrepant testimony that we observe here from many similar examples in the annalistic tradition. Indeed, it would appear that this particular conflict can be easily resolved. Livy, it has been argued, manipulated the legend to make it serve his didactic purpose; Dionysius, on the other hand, has seized upon the pathetic elements in the scene, and elaborated them in conformity with the principles of tragic history.[29] Despite the inherent plausibility of this explanation, however, in the last decade many students of Roman history have come to the conclusion that source conflicts of this type often harbor a deeper meaning. In a widely read and quite influential article, for example, Paul Veyne has argued that the transition from Republic to Empire had a profound impact upon conjugal relations within the Roman elite. In the highly competitive political environment of the Republic, marriage within the elite was viewed largely as a means of forming political alliances and conveying property, but in the quite different atmosphere of the Principate, romantic love became for the first time an acknowledged and valued feature of the marital union. In the final analysis, he claims, it is this growing capacity for emotional expression that is responsible for many of the discrepancies that we observe in republican and imperial accounts of a given event.[30]

Jean-Pierre Neraudau, Michel Manson, Suzanne Dixon and Thomas Wiedemann have extended Veyne's argument to the bond between the aristocratic parent and child. Here as well, they remark, the values that were so widely admired during the Republic evolved into something quite different under the Principate. In the former period, the emphasis was upon training the child to carry out his or her future responsibilities; satisfaction of the child's immediate emotional needs was deemed to be of little or no importance. Plautus takes us to the very core of this value system when, in an awkward architectural metaphor, he writes that

> parents are the builders of their children. They lay the bases of their children's lives. They raise them up, take great pains to put their lives on a firm foundation. They stop at nothing to make them useful and upright, both as men and citizens, nor do they reckon money spent on this effort as an expense.

Because their emotional investment in their offspring was so small, parents were neither expected nor encouraged to mourn those who died in infancy or childhood; indeed, it is quite clear from Cicero's defensiveness in this regard that an adult who paid close attention to small children was behaving in an inappropriate manner. In startling contrast, as all of these authors again note, throughout the Principate fathers and mothers alike took a keen interest in their children's activities, nurtured them emotionally, and mourned their premature decease with such intensity that a new literary genre, the *consolatio*, was called into being. Admittedly, the recipient of such a treatise was typically a woman, but Quintilian's devastated reaction to the deaths of his two sons – a reaction for which there are ample parallels – warns us not to accept at face value the letter in which Seneca reproaches his friend Marullus for an unseemly display of grief.[31]

There is, then, among those who have studied the issue closely, general agreement that the emotional content of the two central relationships in Roman society, husband and wife, and parent and child, witnessed a profound change that began in the Republic and climaxed during the first decades of the Principate. This consensus should not be allowed, however, to conceal the deep divisions of opinion that still exist with regard to the dimensions of this development, its more precise timing, and its causes. The most schematic (and therefore untenable) position has been adopted by Veyne, who maintains that conubial relations were deeply affected at every level of Roman society, and that the conjoining of love and marriage was a natural outcome of the political revolution that ushered in the Principate. He stipulates, that is to say, that this trend first surfaced among the elite, who had to formulate a new *raison d'être* for marriage since it could no longer facilitate traditional political objectives, and spread from there to the rest of society. This position compels him to argue, *inter alia*, that slave marriage (*contubernium*) not only developed in the imperial period but was actually an indirect consequence of a political revolution – a most perilous position indeed![32] Neraudau, on the other hand, also believes that the advent of the Principate marked the climactic moment in this great drama, but he attributes the growing emphasis upon mutually affective relationships to the commensurately gradual but steady erosion of *patria potestas*.[33] Manson and Dixon, it might be added, are quite vague about the origins and devolution of this extraordinary development, but both are clearly of the opinion that it was already well advanced by the end of the Republic.[34]

The current debate over these basic points seems destined to continue indefinitely, in part at least because the body of evidence upon which historians construct their interpretations is itself contradictory. Early in the second century BC, we find grieving fathers in Plautus' comedies, and indulgent parents in Terence. Conversely, in the first and second centuries AD, when parental indulgence of children and overt displays of affection for them were both commonplace, Seneca and Tacitus continue to advocate the conservative doctrine that a parent's foremost responsibility was 'to shape the child's sense of morality and mould it, for the principles that are impressed in the formative years penetrate to the very core of one's being.' At about the same time, Plutarch is openly critical of mothers who neglect their children while they are alive, yet put on a histrionic display of grief when they die. In the late Republic, Catullus and Lucretius manifest the kind of sentimental tenderness toward children that caused Cicero such embarrassment, yet while the latter counseled his readers to accept the death of their children with Stoic calm, he himself was overwhelmed by grief on the death of his daughter Tullia.[35]

Confronted with such intractable contradictions, perhaps the most prudent course for the historian to follow is to try and elucidate prevalent attitudes and values, while conceding that any given finding will in all likelihood admit of many individual exceptions. Thus, in the course of an exemplary study of the social implications of wet-nursing in Italian society, Keith Bradley comes to the conclusion that a man's *amici* would measure the grief that he displayed upon the death of a child against the child's age. Mourning that would be considered proper for a child of 14, for example, would be thought excessive for a child of 5, and still more inappropriate in the case of an infant. This particular element of the Roman value system is clearly displayed in Plutarch's letter of condolence to his wife on the death of their daughter Timoxena, and it was the violation of this code that inspired Seneca's seemingly inhuman criticism of his friend Marullus. Seneca might have proven more sympathetic, in short, if the child for whom Marullus grieved had been somewhat older at the moment of his death. Nevertheless, this excessive display of grief on Marullus' part shows how a value that is endorsed in the abstract may be found wanting when put to the test.[36]

These cautionary remarks should be kept firmly in mind when assessing the results of the semantic approach that Manson has employed to probe changes in the parent–child relationship. As he points out, early in the second century BC the vocabulary used to describe infancy and early childhood was still vague and in flux. Thus there is no single word equivalent to our modern 'baby'; instead, the Romans made do with terms that reflected the new-born's diminutive size (*parvus/parvulus*). Adverbial phrases, such as Terence's *a parvolo* or *a pueris parvolis*, were used to connote both infancy and childhood, and it is often impossible to determine which meaning the author has in mind in a given line. Two centuries later, in contrast, the terms *infans* and *infantia* are used routinely with reference to the period from birth to age 7, and thereafter the vocabulary of childhood becomes still more specialized, with diminutives such as *infantulus, anniculus, bimulus, trimulus* and *quadrimulus* designating precise moments within this seven-year period. All of this led Manson rightly to conclude that, in the interim, the small child 'took on substance and became personalized and individualized.'[37]

   This growing awareness of the child as a unique personality is, however, only one element in the changing pattern of parent–child relations. Semantic analysis further reveals that, in this same time period, aristocratic parents increasingly began to feel that small children should be treated with love and tenderness, and no longer simply be viewed as the impassive instruments by means of which one perpetuated lineage, wealth and social standing. Here Manson does not have in mind such puerile remarks as Cicero's frequently cited dictum that human beings instinctively love children – a proposition which is not in fact as self-evident as it might appear, and with which his friend Atticus, for a very long time, strongly disagreed.[38] Rather, he draws our attention to the contexts in which Latin authors used the adjectives *dulcis, suavis* and *mellitus* to express the concept of sweetness, and how they changed over time. In Plautus, Terence and the fragments of Lucilius, these terms are never applied to children; in the late Republic and early Empire, in contrast, *liberi* are repeatedly described as 'sweet' in both prose and poetry, while this quality is attributed to them on scores of funerary inscriptions dating from the Principate.[39] Again, in Ciceronian Latin *diligentia* conveys the tender and protective concern that a parent feels for his child; in Plautus, this noun (or the verb *diligere*) occurs in ten passages, not one of which involves children.[40] Similar shifts of meaning take place in other word groups, which need not be surveyed here; the seminal point is that, between Plautus and Terence in the early second century, and Catullus and Cicero in the middle of the first, the small child not only came to be valued as an individual but also to be looked upon with love and affection.[41] It remains to try to account for this phenomenon, and we shall begin by examining Neraudau's bald but seemingly plausible contention that the dynamic element in this situation was the erosion of the *patria potestas*. This supposition, it will be argued, is wholly in error – a point that can best be demonstrated by drawing upon some of the large body of comparable evidence deployed by anthropologists who have probed the formative elements of the parent–child relationship in modern societies.

PATRIA POTESTAS, MATERNA AUCTORITAS

We have already reviewed in some detail the various ways in which primitive Roman law allowed fathers to exercise authority over their legitimate children, so a brief recapitulation should suffice at this point.[42] Foremost among these powers was the *ius vitae et necis*, the power of life and death over all children still *in manu*. Although Dionysius of Halicarnassus asserts that a father was legally required to rear all of his sons as well as his first-born daughter – a constraint that he attributes to Romulus – in fact it is generally agreed that the fate of every child was subject to his whim. Immediately upon delivery, the new-born infant was placed on the ground at the father's feet, and the latter acknowledged both paternity and his intention to rear the child by picking it up (*tollere liberos*). Those whom he refused to recognize were then exposed or killed: the Law of the Twelve Tables compelled him to dispose of the deformed in this fashion, but it is equally obvious that superfluous daughters and the illegitimate of both sexes were also very much at risk.[43]

In theory at least, every unemancipated son or unmarried daughter ran the risk of being put to death so long as his or her father remained alive, but it is impossible to judge how many parents would have been willing to resort to such an extreme measure even with the greatest provocation. To be sure, some fathers did make use of this power, but it should be noted that in every case of which we have knowledge, the son or daughter who was executed had reached adulthood, while there is no evidence that such action was ever taken capriciously; furthermore, it is not always clear whether the young men in question were victims of *patria potestas* or magisterial *imperium*. This ambiguity, for example, surrounds the three most notorious and tragic cases in the annalistic record, when L. Junius Brutus exercised his consular authority to order the execution of his sons for treason (509 BC), and the generals A. Postumius Tubertus and T. Manlius Imperiosus Torquatus (431 and 340 BC) similarly dispatched their sons for truly egregious lapses in military discipline.[44] The legendary Spurius Cassius, according to one tradition at least, was also put to death by his father after a domestic *consilium* found him guilty of treasonable activities during his consulship (486 BC). Centuries later, the charges levelled against D. Iunius Silanus, Aemilius Scaurus and A. Fulvius were equally heinous. Silanus committed suicide after his father declared him guilty of *repetundae* during his governorship in Macedon (140 BC). Scaurus similarly killed himself when he was barred from his father's presence after running away in battle against the Cimbri; Fulvius was executed by his parent for his role in the Catilinarian conspiracy (*circa* 102 and 63 BC).[45] These episodes all involved public misconduct in one form or another, but the few tribunals in which fathers are known to have judged their sons for purely private offenses also dealt with extremely grave charges. In the Augustan period, to cite but one well-known case, a certain Tarius sent his son into exile after a *consilium* found him guilty of attempted patricide. For all intents and purposes, then, whether or not a parent was formally prohibited at law from invoking the *ius vitae et necis* except *ex iusta causa*, the force of public opinion certainly would have discouraged most people from using this awesome power lightly.[46]

This same caveat also applies to the father's ability to punish his child. There was no legal sanction that could prevent him from abusing this element of his *potestas*, as we see in an annalistic *cause célèbre* whose central figure was the above-mentioned T. Manlius Imperiosus Torquatus. He lived up to his *cognomen* by sending his son to labor in a rural *ergastulum* simply because he was slow-witted. He was legally empowered to do so, but such arbitrary behavior so enraged the general populace, amongst whom Torquatus was unpopular to begin with, that a plebeian tribune is said to have brought charges against him. In the event, we are told, the unfortunate youth displayed his filial piety by threatening to murder the tribune unless he abandoned his prosecution. This brought the matter to a close, but whether there is any truth in this annalistic tale or not, the real point to be grasped here is that public opinion would sharply condemn anyone who chastised his sons or daughters without reasonable cause.[47] Similarly, throughout most of the Republic parents who chose explicitly to disinherit one or more of their *sui heredes* were not legally accountable for their actions, but the public at large would countenance such an unnatural act only if the child in question was demonstrably dissolute, or had plainly failed to discharge its filial obligations. Indeed, this sentiment was so strong that, by the end of the Republic, the praetors were prepared to set aside any will in which a *suus heres* had been disinherited for all but the most compelling of reasons (*querella inofficiosi testamenti*).[48] All of this, in turn, makes it intrinsically unlikely that public opinion would have permitted fathers to sell their children into slavery *trans Tiberim* or *mancipium* at Rome as a punitive measure. This course of action was undoubtedly tolerated only when the parent found himself in the most desperate of circumstances, but even then he would be forever marked by *infamia*. In Plautus' *Persa*, this point is driven home to the parasite Saturio by his daughter, whom he threatens to sell in order to escape the threat of starvation.[49]

In the *Stichus*, as we have already seen, Plautus also makes it clear that fathers could order their married children to divorce whether they wished to or not. Once again, however, it is not at all likely that this privilege was widely abused. Since Roman marriages were invariably arranged, and typically involved transfers of property in the form of dowry, for the most part the uncertain financial consequences of divorce must have effectively deterred the *pater familias* from acting capriciously in this regard. Normally, of course, the father of the bride would expect to recover the dotal property or its cash equivalent from the groom's family, but it must always be kept in mind that, starting late in the third century BC, the latter could sue for damages (the *actio rei uxoriae*) in an attempt to retain some or all of the dowry for child support (*retentio propter liberos*) or as compensation for the wife's injurious behavior (*retentio propter mores*).[50]

With the introduction of property, we have arrived at what is undoubtedly the most complex and contentious element of the *patria potestas*. In principle, the *pater familias* was the absolute master of the entire family estate (the *patrimonium*). His unemancipated *filii*, even if they were adults in their own right, could not own property, and anything that they actually acquired served merely to swell the *patrimonium*. To be sure, a father might cede property to his sons in the form of *peculium* so that they could maintain their own residences, but equally he might decide to limit them to an annual allowance. Both arrangements are clearly attested in the sources: Cicero tells us, on the one hand, that Sextus Roscius enjoyed the usufruct from three of his father's estates, while young Marcus Caelius paid for his apartment on the Palatine from his allowance. He neither kept accounts, on the premise that *tabulas qui in patris potestate est nullas conficit*, nor borrowed money – presumably because no one would lend it to him.[51] We are thus presented, as Veyne has properly emphasized, with a truly fascinating social environment. In every generation, there will have been a significant number of young adults who, having become *sui iuris* on the deaths of their fathers, owned and administered their own property.[52] At the same time, however, many of their peers as well as a somewhat smaller group of still older individuals would have remained *in potestate* and without the legal capacity to own anything at all simply because their fathers were still alive. There was in this anomalous situation, as Veyne again stresses, a very real possibility that many young Romans would develop feelings of anger and resentment for their fathers.[53] Happily, we do not have to rely upon anecdotal evidence to demonstrate that this was in fact the case; by briefly surveying the cult of the dead, and focussing in particular upon the feelings that the living displayed toward their deceased parents, we may obtain some insight into how widespread these negative emotions really were. At the same time, this approach will also serve to disprove Neraudau's claim that children became valued individuals in the latter stages of the Republic because of the increasing irrelevance of the *patria potestas*.

Although Roman society sported its atheists and agnostics, in all periods the vast majority of the populace seem to have believed in some kind of continuing spiritual existence after physical death. Throughout the Republic and early Empire, it was also commonly believed that, except for the fortunate few who ascended to heaven in the manner of Caesar, this afterlife would be closely tied to the grave in which one's remains were laid to rest. The sepulcher was, therefore, logically called the *domus aeterna*, and at one point in the *Satyricon*, Petronius neatly captures the sentiments that must have prevailed among many Roman citizens when they actually thought about their tombs and the life to come: 'It is assuredly wrong to embellish the houses in which we now live,' he has the fictional Trimalchio remark, 'and yet not trouble about those which we must inhabit for a far longer time.' It is this conviction that underwrites the elaborate kitchens (*culinae*), dining-chambers (*triclinia*) and gardens (*horti*) that the wealthy sometimes chose to incorporate into their mortuary establishments.[54]

Once resident in their tombs, then, the shades of the dead (the *di manes*) were obviously thought to go on feeling the same physical pleasures and discomforts that they had experienced in life. This belief inspired the formula *sit tibi terra levis* ('may the earth rest lightly upon you'), which is encountered on so many tombstones,[55] as well as the imposing, but far more rare, mortuary dining facilities alluded to above. What the *di manes* required above all, that is to say, was the necessities of life itself, in the form of periodic sacrifices of food and drink. If these offerings were made on a timely basis, then the spirits would be content, and would manifest themselves to the living in a benevolent and protective guise; when, however, they were not forthcoming, their only defense against the terrifying possibility of suffering perpetual hunger and thirst was to rise from the grave in order to seek out and punish those guilty of such *impietas*. The infamous emperor Caligula provides what is perhaps the single most interesting example of an isolated spirit driven to haunt the living in this fashion. After his assassination, Caligula's corpse was denied proper burial, and naturally he received no offerings whatsoever. In due course, his spirit began to haunt the gardens in which his remains had been hastily interred, as well as the house in which he had been slain. These apparitions were ignored, however, until the house was burnt to the ground. At this point, his sisters were permitted to dig up his body and transfer it to a proper tomb – and thereafter, the spirit of Caligula was seen no more.[56]

It was thus the individual spirit that was typically to be feared, but the *res publica* also set aside certain days during the course of the year in which the citizenry at large had a standing obligation to propitiate the dead. The most important such occasion was the *parentalia*, and Ovid has left us a chilling description of the lethal results that ensued on the one occasion when the community neglected this ritual act:

> This did not go unpunished, for it is said that from that ominous day Rome glowed with the funeral fires without the city. Indeed they say, although I can scarcely credit it, that the ancestors went forth from the tombs to wail in the hours of darkest night, and hideous ghosts, they say, a spectral throng, howled throughout the city streets and the wide fields. Afterwards, the honors which had been neglected were again paid to the tombs, and a limit was set to prodigies and funerals.[57]

Today there are literally scores of societies in which a cult of the dead continues to be observed, and virtually all of them are similar to the Roman in that offerings of food and drink on appropriate occasions constitute the most tangible element of the ritual. It is much more rare, however, to encounter cults in which the living regard the dead with such ambivalence, viewing them as equally capable of benevolent and malevolent intervention in human affairs. Anthropologists have studied a number of these cults at first hand, and their findings offer some interesting insights into the relationship between father and son in early Rome.

To date, the most fruitful such studies have been conducted among the Nayars in India, the LoDagaa in Africa, and especially in China. In India, for example, Gough has drawn our attention to the fact that, while Brahman ancestors treat their descendants with considerable indulgence, and are in turn typically viewed with affection, among the Nayars the spirits of the deceased are objects of fear. They can, to be sure, benefit the living by protecting their children, cattle and crops, but they are nevertheless feared because the punishments that they inflict upon their descendants are so often completely disproportionate to the offenses that occasioned them. As was clearly the case in Rome as well, the most common offense among the Nayars is neglect of the obligatory offerings. There are, however, many other ways in which one might arouse the wrath of the spirits, and equally, many ways in which they can express their wrath.

> The misfortunes inflicted by lineage ghosts include many forms of sickness, mental disorder, female barrenness and miscarriages, all of which are attributed to actual bodily possession by a ghost. Financial loss, crop failure and the deaths of babies or cows may also result from the ghosts' displeasure.[58]

Ritual neglect is also a commonplace failing among the LoDagaa; indeed, although the members of this tribe fully expect to be punished savagely for their misbehavior, they often choose deliberately to ignore their ritual obligations until the deceased retaliate against them. In other African tribes as well, including those in which the ancestral spirits are generally regarded as beneficent, failure to propitiate the dead in a timely and ritually correct manner will similarly result in sickness or some other misfortune.[59] It is, however, in China that the ambivalent relationship between the living and the dead is most vividly on display. After prolonged investigation in the pseudonymous Yunnan community of 'West Town', F.L.K. Hsu came to the conclusion that 'to living descendants their own ancestral spirits are always benevolent, never malicious.'[60] The evidence that he presents in support of this bluntly stated position is certainly impressive, and today few if any would quarrel with his findings. Before they can be applied to

Chinese society at large, however, anthropologists who have closely studied the problem are equally in agreement that Hsu's conclusions must be qualified in one important (and now predictable) respect. When the ancestral spirits choose to intervene in human affairs, these scholars contend, it is indeed the case that they will normally do so in order to protect and support their own lineage members; nevertheless, when legitimately provoked, they will punish their kinsmen without hesitation. This school of thought may be most economically summarized by citing Arthur Wolf's observation that 'neglect of worship is the most common reason given for misfortunes attributed to the agency of the ancestors'. In the present context, this bland statement will hardly occasion surprise,[61] but Wolf's own field-work in the Taiwanese village of San-hsia actually calls to mind the harsh and unforgiving spirits of the Nayars or LoDagaa rather than the benign ancestors of Hsu's 'West Town'. In fifteen case-histories that Wolf collected in this community, aggrieved spirits are not only charged with responsibility for assorted illnesses but are considered equally liable for deaths in three different families, as well as the grinding poverty that afflicts a fourth.[62] In these cases, the punishments meted out by the ancestors seem to be utterly capricious, which is precisely the term that Emily Ahern employs to characterize ancestral behavior in her seminal study of the Taiwanese community of Ch'i-nan. Here, as one of Ahern's informants bluntly puts it, 'you can make lavish offerings on all the proper occasions, but you never know that the ancestors won't come back and make trouble.' Obviously, there was no guarantee that an ancestor who had been offended would be appeased by propitiatory offerings, as an elderly man in the village discovered to his cost. He had suffered from a bad back for many years, and his condition was attributed to the malice of a particular ascendant in his grandfather's generation. The victim's family had made numerous attempts to propitiate this spirit, but all their efforts had failed. 'That ancestor just has a bad heart,' Ahern was told. 'That's why the man has that trouble with his back. The ancestor is causing it out of meanness.'[63]

The ambivalent attitude that the *di manes* harbored for their descendants in ancient Rome, it should now be clear, constitutes a kind of middle ground between the extreme forms of ancestral behavior represented by the capricious spirits of Ch'i-nan on the one hand, and their wholly benevolent counterparts in 'West Town' on the other. It is this middle ground, which the Romans share with the Nayars and many other tribes, that has captured the attention of anthropologists. Their field-studies have yielded two radically different and seemingly competing explanations for the behavior, protective one moment and punitive the next, that the living attribute to the deceased in these communities.

One of these explanations was first articulated some thirty years ago, in a highly influential study published by Lambert, Triandis and Wolf. After examining 62 different societies in which supernatural agents were characterized as, in the main, either aggressive or benevolent, these authors came to the conclusion that there was a high degree of correlation between the pattern of supernatural activity in a given society, and the principles of infant- and child-rearing that it endorsed. In communities, that is to say, where the small child is indulged, the supernatural powers are generally regarded as indulgent as well; conversely, in those societies in which the behavior of infants and small children is manipulated through punishment, these same powers become objects of fear because they are widely regarded as predominantly punitive in nature.[64]

At virtually the same moment in time, Gough elaborated the contrasting point of view in her study of the Nayars. Here she suggested that 'cults of predominantly punitive ancestors are likely to be accompanied by kinship relationships in which the senior generation retains control over the junior until late in life.' A few years later, Jack Goody drew the same conclusion in his work on the LoDagaa. The senior generation of this tribe, he discovered, clings tenaciously to its women, property and social position right up to the moment of death. For the younger generation, the death of a father is 'an event that is therefore hoped for as well as feared; when it comes, the death arouses joy as well as sadness, the inheritance brings guilt as well as pleasure.' Then, as Freud pointed out long ago, the new property-holder deals with his own ambivalent feelings by projecting them onto his deceased parent. Guilt, in short, inspires among the living a natural inclination to blame any subsequent misfortune on an injured and presumably vengeful ancestor.[65]

These two constructs have strongly influenced the more recent debate on ancestral behavior in China. Maurice Freedman, for example, claims that the Chinese typically regard their ancestors as kindly and supportive precisely because sons do not have to wait until their fathers' deaths to attain their economic and ritual majority.

184

From this fundamental characteristic of the Chinese family flows what, in the light of the comparative ethnographic evidence, appears to be the relative ineffectiveness of Chinese ancestors, their general air of benevolence, and doubtless too the lack of strong feelings of hatred or guilt towards them on the part of their descendants.[66]

These principles of social organization do not, however, apply to Ch'i-nan: here, in conspicuous contrast, a son remains ritually subordinate until the death of his father, which in most cases also brings him a substantial landed inheritance. Moreover, as Ahern points out at considerable length, this is also a community in which infants and small children are routinely exposed to systematic ridicule and harsh corporal punishment. It would seem, therefore, that Ch'i-nan is a place in which *both* explanations must be brought into play to explain the unusually harsh and capricious behavior of its ancestral spirits.[67] In fact, this premise can be put to the test, and verified, by drawing upon an unexpected source, namely, Hsu's 'West Town'. Here, let us keep in mind, even by Chinese standards the ancestors appear to behave in an extraordinarily benevolent manner. This is also a community, however, in which fathers regard their sons as their ritual and economic equals as soon as they marry and have children, and in which the latter are never subjected to severe punishment.[68] Given the coherent patterns of behavior that we find in Ch'i-nan and 'West Town', then, it seems self-evident that in China at large an individual's relationship with his ancestors is merely one part of a larger social matrix, and that it is conditioned above all first by the indulgent or punitive nature of the parent–child relationship, and still later by the ritual and economic relationship between young adults and their parents.

By this point, it should of course be equally self-evident that the ambivalent feelings which the Romans harbored for their deceased ancestors are part of the same matrix. In the early Republic – the period in which these mixed emotions must have crystallized – the *patria potestas* was at its most oppressive. The ritual, jural and economic subordination of a son only ended with the death of his father, and we may readily believe that the hostility which Romans projected onto their ancestors reflects the same set of conflicting emotions, and concomitant guilt, that Goody encountered among the LoDagaa, and which we occasionally glimpse in the sources.[69] At the same time, there is considerable evidence to suggest that, within the Roman elite at least, children were not only emotionally distanced from their parents but also subject to the floggings and other forms of corporal punishment for which schoolmasters were later so notorious.[70] Precisely as in China, then, and above all in Ch'i-nan, this combination of circumstances encouraged the Romans to fear their ascendants even as they revered them; indeed, one suspects that Meyer Fortes' famous description of the Tallensi, a tribe in which the *patria potestas* is about as all-embracing as it was in early Rome, applies equally well to the early *cives Romani*:

> The figures of the dead parents are clothed in qualities that are in part highly magnified versions of their most praiseworthy qualities in real life and in part distorted reflections of the tensions that exist between parents and children in reality. It is no misrepresentation to describe them as a standardized and highly elaborated picture of the parents as they might appear to a young child in real life – mystically omnipotent, capricious, vindictive, and yet beneficent and long-suffering.[71]

Once again, however, it must be emphasized that in any society the pattern of social forces that gives meaning to such a generalization is hardly immutable. While one might, for example, apply Fortes' description to the citizens of primitive Rome, it would become increasingly awkward to do so during the last century and a half of the Republic. In this period, as we have already seen, children became for the first time objects of love and affection, and as we shall see below, it is likely that these decades also witnessed considerable erosion of the *patria potestas*. It is hardly surprising, therefore, that the punitive capacity of the *di manes* gradually faded from view as well, and that during the imperial period, *exempli gratia*, people had to devise new mechanisms to prevent desecration of their tombs.[72] Clearly, we are confronted here with a complex and highly interdependent, yet delicately balanced, social matrix. The affective relationship between parents and small children, and at a later point in time, the ritual, economic and jural ties between parents and adult children still *in potestate*, are both elements of this matrix. Nevertheless, this ethnographic material, and the convincing way in which anthropologists have interpreted it, should make us hesitate to accept Neraudau's contention that the slow dissolution of the *patria potestas* remorselessly led to equally fundamental shifts on the affective level. Rather, we should look for a feature of this period sufficiently dynamic to have influenced both of these elements of the matrix simultaneously. The suggestion that Rome's wars of transmarine conquest were ultimately responsible for both the gradual collapse of the *patria potestas* and the changing emotional relationship between Roman parents and their children, for example, supplies from the methodological point of view a far more satisfactory explanation for these phenomenona than Neraudau's hypothesis. Simply put, the central weakness of his argument is that he posits a cause–effect relationship between these two patterns of behavior, although even he concedes that they both experienced palpable change during the second and first centuries BC. If we endorse his view, that is to say, then we must still account for the ongoing erosion of the *patria potestas* in the middle and late Republic; it is, however, eminently probable that historical forces sufficiently potent to undermine such well-established patriarchal authority would have also exercised some influence on the affective ties between parents and their children. In fact, one can demonstrate that the diminution of paternal authority was not the force for change that Neraudau makes it out to be, and that the emotional and jural changes that we observe within the family are in all probability to be numbered among the domestic consequences of Rome's extraordinary expansion during this period.

The first purely formal attempt to mitigate the *patria potestas* occurred during the reign of Augustus. The latter was determined to promote marriage and procreation, and in furtherance of this objective, decided to permit a son or daughter *in potestate* who wished to marry but whose father unreasonably opposed the union to seek magisterial assistance.[73] Some 150 years later, Antoninus Pius strengthened this Augustan initiative by finally putting an end to the father's age-old right to break up his children's marriages against their will *(bene concordans matrimonium)*.[74] Antoninus further decreed that, when a marriage which had produced children ended in divorce, the mother might petition a magistrate to take the father's character into account and give her custody of the children. In theory at least, the father's *potestas* remained unimpaired, but whether he was able to exercise it or not, he could in any event be ordered to pay child support.[75]

The various measures enacted to curb the *ius vitae et necis*, and to protect children from physical abuse disguised as corporal punishment, were similarly of imperial vintage. While exposure and infanticide were not formally outlawed until AD 374, a passage excerpted from Paul's *Ad Sabinum* refers to this paternal prerogative in the past tense. Gardner takes this to mean that the Severan jurists already regarded these acts as tantamount to murder, and she may well be right: a *senatusconsultum Plancianum*, which was promulgated at the latest during the reign of Trajan, stipulated that a woman who discovered she was pregnant within thirty days after her divorce had to communicate this fact to her former husband. The latter could deny paternity, or recognize the child as his own, but he could no longer invoke his *potestas* and order it to be exposed or put to death.[76] Finally, and as one might expect, lawyers and emperors who exhibited such solicitude for the new-born were even more determined to defend older children and young adults still *in potestate* from paternal abuse. Hadrian, for example, deported a father who killed a son guilty of adultery with his stepmother; in the third century, Severus Alexander and Valerian both ruled that fathers who wished to punish their sons for unfilial behavior could use their *potestas* to do so, but they reserved the harsher forms of punishment for the magistrates, before whom offended parents would have to lay their grievances.[77]

In adopting these positions, the jurists were occasionally in advance of society at large: their unsympathetic view of exposure and infanticide – practices circumscribed as early as the second century and formally abolished in the fourth – offers a case in point. For the most part, however, their attempts to diminish the *patria potestas* were merely a belated concession to a public that had long since displayed its displeasure with certain aspects of this institution. Thus during the principate of Augustus, or more than a century before Hadrian took action against a father who had killed his son, an *eques* named Tricho flogged his son to death, and then barely escaped with his life when an infuriated crowd attacked him in the Forum.[78] Sepulchral inscriptions from the early Empire occasionally introduce us to children who continued to live with their mother after the break-up of her marriage; these epitaphs make it clear that Antoninus Pius was not the first Roman to deviate from the principle that fathers were the natural custodians of their children.[79] More importantly, as Kajanto has correctly observed, the many inscriptions in which children bear two *gentilicia* – one taken from the father and the other from the mother – testify to the loss of faith among ordinary Romans in the hallowed principle that children belonged to the father's family and not the mother's.[80] Such widespread disregard for one of the cornerstones of the *patria potestas* did not, to be sure, happen overnight; rather, it was the culmination of a historical trend that began in the middle Republic, when the force of events forever altered the political, social and economic life of primitive Rome, and thus destroyed the foundations upon which its principles of social organization rested.

On reflection, it should be apparent that the institutionalized authority which the *pater familias* exercised over his legitimate offspring in the early Republic depended upon a political, social and economic structure that allowed fathers and sons to live in close proximity to one another until death severed the relationship between them. While it might have been possible, for example, for Roman fathers to emulate their Egyptian counterparts and *in absentia* order a new-born child to be exposed,[81] it is simply inconceivable that a parent could have arranged for a mature son or unmarried daughter *in potestate* to be put to death without being physically present to hear the charges brought against them. It would have been similarly unthinkable for a son to be sold into *mancipium* at Rome or into slavery across the Tiber in his father's absence, nor is it likely that a father could have arranged to settle a debt by surrendering his son's labor without being present personally to endorse the agreement. In practice, however, this should not have caused many problems in the early Republic, for primitive Rome was, at bottom, an agricultural and pastoral community that prosecuted tribal warfare on a seasonal basis. With the onset of the First Punic War, however, this pattern of conflict abruptly changed, and for the duration of the Republic's history scores of thousands of citizen-soldiers were sent abroad for prolonged periods of time in every generation. A common soldier or centurion such as Spurius Ligustinus, whom we discussed at some length in the previous chapter, could hardly exercise his *potestas* from Spain or Macedon, but it needs to be emphasized that the same also held true for the senatorial staff officers and generals under whom he served. Here it will be useful to recall the practical difficulties that Cicero encountered when he tried to find a new husband for his daughter Tullia while serving as governor of Cilicia, and still more, Cn. Cornelius Scipio Calvus' frequently described request to be relieved of his command in Spain so that he might return to Rome and negotiate his daughter's marriage.[82] Nothing, in short, undermined the early Roman concept of *patria potestas* quite as effectively as the physical distance that the wars of the middle and late Republic interposed between fathers and sons.

At some point late in the 190s BC, the Senate displayed its awareness of the negative influence that prolonged campaigning was exerting on the *patria potestas* by passing a measure that was clearly meant to check its single most alarming consequence, namely the premature emancipation of large numbers of youths whose fathers had become casualties of war. Heretofore the onset of puberty, which seems originally to have been determined on a case-by-case basis, but which the jurists ultimately fixed at 14 for boys and 12 for girls, marked the great social divide in Roman life.[83] It was at this moment that the *puer* became a *iuventus*, which meant above all that he was now elegible to marry and raise a family of his own. It does not, of course, necessarily follow that young men rushed to take advantage of this privilege, but more to the point, in the early Republic the legal capacity of the vast majority of youths would still have been open to question. To be sure, *iuvenes* were now free to sign contracts, but the praetors may have already barred anyone under the age of 17 from representing himself in court. In any event, the seminal point is that a person *in potestate* would be represented at law by his father, could not own property, and therefore could not dispose of it by gift or will.[84] Hence the only adolescents who would have acquired full legal capacity at the age of 14 were those previously *in tutela*, who then became *sui iuris*.[85] There must always have been some *iuvenes* who thus came fully of age at 14, but it can hardly be a coincidence that, in the decade after the Hannibalic war and its unprecedented casualty rates, the Senate finally decided to draft legislation that would protect these fully emancipated but wholly inexperienced youths from those who were prepared to defraud them. The *lex Plaetoria* (or *Laetoria*) permitted any interested citizen to bring an action before the praetor against a person suspected of cheating a *iuvenis* aged 14–25 in a financial transaction; conviction brought both a fine and *infamia*.[86] In addition, the praetor was also directed to grant the youth an *exceptio* in order to prevent a creditor who had fraudulently persuaded him to enter a contract from subsequently bringing suit against him. Since the creditor was burdened with proving that he had not set out to cheat his young client, in the short term the law effectively discouraged creditors from lending money to anyone under the age of 26.[87] It is, however, the long-term repercussions of this measure that are of the greatest interest to us. First, for all intents and purposes it established a third legal stage of life between *pueritia* and *iuventa*, which gradually came to be known as *adulescentia*.[88] Secondly, since it was obvious from the outset that men in this age bracket would often have a legitimate need to borrow money, some mechanism had to be devised that would allow creditors to lend it to them without risking indictment under the *lex*. We do not know the precise moment in time at which the precedent was set, but at some point it became established procedure for the praetor to appoint a *curator* at the request of the *adulescens*, who would assist him in a particular transaction. Once this figure had given his consent to the matter at hand, in practice the praetor would refuse to sanction an action against the creditor, and equally refuse to grant the borrower an *exceptio* against him. It was in this fashion that the credit of minors was initially restored, and when Marcus Aurelius eventually ruled that all transactions involving minors must be approved by a *curator*, a new institution arose, the *cura minorum*.[89]

There is no evidence to suggest that *curatores* were being appointed as early as the second century BC, but even if this were the case, the substantive differences between their responsibilities and those of a *tutor* should be kept firmly in mind. In particular, it should be noted that a guardian's consent was an essential preliminary to any financial undertaking involving the property of his ward, and that the latter had no voice in the selection of his *tutor*. The earliest *curatores* were not, then, surrogate guardians; the law discouraged adolescents from unwisely putting their property at risk, but it did not prevent them from doing so. One might, therefore, quickly come to the conclusion that in this area as in so many others, the *patres* contented themselves with a half-measure. In fact, however, the Senate's deliberations seem to have been influenced from the outset by an element in the situation that historians today can easily overlook: an adolescent who became *sui iuris* at 14 acquired full legal capacity, but it does not inevitably follow that he was thereby freed of all constraints and able to exercise his rights at will. We have already remarked that *iuvenes* did not take brides as a matter of course once they became *sui iuris*; on reflection, it should be equally obvious that few if any would take instant advantage of their right to establish an independent household. Accordingly, although the senators had good reason to distrust the judgement of (*inter alios*) an *adulescens* who had not even assumed the *toga virilis*, its legislative response was probably tempered by the expectation that such youths would continue to live with their widowed mothers, or in a stepfather's household, and that the mother's influence would still serve as a check on her son's youthful intemperance.[90]

It thus seems clear that the Senate fully expected *materna auctoritas* to be an adequate substitute for the increasingly evanescent *patria potestas* – and if the Senate's judgement was well-founded, then Neraudau's claim that the breakdown of patriarchal authority led insensibly to more affective parent–child relationships cannot possibly be right. Unfortunately, the evidence that can be brought to bear on this crucial point is exceptionally sparse, and even worse, we cannot say with absolute assurance that the point of view which it advocates was endorsed by anyone outside the literate minority of Roman society. Still, as even Neraudau concedes, however sketchy it may be, the picture that can be drawn from our sources is at the very least remarkably consistent. The most celebrated widows in Roman history were not those who indulged their sons, but rather those who continued to subject them to the *disciplina ac severitas* that we customarily associate with the *patria potestas*. Here one thinks again of Livy's Veturia, and the manner in which she overawed her son Coriolanus. Whether or not this dramatic scene unfolded in the manner that Livy describes is immaterial; the value of the passage lies in what it tells us about how widowed mothers and their sons were expected to interact in aristocratic families of the late Republic.[91] Looking back at this turbulent period from the vantage point of the early Principate, the notoriously conservative historian Tacitus decried the fact that in his own day one could no longer find mothers such as Cornelia, Aurelia and Atia. With their *disciplina ac severitas*, the orator Vipstanus Messalla is made to remark,

> they aimed at this alone – that the natural disposition of each one of their children, which was pure, unspoiled and still not warped by vice in any form, should seize at once and with whole heart upon virtuous pursuits; and, whether its inclination lay in the direction of military affairs, the study of law, or the pursuit of eloquence, that it would focus on this alone, and drain it to the full.[92]

Cornelia, the mother of Tiberius and Caius Gracchus, enjoyed a reputation in her own lifetime that the passage of the centuries only continued to enhance. Thus Cicero remarks at one point that 'her sons were nursed no less on her speech than at her breast,' while Plutarch adds that their virtues were widely believed to stem more from her tutelage than from their own innate dispositions. It is a still more telling indicator of her *auctoritas*, however, that during his first plebeian tribunate Caius bowed to her wishes and withdrew a bill that he had proposed to secure the disgrace of M. Octavius, the tribune who had played such a critical role in the events leading up to Tiberius' murder.[93] Aurelia seems to have played an active role in shaping Caesar's rhetorical skills; and Atia, we are told, continued personally to supervise the education of her son Octavius (the future emperor Augustus) even after her marriage to L. Marcius Philippus. Both women exhibited a strong interest in their sons' political careers, and it is again an indication of what was expected of a young *nobilis* that Octavius sought out his mother's counsel before deciding to take up Caesar's inheritance.[94] Octavian, as it turned out, spurned her advice, but it would be a serious mistake to presume that he did not give it respectful consideration. It is clear, for example, that M. Iunius Brutus, the Caesarian assassin, never escaped the influence of his mother Servilia, a formidable lady whom Cicero characterizes at one point as a *prudentissima et diligentissima femina*. Brutus lost his like-named father in 77 BC, at the age of 8, and followed his mother into the household of her second husband, D. Iunius Silanus. When he was in his 30s, he still solicited her political counsel: we know of one famous meeting at Antium, in the months immediately following Caesar's assassination, during the course of which she even managed to silence Cicero. The fact that Brutus continued to defer to her should not be taken as a sign of weakness in his own personality, for Servilia is also said to have exercised a mother's *auctoritas* over her half-brother Cato, clearly one of the most strong-willed figures of this generation.[95]

Tacitus' protestations to the contrary notwithstanding, widows of this sort continue to surface in the sources for the early Empire. Ironically, in Iulia Procilla and the younger Agrippina Tacitus himself furnishes the two most well-known examples. Iulia Procilla was the mother of the historian's father-in-law, Cn. Iulius Agricola; in his youth the latter had exhibited an altogether un-healthy interest in philosophy, which his mother quickly checked. Apparently, therefore, she was personally supervising his education, whereas the imperious Agrippina left her son Nero's instruction to Seneca, but closely monitored the curriculum to which he was exposed.[96]

Fortunately, there are more casual references to *materna auctoritas* in our literary sources, and these passages strongly reinforce this anecdotal evidence. Some mothers, Cicero says, came to funerals with whips ready to hand; if their children did not grieve in the approved manner, a flogging would nicely cause their tears to flow! In still more casual contexts, Horace alludes to the *severitas* of Sabinic peasant women, and to the *dura custodia* with which widowed mothers in general keep their young sons in check.[97] In short, all of our literary evidence points to a single conclusion: when sons lost their fathers at an early age, it was far more likely that their mothers would treat them with greater strictness than with greater indulgence.[98]

Such women could not have failed to earn the respect and trust of their husbands, but one may still question how commonplace such values were outside the literate elite. Happily, in the rich corpus of legal sources we may at last find confirmation that maternal *disciplina ac severitas* were actually quite widespread. In Roman Egypt, with its substantially different historical traditions about the role of women in society, it was fairly common to find husbands who bequeathed their property to their minor children, and who appointed *tutores* for them in conformity with the law. At the same time, however, they also made it clear in their wills that the estate should actually be controlled by their wives, and that these guardians should regard their role in the administration of the property as a mere formality. Alternatively, it was an equally common practice for husbands to nominate their legitimate heirs as the ultimate recipients of the estate, but to allow the wife to enjoy the usufruct of some or all of it for a specified period of years – or even the balance of her lifetime – so that she might be positioned to protect her children's interests.[99] We have already stressed that in the second century BC Roman husbands also resorted to this latter tactic as a means of evading the *lex Voconia*.[100] It should now be obvious that, in a period when *tutela mulierum* was being increasingly ignored, *usufruct* could be used just as well to leave control of the estate in the hands of a wife whose judgement the husband trusted, and thus avoid the risk of having it managed by a less interested *tutor impuberis*. Admittedly, there is no source that actually alludes to a Roman husband giving his wife usufruct of his property for this particular purpose, but the supposition derives some support from the fact that, like their counterparts in Egypt, Roman fathers often tried to reduce the guardian's role to that of a rubber stamp, and leave the effective management of the estate in the wife's hands.[101] Indeed, in their wills some husbands even went so far as explicitly to appoint their wives to serve as the guardians of their children; despite the staunch opposition of the classical jurists, in AD 390 this hitherto alien concept was finally incorporated into the law. This furnishes still another example of how prolonged tension between an abstract principle of law and the realities of Roman social life ultimately climaxed with the modification of the legal principle.[102]

This legal vindication of *materna auctoritas* was, however, perhaps the single most belated concession to reality in the whole roster of legal reforms affecting women that we have surveyed to this point. Centuries earlier, the classical jurists had already staked out conflicting positions on whether or not transactions undertaken by women on behalf of their children should be regarded as legally enforceable when it was clear that the deceased husband wished his wife to represent their interests in this fashion.[103] Women had also been warned that their failure to seek out *tutores* for their children could result in forfeiture of their right to the latter's property under the intestate provisions of the *senatusconsultum Tertullianum*.[104] As Gardner rightly points out, all of this certainly suggests that many women never went to the trouble of obtaining guardians for their offspring; for these women, 'occasions may seldom or never have arisen when the validity of a transaction came into question and the lack of tutorial authorisation became important.'[105] Doubtless this was not the case within the elite, but Seneca makes it clear that his mother Helvia personally administered the *patrimonium* that he would eventually inherit, and Cicero similarly refers to a noblewoman in Sicily who looked after her daughter's affairs on a day-to-day basis.[106] If our sources for the second century BC were fuller, it is thus reasonable to assume that Cornelia, the mother of the Gracchi, would not furnish its only clear-cut example of *materna tutela*.[107]

SLAVERY AND SURROGATE PARENTING

It still remains for us to try and account, therefore, for the emergence of the small child as a distinct and valued personality in the Roman household of the late Republic and early Empire. Here we cannot hope to exhaust a topic for which the groundwork is still incomplete,[108] but it is worth pointing out that Rome's immensely profitable wars of transmarine conquest in the post-Hannibalic period radically altered both the structure of the urban *familia* and the traditional concept of parental responsibility. These changes, it should be added, are particularly and predictably evident in the elite households from which so much of our literary evidence stems.

'In the good old days,' Tacitus has Vipstanus Messalla lament,

> every child born in holy wedlock was brought up not in the cramped chamber of a hired nurse but in its mother's lap and embrace. A woman of this sort gloried above all in keeping her home in good order and personally attending to her children.

Such households had existed in the past; indeed, Plutarch lavishly praises the elder Cato and his wife for upholding these pristine values. The latter, he tells us, not only breast-fed her own child but those of her slaves as well; in turn, Cato first taught his son how to read, then instructed him in the principles of Roman law, and finally took personal charge of his physical education.[109]

Cato did have at least one well-educated slave in his household – a Greek schoolmaster named Chilo, who did in fact teach a number of other children. Plutarch adds, however, that most of his slaves were rude herdsmen and field workers, and that he never wasted his money buying domestic servants.[110] In this as in so many other ways Cato was, of course, badly out of touch with his times: early in the second century BC, the urban households of Roman aristocrats were already swelling dramatically in size, with Greek captives constituting the most visible and valued element in the rapidly growing slave *familia*. It was to these slaves that the Roman *nobilis* and his wife increasingly delegated the menial aspects of child-rearing, erecting in the process a physical and emotional barrier between themselves and their children that could only serve to exaggerate, for example, the mother's *auctoritas*. This also meant, however, that from infancy the child was placed in the hands of one or more surrogate parents, often referred to in sepulchral inscriptions as the baby's *mamma* or *tata*; these servants, it need hardly be added, did not necessarily share the values of their owners, much less pass them on to the child.[111] Conservative thinkers such as Tacitus decried this approach to child-rearing, for they regarded it as the ultimate source of the moral decay that seemingly had their own generations in its grip. 'Nowadays,' his Vipstanus Messalla once again remarks,

> at birth our children are handed over to some silly little Greek
> serving girl and some male slave or other – typically the most
> worthless fellow in the whole household, someone not suited
> for any kind of serious work. From the very outset they fill
> the children's tender and gullible minds with their stuff and
> nonsense, and not one person in the entire establishment gives
> a thought to what he should say or do in the presence of his
> infant master. Moreover, even the parents themselves accustom
> their offspring to lewdness and glib talk in lieu of goodness and
> modesty, as a result of which they gradually lose their sense of
> shame and become equally contemptuous of themselves and
> others.'

It is in this environment, Vipstanus goes on to declare, that a
young man's passion for actors, gladiators and the horses is forged
– and one wonders if it was the emperor Nero that he had in
mind. Reared by two servile nurses, Egloge and Alexandria, and
initially educated in the household of his aunt Domitia Lepida by
a dancer and a barber, in his adolescence Nero was already an
enthusiastic devotee of the stage, the arena, and the circus.[112] The
stern instruction that he had received in the interim from Agrippina
and Seneca conspicuously failed, in short, to compensate for the
spoilt and frivolous nature that these surrogate parents apparently
allowed to develop unchecked in Nero's formative years.

Nero thus embodies the modern conviction that a child learns
most from those to whom it is first exposed. If we can extrapolate
from his experience, then it may well be the case that the unprecedented recognition of and affection for small children in late
republican society is directly connected to these equally fundamental
changes in child-rearing – changes that were themselves the direct
result of Rome's conquest of the East. When, that is to say, Roman
parents surrendered the admittedly tedious task of coping with their
infants and young children to servile surrogates, as Tacitus himself
shrewdly recognized, they were simultaneously passing on to these
individuals the responsibility for molding their values. Since slaves
of Greek extraction were, as both Tacitus and the Greek physician
Soranus remark in quite different contexts, always preferred for
this work,[113] it should be obvious that we need to examine
Greek child-rearing practices in order to test this hypothesis.
Unfortunately, very little research has been conducted in this

area, so at present we cannot draw any definitive conclusions. Nevertheless, it is worthy of note that in the one study so far concluded, it is forcefully argued that in classical Athens children were deeply loved, and not simply regarded as instruments for the perpetuation of the family in its political, economic, jural and ritual aspects.[114] Since it seems safe to assume that children continued to be valued in this fashion in Hellenistic Athens, it therefore follows that an Athenian woman working as a *nutrix* in a Roman household, in either a servile or mercenary capacity, would have frequently brought these values to her work, and subtly communicated them to her young charge.[115] If, in fact, it should turn out that the majority of these Greek *nutrices* viewed children in this manner, then one may readily comprehend how aristocratic children at large came gradually to be valued as individuals in their own right in the last 150 years of the Republic. Moreover, keeping in mind that the influence which a *nutrix* initially brought to bear on her ward's attitudes and values was often reinforced by a deep sense of mutual affection that continued throughout their lives,[116] it is also easy to understand how at least some of these children, when they grew up to marry and have sons and daughters of their own, would have developed a more affective relationship with them. In the course of several generations – precisely the generations that separate Plautus and Catullus – the cumulative impact of such shifts in individual behavior, especially within so well-defined a group as the Roman elite, could easily have been sufficiently far-reaching to produce the fundamental changes in the literary presentation of children that the semantic analysis of Manson has revealed.

As we have already remarked, in his provocative article on the gradual acceptance of homosexuality in Roman society, Verstraete appropriately stresses that it was not only the Hellenization of Roman values in the second and first centuries BC that made it possible but also the ready availability of slaves. After all, sexual relations with male slaves, regardless of their age, did not expose a citizen to indictment for *stuprum*.[117] This was certainly one of the unanticipated consequences of Rome's expansion east of the Adriatic, and we may suitably conclude by observing that the flow of Greek slaves and Greek values seems in the end to have played a similar role in undermining the traditional relationship between aristocratic Roman parents and their children. If future research should bear out this hypothesis, then we may add this to the already long catalog of changes that systemic warfare brought to the lives of Roman woman and children.

NOTES

1   Cf. the still more cautious (and exasperated) judgement of B. Kytzler, *M. Minuci Felicis Octavius* (Leipzig, 1982) vi: 'quo tempore Minucius Felix *Octavium* scripsisset homines docti maximo ardore minimo effectu diu multumque disputabant. Neque enim de anno vel de saeculo, quo auctor opusculum perfecerit, nec de relatione quae intercedat inter Minucii *Octavium* et *Apologeticum* Tertulliani nos adhuc aliquid certi scire valde dolendum est.' Fortunately, the date of the essay is not critical to this argument, for the passage that interests us is but one of many such from the imperial period, in both pagan and Christian literature.

2   *Octavius* 3.5–6.

3   Pliny, *Epistulae* 9.33; cf. Pliny, *Naturalis Historia* 9.26, who offers a different version of this same story. A similar incident occurred in New Zealand in 1956; for fuller discussion, see A.N. Sherwin-White, *The Letters of Pliny. A Historical and Social Commentary* (Oxford, 1966) 514–515.

4   Horace, *Satirae* 2.3.251–252; Seneca, *De Constantia Sapientia* 12.2.

5   Horace, *Ars Poetica* 417; *Epistulae* 1.1.59 (tag); Martial 14.20 (soldiers); Rufinus, *Historia Ecclesiastica* 10.15 (the child Athanasius pretending to be a bishop); Seneca, *De Constantia Sapientia* 12.2; Plutarch, *Cato Minor* 2.5; S.H.A., *Severus* 1.4 (play magistrates).

6   Balls and ball games: Ovid, *Tristia* 2.485–486; cf., *inter alia*, Plautus, *Curculio* 296; Martial 4.19, 7.32, 7.72, 12.82, 14.45–48; along with the discussions in A. Mau, 'Ballspiel,' *RE* 2B (1896) 2832–2834; and J.-P. Neraudau, *Etre enfant à Rome* (Paris, 1984) 300–301; see also 294 (leap-frog) and 300 (blind-man's bluff). The *lex Aquilia*, we are told, actually considered compensation for injury or death caused by the negligence of people playing ball in the streets (*Digesta* 9.2.11, 9.2.52.4).

7   Macrobius, *Saturnalia* 1.7.22 (heads or tails); Horace, *Satirae* 2.3.248 (odd and even); Cicero, *De Officiis* 3.19.77, 3.23.90; Varro, in Nonius, *De Compendiosa Doctrina* v. *micare* [*morra*].

8   Suetonius, *Divus Augustus* 71; for the darker side of this Roman addiction, see such sources as Ovid, *Ars Amatoria* 3.372–376; and Juvenal 1.87–93. Cf. Ovid, *Tristia* 471–484 (treatises on dice games); Plautus, *Miles Gloriosus* 164–165; Cicero, *De Oratore* 3.58; Horace, *Carmina* 3.24.58; *Satirae* 2.3.168–178; Ovid, *Nux* 73–86; Persius, *Satirae* 3.44–52; Seneca, *De Constantia Sapientia* 12.2; and Martial 5.84, 14.18, 14.185 (children's games of chance).

9   Persius, *Satirae* 2.70; Lactantius, *Divinae Institutiones* 2.4.13 (dolls); Virgil, *Eclogues* 8.30; Catullus 61.122–136 (nuts).

10 Plutarch, *Moralia* 608d.

11 Persius, *Satirae* 3.51; Tibullus 1.5.3–4; Virgil, *Aeneid* 7.378–383; Marcus Aurelius, *Meditationes* 5.36; Augustine, *Epistulae* 133.104 (tops); Horace, *Satirae* 2.3.247–248; Galen, *De Sanitate Tuenda* 1.8 (riding sticks and miniature carts). If we may believe Valerius Maximus 8.8.ext. 1, even Socrates entertained his children by riding on a broomstick!

12 Sometimes with tragic results; cf. *CIL* VI.10078 = *ILS* 5300, and XIV.1808.

13 *CIL* VI.19007 (Geminia Agathe); *CLE* 1167: *ludite, felices, patitur dum vita, puellae, saepe et formosas fata sinistra trahunt* (Crocale); cf. Cicero, *De Finibus* 5.55; Ovid, *Remedia Amoris* 23–24; Quintilian, *Institutio Oratoria* 1.12.10; and Augustine, *Confessiones* 1.10. For further discussion of children's toys

and games, and the role that they played in preparing children for adulthood, see now T. Wiedemann, *Adults and Children in the Roman Empire* (London, and New Haven, 1989) 146–153. One should not, however, neglect the older but absolutely delightful commentary of D'A.W. Thompson, 'Games and Playthings,' *G&R* 2 (1933) 71–79.

14   The distinction between exposure and infanticide, particularly in the context of population studies of Greece and Rome, has too often been ignored by the social historian of antiquity – a point rightly emphasized by J.E. Boswell, '*Expositio* and *Oblatio*: the Abandonment of Children and the Ancient and Mediaeval Family,' *AHR* 89 (1984) 12–16. In some cases, this may simply reflect conceptual ambiguities in the ancient sources themselves, as both M.K. Hopkins, 'Contraception in the Roman Empire,' *CSSH* 8 (1965–66) 136–142; and R. Etienne, 'La conscience médicale antique et la vie des enfants,' *Annales de Démographie Historique* 9 (1973) 15–46 = 'Ancient Medical Conscience and the Life of Children,' *Journal of Psychohistory* 4 (1976) 131–161, especially 131–143, stress. There is a further danger that the historian's own views on such currently sensitive issues as abortion will color his or her interpretation of the data. This failing is noticeable above all in the massive study of E. Nardi, *Procurato aborto nel mondo greco romano* (Milan, 1971), as S. Dickison rightly points out in her lengthy critique of this work; see 'Abortion in Antiquity,' *Arethusa* 6 (1973) 159–166. In the last decade, the literature increasingly has come to be dominated by attempts to establish a statistical model for infanticide and exposure in the classical world. The argument for a very low rate of infanticide elaborated by D. Engels, 'The Problem of Female Infanticide in the Greco-Roman World,' *CP* 75 (1980) 112–120, was rightly rejected by W.V. Harris, 'The Theoretical Possibility of Extensive Infanticide in the Graeco-Roman World,' *CQ* new series 32 (1982) 114–116; and independently and at much greater length by M. Golden, 'Demography and the Exposure of Girls at Athens,' *Phoenix* 35 (1981) 316–331. Golden himself argues for a rate of female infanticide of 10 percent or higher (p. 330), and this in turn is endorsed by S.B. Pomeroy, 'Infanticide in Hellenistic Greece,' in A. Cameron and A. Kuhrt (eds), *Images of Women in Antiquity* (Detroit, 1983) 207–222. She draws upon Golden in support of her own attempt to extrapolate a high rate of female infanticide from a set of Milesian inscriptions; her demographic findings, like those of Engels and Golden, are firmly rejected in the recent and quite sensible study of C. Patterson, ' "Not Worth the Rearing": the Causes of Infant Exposure in Ancient Greece,' *TAPA* 115 (1985) 103–123. For a broad introduction to the subject, one might profitably begin with W.L. Langer, 'Infanticide: a Historical Survey,' *History of Childhood Quarterly* 1 (1973–74) 353–366.

15   Petronius, *Satyricon* 75; Martial 1.31, 1.58, 3.71, 3.73, 4.42, 9.21, 9.59, 11.43, 11.70, 11.78, 12.16, 12.33, 12.86, 12.96–97; cf., *inter alia*, Catullus 15, 61. The best discussions of this phenomenon are those of P. Veyne, 'Homosexuality in Ancient Rome,' in P. Ariès and A. Béjin (eds), *Western Sexuality*, trans. A. Forster (Oxford, 1985) 26–35; and B.C. Verstraete, 'Slavery and the Social Dynamics of Male Homosexual Relations in Ancient Rome,' *Journal of Homosexuality* 5 (1980) 227–236. Still, readers of the latter article should be aware that Verstraete has misconstrued the evidence for homosexual relations between free-born Roman citizens, which will be taken up below. *Deliciae* were not, of course, invariably subject to sexual abuse; some seem to have been treasured as virtual pets, and Martial's Erotion apparently had as much or more time for play than a girl of free birth (5.34).

16   Pliny, *Naturalis Historia* 32.135 (depilatories); 21.170, 30.41 (delay puberty).

17   Martial 2.60, 3.58, 6.67, 10.91, 11.81; Ammianus Marcellinus 18.4.5. For the

legislation, see Statius, *Silvae* 3.4.74–76, 4.3.13–15; Martial 9.6, 9.8; Suetonius, *Domitianus* 7; Dio Cassius 67.2.3, 68.2.3 (Domitian); *Digesta* 48.8.6 (Nerva), 48.8.4.2, 5 (Hadrian). In the end, conviction under the *lex Cornelia de sicariis et veneficiis* resulted in confiscation of property and deportation to an island for *honestiores*, and execution for *humiliores* (Paulus, *Sententiae* 5.23.13). The best study of the increasing influence of eunuchs in Roman society and politics is that of M.K. Hopkins, *Conquerors and Slaves* (Cambridge, 1978) 172–196, especially 193–195.

18 Neraudau, *Etre enfant*, 366; for the physical and sexual abuse of slaves, see J. Kolendo, 'L'esclavage et la vie sexuelle des hommes libres à Rome,' *Index* 10 (1981) 288–297; R.P. Saller, 'Slavery and the Roman Family,' in M.I. Finley (ed.), *Classical Slavery* (Cambridge, 1987) 78–79; and K.R. Bradley, *Slaves and Masters in the Roman Empire: a Study in Social Control* (Oxford, 1987) 113–137. Cf. C. Ritter (ed.), *M. Fabii Quintiliani Declamationes Quae Supersunt CXLV* (Leipzig, 1884) 175 (*Decl.* 298); and *Institutio Oratoria* 2.5.11 (physical abnormality).

19 Plutarch, *Marius* 27. The relevant evidence may be conveniently consulted in K.R. Bradley, 'On the Roman Slave Supply and Slave Breeding,' in M.I. Finley (ed.), *Classical Slavery* (Cambridge, 1987) 50–54. Bradley argues that breeding was an essential complement to the generation of slaves from war and commerce as early as the post-Hannibalic period. He presses his evidence too hard – one can rarely determine how the children who appear in the sources for this period actually entered slavery – but it is nonetheless the case that scholars at large have underestimated the incidence of child enslavement in the Republic.

20 Verstraete, 'Male Homosexual Relations,' 227–236.

21 Seneca, *De Constantia Sapientia* 12.3; Horace, *Epistulae* 2.1.70–71; Suetonius, *De Grammaticis* 9 (*si quos Orbilius ferula scuticaque cecidit*).

22 *CIL* IV. 4208; cf., for example, Plautus, *Bacchides* 440–446; Ovid, *Amores* 1.13.17–18; Martial 9.68, 14.18, 14.80; Juvenal 1.15; Plutarch, *Cato Maior* 20.4; Libanius, *Epistulae* 1330; Ausonius, *Liber Protrepticus ad Nepotem* 24–32; Augustine, *Confessiones* 1.10, 1.14, 1.19; *De Civitate Dei* 21.14; and *Epistulae* 133.104, 153.16. A fresco has also survived from Herculaneum, in which a schoolboy is receiving a flogging from his *magister*; see plate 10.

23 *CIL* IV.4201, 4206, 4209; Juvenal 10.224; Suetonius, *De Grammaticis* 23; *CIL* X.3969 = *ILS* 7763 (*summa quom castitate in discipulos suos, idemque testamenta scripsit cum fide, nec quoiquam pernegavit, laesit neminem*).

24 Artemidorus, *Oneirocritica* 1.78–79; Martial 2.4 (cf. Juvenal 6.133–135); Tacitus, *Annales* 6.1; Suetonius, *Tiberius* 43–44; *Gaius Caligula* 16; *Vitellius* 3 (*spintriae*). Caligula, we are told, opened a *lupanar* in the palace, and staffed it with noblewomen and children; see Suetonius, *Gaius Caligula* 41; Dio Cassius 59.28.9; and the discussion in T.A.J. McGinn, 'The Taxation of Roman Prostitutes,' *Helios* 16 (1989) 83–86. Verstraete, 'Male Homosexual Relations,' 228, argues that 'a homosexual relationship between citizens would have scandalized the most tolerant circles of Roman society'. On the basis of this generalization, he then argues that all of the *pueri* who were sodomized were slaves, whether or not they are explicitly identified as such in the sources. Since the generalization is demonstrably false, however, there is no good reason to claim servile status for, *inter alia*, the youths in Lucilius 74M, 173M; Tibullus' Marathus (1.4, 1.8–9); or even the entire roster of youths in Martial's epigrams that was cited in note 15 above.

25 *De Civitate Dei* 21.14. For the physical and sexual abuse of free-born children, see further Wiedemann, *Adults and Children*, 27–31, 87, 106, 165, and 203.

26 Plautus, *Captivi* 1002–1003; *Poenulus* 1072–1074; see M. Manson, 'The Emergence of the Small Child in Rome (Third Century BC–First Century

AD),' *History of Education* 12 (1983) 155–156.

27 Livy 2.39–40; Dionysius of Halicarnassus, *Antiquitates Romanae* 8.39–54; Plutarch, *Coriolanus* 33–36.

28 Livy 2.40.12; Dionysius of Halicarnassus, *Antiquitates Romanae* 8.55.3–5; Plutarch, *Coriolanus* 37.

29 See, for example, R.M. Ogilvie, *A Commentary on Livy, Books 1–5* (Oxford, 1965) 314.

30 P. Veyne, 'La famille et l'amour sous le haut-empire romain,' *Ann(ESC)* 33 (1978) 35–63. The first part of this equation has been widely endorsed throughout most of this century, first and foremost by those who rely upon prosopography as a tool of historical analysis, but also by social historians. Cf., *inter alia*, P. Grimal, *Love in Ancient Rome*, trans. A. Train, Jr. (Norman, Okla., 1986) 71: 'a marriage was above all the means of concluding alliances between families, of establishing or consolidating friendships, of making sure of the backing of one's fellow citizens in the City-State.'

31 Plautus, *Mostellaria* 120–125 (philosophy of child-rearing); Publilius Syrus 401; Cicero, *Tusculanae Disputationes* 1.93; *De Amicitia* 9; Valerius Maximus 5.10.1–3 (calm acceptance of death); *De Finibus* 5.55 (undue interest in children); Seneca, *Epistulae* 99.1 (excessive grief); Quintilian, *Institutio Oratoria* 6.*pr.*; cf., *inter alia*, Pliny, *Epistulae* 4.2, 5.16; Tacitus, *Annales* 15.23; Juvenal 15.138–140; Ausonius, *Parentalia* 10–11 (the mourning of children). For these and other passages that sustain the comparison, see Manson, 'Emergence of the Small Child,' 149–159; Neraudau, *Etre enfant*, 379–385; S. Dixon, *The Roman Mother* (Norman, Okla., 1988) 104–120; and Wiedemann, *Adults and Children*, 89–99.

32 Veyne, 'La famille et l'amour,' 40 *et passim* (the elite), 55 (*contubernium*). R.P. Saller and B.D. Shaw, 'Tombstones and Family Relations in the Principate: Civilians, Soldiers and Slaves,' *JRS* 74 (1984) 134–136, are especially (and rightly) critical of Veyne's extravagant claims about the political origins of marriage within the lower classes.

33 *Etre enfant*, 163–164: 'perte de pouvoir d'un côté et raidissement des droits de l'autre, voilà une incohérence qui mit le père de famille encore plus en demeure de trouver à la solidité familiale un autre ciment que sa puissance. D'ailleurs libéré de ses contraintes familiales et politiques, il sera jeté au-devant de lui-même, et plus apte à découvrir les joies de l'amour conciliées ou non avec celles de la paternité.'

34 Manson, 'Emergence of the Small Child,' 153 *et passim*; Dixon, *Roman Mother*, especially 104–105, and 111–113. Wiedemann, *Adults and Children*, alone argues for a date in the second century AD. He rightly observes, for example, that in the correspondence between Fronto and Marcus Aurelius 'we have already moved a long way from the classical world's lack of interest in children when we find that Fronto should think of applying the stock theme that "those whom the gods love, die young" to a *child*, rather than just a young adult. The dividing line between the child and the adult is no longer as clear-cut as it had still been to Pliny' (97). All this really tells us, however, is that Pliny endorsed Seneca's thinking on the proper adult response to a child's illness and death, while Fronto exhibited the same overt concern and grief that Quintilian and Marullus had shown a century earlier. The anecdotal method of analysis that Wiedemann uses at this point cannot by its very nature date this kind of historical development with any precision, but as we shall see below, this particular problem lends itself to semantic analysis that is at once more reliable and clearly points to a date considerably earlier than the second century AD.

35 Plautus, *Menaechmi* 31–36; *Poenulus* 64–69; Terence, *Adelphoe* 57–67; *Heautontimorumenos* 991–992; Seneca, *Ad Helviam* 18.8; Tacitus, *Dialogus de*

Oratoribus 28.6 (29.2, however, makes it clear that the views of Seneca and Tacitus, which were also espoused in this period by Plutarch, *Moralia* 3e–f, are no longer widely shared); Plutarch, *Moralia* 609e; Catullus 61.212–216; Lucretius, *De Rerum Natura* 3.895–896; Cicero, *Tusculanae Disputationes* 1.93; *De Amicitia* 9; *Epistulae ad Familiares* 4.5–6.

36 Plutarch, *Moralia* 608c, 609a–b; Seneca, *Epistulae* 99.1; K. Bradley, 'Wet-Nursing at Rome: a Study in Social Relations,' in B. Rawson (ed.), *The Family in Ancient Rome* (London, 1985) 216–218.

37 Manson, 'Emergence of the Small Child,' 150–153; cf. W.B. Sedgwick, 'Babies in Ancient Literature,' *The Nineteenth Century* 104 (1928) 375; and Neraudau, *Etre enfant*, 56–58. For examples of vague terminology in Terence, see *Adelphoe* 48, 494; and *Andria* 35.

38 *De Finibus* 1.23, 3.62, 4.17; *Pro Roscio Amerino* 53; *Epistulae ad Atticum* 7.2. Contra V. French, 'History of the Child's Influence: Ancient Mediterranean Civilizations,' in R.Q. Bell and L.V. Harper (eds), *Child Effects on Adults* (Hillsdale, NJ, 1977) 22, one also should not make too much of such purely rhetorical statements as Sallust, *Bellum Iugurthinum* 14.25.

39 Cf., *inter alia*, Lucretius 3.894–896; Horace, *Epodi* 2.39–40 ('quod si pudica mulier in partem/iuvet domum atque dulces liberos . . .'); and *CIL* VI.7303 = *ILS* 7863 (the epitaph of Spendusa, who died at the age of 5 months, and who is called the *dulcissima filia* of Torquatianus and Primigenia).

40 *In Verrem* 2.1.112; *De Finibus* 3.9; cf. Catullus 72, where parental *diligentia* is explicitly distinguished from romantic love or sexual passion. Only two of the ten appearances of *diligere* in Plautus involve any expression of affection (*Amphitruo* 509; *Bacchides* 816); normally, he employs the term in the emotionally neutral sense of 'to attend to' (cf. *Amphitruo* 973; *Captivi* 115; *Rudens* 820).

41 Manson, 'Emergence of the Small Child,' 153–154.

42 It is worth stressing that only the legitimate offspring of citizen parents were subject to *patria potestas*. *Spurii*, for example, took the legal status of their mothers, and in the period from Augustus to Marcus Aurelius were not even subject to the procedures that the *leges Aelia-Sentia* and *Papia Poppaea* established for the registration of the new-born. See F. Schulz, 'Roman Registers of Birth and Birth Certificates,' *JRS* 32 (1942) 78–91; 33 (1943) 55–64; and M. Lemosse, 'L'enfant sans famille en droiṭ romain,' *Recueils de la Société Jean Bodin* 35 (1975) 257–270.

43 Dionysius of Halicarnassus, *Antiquitates Romanae* 2.15.2; Cicero, *De Legibus* 3.19 (elimination of the deformed). A father could also expose a child whom he had begun to rear, as we see in Suetonius, *Divus Claudius* 27.1. The ritual aspects of raising up the child are placed in their anthropological context by N. Belmont, 'Levana, ou comment "elever" les enfants,' *Ann(ESC)* 28 (1973) 77–89 = 'Levana: or How to Raise Up Children,' in R. Forster and O. Ranum (eds.), *Family and Society* (Baltimore and London, 1976) 1–15.

44 Cf. Livy 2.4–5; Dionysius of Halicarnassus, *Antiquitates Romanae* 8.79.2; Valerius Maximus 5.8.1 (Brutus); Diodorus Siculus 12.64; Livy 4.29.5–6; Valerius Maximus 2.7.6; Aulus Gellius, *Noctes Atticae* 17.21.17 (Postumius); Livy 8.7; Dionysius of Halicarnassus, *Antiquitates Romanae* 8.79.2; Valerius Maximus 2.7.6 (Torquatus).

45 Livy 2.41.10–12; and Dionysius of Halicarnassus, *Antiquitates Romanae* 8.79.1, are equally skeptical of the tradition that Spurius Cassius was killed by his father; Valerius Maximus 5.8.2, however, accepts this version of the story without hesitation. Cf. Valerius Maximus 5.8.3 (suicide of Silanus), 5.8.4; Frontinus, *Strategemata* 4.1.13 (Scaurus); Sallust, *Coniuratio Catilinae* 39.5; Valerius Maximus 5.8.5; and Dio Cassius 37.36.4 (execution of Fulvius).

Orosius 4.13.18 claims that M. Fabius Buteo (cos. 245) put his son to death for theft, but in the absence of any earlier corroborative evidence, this story should be treated with caution.

46 Seneca, *De Clementia* 1.15.2–7; for an example of a domestic tribunal convened to investigate a youth suspected of planning to commit matricide, see Valerius Maximus 5.9.1. For examples of daughters being executed, see Valerius Maximus 6.1.3 and 6.1.6. In the period 104–102 BC, Q. Fabius Maximus Eburnus (cos. 116) executed his son for a sexual offence; although he undoubtedly invoked his *potestas*, he was nevertheless tried, convicted and sent into exile (Cicero, *Pro Balbo* 28; pseudo-Quintilian, *Declamationes* 3.17; Valerius Maximus 6.1.5; Orosius 5.16.8). This lends support to R. Yaron, 'Vitae Necisque Potestas,' *TRG* 30 (1962) 249; W. Kunkel, 'Das Konsilium im Hausgericht,' *ZRG* 83 (1966) 241–246; and A. Watson, *Rome of the XII Tables* (Princeton, 1975) 42–44, all of whom argue that the *ius vitae et necis* was legally delimited; *contra*, A. Guarino, *Labeo* 13 (1967) 124; and J.-P. Neraudau, *La Jeunesse dans la littérature et les institutions de la Rome républicaine* (Paris, 1979) 170. Seneca, *De Clementia* 1.15.1 also tells us that Augustus had personally to intervene to save an *eques* named Tricho from a lynch-mob in the forum; the latter had flogged his son to death, for reasons that the populace self-evidently found insufficient. This sort of violent reaction, which could be anticipated in advance, must have deterred all but the most stubborn or intemperate from using the *ius vitae et necis* too rashly. For further analysis of the various episodes discussed here, see now W.V. Harris, 'The Roman Father's Power of Life and Death,' in R. S. Bagnall and W.V. Harris (eds), *Studies in Roman Law in Memory of A. Arthur Schiller* (Leiden, 1986) 81–95.

47 See Livy 7.4–5; Valerius Maximus 5.4.3.

48 Cicero, *Pro Roscio Amerino* 53 puts this point quite bluntly, and there are many concrete examples in Valerius Maximus 7.7–8 of wills that were or could have been overturned because a parent disinherited a son or daughter without just cause. For the *querella inofficiosi testamenti*, see, *inter alia*, F. Schulz, *Classical Roman Law* (Oxford, 1951) 275–278; A. Watson, *The Law of Succession in the Later Roman Republic* (Oxford, 1971) 62–63; and W.W. Buckland, *A Textbook of Roman Law from Augustus to Justinian³* (rev. P. Stein, Cambridge, 1963) 327–331.

49 Plautus, *Persa* 329–399; cf. Cicero, *Pro Caecina* 98; *De Oratore* 1.181 (sale into slavery); Gaius, *Institutiones* 1.117 (sale *in mancipio*).

50 Plautus, *Stichus* 17, 27–28, 51–54, 68–74, 130–131, and 141–142 speak to a father's right to arrange divorces for his daughters (and, presumably, his sons) against their will, but as we have also seen, Cicero's long-delayed decision to divorce his daughter Tullia from P. Cornelius Dolabella out of fear that he would be unable to recover her dotal payments (*Epistulae ad Atticum* 11.23.3, 16.15.2; *Epistulae ad Familiares* 6.18.5) eloquently reveals how financial considerations could discourage divorce proceedings.

51 Cicero, *Pro Roscio Amerino* 44; *Pro Caelio* 17–18; cf. Seneca, *De Clementia* 1.15.2, where Tarius generously decides to go on paying an allowance to his son even after exiling him to Massilia for attempted patricide. Cicero also assigned an allowance to his son, setting aside the rents from certain properties in order to generate it on a monthly basis (*Epistulae ad Atticum* 15.20.4). For humorous examples of the difficulty that *adulescentes* encountered when they tried to borrow money, and the legal reasons for the reluctance of would-be creditors, see Plautus, *Pseudolus* 303–304, 506; and *Rudens* 1380–1382.

52 After the passage of the *lex Plaetoria* (or *Laetoria*) around 192 BC, *adulescentes* between the ages of 14 and 25 who were *sui iuris* may have had to seek the approval of a *curator*, who could refuse his consent to their proposed financial

dealings, before anyone would grant them credit. Sulla later raised the age of *adulescentia* to 30, before Augustus set it permanently at 25. The implications of the *lex Plaetoria*, and particularly of the curatorship, will be discussed below.

53 'La famille et l'amour,' 36. Here the recent attempt to minimize the impact of *patria potestas* upon adult sons by R.P. Saller, 'Men's Age at Marriage and Its Consequences in the Roman Family,' *CP* 82 (1987) 21–34, is explicitly rejected. Drawing upon sepulchral inscriptions from the second and third centuries AD, Saller attempts to establish the age of first marriage for men by isolating the relationship between the deceased and his commemorator for different age cohorts. In the 15–19 age bracket, for example, not one out of 128 dedications stems from a wife. Seventy-five per cent of those in the 20–25 age cohort are also commemorated by both parents; it is only after 25 that wives begin to take over as commemorators, and with increasing frequency as the age of the deceased increases. This leads him to the conclusion that the modal age for men's first marriages was 'at least 25 years of age for men in all areas of the Latin-speaking Empire outside the capital city for which data are available' (29). As he then notes, this pattern, in tandem with a 'premodern' mortality rate, would minimize the number of adults *in potestate*, and particularly would cast doubt upon the relevance of a father's authority to dissolve his son's marriage as well as ease many of the tensions associated with the father's absolute control of the *patrimonium*. Sixty per cent of all sons, he says, would have lost their fathers by or in their twenties, 80 per cent in their thirties, and virtually everybody would have gained emancipation in their forties (32).

It is disquieting that Saller must exclude the *plebs rustica* from his analysis for lack of evidence, and even more disconcerting that he deliberately excludes Rome from the study 'because of the large proportion of slaves and ex-slaves in the population' (25). In fact, one would have thought that the evidence for *contubernium* in Rome offers the one meaningful vehicle for glimpsing marriage patterns in the Roman lower classes. In any event, this study is vitiated by two equally grave errors. First, Saller's conclusion rest squarely upon the unconscious, untested and ultimately unproveable assumption that, when a son married, his parents invariably passed on the duty of commemorating him to his wife. In Spain, however, as he duly observes, parents routinely continued to commemorate their sons after their marriages. Second, a fundamental demographic inconsistency has slipped into his argument. Since he accepts that Roman society has a high ('premodern') mortality rate, it is clear that he is not measuring the life expectancy of would-be husbands from birth, but from some more advanced age. In calculating the percentage of fathers who would still be alive to exercise their *potestas* over sons in different age cohorts, however, he is just as obviously measuring their life expectancy from birth itself. Self-evidently, for his argument to possess any value at all, he must employ the same base-standard for measuring the life expectancy of father and son alike.

54 Suetonius, *Divus Iulius* 88; Petronius, *Satyricon* 71. For funerary inscriptions that invoke the term *domus aeterna*, cf., *inter alia*, *ILS* 7814, 8077, 8079, 8081, 8240, 8246, and 8341. On the *culina*, see Festus, *Glossaria Latina* v. *culina*; and *CIL* I².1059, V.7459 = *ILS* 8342. The full range of funerary amenities is described in F. Cumont, *After Life in Roman Paganism* (New Haven, Conn., 1922) 53–57; and still more briefly in J.M.C. Toynbee, *Death and Burial in the Roman World* (London, 1971) 51. The argument that unfolds here is adapted from J.K. Evans, 'The Cult of the Dead in Ancient Rome and Modern China: a Comparative Analysis,' *Journal of the Hong Kong Branch of the Royal Asiatic Society* 25 (1985) 119–151.

55 Thus *ILS* 7583, 8426, and 9143. The abbreviation *S.T.T.L* is far more common; see, *inter alia*, *ILS* 1555, 1659, 2514, 2654, 4960, 6801, 7594–7595, 7749, 7766,

7802, 8100, 8131, 8421, and 8445. R. Lattimore, *Themes in Greek and Latin Epitaphs* (Urbana, Ill., 1942) 65–74, examines this and other formulae that presume a belief in sensation after death.

56 Suetonius, *Gaius Caligula* 59; cf. Plautus, *Mostellaria* 499–504. Plato believed that murderers should suffer not only capital punishment but also eternal torment, hence he recommended that their remains should be denied proper burial (*Leges* 874b).

57 *Fasti* 2.549–556.

58 E.K. Gough, 'Cults of the Dead among the Nayars,' *Journal of American Folklore* 71 (1958) 446–478, at 449–450. It is worth emphasizing here that Roman ghosts might also demand a blood-sacrifice for reasons other than ritual neglect. The spirit of Verginia, for example, only ceased to haunt the living when all of the individuals responsible for her own demise had met with violent deaths, or worse still, suffered exile and complete confiscation of their property (Livy 3.58.11).

59 J. Goody, *Death, Property and the Ancestors* (Stanford, Calif., 1962) 393–394, 401; cf. M. Fortes, *The Web of Kinship among the Tallensi* (Oxford, 1949) 234–235; and A.R. Radcliffe-Brown, 'Religion and Society,' in *Structure and Function in Primitive Society* (Glencoe, Ill., 1952) 175.

60 F.L.K. Hsu, *Under the Ancestors' Shadow* (Garden City, NY, 1967) 210; cf. *Clan, Caste and Club* (Princeton, 1963) 45–46, where Hsu extends this generalization from 'West Town' to 'every part of China.'

61 A.P. Wolf, 'Gods, Ghosts and Ancestors,' in A.P. Wolf (ed.), *Religion and Ritual in Chinese Society* (Stanford, Calif., 1974), 160; cf., *inter alia*, R.F. Johnston, *Lion and Dragon in Northern China* (New York, 1910) 286–287; Hsiao-tung Fei, *Peasant Life in China: a Field Study of Country Life in the Yangtze Valley* (London, 1939) 78; M.C. Yang, *A Chinese Village: Taitou, Shantung Province* (New York, 1945) 45; M. Freedman, 'Ancestor Worship: Two Facets of the Chinese Case,' in M. Freedman (ed.), *Social Organization, Essays Presented to Raymond Firth* (Chicago, 1967) 92–93; and D.K. Jordan, *Gods, Ghosts and Ancestors* (Berkeley, 1972) 97.

62 Wolf, 'Gods, Ghosts and Ancestors,' 164–167.

63 E. Ahern, *The Cult of the Dead in a Chinese Village* (Stanford, Calif., 1973) 199–201, *et passim*.

64 W.W. Lambert, L.M. Triandis, and M. Wolf, 'Some Correlates of Beliefs in the Malevolence and Benevolence of Supernatural Beings: a Cross-Societal Study,' *Journal of Abnormal and Social Psychology* 58 (1959) 162–169.

65 Gough, 'Cults of the Dead,' 457; Goody, *Death, Property and the Ancestors*, 328, 409–410; S. Freud, *Totem and Taboo* (New York, 1952) 58–61.

66 M. Freedman, *Chinese Lineage and Society: Fukien and Kwantung* (London, 1966) 151; cf. 'Ancestor Worship,' 95, 98.

67 Ahern, *Cult of the Dead*, 191–203, 213–218.

68 Hsu, *Ancestors' Shadow*, 65, 223.

69 See, for example, Plautus, *Mostellaria* 233–234; and Terence, *Adelphoe* 107–110, and 874, the earliest such references, and telling ones despite their comical setting.

70 For freeborn children being whipped in the Republic, cf., *inter alia*, Terence, *Adelphoe* 64–71; and Cicero, *Tusculanae Disputationes* 3.64. In the early Principate, let us further recall, Seneca strongly advocated the beating of children as the only effective means of instilling correct behavior in them (*De Constantia Sapientia* 12.3). Despite his frail physique, the emperor Claudius was abused in this fashion throughout childhood (Suetonius, *Divus Claudius* 2.2).

71 Fortes, *Web of Kinship*, 234–235; for the *potestas* of Tallensi fathers, see

138–139.

72 This particular outgrowth of the waning fear of the ancestral spirit's punitive capacity is further discussed by Evans, 'Cult of the Dead in Ancient Rome and Modern China,' 140–142.

73 *Digesta* 23.2.19.

74 Paulus, *Sententiae* 5.6.15; cf. 2.19.2; *Codex Iustinianus* 5.17.5; *Digesta* 24.1.32.19, and 43.30.1.5.

75 *Digesta* 25.3.5.14, 43.30.1.3, 43.30.3.5–6; *Codex Iustinianus* 5.25.3.

76 *Codex Iustinianus* 9.16.8; *Digesta* 28.2.11 (cf. 25.3.4, where Paul makes it clear that he regards smothering a child, denying it food, exposing it, or abandoning it as merely different forms of infanticide); 25.3.1; and J.F. Gardner, *Women in Roman Law and Society* (Bloomington and Indianapolis, 1986) 155–156. This does not, of course, mean that society at large viewed infanticide as murder, and infants certainly continued to be eliminated by one means or another long after AD 374. Boswell, '*Expositio* and *Oblatio*,' 10–33, discusses this point at some length.

77 *Digesta* 48.9.5 (Hadrian); 1.16.9.3; *Codex Iustinianus* 8.47.3–4 (Severus Alexander and Valerian).

78 Seneca, *De Clementia* 1.15.1.

79 See, for example, *CIL* VI.14170, and the discussion in I. Kajanto, 'On Divorce among the Common People in Rome,' *Mélanges Marcel Durry* (Paris, 1970) 99–113.

80 I. Kajanto, *Onomastic Studies in the Early Christian Inscriptions of Rome and Carthage* (Acta Instituti Romani Finlandiae II.1, Helsinki, 1963) 19–21.

81 The most celebrated instance remains *P.Oxy.* 744 = A.S. Hunt and C.C. Edgar (eds.), *Select Papyri* I (Cambridge, Mass., 1932) 105.

82 Cicero, *Epistulae ad Familiares* 3.12.2; Valerius Maximus 4.4.10 (Scipio).

83 In the imperial period, the Sabinians continued to advocate the archaic custom of fixing puberty by means of individual physical examinations, but it was the Proculian view that prevailed (Gaius, *Institutiones* 1.196); for further discussion, see, *inter alia*, Schulz, *Classical Roman Law*, 164–165.

84 See *Digesta* 3.1.3 (those under 17 barred from court in classical law); 44.1.14 (*patres* sue on behalf of their sons *in potestate*); Cicero, *De Legibus* 2.50 (sons *in potestate* cannot give gifts without parental consent); *Institutiones Iustiniani* 2.12.*pr.*–1 (capacity to make a will limited to those who are *sui iuris* and pubescent).

85 For the summary conclusion of *tutela* at the onset of *pubertas*, see again Gaius, *Institutiones* 1.196.

86 Cf. Cicero, *De Natura Deorum* 3.74 (the *actio popularis* and fine); and *CIL* I².593 = *ILS* 6085, 112 (*infamia*).

87 Both the *exceptio* and the reluctance of money-lenders to deal with *iuvenes* are clearly in evidence in Plautus, *Rudens* 1380–1382; and *Pseudolus* 303–304, 506.

88 Cf., on this point, E. Eyben, ' "Antiquity's View of Puberty," *Latomus* 31 (1972) 677–697; 'Was the Roman "Youth" an "Adult" Socially?,' *AC* 50 (1981) 328–350; and Neraudau, *Etre enfant*, 23–28.

89 See *Digesta* 4.4.1; *Codex Iustinianus* 5.31.1, 6; and S.H.A., *Marcus* 10.12. The genesis of the *cura minorum*, and the difficulties that this institution have posed for students of Roman law, are ably discussed by Schulz, *Classical Roman Law*, 190–197.

90 Dixon, *Roman Mother*, 63–64, draws the same conclusion, although she arrives at it from a quite different and more narrowly legal point of departure.

91 Livy 2.40.1–9; cf. Plutarch, *Coriolanus* 4, where we are told that this strong and proudly independent man married a woman of his mother's choosing, and

continued to live under her roof even after he had fathered his children.

92   Tacitus, *Dialogus de Oratoribus* 28.6.

93   Cicero, *Brutus* 211; Plutarch, *Tiberius Gracchus* 1.4–5; *Gaius Gracchus* 4.1–3.

94   Cicero, *Brutus* 252, cryptically remarks that Caesar's oratorical skills stemmed in the first instance from *domestica consuetudine*; this may be what Tacitus has in mind in the *Dialogus*. For Aurelia's later involvement in Caesar's political career, cf. Suetonius, *Divus Iulius* 13; and Plutarch, *Caesar* 7. For Atia and Augustus, see F. Jacoby (ed.), *Die Fragmente der griechischen Historiker* (Leiden, 1923–1958) 90 F 127 (Nicolaus Damascenus); Dio Cassius 45.1.1; Velleius Paterculus 2.59.2–60.2; Appian, *Bella Civilia* 3.10–11; and Suetonius, *Divus Augustus* 8.

95   Cf. Cicero, *Epistulae ad Brutum* 26.1 (his characterization of Servilia); *Epistulae ad Atticum* 15.11 (the meeting at Antium); and Asconius 17KS (her *auctoritas* over Cato). For further discussion, see especially J.P. Hallett, *Fathers and Daughters in Roman Society* (Princeton, 1984) 49–52.

96   Tacitus, *Agricola* 4.3; *Annales* 12.8; Suetonius, *Nero* 52. Seneca, *Ad Marciam* 24.1–2 supplies still another example in the persons of Marcia and her son. The latter refused to undertake military service because it would mean abandoning his mother's household.

97   Cicero, *Tusculanae Disputationes* 3.64; Horace, *Carmina* 3.6.33–40; *Epistulae* 1.1.21–22.

98   This point was first articulated by T.W. Africa, 'The Mask of an Assassin: a Psychohistorical Study of M. Iunius Brutus,' *Journal of Interdisciplinary History* 8 (1978) 599–626. It has been most fully elaborated by Dixon, *Roman Mother*, xv, 2–4, 109–111, 131, *et passim*. Cf. also Neraudau, *Etre enfant*, 171–173; and Hallett, *Fathers and Daughters*, 251–252.

99   Cf., *inter alia*, *PSI* 1027 (AD 151); and *P.Oxy.* 494 = Hunt and Edgar (eds.), *Select Papyri* I.84 (AD 156–165).

100 Cf. again Cicero, *Pro Caecina* 11; and *Topica* 3.17 – the two most pertinent passages for the late Republic.

101 Thus *Digesta* 26.7.5.8.

102 Cf. *Digesta* 26.2.26.*pr.* (appointment of a *tutrix* illegal in classical law); *Codex Theodosianus* 3.17.4; *Codex Iustinianus* 5.35.2–3 (women empowered in certain circumstances to serve as guardians in AD 390). See further Gardner, *Women in Roman Law and Society*, 149–154.

103 Cf. *Digesta* 3.5.31.6; and 46.3.88.

104 *Digesta* 38.17.2.23–46.

105 Gardner, *Women in Roman Law and Society*, 149.

106 Seneca, *Ad Helviam* 14.3; Cicero, *In Verrem* 2.1.104–106.

107 Dixon, *Roman Mother*, 47–60, tentatively suggests that the system of usufruct may have strengthened the *auctoritas* of Roman mothers, and that the ability to pass on or withhold their own property from their children will have given them still greater leverage. Both of these observations are, however, open to question. As Dixon herself points out, the principles of agnatic inheritance enshrined in the intestate regulations of the Law of the Twelve Tables were already being ignored in the mid-second century BC. It was at this point that Papiria, for example, bequeathed her property to a son (Scipio Aemilianus) who had been adopted out of his natal family, and with whom in consequence she no longer had any legally recognized ties (Polybius 31.28.7–9). Such practices may have already been well established by this point in time, but the more immediately relevant point is that, during the Republic, the *populus Romanus* had already come to the conclusion that a mother should leave her property to her children. Here again, the codification of this principle in AD 321, when it was first formally decreed that children who had observed their filial responsibilities

could challenge their mother's will if they were not left one-quarter of her property (*Codex Theodosianus* 2.19.2), was merely a much belated concession to this social reality. Augustus, for example, had long since struck down a will in which a certain Septicia had capriciously disinherited her two sons (Valerius Maximus 7.7.4), while the testament of Aebutia, the wife of Menenius Agrippa, was deemed *plenae furoris* because she completely passed over one of her two daughters, *animi sui potius inclinatione provecta quam ullis alterius iniuriis aut officiis commota*. Valerius makes it clear that here as well, the will would have been set aside if the injured daughter had opted to challenge it in court, since the mother had no rational grounds for disinheriting her (7.8.2). In this social environment, therefore, it seems highly unlikely that a woman's *auctoritas* was effectively enhanced by an increasingly questionable ability to withhold her property from her offspring.

108 Other approaches that might be profitably explored in order fully to account for this extraordinary phenomenon include, *inter alia*, comparative analysis of the presentation of children in Hellenistic and Roman poetry; and careful study of the theories of child-rearing promoted by the various schools of Greek philosophy that found adherents within the Roman elite.

109 Tacitus, *Dialogus de Oratoribus* 28.4; Plutarch, *Cato Maior* 20.

110 Cf. *Cato Maior* 4 (the composition of his slave *familia*), and 21 (Chilo).

111 For the meaning of these terms, and a fuller analysis of the relevant inscriptions, see especially S. Dixon, 'Roman Nurses and Foster-Mothers: Some Problems of Terminology,' *AULLA* 22 (1984) 9–24.

112 Tacitus, *Dialogus de Oratoribus* 29; Suetonius, *Nero* 6.3, 50. Claudius, it might be added, was raised by a retired muleteer, but he favored Seneca's abusive approach to child-rearing. If Claudius turned out better than his successor, a conservative Roman might logically have concluded that this merely reflected the different ways in which they had been brought up.

113 Tacitus, *Dialogus de Oratoribus* 29; Soranus, *Gynaikeia* 1.19–20; cf. Quintilian, *Institutio Oratoria* 1.1.12; pseudo-Plutarch, *De Liberis Educandis* 3e–f.

114 M.-Th. Charlier and G. Raepsaet, 'Etude d'un comportement social: les relations entre parents et enfants dans la société Athénienne à l'epoque classique,' *AC* 40 (1971) 589–606. M. Golden, 'Did the Ancients Care When Their Children Died?,' *G&R* second series 35 (1988) 152–163 reaches the same conclusion in a still more rapid survey of this evidence. For a typical example drawn from the literary sources, see Euripides, *Hercules Furens* 634–636. M. Golden, *Children and Childhood in Classical Athens* (Baltimore and London, 1990), appeared too late to be incorporated into this analysis. Golden does, however, conclude that 'the weight of the evidence seems overwhelmingly to favor the proposition that the Athenians loved their children and grieved for them deeply when they died' (p. 89).

115 It does not follow that they would have invariably done so, for as noted by Bradley, 'Wet-Nursing at Rome,' 220–222, many slave *nutrices* must have resented having to breast-feed their master's child, especially if this involved the prolonged period of enforced celibacy that we discussed earlier. For enslaved Greek *nutrices* in post-Hannibalic Rome, see Plautus, *Aulularia* 698; *Poenulus* 28–31; *Trinummus* 512–513; and Terence, *Adelphoe* 972–977.

116 The obvious example here is Pliny the Younger, who gave his old *nutrix* a farm worth HS 100,000 (*Epistulae* 6.3), but the enduring affection between nurse and ward is equally obvious in the funerary inscriptions that they dedicated to one another; see again Dixon, 'Roman Nurses and Foster-Mothers,' 9–24; and Bradley, 'Wet-Nursing at Rome,' 220–222.

117 Verstraete, 'Male Homosexual Relations,' 227–236.

APPENDICES

i ROMAN CRAFTS AND TRADESWOMEN

Profession	Status	Male present?	Source
auri netrix (spinner of gold thread)	Inc.	No	*CIL* VI.9213 = *ILS* 7691
auri vestrix (embroiderer in gold thread?)	Inc.	Mar./Inc.	*CIL* VI.9214a = *ILS* 7692
aurifex (goldsmith)	Lib. Inc.	No Inc.	*CIL* VI.4430 *CIL* VI.9207
brattiaria (worker in gold leaf)	Lib. Inc.	Lib. Lib.	*CIL* VI.6939 *CIL* VI.9211
calcaria (dealer in burnt lime)	Inc.	No	*ILS* 7663
carnaria? (dealer in meat)	Inc.	Mar./Inc.	*CIL* VI.9685
clavaria (dealer in nails)	Lib.	Mar./Civ.	*CIL* V.7023 = *ILS* 7636
conditaria (dealer in preserved foods)	Inc.	Mar./Inc.	*CIL* VI.9277
coronaria (maker of crowns and garlands)	–	–	Pliny, *Naturalis Historia* 21.3
fabaria (dealer in beans)	Inc.	Inc. (same name)	*CIL* III.153 = 6672
faeneratrix (money-lender)	Inc.	No	*CIL* IV.4528, 8203–8204

furnaria	*Lib.*	*Lib.*	*CIL* VIII.24678
(baker)	*Lib.*	No	*CIL* IX.4721–4722
gemmaria	*Lib.*	*Lib.*	*CIL* VI.9435
(gem-cutter)			
hordeum vendit	*Inc.*	No	*CIL* VI.9684
(dealer in barley)			
lagunaria	*Inc.*	No	*CIL* VI.9488
(dealer in			
bottles)			
linaria/	*Inc.*	No	*CIL* II.4318*a* = *ILS* 7562
lintearia	*Lib.*	*Lib.*	*CIL* V.5923 = *ILS* 7560
(dealer in cloth)			
margaritaria	*Lib.*	No	*CIL* VI.5972
(pearl-setter)			
negotiatrix	*Inc.*	*Inc.*	*CIL* VI.814
(dealer in	*Inc.*	*Mar.*	*CIL* XII.4496
cereals?)			
negotiatrix	*Lib.*	*Mar./Lib.*	*CIL* VI.9683 = *ILS* 7488
frumentariae et			
legumenariae			
(dealer in cereals			
and vegetables)			
negotiatrix	*Inc.*	*Mar./Inc.*	*AE* 1973, 71
olearii et vini			
(dealer in oil			
and wine)			
officinatrix	*Inc.*	No	*CIL* VI.9715
(manager or owner			
of a workshop)			
piscatrix	*Lib.*	*Lib.*	*CIL* VI.9801 = *ILS* 7500
(fishmonger)			
plumbaria	*Inc.*	*Mar./Inc.*	*CIL* III.2117
(dealer in lead)			
pomaria	*Inc.*	*Mar./Inc.*	*CIL* VI.37819
(dealer in fruit)			
purpuraria	*Inc.*	*Inc.*	*CIL* II.1743
(dealer in	*Lib.*	*Mar./Lib.*	*CIL* VI.37820 = *ILS* 9428
purple-dyed	*Lib.*	No	*CIL* VI.9846
cloth)	*Inc.*	*Inc.*	*CIL* VI.9848
	Lib.	*Mar./Inc.*	*CIL* XIV.2433 = *ILS* 7597
	Lib.	*Mar./Lib.*	*NS* 1922, 144
resinaria	*Inc.*	No	*CIL* VI.9855 = *ILS* 7658
(dealer in resin)			
sarcinatrix	*Lib.*	*Mar./Lib.*	*CIL* VI.9884 = *ILS* 7567
(needlewoman)			
seminaria	*Inc.*	*Mar./Inc.*	*CIL* XIV.2850 = *ILS* 3689
(dealer in seeds)			

siricaria	*Inc.*	No	*CIL* VI.9892
(dealer in silk)			
sutrix	*Inc.*	*Inc.*	*CIL* XIV.4698
(shoe-maker)			
tesseraria	*Lib.*	No	*CIL* V.7044 = *ILS* 7288
lignaria			
(mosaic worker)			
thuraria	*Lib.*	*Lib.*	*CIL* VI.9933
(dealer in incense)	*Lib.*	*Mar./Lib.*	*CIL* VI.9934
unguentaria	*Inc.*	*Mar./Inc.*	*CIL* VI.10006
(dealer in perfume)	*Inc.*	*Inc.*	*CIL* VI.33928
		(same name)	
	Inc.	No	*CIL* X.1965
	Inc.	No	*CIL* XII.1594
vestiaria	*Lib.*	*Lib.*	*CIL* VI.33920
(tailor)	*Lib.*	*Mar./Lib.*	*CIL* VI.37826

Abbreviations: *Civ.* = free-born citizen
Inc. = uncertain
Lib. = freedman/woman
Mar. = husband

ii PROFESSIONAL WOMEN

Profession	*Status*	*Source*
medica/	Civ.?	*CIL* II.497 = *ILS* 7802
iatromea	Inc.	*CIL* II.4314 = *ILS* 5299
(physician)	Civ.?	*CIL* II.4380
	Ser.	*CIL* V.3461
	Ser.	*CIL* VI.6851
	Civ.	*CIL* VI.7581 = *ILS* 7804
	Ser.	*CIL* VI.8639.*b*.9
	Ser.	*CIL* VI.8711 = *ILS* 7803
	Lib.?	*CIL* VI.8926
	Ser.	*CIL* VI.9084
	Inc.	*CIL* VI.9477 = *ILS* 7806
	Inc.	*CIL* VI.9478
	Ser.	*CIL* VI.9510
	Inc.	*CIL* VI.9614
	Lib.	*CIL* VI.9615 = 33812
	Lib.	*CIL* VI.9616
	Lib.	*CIL* VI.9617
	Inc.	*CIL* VIII.806
	Civ.	*CIL* VIII.24679
	Lib.	*CIL* IX.5861
	Civ.?	*CIL* X.3980 = *ILS* 7805
	Civ.?	*CIL* XII.3343
	Civ.?	*CIL* XIII.2019

	Civ.	*CIL* XIII.4334
	Lib.?	*AE* 1972, 83
	Civ.	Pleket, *Epigraphica* II.12
	Civ.	Pleket, *Epigraphica* II.20
	Civ.	Pleket, *Epigraphica* II.26
	Civ.	Pleket, *Epigraphica* II.27
opstetrix	Inc.	*CIL* III.8820
(mid-wife)	Lib.	*CIL* VI.4458
	Ser.	*CIL* VI.6325
	Ser.	*CIL* VI.6647
	Ser.	*CIL* VI.6832
	Lib.	*CIL* VI.8192
	Lib.	*CIL* VI.8207
	Lib.	*CIL* VI.8947 = *ILS* 1840
	Ser.	*CIL* VI.8948
	Lib.	*CIL* VI.8949
	Civ.?	*CIL* VI.9720
	Lib.	*CIL* VI.9721–9721a
	Inc.	*CIL* VI.9722
	Lib.	*CIL* VI.9723
	Civ.?	*CIL* VI.9724
	Inc.	*CIL* VI.9725
	Lib.	*CIL* VI.37810
	Ser.	*CIL* VIII.4896
	Inc.	*CIL* VIII.5155
	Inc.	*CIL* VIII.15593
	Inc.	*CIL* VIII.25394
	Inc.	*CIL* X.1933
	Lib.	*CIL* X.3972
	Civ.?	*CIL* XI.4128
	Inc.	*CIL* XIII.3706
	Inc.	*AE* 1979, 396
	Inc.	*AE* 1980, 936

Abbreviations: Civ. = free-born citizen
Inc. = uncertain
Lib. = freedwoman
Ser. = slave woman

iii WET-NURSES

Familia Caesaris

Status	Source
Lib.	*CIL* VI.4352
Lib.	*CIL* VI.5201 = *ILS* 1837
Lib.	*CIL* VI.8941

Civ.?	*CIL* VI.8942 = *ILS* 1839
Lib.	*CIL* VI.8943 = *ILS* 1838
Lib.	*CIL* VI.10909

Aristocratic *familiae*

Lib.	*CIL* VI.1354
Ser.	*CIL* VI.1365 = *ILS* 1160
Lib.	*CIL* VI.1516 = *ILS* 1202
Lib.	*CIL* VI.4457
Lib.	*CIL* VI.5939
Inc.	*CIL* VI.6072
Ser.	*CIL* VI.6323
Ser.	*CIL* VI.6324 = *ILS* 8539
Lib.	*CIL* VI.7290 = *ILS* 7446
Lib.	*CIL* VI.7355
Lib.	*CIL* VI.7393
Ser.	*CIL* VI.7618
Lib.	*CIL* VI.9245
Lib.	*CIL* VI.9901*b*
Inc.	*CIL* VI.16128
Lib.	*CIL* VI.16440
Lib.	*CIL* VI.16450
Lib.	*CIL* VI.16470
Inc.	*CIL* VI.16587
Inc.	*CIL* VI.16592
Lib.	*CIL* VI.20883
Lib.	*CIL* VI.21661
Lib.	*CIL* VI.23458
Ser.	*CIL* VI.24073
Lib.	*CIL* VI.26539
Lib.	*CIL* VI.28381
Lib.	*CIL* VI.29550

Servae

CIL V.3950	*CIL* VI.20042
CIL VI.7741	*CIL* VI.25301
CIL VI.10554 (2 *nutrices*)	*CIL* VI.25728
CIL VI.12366	*CIL* VI.28120 = *ILS* 8537
CIL VI.12600	*CIL* VI.35123
CIL VI.17564	*CIL* VI.38999

Libertae

CIL II.545	*CIL* VI.11265
CIL V.7277	*CIL* VI.12023

CIL VI.14558
CIL VI.15655
CIL VI.18032
CIL VI.18073
CIL VI.21347
CIL VI.21988
CIL VI.23078 = 34143*b*
CIL VI.27262 = *ILS* 8538
CIL VI.29497 = *ILS* 8538

CIL VI.34383
CIL VI.35037
CIL X.30
CIL X.2669
CIL XII.4797
AE 1964, 274
AE 1972, 434
AE 1980, 326

Ingenuae

CIL VI.32049
AE 1960, 249

Incertae

CIL II.3190
CIL III.2012
CIL III.2450
CIL III.5314
CIL VI.3403 = *ILS* 8203
CIL VI.3899
CIL VI.5063
CIL VI.6686
CIL VI.8660
CIL VI.12133
CIL VI.12299
CIL VI.13683
CIL VI.15377
CIL VI.15952
CIL VI.16329
CIL VI.17157
CIL VI.17490

CIL VI.19155
CIL VI.20938
CIL VI.21151
CIL VI.21710
CIL VI.23128
CIL VI.23589
CIL VI.24297
CIL VI.27134
CIL VI.29191
CIL X.2185
CIL X.3112
CIL X.6006 = *AE* 1982, 157
CIL X.7038
AE 1960, 190
AE 1960, 193
AE 1972, 203
AE 1985, 166

Abbreviations: *Civ.* = free-born citizen
Inc. = uncertain
Lib. = freedwoman
Ser. = slave woman

iv SOME EGYPTIAN WET-NURSING CONTRACTS

Length of contract	Status	Source
6 months	*Civ./Mar.*	*P.Meyer* 11
8 months	*Civ./Mar.*	*BGU* 1110

10 months	Ser.	*BGU* 1109
12 months	Ser.	*BGU* 1112
15 months	Civ.	*BGU* 1108
16 months	Civ.	*BGU* 1107 = *SP* 16
18 months	Civ./Mar.	*BGU* 1106
24 months	Civ./Mar.	*BGU* 297
24 months	Ser.	*BGU* 1058
24 months	Civ.	*P.Bour.* 14
24 months	Civ./Mar.	*P.Oxy.* 37
24 months	Civ./Mar.	*P.Oxy.* 38
24 months	Ser.	*P.Oxy.* 91 = *SP* 79
24 months	Civ./Mar.	*P.Ross.–Georg.* 18
24 months	Civ./Mar.	*P.Ross.–Georg.* 74
24 months	Civ./Mar.	*P.Ryl.* 178
24 months	Civ./Mar.	*PSI* 203
24 months	Ser.	*PSI* 1065
24 months	Civ./Mar.	*SB* 7619
24 months	Civ./Mar.	*ZPE* 14 (1974) 148
30 months	Civ./Mar.	*SB* 7607
36 months	Ser.	*P.Teb.* 399
–	Ser.	*BGU* 1111
–	Civ.	*BGU* 1153
–	Civ.	*P.Grenf.* 75
–	Civ.	*P.Ross.–Georg.* 16
–	Civ.	*P.Ryl.* 342
–	Civ./Mar.	*PSI* 1131

Abbreviations: *Civ.* = free-born citizen
Mar. = married
Ser. = slave woman

v REPUBLICAN AND AUGUSTAN ACTRESSES

Name	Status	Source
Antiodemis	Civ.?	*Anthologia Palatina* 9.567
Arbuscula	Inc.	Cicero, *Epistulae ad Atticum* 4.15.6
Bacchis	Inc.	Cicero, *Epistulae ad Atticum* 15.27.3
Dionysia	Inc.	Cicero, *Pro Roscio Amerino* 23
Ecloga	Ser.	*CIL* VI.10110 = *ILS* 5216
Emphasis?	Inc.	*CIL* I².1359 = VI.33112
Eucharis	Lib.	*CIL* I².1214 = VI.10096 = *ILS* 5213
Galeria Copiola	Inc.	Pliny, *Naturalis Historia* 7.158
Lucceia	Inc.	Pliny, *Naturalis Historia* 7.158
Luria Privata	Inc.	*CIL* VI.10111 = *ILS* 5215
Origo	Inc.	Horace, *Satirae* 1.2.55–59
Quintia	Inc.	*Priapea* 27

Sammula	*Inc.*	Pliny, *Naturalis Historia* 7.159
Sophe	*Inc.*	*CIL* VI.10128
Syrisca	*Inc.*	Pseudo-Virgil, *Copa* 1–4
Telethusa	*Inc.*	*Priapea* 19
Tertia	*Civ.*	Cicero, *In Verrem* 2.3.78
Volumnia Cytheris	*Lib.*	Cicero, *Epistulae ad Atticum* 10.10.5, 10.16.5, 15.22; *Orationes Philippicae* 2.58–62, 69

Abbreviations: *Civ.* = free-born citizen
Inc. = uncertain
Lib. = freedwoman
Ser. = slave woman

vi FEMALE DANCERS AND ENTERTAINERS

Profession	*Status*	*Source*
cantrix/cantatrix	*Ser.*	*CIL* VI.7285
(singer)	*Ser.?*	*CIL* VI.9230
	Lib.	*CIL* VI.33794 = *ILS* 1696
	Inc. (2)	*CIL* VI.37783 = *ILS* 9347
choraule	*Lib.*	*CIL* VI.7286
(flute player)		
citharistria/	*Inc.*	*CIL* VI.10125 = *ILS* 5244
citharoeda		
(cithara player)		
cymbalistria	*Ser.*	*CIL* VI.2254
(cymbal player)		
emboliaria	*Inc.*	*CIL* VI.10127 = *ILS* 5262
(actress performing	*Inc.*	*CIL* VI.10128 = *ILS* 5263
at interludes)		
musica	*Inc.*	*CIL* VIII.126
(musician)		
psaltria	*Lib.*	*CIL* VI.10137 = *ILS* 5249
(lute player)	*Lib.*	*CIL* VI.10138 = *ILS* 5248
	Inc.	*CIL* VI.10139
sambucistria	*Inc.*	*CIL* VIII.25745a
(sambuca player)		
saltatrix	*Inc.*	*CLE* 1166
(dancing girl)	*Inc.*	*CIL* VI.10143
	Lib.	*CIL* VI.10144
	Ser.	*CIL* VIII.12925
sinfoniaca	*Inc.*	*CIL* II.3465 = *ILS* 5256a
(choral musician)		
tibicina	*Lib.*	*AE* 1985, 329
(flute player)		
timpanaria	*Inc.*	*AE* 1972, 715
(drummer)		

Abbreviations: *Inc.* = uncertain
Lib. = freedwoman
Ser. = slave woman

vii POMPEIAN PROSTITUTES

Price	Name	Status	Source (CIL IV)
2 *asses*	Lahis	*Inc.*	1969
	Felicla	*Ver.*	4023
	Athenais	*Inc.*	4150
	Sabina	*Inc.*	4150
	Eutychis	*Inc.*	4592
	Optata	*Ver.*	5105
	Pieris	*Inc.*	5338
	Euche	*Ver.*	5345
	–	*Inc.*	5372
	Arbuscula	*Inc.*	7068
	Afillia Ianuaria	*Inc.*	7764
	–	*Inc.*	8160
	Fortunata	*Inc.*	8185
	Naebris	*Inc.*	8394
	Veneria	*Inc.*	8465
	Spes	*Inc.*	8511
3 *asses*	Libanis	*Inc.*	2028
	Pitane	*Inc.*	4439
5 *asses*	Tyche	*Inc.*	2450
	–	*Ver.*	5204
8 *asses*	Logas	*Ver.*	5203
9 *asses*	Spes	*Inc.*	5127
16 *asses*	Attica	*Inc.*	1751
	–	*Ver.*	5206
1 *denarius*	Drauca	*Inc.*	2193
23 *asses*	Fortunata	*Inc.*	8034
–	Lucilla	*Inc.*	1948
–	–	*Ver.*	4593

Abbreviations: *Inc.* = uncertain
Ver. = woman born in slavery

SELECTED BIBLIOGRAPHY

Adams, J.N., *The Latin Sexual Vocabulary* (Baltimore, 1982).

Africa, T.W., 'The Mask of an Assassin: a Psychohistorical Study of M. Iunius Brutus,' *Journal of Interdisciplinary History* 8 (1978) 599–626.

Afzelius, A., *Die römische Kriegsmacht während der Auseinandersetzung mit den hellenistischen Grossmächten* (Copenhagen, 1944).

Ahern, E., *The Cult of the Dead in a Chinese Village* (Stanford, Calif., 1973).

Amundsen, D.W., and Diers, C.J., 'The Age of Menarche in Classical Greece and Rome,' *Human Biology* 41 (1969) 125–132.

Ankum, H., 'La femme mariée et la loi Falcidia,' *Labeo* 30 (1984) 28–70.

Arthur, M., ' "Liberated" Women: the Classical Era,' *Becoming Visible: Women in European History*, ed. R. Bridenthal and C. Koonz (Boston, 1977) 60–89.

Astin, A.E., *Scipio Aemilianus* (Oxford, 1967).

Astin, A.E., *Cato the Censor* (Oxford, 1978).

Badian, E., 'Tiberius Gracchus and the Beginning of the Roman Revolution,' *ANRW* I.1 (1972) 668–731.

Balsdon, J.P.V.D., *Roman Women: Their History and Habits* (London, 1962).

Bang, M., 'Das gewöhnliche Alter der Mädchen bei der Verlobung und Verheiratung,' in L. Friedländer, *Darstellungen aus der Sittengeschichte Roms*[10] IV (Leipzig, 1922) 133–141.

Barker, G., Lloyd, J., and Webley, D., 'A Classical Landscape in Molise,' *PBSR* n.s. 33 (1978) 35–51.

Beard, M., 'The Sexual Status of Vestal Virgins,' *JRS* 70 (1980) 12–27.

Beaucamp, J., 'Le vocabulaire de la faiblesse féminine dans les textes juridiques romains du IIIᵉ au VIᵉ siècle,' *RD* 54 (1976) 485–508.

Bell, H.I., 'A Musician's Contract,' *JEA* 10 (1924) 145–146.

Belmont, N., 'Levana, ou comment "elever" les enfants,' *Ann(ESC)* 28 (1973) 77–89 = 'Levana: or How to Raise Up Children,' *Family and Society*, ed. R. Forster and O. Ranum (Baltimore and London, 1976) 1–15.

Beloch, K.J., *Die Bevölkerung der griechisch-römischen Welt* (Leipzig, 1886).

Berger, A., *Encyclopedic Dictionary of Roman Law* (Philadelphia, 1953).

219

Bernstein, A.H., *Tiberius Sempronius Gracchus, Tradition and Apostasy* (Ithaca, NY, 1978).

Besnier, M., 'A Propos de la table hypothécaire de Veleia,' *REA* 24 (1922) 118–122.

Best, E.E., Jr., 'Cicero, Livy and Educated Roman Women,' *CJ* 65 (1970) 199–204.

Betz, H.D., *The Greek Magical Papyri in Translation* I (Chicago, 1986).

Biondi, B., *Successione testamentaria donazioni* (Milan, 1943).

Biondi, B., *Il diritto romano cristiano* (Milan, 1952–1954). 3 vols.

Bizzarri, E., 'Titolo Mummiano a Fabrateria Nova,' *Epigraphica* 35 (1973) 140–142.

Bonfante, L., 'The Women of Etruria,' *Arethusa* 6 (1973) 91–101. Reprinted in *Women in the Ancient World: the Arethusa Papers*, ed. J. Peradotto and J.P. Sullivan (Albany, 1984) 229–239.

Bonfante, L., 'Etruscan Women: a Question of Interpretation,' *Archaeology* 26 (1973) 242–249.

Bonfante, L., 'Etruscan Couples and Their Aristocratic Society,' *Women's Studies* 8 (1981) 157–187. Reprinted in *Reflections of Women in Antiquity*, ed. H.P. Foley (New York, 1981) 323–342.

Boren, H.C., 'The Urban Side of the Gracchan Economic Crisis,' *AHR* 63 (1958) 890–902.

Boswell, J.E., '*Expositio* and *Oblatio*: the Abandonment of Children and the Ancient and Mediaeval Family,' *AHR* 89 (1984) 10–33.

Bourne, F.C., 'The Roman Republican Census and Census Statistics,' *CW* 45 (1952) 129–135.

Bourne, F.C., 'The Roman Alimentary Program and Italian Agriculture,' *TAPA* 91 (1960) 47–75.

Boyer, G., 'Le droit successoral romain dans les oeuvres de Polybe,' *RIDA* 4 (1950) 169–187.

Bradley, K.R., 'Sexual Regulations in Wet-Nursing Contracts from Roman Egypt,' *Klio* 62 (1980) 321–325.

Bradley, K.R., 'Wet-Nursing at Rome: a Study in Social Relations,' *The Family in Ancient Rome*, ed. B. Rawson (London, 1985) 201–229.

Bradley, K.R., 'Child Labour in the Roman World,' *Historical Reflections* 12 (1985) 311–330.

Bradley, K.R., 'On the Roman Slave Supply and Slave Breeding,' *Classical Slavery*, ed. M.I. Finley (Cambridge, 1987) 42–64.

Bradley, K.R., *Slaves and Masters in the Roman Empire: a Study in Social Control* (Oxford, 1987).

Bringmann, K., *Die Agrarreform des Tiberius Gracchus* (Stuttgart, 1985).

Briscoe, J., *A Commentary on Livy, Books XXXI–XXXIII* (Oxford, 1973).

Briscoe, J., *A Commentary on Livy, Books XXXIV–XXXVII* (Oxford, 1981).

Broughton, T.R.S., *The Magistrates of the Roman Republic* (Cleveland, 1951–1952). 2 vols.

Brunt, P.A., *Italian Manpower, 225 BC–AD 14* (Oxford, 1971).

Buckland, W.W., *A Textbook of Roman Law from Augustus to Justinian*[3], rev. P. Stein (Cambridge, 1963).

Burford, A.M., 'Heavy Transport in Classical Antiquity,' *EHR* 2nd ser. 13

(1960) 1–18.

Calza, G., and Becatti, G., *Ostia*⁹ (Rome, 1974).

Cantarella, E., *Pandora's Daughters* (Baltimore, 1987).

Carcopino, J., 'La table de Veleia et son importance historique,' *REA* 23 (1921) 287–303.

Carp, T., 'Two Matrons of the Late Republic,' *Women's Studies* 8 (1981) 189–200. Reprinted in *Reflections of Women in Antiquity*, ed. H. Foley (New York, 1981) 343–354.

Carter, J.C. (ed.), *The Territory of Metaponto, 1981–82* (Austin, 1983).

Carter, J.C., Costantini, L., D'Annibale, C., Jones, J.R., Folk, R.L., and Sullivan, D., 'Population and Agriculture: Magna Grecia in the Fourth Century BC,' *Papers in Italian Archaeology IV: the Cambridge Conference*, ed. C. Malone and S. Stoddart, I (Oxford, 1985) 281–312.

Cebeillac-Gervasoni, M., and Zevi, F., 'Révisions et nouveautés pour trois inscriptions d'Ostie,' *MEFR* 88 (1976) 607–637.

Champlin, E., 'Owners and Neighbours at Ligures Baebiani,' *Chiron* 11 (1981) 239–264.

Charlier, M.-Th., and Raepsaet, G., 'Etude d'un comportement social: les relations entre parents et enfants dans la société Athénienne à l'epoque classique,' *AC* 40 (1971) 589–606.

Clark, G., 'Roman Women,' *G&R* 2nd ser. 28 (1981) 193–212.

Coarelli, F., *Guida archeologica di Roma*² (Rome, 1975).

Collins, J.H., 'Tullia's Engagement and Marriage to Dolabella,' *CJ* 47 (1952) 164–168, 186.

Corbett, P.E., *The Roman Law of Marriage* (Oxford, 1930).

Crawford, M.H., 'War and Finance,' *JRS* 54 (1964) 29–32.

Crook, J.A., 'Patria Potestas,' *CQ* n.s. 17 (1967) 113–122.

Crook, J.A., *Law and Life of Rome* (London, 1967).

Crook, J.A., 'Intestacy in Roman Society,' *PCPhS* n.s. 19 (1973) 38–44.

Crook, J.A., 'Women in Roman Succession,' *The Family in Ancient Rome*, ed. B. Rawson (London, 1985) 58–82.

Crook, J.A., 'Feminine Inadequacy and the Senatusconsultum Velleianum,' *The Family in Ancient Rome*, ed. B. Rawson (London, 1985) 83–92.

Cumont, F., *After Life in Roman Paganism* (New Haven, Conn., 1922).

D'Arms, J.H., 'Control, Companionship, and *Clientela*: Some Social Functions of the Roman Communal Meal,' *CV* 28 (1984) 327–348.

Daube, D., 'The Preponderance of Intestacy at Rome,' *Tulane Law Review* 39 (1964/65) 253–262.

Daube, D., *Roman Law. Linguistic, Social and Philosophical Aspects* (Edinburgh, 1969).

D'Avino, M., *The Women of Pompeii*, trans. M.H. Jones and L. Nusco (Naples, 1967).

Della Corte, M., *Case ed abitanti di Pompei*³ (Naples, 1965).

Dickison, S., 'Abortion in Antiquity,' *Arethusa* 6 (1973) 159–166.

Dixon, S., 'Roman Nurses and Foster-Mothers: Some Problems of Terminology,' *AULLA* 22 (1984) 9–24.

Dixon, S., 'Infirmitas Sexus: Womanly Weakness in Roman Law,' *TRG* 52 (1984) 343–371.

Dixon, S., 'Family Finances: Tullia and Terentia,' *Antichthon* 18 (1984) 78–101. Reprinted in *The Family in Ancient Rome*, ed. B. Rawson (London, 1985) 93–120.

Dixon, S., 'Polybius on Roman Women and Property,' *AJPh* 106 (1985) 147–170.

Dixon, S., 'The Marriage Alliance in the Roman Elite,' *JFamHist* 10 (1985) 353–378.

Dixon, S., 'Breaking the Law to Do the Right Thing: the Gradual Erosion of the Voconian Law in Ancient Rome,' *Adelaide Law Review* 9 (1985) 519–534.

Dixon, S., *The Roman Mother* (Norman, Okla., 1988).

Dohr, H., *Die italischen Gutshöfe nach den Schriften Catos und Varros* (Cologne, 1965).

Duncan, G., 'Sutri,' *PBSR* n.s. 13 (1958) 63–131.

Duncan-Jones, R., 'The Purpose and Organisation of the Alimenta,' *PBSR* n.s. 19 (1964) 123–146.

Duncan-Jones, R., *The Economy of the Roman Empire*² (Cambridge, 1982).

Durry, M., 'Le mariage des filles impubères à Rome,' *CRAI* (1955) 84–91. Reprinted in *Mélanges Marcel Durry* (Paris, 1970) 17–24.

Durry, M., 'Le mariage des filles impubères chez les anciens Romains,' *Anthropos* 50 (1955) 430–432.

Durry, M., 'Le mariage des filles impubères dans la Rome antique,' *RIDA* 2 (1955) 263–273.

Durry, M., 'Sur le mariage romain,' *RIDA* 3 (1956) 227–243. Reprinted as 'Autocritique et mise au point,' *Mélanges Marcel Durry* (Paris, 1970) 27–41.

Earl, D.C., *Tiberius Gracchus: a Study in Politics* (Brussels, 1963).

Ehrenberg, V., *The People of Aristophanes*² (Oxford, 1951, reprinted New York, 1962).

Eichenauer, M., *Untersuchungen zur Arbeitswelt der Frau in der römischen Antike* (Frankfurt, 1988).

Engels, D., 'The Problem of Female Infanticide in the Greco-Roman World,' *CP* 75 (1980) 112–120.

Eschebach, H., *Die städtbauliche Entwicklung des Antiken Pompeji*, *MDAI(R)*, supp. vol. 17 (Heidelberg, 1970).

Etienne, R., 'La conscience médicale antique et la vie des enfants,' *Annales de Démographie Historique* 9 (1973) 15–46 = 'Ancient Medical Conscience and the Life of Children,' *Journal of Psychohistory* 4 (1976) 131–161.

Evans, J.K., '*Plebs Rustica*. The Peasantry of Classical Italy I: the Peasantry in Modern Scholarship,' *AJAH* 5 (1980) 19–47.

Evans, J.K., '*Plebs Rustica*. The Peasantry of Classical Italy II: the Peasant Economy,' *AJAH* 5 (1980) 134–173.

Evans, J.K., 'The Cult of the Dead in Ancient Rome and Modern China: a Comparative Analysis,' *Journal of the Hong Kong Branch of the Royal Asiatic Society* 25 (1985) 119–151.

Evans, J.K., 'Resistance at Home: the Evasion of Military Service in Italy during the Second Century BC,' *Forms of Control and Subordination in Antiquity*, ed. T. Yuge and M. Doi (Tokyo and Leiden, 1988) 121–140.

222

Eyben, E., 'Antiquity's View of Puberty,' *Latomus* 31 (1972) 677–697.

Eyben, E., 'Was the Roman "Youth" an "Adult" Socially?,' *AC* 50 (1981) 328–350.

Fei, Hsiao-tung, *Peasant Life in China: a Field Study of Country Life in the Yangtze Valley* (London, 1939).

Finley, M.I., 'The Silent Women of Rome,' *Horizon* 7 (1965) 57–64. Reprinted in *Aspects of Antiquity* (London, 1968) 129–142.

Finley, M.I., *The Ancient Economy*[2] (London, 1985).

Flory, M.B., 'Family in *Familia*: Kinship and Community in Slavery,' *AJAH* 3 (1978) 78–95.

Forbes, C.A., 'The Education and Training of Slaves in Antiquity,' *TAPA* 86 (1955) 321–360.

Fortes, M., *The Web of Kinship among the Tallensi* (Oxford, 1949).

Förtsch, B., *Die politische Rolle der Frau in der römischen Republik* (Stuttgart, 1935).

Fraenkel, E., *Plautinisches im Plautus* (Berlin, 1922).

Frank, T., *An Economic Survey of Ancient Rome* I (Baltimore, 1933).

Frayn, J.M., 'Wild and Cultivated Plants: a Note on the Peasant Economy of Roman Italy,' *JRS* 65 (1975) 32–39.

Frayn, J.M., *Subsistence Farming in Roman Italy* (London, 1979).

Frederiksen, M.W., 'The Contribution of Archaeology to the Agrarian Problem in the Gracchan Period,' *DArch* 4–5 (1970–71) 330–367.

Freedman, M., *Chinese Lineage and Society: Fukien and Kwantung* (London, 1966).

Freedman, M., 'Ancestor Worship: Two Facets of the Chinese Case,' *Social Organization, Essays Presented to Raymond Firth*, ed. M. Freedman (Chicago, 1967) 85–103.

Freis, H., *Historische Inschriften zur römischen Kaiserzeit* (Darmstadt, 1984).

French, V., 'Midwives and Maternity Care in the Roman World,' *Rescuing Creusa: New Methodological Approaches to Women in Antiquity*, ed. M. Skinner, *Helios* 13.2 (1987) 69–84.

French, V., 'History of the Child's Influence: Ancient Mediterranean Civilizations,' *Child Effects on Adults*, ed. R.Q. Bell and L.V. Harper (Hillsdale, NJ, 1977) 3–29.

Freud, S., *Totem and Taboo* (New York, 1952).

Frier, B.W., *Landlords and Tenants in Imperial Rome* (Princeton, 1980).

Frier, B.W., 'Roman Life Expectancy: Ulpian's Evidence,' *HSPh* 86 (1982) 212–251.

Frier, B.W., *The Rise of the Roman Jurists: Studies in Cicero's* Pro Caecina (Princeton, 1985).

Furneaux, H., *The Annals of Tacitus*[2], rev. H.F. Pelham and C.D. Fisher (Oxford, 1896–1907). 2 vols.

Gabba, E., 'Le origini dell'esercito professionale in Roma: i proletari e la riforma di Mario,' *Athenaeum* n.s. 27 (1949) 173–209. Reprinted in *Esercito e società nella tarda repubblica romana* (Florence, 1973) 1–45.

Gabba, E., 'Ancore sulle cifre dei censimenti,' *Athenaeum* n.s. 30 (1952) 161–173.

Galinsky, K., 'Augustus' Legislation on Morals and Marriage,' *Philologus* 125 (1981) 126–144.

Garcia Garrido, M., 'Minor Annis XII Nupta,' *Labeo* 3 (1957) 76–88.

Gardner, J.F., 'The Recovery of Dowry in Roman Law,' *CQ* n.s. 35 (1985) 449–453.

Gardner, J.F., *Women in Roman Law and Society* (Bloomington and Indianapolis, 1986).

Garnsey, P., 'Trajan's Alimenta: Some Problems,' *Historia* 17 (1968) 367–381.

Garnsey, P., 'Urban Property Investment,' *Studies in Roman Property*, ed. M.I. Finley (Cambridge, 1976) 123–136.

Garnsey, P., 'Where Did Italian Peasants Live?,' *PCPhS* 25 (1979) 1–25.

Garnsey, P., 'Independent Freedmen and the Economy of Roman Italy under the Principate,' *Klio* 63 (1981) 359–371.

Garton, C., 'A Republican Mime-Actress?,' *CR* n.s. 14 (1964) 238–239.

Garton, C., *Personal Aspects of the Roman Theater* (Toronto, 1972).

Gaudemet, J., 'Observations sur la *manus*,' *RIDA* 2 (1953) 323–353.

Gelzer, M., *The Roman Nobility*, trans. R. Seager (Oxford, 1969).

Gide, P., *Etude sur la condition privée de la femme*[2] (Paris, 1885).

Girard, P.F., *Manuel élémentaire de droit romain*[8], rev. F. Stenn (Paris, 1929).

Golden, M., 'Demography and the Exposure of Girls at Athens,' *Phoenix* 35 (1981) 316–331.

Golden, M., 'Did the Ancients Care When Their Children Died?,' *G&R* 2nd. ser. 35 (1988) 152–163.

Gomme, A.W., 'The Position of Women in Athens in the Fifth and Fourth Centuries,' *CP* 20 (1925) 1–25. Reprinted in *Essays in Greek History and Literature* (Oxford, 1937) 89–115.

Goody, J., *Death, Property and the Ancestors* (Stanford, Calif., 1962).

Gough, E.K., 'Cults of the Dead among the Nayars,' *Journal of American Folklore* 71 (1958) 446–478.

Gould, J.P., 'Law, Custom and Myth: Aspects of the Social Position of Women in Classical Athens,' *JHS* 100 (1980) 38–59.

Grant, M., De Simone, A., and Merella, M.T., *Eros in Pompeii: the Secret Rooms of the National Museum of Naples* (New York, 1975).

Gratwick, A.S., 'Free or Not So Free? Wives and Daughters in the Late Roman Republic,' *Marriage and Property*, ed. E.M. Craik (Aberdeen, 1984) 30–53.

Grimal, P., 'A propos du *Truculentus*. L'antiféminisme de Plaute,' *Mélanges Marcel Durry* (Paris, 1970) 85–98.

Grimal, P., *Love in Ancient Rome*, transl. A. Train, Jr. (Norman, Okla., 1986).

Gruen, E., *The Last Generation of the Roman Republic* (Berkeley, 1974).

Gruen, E., *The Hellenistic World and the Coming of Rome* (Berkeley, 1984). 2 vols.

Guarino, A., 'Appunti sulla "ignorantia iuris" nel diritto penale romano,' *Annali della R. Università di Macerata* 15 (1941) 166–205.

Guarino, A., *Le collazioni ereditarie, corso di diritto romano* (Naples, 1945).

Guarino, A., 'Collatio Dotis,' *BIDR* n.s. 8–9 (1947) 259–276.

Gummerus, H., 'Die römische Industrie I: das Goldschmied und Juweilergewerbe,' *Klio* 14 (1915) 129–189; 15 (1918) 256–302.

Hadas, M., 'Observations on Athenian Women,' *CW* 29 (1936) 97–100.

Hallet, J.P., *Fathers and Daughters in Roman Society* (Princeton, 1984).

Harkness, A.G., 'Age at Marriage and at Death in the Roman Empire,' *TAPA* 27 (1896) 35–72.

Harris, W.V., *War and Imperialism in Republican Rome, 327–70 BC* (Oxford, 1979).

Harris, W.V., 'The Theoretical Possibility of Extensive Infanticide in the Graeco-Roman World,' *CQ* n.s. 32 (1982) 114–116.

Harris, W.V., 'The Roman Father's Power of Life and Death,' *Studies in Roman Law in Memory of A. Arthur Schiller*, ed. R.S. Bagnall and W.V. Harris (Leiden, 1986) 81–95.

Harrison, A.R.W., *The Law of Athens: the Family and Property* (Oxford, 1968).

Hemphill, P., 'The Cassia–Clodia Survey,' *PBSR* n.s. 30 (1975) 118–175.

Hermansen, G., *Ostia: Aspects of Roman City Life* (Edmonton, 1981).

Herrmann, C., *Le Rôle judiciaire et politique des femmes sous le République romaine* (Brussels, 1964).

Herrmann, J., 'Die Ammenverträge in den gräko-ägyptischen Papyri,' *ZRG* 76 (1959) 490–499.

Herter, H., 'Die Soziologie der antiken Prostitution im Lichte des heidnischen und christlichen Schrifttums,' *JbAC* 3 (1960) 70–111.

Heurgon, J., 'Valeurs féminines et masculines dans la civilisation étrusque,' *MEFR* 73 (1961) 139–160.

Hobsan, D., 'Women as Property Owners in Roman Egypt,' *TAPA* 113 (1983) 311–321.

Hobsan, D., 'The Role of Women in the Econonic Life of Roman Egypt: a Case Study from First Century Tebtunis,' *CV* 28 (1984) 373–390.

Hopkins, M.K., 'The Age of Roman Girls at Marriage,' *Population Studies* 18 (1965) 309–327.

Hopkins, M.K., 'Contraception in the Roman Empire,' *CSSH* 8 (1965–66) 124–151.

Hopkins, M.K., 'On the Probable Age Structure of the Roman Population,' *Population Studies* 20 (1966) 245–264.

Hopkins, M.K., *Conquerors and Slaves* (Cambridge, 1978).

Hopkins, M.K., 'Brother–Sister Marriage in Roman Egypt,' *CSSH* 22 (1980) 303–354.

Hörle, J., *Cato's Hausbücher* (Paderborn, 1929).

Hsu, F.L.K., *Clan, Caste and Club* (Princeton, 1963).

Hsu, F.L.K., *Under the Ancestors' Shadow* (Garden City, NY, 1967).

Hunt, A.S., and Edgar, C.C., (eds) *Select Papyri* (Cambridge, Mass., 1932–1934). 2 vols.

Jacoby, F., *Die Fragmente der griechischen Historiker* (Leiden, 1923–1958).

Jocelyn, H.D., *The Tragedies of Ennius* (Cambridge, 1967).

Johnston, P.A., *'Poenulus* I, 2 and Roman Women,' *TAPA* 110 (1980) 143–159.

Johnston, R.F., *Lion and Dragon in Northern China* (New York, 1910).

Jones, G.D.B., 'Capena and the Ager Capenas,' *PBSR* n.s. 17 (1962)

116–210; 18 (1963) 100–158.

Jordan, D.K., *Gods, Ghosts and Ancestors* (Berkeley, 1972).

Just, R., 'Conceptions of Women in Classical Athens,' *Journal of the Anthropological Society of Oxford* 6 (1975) 153–170.

Kahane, A., Threipland, L.M., and Ward-Perkins, J.B., 'The Ager Veientanus, North and East of Rome,' *PBSR* n.s. 23 (1968).

Kahrstedt, U., *Die wirtschaftliche Lage Grossgriechenlands in der Kaiserzeit* (Wiesbaden, 1960).

Kajanto, I., *Onomastic Studies in the Early Christian Inscriptions of Rome and Carthage* (Acta Instituti Romani Finlandiae II, 1, Helsinki, 1963).

Kajanto, I., 'On the Problem of the Average Duration of Life in the Roman Empire,' *Soumalainen Tiedeakatemia* 153 (1968) 1–30.

Kajanto, I., 'On Divorce among the Common People of Rome,' *Mélanges Marcel Durry* (Paris, 1970) 99–113.

Kajanto, I., 'Women's Praenomina Reconsidered,' *Arctos* n.s. 7 (1972) 13–30.

Kajanto, I., 'On the First Appearance of Women's *cognomina*,' *Akten des VI. Internationalen Kongresses für griechische und lateinische Epigraphik, München 1972* (Munich, 1973) 402–404.

Kajanto, I., 'On the Peculiarities of Women's Nomenclature,' *L'Onomastique latine* (Paris, 1977) 147–159.

Kampen, N.B., *Image and Status: Roman Working Women in Ostia* (Berlin, 1981).

Kampen, N.B., 'Social Status and Gender in Roman Art: the Case of the Saleswoman,' *Feminism and Art History*, ed. N. Broude and M.D. Garrard (New York, 1982) 63–77.

Karlowa, O., *Römische Rechtsgeschichte* (Leipzig, 1901). 2 vols.

Kaser, M., *Roman Private Law*[3], trans. R. Dannenbring (Pretoria, 1980).

Keuls, E.C., *The Reign of the Phallus: Sexual Politics in Ancient Athens* (New York, 1985).

Kierdorf, W., *Laudatio Funebris. Interpretationen und Untersuchungen zur Entwicklung der römischen Leichenrede* (Meisenheim am Glan, 1980).

Kitto, H.D.F., *The Greeks* (Harmondsworth, 1951).

Kleberg, T., *Hôtels, restaurants et cabarets dans l'antiquité romaine* (Uppsala, 1957).

Kolendo, J., 'L'esclavage et la vie sexuelle des hommes libres à Rome,' *Index* 10 (1981) 288–297.

Konstan, D., 'Plot and Theme in Plautus' *Asinaria*,' *CJ* 73 (1978) 215–221.

Kornhardt, H., 'Recipere und servus recepticius,' *ZRG* 58 (1938) 162–164.

Kromayer, J., 'Die wirtschaftliche Entwicklung Italiens im II. und I. Jahrhundert vor Chr.,' *NJA* 33 (1914) 145–169.

Krüger, P., 'Anecdoton Livianum,' *Hermes* 4 (1870) 371–372.

Kübler, B., 'Das Intestaterbrecht der Frauen im alten Rom,' *ZRG* 41 (1920) 15–43.

Kunkel, W., 'Das Konsilium im Hausgericht,' *ZRG* 83 (1966) 219–251.

La Rocca, E., and de Vos, M. and A., *Guida archeologica di Pompei*[2] (Rome, 1981).

Lacey, W.K., *The Family in Classical Greece* (London, 1968).

Lambert, W.W., Triandis, L.M., and Wolf, M., 'Some Correlates of Beliefs in the Malevolence and Benevolence of Supernatural Beings: a Cross-Societal Study,' *Journal of Abnormal and Social Psychology* 58 (1959) 162–169.

Lanfranchi, F., *Il diritto nei retori romani* (Milan, 1938).

Langer, W.L., 'Infanticide: a Historical Survey,' *History of Childhood Quarterly* 1 (1973–74) 353–366.

Lattimore, R., *Themes in Greek and Latin Epitaphs* (Urbana, Ill., 1942).

Le Gall, J., 'Métiers de femmes au *Corpus Inscriptionum Latinarum*,' in *Mélanges Marcel Durry* (Paris, 1970) 123–130.

Lemosse, M., 'L'enfant sans famille en droit romain,' *Recueils de la Société Jean Bodin* 35 (1975) 257–270.

Leonhard, R., 'Diffareatio,' *RE* 5 (1903) 481.

Lepore, E., 'Orientamente per la storia sociale di Pompei,' in *Pompeiana. Raccolta di studi per il secondo centenario degli scavi di Pompei* (Naples, 1950) 144–166.

Levick, B., 'The *Senatus Consultum* from Larinum,' *JRS* 73 (1983) 97–115.

Lewis, N., 'On Paternal Authority in Roman Egypt,' *RIDA* 3rd ser. 17 (1970) 251–258.

Luck, G., *Arcana Mundi* (Baltimore, 1985).

MacCormack, G., 'Wine Drinking and the Romulan Law of Divorce,' *IJ* 10 (1975) 170–174.

MacCormack, G., '*Coemptio* and Marriage by Purchase,' *BIDR* 3rd ser. 20 (1978) 179–199.

MacMullen, R., *Paganism in the Roman Empire* (New Haven, 1981).

Manson, M., 'The Emergence of the Small Child in Rome (Third Century BC–First Century AD),' *History of Education* 12 (1983) 149–159.

Marks, M.C., 'Heterosexual Coital Positions as a Reflection of Ancient and Modern Cultural Attitudes' (Diss. SUNY Buffalo, 1978).

Marshall, A.J., 'Ladies at Law: the Role of Women in the Roman Civil Courts,' *Studies in Latin Literature and Roman History*, V, ed. C. Deroux, (Brussels, 1989) 35–54.

Martino, F. de, 'L' "ignorantia iuris" nel diritto penale romano,' *SDHI* 3 (1937) 387–418.

Matringe, G., 'La puissance paternelle et le mariage des fils et filles de famille en droit romain (sous l'Empire et en Occident),' *Studi in onore di Eduardo Volterra* V (Milan, 1971) 191–237.

Mau, A., 'Ballspiel,' *RE* 2B (1896) 2832–2834.

Maxey, M., *Occupations of the Lower Classes in Roman Society* (Chicago, 1938).

McDonnell, M., 'Divorce Initiated by Women in Rome,' *AJAH* 8 (1983) 54–80.

McDonnell, M., 'The Speech of Numidicus at Gellius, *N.A.* 1.6,' *AJPh* 108 (1987) 81–94.

McGinn, T.A.J., 'The Taxation of Roman Prostitutes,' *Helios* 16 (1989) 79–110.

Meise, E., *Untersuchungen zur Geschichte der Julisch-Claudischen Dynastie* (Munich, 1969).

Mohler, S.L., 'Slave Education in the Roman Empire,' *TAPA* 71 (1940) 262–280.

Mommsen, Th., 'Die italische Bodentheilung und die Alimentartafeln,' *Hermes* 19 (1884) 393–416. Reprinted in *Gesammelte Schriften* V (Berlin, 1908) 123–145.

Mommsen, Th., *Römisches Staatsrecht*³ III (Berlin, 1888).

Montevecchi, O., 'Ricerche di sociologia nei documenti dell'Egitto greco-romano, II: i contratti di matrimonio e gli atti di divorzio,' *Aegyptus* 16 (1936) 3–83.

Montevecchi, O., *La papirologia* (Turin, 1973).

Münzer, F., *Römische Adelsparteien und Adelsfamilien* (Stuttgart, 1920).

Münzer, F., 'Megullia,' *RE* 15 (1931) 333.

Münzer, F., 'Tuccia,' *RE* 7A (1939) 768.

Nagle, D.B., 'The Etruscan Journey of Tiberius Gracchus,' *Historia* 25 (1976) 487–489.

Nagle, D.B., 'Towards a Sociology of Southeastern Etruria,' *Athenaeum* n.s. 57 (1979) 411–441.

Nardi, E., *Procurato aborto nel mondo greco-romano* (Milan, 1971).

Neeve, P.W. de, *Peasants in Peril: Location and Economy in Italy in the Second Century BC* (Amsterdam, 1984).

Neraudau, J.-P., *La Jeunesse dans la littérature et les institutions de la Rome républicaine* (Paris, 1979).

Neraudau, J.-P., *Etre enfant à Rome* (Paris, 1984).

Nicholas, B., *An Introduction to Roman Law* (Oxford, 1962).

Nicolet, C., *The World of the Citizen in Republican Rome*, trans. P.S. Falla (London, 1980).

Noailles, P., 'Les tabous du mariage dans le droit primitif des Romains,' *Annales Sociologiques* ser. C fasc. 2 (Paris, 1937) 6–34.

North, J.A., 'Religious Toleration in Republican Rome,' *PCPhS* n.s. 25 (1979) 85–103.

Ogilvie, R.M., 'The Maid of Ardea,' *Latomus* 21 (1962) 477–483.

Ogilvie, R.M., 'Eretum,' *PBSR* n.s. 20 (1965) 70–112.

Ogilvie, R.M., *A Commentary on Livy, Books 1–5* (Oxford, 1965).

Pachtere, F.G. de, *La Table hypothécaire de Veleia* (Paris, 1920).

Pape, M., *Griechische Kunstwerke aus Kriegsbeute und ihre öffentliche Aufstellung in Rom* (Diss. Hamburg, 1975).

Patterson, C., ' "Not Worth the Rearing": the Causes of Infant Exposure in Ancient Greece,' *TAPA* 115 (1985) 103–123.

Pearce, T.E.V., 'The Role of the Wife as *Custos* in Ancient Rome,' *Eranos* 72 (1974) 16–33.

Peek, W., *Neue Inschriften aus Epidauros. Abhandlungen der sächsischen Akademie der Wissenschaften zu Leipzig. Philologisch-historische Klasse* 63.5 (Leipzig, 1972).

Philipp, H., and Koenigs, W., 'Zu den Basen des L. Mummius in Olympia,' *MDAI(A)* 94 (1979) 193–216.

Phillips, J.E., 'Roman Mothers and the Lives of Their Adult Daughters,' *Helios* 6 (1978) 69–80.

Pieri, G., *Histoire du cens à Rome des ses origines à la fin de la République* (Sirey, 1967).

Pleket, H.W., *Epigraphica II: Texts on the Social History of the Greek World* (Leiden, 1969).

Pomeroy, S.B., *Goddesses, Whores, Wives, and Slaves. Women in Classical Antiquity* (New York, 1975).

Pomeroy, S.B., 'The Relationship of the Married Woman to Her Blood Relatives in Rome,' *AncSoc* 7 (1976) 215–227.

Pomeroy, S.B., 'Women in Roman Egypt,' *Reflections of Women in Antiquity*, ed. H.P. Foley (New York, 1981), 303–322.

Pomeroy, S.B., 'Infanticide in Hellenistic Greece,' *Images of Women in Antiquity*, ed. A. Cameron and A. Kuhrt (Detroit, 1983) 207–222.

Pomeroy, S.B., *Women in Hellenistic Egypt from Alexander to Cleopatra* (New York, 1984).

Post, L.A., 'Woman's Place in Menander's Athens,' *TAPA* 71 (1940) 420–459.

Potter, T.W., *Roman Italy* (Berkeley, 1987).

Radcliffe-Brown, A.R., 'Religion and Society,' *Structure and Function in Primitive Society* (Glencoe, Ill., 1952) 153–177.

Raditsa, L.F., 'Augustus' Legislation Concerning Marriage, Procreation, Love Affairs and Adultery,' *ANRW* II.13 (1980) 278–339.

Rantz, B., 'Les droits de la femme romain tels qu'on peut les apercevoir dans le *pro Caecina* de Ciceron', *RIDA* 29 (1982) 265–280.

Rathbone, D.W., 'The Development of Agriculture in the "Ager Cosanus" during the Roman Republic: Problems of Evidence and Interpretation,' *JRS* 71 (1981) 10–23.

Rawson, B., 'The Roman Family,' *The Family in Ancient Rome*, ed. B. Rawson (London, 1985) 1–57.

Rawson, E., 'The Ciceronian Aristocracy and Its Properties,' *Studies in Roman Property*, ed. M.I. Finley (Cambridge, 1976) 85–102.

Reinach, J., 'Puberté féminine et mariage romain,' *RD* 34 (1956) 268–273.

Reynolds, J., Beard, M., Duncan-Jones, R., and Roueché, C., 'Roman Inscriptions, 1976–80,' *JRS* 71 (1981) 121–143.

Richlin, A., 'Approaches to the Sources on Adultery at Rome,' *Women's Studies* 8 (1981) 225–250. Reprinted in *Reflections of Women in Antiquity*, ed. H. Foley (New York, 1981) 379–404.

Richter, D.C., 'The Position of Women in Classical Athens,' *CJ* 67 (1971) 1–8.

Ruggiero, A., 'Il matrimonio della impubere in Roma antica,' *AAN* 92 (1981) 63–71.

Sachers, E., 'Tutela,' *RE* 7A (1948) 1498–1599.

Ste. Croix, G.E.M. de, 'Some Observations on the Property Rights of Athenian Women,' *CR* n.s. 20 (1970) 273–278.

Saller, R.P., 'Men's Age at Marriage and Its Consequences in the Roman Family,' *CP* 82 (1987) 21–34.

Saller, R.P., 'Slavery and the Roman Family,' *Classical Slavery*, ed. M.I. Finley (Cambridge, 1987) 65–87.

Saller, R.P., and Shaw, B.D., 'Tombstones and Roman Family Relations in the Principate: Civilians, Soldiers and Slaves,' *JRS* 74 (1984) 124–156.

Sanctis, G. De, *Storia dei Romani* III.2 (Turin, 1917).

Sanders, I.T., *Rainbow in the Rock, the People of Rural Greece* (Cambridge, Mass., 1962).

Scarborough, J., *Roman Medicine* (London, 1969).

Schaps, D.M., 'Women in Greek Inheritance Law,' *CQ* n.s. 25 (1975) 53–57.

Schaps, D.M., 'The Woman Least Mentioned: Etiquette and Women's Names,' *CQ* n.s. 27 (1977) 323–330.

Schaps, D.M., *Economic Rights of Women in Ancient Greece* (Edinburgh, 1979).

Schuhmann, E., 'Zur sozialen Stellung der Frau in den Komödien des Plautus,' *Das Altertum* 24 (1978) 97–105.

Schulz, F., 'Roman Registers of Birth and Birth Certificates,' *JRS* 32 (1942) 78–91; 33 (1943) 55–64.

Schulz, F., *Classical Roman Law* (Oxford, 1951).

Scullard, H.H., *Roman Politics 220–150 BC*[2] (Oxford, 1973).

Sedgwick, W.B., 'Babies in Ancient Literature,' *The Nineteenth Century* 104 (1928) 374–383.

Segal, E., *Roman Laughter*[2] (Cambridge, Mass., 1987).

Seltman, C., 'The Status of Women in Athens,' *G&R* 2nd ser. 2 (1955) 119–124.

Shaw, B.D., 'The Age of Roman Girls at Marriage: Some Reconsiderations,' *JRS* 77 (1987) 30–46.

Shatzman, I., 'The Roman General's Authority over Booty,' *Historia* 21 (1972) 177–205.

Shatzman, I., *Senatorial Wealth and Roman Politics* (Brussels, 1975).

Sherwin-White, A.N., *The Letters of Pliny. A Historical and Social Commentary* (Oxford, 1966).

Sherwin-White, A.N., *Roman Foreign Policy in the East, 168 BC to AD 1* (London, 1984).

Simonius, P., *Die Donatio Mortis Causa im klassischen römischen Recht* (Basel, 1958).

Smith, R.E., *Service in the Post-Marian Roman Army* (Manchester, 1958).

Solazzi, S., 'Infirmitas aetatis e infirmitas sexus,' *AG* 4th ser. 20 (1930) 3–31.

Solazzi, S., 'Glosse a Gaio,' *Studi in onore di Salvatore Riccobono* I (Palermo, 1936) 71–191.

Solazzi, S., '*Servus recepticius et dos recepticia*,' *SDHI* 5 (1939) 222–225.

Spurr, M.S., *Arable Cultivation in Roman Italy* (London, 1986).

Steiner, G., 'The Fortunate Farmer: Life on the Small Farm in Ancient Italy,' *CJ* 51 (1955) 57–67.

Steinwenter, A., 'Lex Furia *testamentaria*,' *RE* 12 (1925) 2356–2360.

Steinwenter, A., 'Lex Voconia,' *RE* 12 (1925) 2418–2430.

Stockton, D., *The Gracchi* (Oxford, 1979).

Syme, R., 'Bastards in the Roman Aristocracy,' *PAPhS* 104 (1960) 323–327. Reprinted in *Roman Papers* II, ed. E. Badian (Oxford, 1979) 510–517.

Syme, R., 'The Historian Servilius Nonianus,' *Hermes* 92 (1964) 408–414. Reprinted in *Ten Studies in Tacitus* (Oxford, 1970) 91–109.

Syme, R., *Sallust* (Berkeley, 1964).

Thomas, Y., 'Mariages endogamiques à Rome. Patrimoine, pouvoir et parenté depuis l'époque archaïque,' *TRG* 58 (1980) 345–382.

Tibiletti, G., 'Ricerche di storia agraria romana,' *Athenaeum* n.s. 28 (1950) 183–266.

Toynbee, A.J., *Hannibal's Legacy* (London, 1965). 2 vols.

Toynbee, J.M.C., *Death and Burial in the Roman World* (London, 1971).

Tracy, V.R., 'The *leno-maritus*,' *CJ* 72 (1976) 62–64.

Treggiari, S., 'Libertine Ladies,' *CW* 64 (1971) 196–198.

Treggiari, S., 'Domestic Staff at Rome in the Julio-Claudian Period, 27 BC to AD 68,' *Histoire sociale* 6 (1973) 241–255.

Treggiari, S., 'Family Life among the Staff of the Volusii,' *TAPA* 105 (1975) 393–401.

Treggiari, S., 'Jobs in the Household of Livia,' *PBSR*, n.s. 30 (1975) 48–77.

Treggiari, S., 'Jobs for Women,' *AJAH* 1 (1976) 76–104.

Treggiari, S., 'Lower Class Women in the Roman Economy,' *Florilegium* 1 (1979) 65–86.

Treggiari, S., 'Concubinae,' *PBSR* n.s. 36 (1981) 59–81.

Treggiari, S., 'Consent to Roman Marriage: Some Aspects of Law and Reality,' *CV* 26 (1982) 34–44.

Treggiari, S., Digna Condicio: Betrothals in the Roman Upper Class,' *CV* 28 (1984) 419–451.

Vahlen, J., *Ennianae Poesis Reliquiae*[3] (Leipig, 1928).

Van Lith, S.M.E., 'Lease of Sheep and Goats / Nursing Contract with Accompanying Receipt,' *ZPE* 14 (1974) 145–162.

Verstraete, B.C., 'Slavery and the Social Dynamics of Male Homosexual Relations in Ancient Rome,' *Journal of Homosexuality* 5 (1980) 227–236.

Veyne, P., 'La table des Ligures Baebiani et l'institution alimentaire de Trajan,' *MEFR* 69 (1957) 81–135.

Veyne, P., 'Les *Alimenta* de Trajan,' in *Les Empereurs romains d'Espagne* (Paris, 1965) 163–179.

Veyne, P., 'La famille et l'amour sous le haut-empire romain,' *Ann(ESC)* 33 (1978) 35–63.

Veyne, P., 'Homosexuality in Ancient Rome,' *Western Sexuality*, ed. P. Ariès and A. Béjin, trans. A. Forster (Oxford, 1985) 26–35.

Vigneron, R., 'L'antiféministe loi Voconia et les "Schleichwege des Lebens",' *Labeo* 29 (1983) 140–153.

Villers, R., 'A propos de la disparition de l'*usus*,' *RD* 28 (1950) 538–547.

Villers, R., 'Le statut de la femme à Rome jusqu'à la fin de la République,' *Recueils de la Société Jean Bodin XI: la Femme* (1959) 177–189.

Villers, R., '*Manus* et mariage,' *IJ* 4 (1969) 168–179.

Villers, R., *Rome et la droit privé* (Paris, 1977).

Vogt, H., *Studien zum Senatus Consultum Velleianum* (Bonn, 1952).

Vollmer, F., *Laudationum Funebrium Romanorum Historia et Reliquiarum Editio* (Leipzig, 1891).

Volterra, E., 'Sulla capacità delle donne a far testamento,' *BIDR* n.s. 7 (1941) 74–87.

Volterra, E., 'Ancora sulla manus e sul matrimonio,' *Studi in onore di Siro Solazzi* (Naples, 1948), 675–688.

Volterra, E., 'Sul diritto familiare di Ardea nel V secolo a.C.,' *Studi in onore di Antonio Segni* IV (Milan, 1967) 657–677.

Walbank, F.W., *A Historical Commentary on Polybius* (Oxford, 1957–1979). 3 vols.

Ward-Perkins, J.B., 'Notes on Southern Etruria and the Ager Veientanus,' *PBSR* n.s. 10 (1955) 44–72.

Watson, A., 'The Divorce of Carvilius Ruga,' *TRG* 33 (1965) 38–50.

Watson, A., *The Law of Persons in the Later Roman Republic* (Oxford, 1967).

Watson, A., *The Law of Succession in the Later Roman Republic* (Oxford, 1971).

Watson, A., *Roman Private Law around 200 BC* (Edinburgh, 1971).

Watson, A., 'Roman Private Law and the *Leges Regiae*,' *JRS* 62 (1972) 100–105.

Watson, A., *'Enuptio Gentis,' Daube Noster*, ed. A. Watson (Edinburgh, 1974) 331–341.

Watson, A., *Rome of the XII Tables* (Princeton, 1975).

Watson, A., 'The Origins of *usus*,' *RIDA* 3rd ser. 23 (1976) 265–270.

Weaver, P.R.C., *Familia Caesaris* (Cambridge, 1972).

Wesel, U., 'Ueber den Zusammenhang der *lex Furia, Voconia* und *Falcidia*, *ZRG* 81 (1964) 308–316.

Westermann, W.L., 'The Castanet Dancers of Arsinoe,' *JEA* 10 (1924) 134–144.

White, K.D., 'Latifundia,' *BICS* 14 (1967) 62–79.

White, K.D., *Roman Farming* (London, 1970).

Wieacker, F., 'Die XII Tafeln in ihrem Jahrhundert,' *Les Origines de la république romaine* (Geneva, 1967).

Williams, G., 'Some Aspects of Roman Marriage Ceremonies and Ideals,' *JRS* 48 (1958) 16–29.

Wolf, A.P., 'Gods, Ghosts and Ancestors,' *Religion and Ritual in Chinese Society*, ed. A.P. Wolf (Stanford, Calif., 1974) 131–182.

Wolf, A.P., and Huang, Chieh-shan, *Marriage and Adoption in China, 1845–1945* (Stanford, 1980).

Wolff, H.J., 'Trinoctium,' *TRG* 16 (1938) 145–183.

Wright, F.A., *Feminism in Greek Literature: from Homer to Aristotle* (London, 1923, reprinted Port Washington, NY, 1969).

Yang, M.C., *A Chinese Village: Taitou, Shantung Province* (New York, 1945).

Yaron, R., 'Minutiae on Roman Divorce,' *TRG* 28 (1960) 1–12.

Yaron, R., 'Vitae Necisque Potestas,' *TRG* 30 (1962) 243–251.

Yeo, C.A., 'Land and Sea Transportation in Imperial Italy,' *TAPA* 77 (1946) 221–244.

Yeo, C.A., 'The Development of the Roman Plantation and Marketing of Farm Products,' *Finanzarchiv* n.s. 13 (1951) 321–342.

Zilletti, U., *La dottrina dell'errore nella storia del diritto romano* (Milan, 1961).

Zulueta, F. De, *The Institutes of Gaius* (Oxford, 1946–1953). 2 vols.

INDEX OF SOURCES

1. LITERARY SOURCES

3. INSCRIPTIONS

INDEX OF PERSONS

1. WOMEN

2. MEN

All dates are BC unless
otherwise indicated.

INDEX OF SUBJECTS

INDEX OF SUBJECTS

261